Reforming Jim Crow

Reforming Jim Crow

Southern Politics and State in the Age before *Brown*

Kimberley Johnson

2010

OXFORD
UNIVERSITY PRESS

Oxford University Press, Inc., publishes works that further
Oxford University's objective of excellence
in research, scholarship, and education.

Oxford   New York
Auckland   Cape Town   Dar es Salaam   Hong Kong   Karachi
Kuala Lumpur   Madrid   Melbourne   Mexico City   Nairobi
New Delhi   Shanghai   Taipei   Toronto

With offices in
Argentina   Austria   Brazil   Chile   Czech Republic   France   Greece
Guatemala   Hungary   Italy   Japan   Poland   Portugal   Singapore
South Korea   Switzerland   Thailand   Turkey   Ukraine   Vietnam

Copyright © 2010 by Oxford University Press, Inc.

Published by Oxford University Press, Inc.
198 Madison Avenue, New York, NY 10016

www.oup.com

Oxford is a registered trademark of Oxford University Press

All rights reserved. No part of this publication may be reproduced,
stored in a retrieval system, or transmitted, in any form or by any means,
electronic, mechanical, photocopying, recording, or otherwise,
without the prior permission of Oxford University Press.

Library of Congress Cataloging-in-Publication Data
Johnson, Kimberley S., 1966–
Reforming Jim Crow : Southern politics and state in the age
before Brown / Kimberley Johnson.
p.   cm.
Includes bibliographical references and index.
ISBN 978-0-19-538742-1
1. African Americans—Segregation.
2. African Americans—Civil rights.
3. Civil rights—Southern States—History.
4. Brown, Oliver, 1918–1961.
5. Segregation in education—Southern States—History.
6. Southern States—Race relations.
7. Southern States—Politics and government.   I. Title.
E185.61.J694 2010
323.1196'073—dc22   2009023879

9 8 7 6 5 4 3 2 1

Printed in the United States of America
on acid-free paper

Contents

Acknowledgments	vii
Introduction	1
1 The Problem of the South and the Beginning of Reform	19
2 Lynching, Legitimacy, and Order	43
3 Southern Reform and the New Deal	66
4 Democratization for the White South	91
5 The Natural Way: Education in the Jim Crow Order	116
6 Higher Education for Blacks in the South: Pragmatism and Principle?	144
7 Building the Jim Crow University System	169
8 Jim Crow Reform and the Rebirth of Black Political Citizenship	190
9 The End of Jim Crow Reform	223
Race, Region, and American Political Development: An Analytical Coda	240
Notes	251
Bibliography	281
Index	317

Acknowledgments

This work would not have come about without the support of a variety of people and institutions. Barnard College has been a consistently warm and supportive community as I worked through the intellectual, personal, and financial logistics of this project. A great thank you is extended to my colleagues, the administration, and the research assistants. A special thank you goes to the following institutions for providing critical support for a project that straddled disciplinary boundaries: Columbia University ISERP seed grant research program, the National Endowment for the Humanities Summer Research Grant Program, and the APSA Public Administration section for awarding me a Volcker Junior Scholar Research Award.

A work that depends on historical documents also depends on librarians and archivists. In addition to the Columbia University libraries, especially its invaluable Oral History Library, I want to thank staff at the following places for graciously accommodating my numerous requests for material: the University of Alabama, Atlanta University, the British Library, Emory University, Fisk University, Georgia State University, the Rockefeller Archive Center, Syracuse University, the South Caroliniana Library, the Richmond History Center, and the Vere Harmsworth Library and Rothermere Institute Library at the University of Oxford. I want to particularly thank Lucious Edwards, university archivist at Virginia State University, whose deep knowledge of southern African American politics proved to be a tremendous help in the initial stages of this project. I also want to thank some unsung and neglected scholarly heroes, the African American political scientists and historians whose unpublished works on southern politics, and especially southern African American politics, from the 1920s to the 1950s provided me with a critical entry into the world of Jim Crow.

I owe a tremendous debt to colleagues in political science who have all provided critical and helpful feedback on this project over the years, in particular Paul Frymer, Matthew Holden, Ira Katznelson, Desmond King, Dan Kryder, Robert Lieberman, Joe Lowndes, Eileen McDonagh, Rob Mickey, Lori Minnitee, Julie Novkov, Alice O'Connor, Diane Pinderhughes, Wilbur Rich, Ray Smith, Scott Spitzer, Rick Vallely, and Dorian Warren.

My last, though not least, thanks go to family and friends who provided much need support and encouragement. In some cases they provided a place to lay my head as I toured southern university archives: thanks especially to Bethany and Daniel, and Angelina and Melvin. Kerlene, Carla, and Marilyn have always lit the way. My children wanted to see their names in print again, so here it is: Thank you Milo, Aaron, and Liza for your inspiration and love. Finally, words cannot convey my thanks, as always, to Daniel.

Reforming Jim Crow

Introduction

> Rosa
> How she sat there,
> the time right inside a place
> so wrong it was ready.
>
> That trim name with
> its dream of a bench
> to rest on. Her sensible coat.
>
> Doing nothing was the doing:
> the clean flame of her gaze
> carved by a camera flash.
>
> How she stood up
> when they bent down to retrieve
> her purse. That courtesy.
>
> Rita Dove, *On the Bus with Rosa Parks: Poems*

Rosa Parks, it's been said, was tired. She sat down on a bus seat at the end of one day and the civil rights revolution began. Rosa Parks did indeed sit down, but not alone. She sat down as a person intertwined within developing networks of individuals and groups committed to the proposition that the South at long last had to rejoin the United States and that the United States had to fulfill its moral and legal obligations to its African American citizens. When Rosa Parks sat down, she sat down as a member of interracial organizations such as the NAACP and the Highlander School. She sat down as an employee of one of the South's leading white liberals and former New Dealers. Rosa Parks sat down as a voter in a city where African Americans were beginning to reenter the political realm and reclaim their political citizenship. When Rosa Parks sat down she sat down as the embodiment, at the very least, of two decades of renewed struggle in the South to reclaim full African American citizenship. This struggle for citizenship rested of course on an even longer historical undertaking. When Rosa Parks sat down she marked a turning point, from a movement to reform the South to a movement that would ultimately transform the South and the nation.

The world that shaped Rosa Parks and against which she protested was a world that was shaped by the efforts of whites and blacks, working separately and at times together, to reform the South and its Jim Crow order. From the 1920s through the early 1950s southern reformers attempted to manage, reconcile, and smooth over the stresses and strains within the disparate elements of the Jim Crow order and between the Jim Crow order and other existing orders within the American state.

Southern reformers engaged in bounded reform. Most reformers by definition and by belief were not revolutionaries; they did not seek to eliminate the order, they simply wanted it to perfect it. For those reformers who did seek to end the Jim Crow order, reform was just one strategy, one alternative, in a world in which possibilities for immediate change seemed remote.

Whatever their ultimate goals and motivations, in their quest to make the South more equal while still separate southern reformers unintentionally exposed what the integrationist NAACP argued before the Supreme Court in the *Brown v. Board of Education* case: separate could never be equal in a political order that was based on explicit as well as hidden inequalities based on race and class.

By tracing the rise and fall of the Jim Crow reform movement I will show how this reform effort critically shaped the initial paths taken by the civil rights movement. Rather than an empty shell waiting to be collapsed by forces from above or below, the Jim Crow order itself, as partially shaped by the southern reformers, played an important role in structuring the paths (not) taken by the civil rights movement and the subsequent transformation of the South.

The actors in the civil rights movement, both black and white, like Rosa Parks did not emerge fully formed on history's stage ready to engage in what we know as the civil rights movement. They emerge as the poet Rita Dove so eloquently says in her poem "Rosa," "[At a time] right inside a place so wrong it was ready."

Jim Crow and Its Reformers

Jim Crow reformers—men and women, whites and blacks—like reformers elsewhere in time and place, sought to make a difference. Too young to have experienced the "forgotten alternatives" (or tragedy, if that was their outlook) of Reconstruction, the southern reformers were instead surrounded and molded by the Jim Crow order.

The Jim Crow South was a world in which white supremacy was not only intellectually and morally acceptable, but had been legitimated by intellectuals and the mass media. White supremacy was not only a social hierarchy; it reflected a political and economic hierarchy as well. Alongside, though not supplanting the racial hierarchy of white supremacy were hierarchies based on class and gender. These multiple hierarchies were in turn institutionalized in the South's political and bureaucratic structures. The Jim Crow order was a complex and intertwined order based on a "system of myths, authority, law, statecraft, prejudice, domination, and psychopathology."[1] Yet far from foreclosing reform, the very complexities and discordances of the Jim Crow order resulted in a very narrow range of possibilities available to those who wished to change the order.

Out of the complexity of the Jim Crow order emerged southern reformers, a small group of whites and blacks within the South's now segregated elite. Although chapter 1 will discuss these reformers, their goals and their organizations in greater depth, as they are the central characters in this analysis a brief introduction is offered here. Many of the most prominent were journalists; others were academics or lawyers. Some were members of the clergy, and a few were civic-minded businessmen. Although individuals often advanced a reform agenda, Jim Crow reform mostly emerged from a variety of institutional sources—southern universities, religious organizations, women's groups, and civic groups—and interracial organizations such as the Commission on Interracial Cooperation and the Southern Conference for Human Welfare. Southern reformers and their organizations were heavily reliant on aid from northern foundations such as the Rockefeller Foundation and the Julius Rosenwald Fund or from state support, in the case of southern state universities.

Typical of Jim Crow reformers and their background was the strong belief in the South that "managed race relations" were best left to the "better classes" of both races.[2] The Progressive leanings of many these southerners (of both races) also shaped the course of reform. Like Progressives elsewhere, southerners also held to the belief that society could be shaped by using rational means based on intensive, scientific, objective, and "realistic" investigation, analysis, and education. True to their belief in southern exceptionalism (and reflecting the closed nature of some parts of southern society), these reformers believed that analysis conducted by (white) southerners for (white) southerners was the only effective way to influence the actions and beliefs of white politicians and white citizens.

For white southern Progressives, progress and reform could come about only with the strict separation of races. In this they showed themselves to be still captured by the belief that racial inequality was not the result of state action but the result of folkways, the customs, habits, and cultures of the South that had been in place since time immemorial. Reformers thus accepted the boundaries of the Jim Crow order and mostly worked for change within this order. Some were "fair play" segregationists, who supported greater equality within a framework of racial separation.[3] Others supported reform out of a sense of Christian morality or white paternalism. Much of this support, among whites but more so among blacks, was driven by pragmatism. For whites, reducing the frictions caused by Jim Crow was essential for keeping social peace, encouraging economic development, and keeping the Jim Crow order stable and legitimate in the eyes of those within and outside of the South. For blacks, given the rigid boundaries of the Jim Crow order and the lack of clear alternatives and possibilities, reform offered the chance of making the best of a bad situation.

The presence of Jim Crow reform thus directly challenges one of the master narratives of southern history, and by extension American history, about the Jim Crow South. The South was not simply a region locked in a state of suspended animation for the first half of the twentieth century. Ongoing and sometimes violent struggles over power lay thinly buried under the moonlight and magnolias imagery favored by the New South boosters eager to attract investors. The struggle over the South was not simply between a backward and recalcitrant South and a more progressive and enlightened North. Nor was the struggle simply between conservative elites and the radical white supremacists such as the Ku Klux Klan, or between these elites and the short-lived interracial organizations on the left such as the Southern Tenant Farmers Union.

All of these struggles played a part in shaping the South, but what shaped the region the most was a struggle within, a battle fought every day in schools and legislatures, in fields and prisons, about the very nature of authority and the legitimacy of the Jim Crow order. By examining the active role that southern governments played in shaping, maintaining, and defending the Jim Crow order, this story focuses on the key role of the state in shaping racial orders.[4] Although racial inequality could be attributed to folkways, it was stateways that gave the color line the force of law.

By focusing on Jim Crow reform this book enables the modern-day observer to suspend the aura of inevitability that surrounds the emergence of the civil rights movement. Arguably the Supreme Court's decision to put an end to *Plessy v. Ferguson* and American apartheid was not only logical and necessary, but also inevitable, given the broad forces of modernization and urbanization, the external push of cold war concerns, and the intraparty politics of the Democratic Party. The very same forces that would lead to the *Brown v. Board of Education* decision were also responsible for nurturing the conditions needed for greater black militancy. Yet the civil rights movement, let alone the *Brown* decision, was not foreordained by these largely external forces. For whites and blacks surveying the political, social, and economic landscape of the South in 1934 (or for that matter, the nation at large), the notion that the Jim Crow order would end within their lifetime was simply a remote possibility (or nightmare). That it would lose its judicial, political, and moral legitimacy in twenty years was simply fantastical. Individuals can and do speculate about the future, but the political strategies and opportunities that individuals and groups choose are partially shaped by, or in reaction to, the political, economic, and social context within which they exist.

Jim Crow reformers, along with others, played a significant role in shaping the political, economic, and social context in which both the civil rights movement and its counterpart, massive resistance, emerged. The policy successes and failures of Jim Crow reform examined in this book played a critical role in shaping the stage onto which history's actors would step. Although arising from competing and often less than benign motives, Jim Crow reform created temporary and uneasy coalitions, based on expediency as well as principles, between unlikely allies. Jim Crow reform exposed the possibilities as well as the limits of reform within a deeply flawed democratic order.

Southern Reform and the Shaping of American Democracy

I examine the nature and structure of American politics and democracy by revisiting an era, from roughly 1920 to 1954, in which democracy and citizenship were effectively stripped from millions of Americans, black and white. This repudiation of democracy raises important questions about the meaning of democracy and citizenship in the United States. If the popular political history of the United States is one of ever expanding democracy and an intermittent desire to export American democratic values, then the post–Civil War era stands as an aberration and a warning. Constitutional mandates creating citizenship rights for African Americans and guaranteeing access to democratic institutions were fairly quickly set aside as the first Reconstruction came to a bitter end for blacks. One could argue that this easy disposal of citizenship and democracy for the formerly enslaved was due to their problematic relationship with white American national identity. Nonetheless the fact that the national government could walk away from these democratic commitments for a variety of reasons, including political expediency, suggests that the robustness of American democracy is not something that can be taken for granted, let alone assumed.[5]

Southern whites, less so than southern blacks, also suffered from massive disenfranchisement in this post-Reconstruction era. For whites across the nation, political participation plummeted in the wake of Progressive electoral reforms that sought to purify the ballot. For southern whites, however, this decline in political participation was exceptional and longer lasting. Unlike in other areas of the nation, southern whites' political de-incorporation was openly justified by the elitist argument that politics ought to be left to the better classes. This rhetorical exclusion was accompanied by instruments such as the poll tax, which ensured that this was a self-fulfilling justification. Without the benefit of organized political competition nonelite whites depended on a variety of insurgents, outsiders, demagogues, and upstarts, who in turn found that their occasional victories could not prevail against the entrenched power of the South's political and economic elites.

The antidemocratic wave that swept the South occurred with (at least) the silent acquiescence, if not active involvement, of the national government. For most of this era much of the national media tacitly and unquestioningly accepted these antidemocratic arrangements. Intellectual support for this partial dismantling of democracy was initially widespread, emerging from America's nascent social and physical sciences, which in turn received funding from newly formed public interest foundations such as the Rockefeller Foundation. Arrayed against this widespread support for limiting democracy and citizenship to select groups were scattered individuals and organizations such as the newly established NAACP, all of whom initially had little political, economic, or social power to reverse this antidemocratic tide.

Far from reflecting the enduring values of America, and far from exhibiting resilience and robustness, democracy and citizenship especially in the South came to be redefined first by state legislatures and then sanctioned by the U.S. Supreme Court. Rather than protecting the rights of minorities (whether political, cultural, or numerical), as the framers of the Constitution had intended, the American federal system instead facilitated the development of multiple nondemocratic polities, which were essentially republics in name only. While this may simply be a case of enduring southern exceptionalism (that is, given its heritage of slavery, the South has always been antidemocratic), the fact is that through federal institutional arrangements the South throughout this era was able to exert a disproportionate effect on American politics and public policy. Modern American democracy as well as the modern American state bears traces of this racial and regional antidemocratic legacy.

Thus to understand not only the modern American state but also the nature of American democracy one must understand the antidemocratic and regional roots that contributed to its growth. If the Civil War was a war over ideas, then the South had won.[6] First, the South rejected the American ideal that all men (and women) were created equal. Second, the South created a new role for government: it was the government's (not society's or the market's) affirmative duty to not only define, but also to actively enforce and if necessary reproduce that inequality, whether based on race, class, or gender. These definitions varied, ranging from rules defining racial status to rules determining union organizing. The methods of enforcing this inequality could be the police power possessed by the streetcar conductor to enforce segregated seating, the largely African American convict labor that built the South's highways, or the segregated and unequal school system. The Jim Crow order was based not only on statutory law, but on bureaucratic organization, implementation, and enforcement. In short, the modernization of the American state went hand-in-hand with the emergence of this antidemocratic moment.[7]

The Jim Crow order was built on a complex array of institutions, policies, and political identities. Once established these new identities and arrangements did not remain static. For example, the institutional arrangements and ideational commitments that defined the boundaries of southern democracy shifted over time as political competition periodically opened and then constricted the southern white electorate. This interplay between policies and political processes is what some political scientists call *policy feedback*. As Theda Skocpol and others argue, although politics creates policies, policies can in turn reshape politics through the "transform[ation of] state capacities" and through "[new] changes in social groups and their political goals and capabilities."[8]

These two effects of policy choice—transformation of state capacity and the creation of new group identity or capacities—can in turn affect the adoption of later policies. In the case of the South, Jim Crow reform led to new institutional and political arrangements, as well as the creation of new political goals and political capacities among a range of groups, from non-elite whites to middle- class black professionals. Jim Crow reform also had short- as well as long-term policy feedback effects.

In the short run Jim Crow reforms seemed to increase the stability and legitimacy of the order. White Southerners could point to the reforms as the key to their success in handling the South's "race problem." With the reforms' promise of social calm and order, some southern elites believed that the reforms would aid their efforts to encourage further investment in the region's textile and manufacturing sector. White southerners could also use the existence of reform efforts as a means to stifle or co-opt any remaining dissent among whites as well as blacks. Many southern blacks, whether they were members of the region's small middle-class or worked in the South's vast agricultural or service sector, saw these incremental reforms as a more realistic approach. Jim Crow reforms offered concrete results as opposed to the emotional appeal of the black nationalism of Marcus Garvey or the litigation-based approach of the NAACP, neither of which had produced significant victories for black southerners by the late 1920s.[9]

The long-term policy feedback effects of reform, however, were not entirely positive for the stability of the Jim Crow order. If the purpose of segregation was to create a parallel though separate and subordinate society, then the case for the Jim Crow order was strengthened by the establishment and expansion of a black professional and managerial class. Yet the creation of a managerial class of blacks did not result in acquiescence to the status quo, although certainly that did exist. Rather, for ideological reasons as well as self-interest, members of the southern black middle and professional classes would increasingly turn the logic of Jim Crow back on itself. If the white South insisted on the separation of races in educational and other public services and amenities, then the black South could in return begin to insist on equality in public service provision ranging from street lights to parks to golf courses. Reforms, whether carried out or not, thus threatened to equalize the very real inequalities in public services and spending between whites and blacks. These visible displays of inequality were used by white elites to secure the support of less privileged whites and were seen by ordinary whites as proof of their superior status.[10] Indeed educational reforms for blacks as well as whites exacerbated divisions among southern elites. For example, many planters were against reforms, fearing that education would ruin a good field hand. Yet better schools could provide a stationary labor force helpful for textile mill owners seeking a docile workforce and for industrialists in search of skilled (though still cheap) labor. In the long run, then, reform efforts, especially those centering on education, constituted an important step in weakening the intellectual, economic, and social foundation of the Jim Crow order.

State administrative and electoral reform, especially poll tax reform, was even more threatening to the Jim Crow order, as it reintroduced political competition and accountability to a political system that had been built on the exclusion of these conditions. The political reincorporation of millions of whites also challenged the social and economic hierarchies of the Jim Crow order. Whereas an older generation of whites had been socialized to believe that politics was a spectator sport that was ultimately dominated by a coterie of courthouse gangs, a new generation led by southern New Dealers and later World War II veterans emerged to challenge these older groups. Not all of these new challengers were liberal; indeed some of them became the leaders of the South's massive resistance to the civil rights movement. Nonetheless these challengers destabilized existing Democratic Party structures and helped to pave the way for the reemergence of the Republican Party in the South.[11]

By the beginning of the 1950s those attempting to overturn the Jim Crow order confronted not the crude Jim Crow South of 1910, but a newer New South that in many instances had defeated or co-opted a variety of internal and external challenges to the region's political, institutional, economic, and social arrangements. It was a South that, though still self-conscious (or obsessive) about its exceptionalist identity, had gradually adapted to its growing convergence with and incorporation into a changing American political order. Despite this adaptation, as a result of piecemeal political reforms, intensified economic development, and its own internal state development the Jim Crow order faced a much stronger array of internal challengers. In addition, unlike in 1910, the Jim Crow order faced not silent acquiescence but public repudiation from a growing number of national political elites. Unlike in 1910, a broad array of national organizations, ranging from the NAACP to the Congress of Industrial Organizations (CIO), were deploying people and resources to confront and overturn the Jim Crow order.

The rise and fall of the Jim Crow order, and the role of Jim Crow reform in that process, reveals a complicated story about American democracy. It is a story not only about how political opportunities can be, in the words of C. Vann Woodward, "forgotten," foreclosed, or lost, but also about how political opportunities can be created and exploited. The multiplicity of interests and the competing and conflicting goals of the institutions and actors involved in this process suggest that the path toward a more democratic and more modern South—and by extension America—was incredibly complex and far from straightforward. The story of Jim Crow reform thus challenges one of the most enduring narratives of American history, that of the solid—and unchanging—South.

The process of Jim Crow reform was the culmination of a strategy that had attempted in some ways to more fully elaborate the Jim Crow order. It was an attempt in the name of *southern* liberalism as well as strategic conservatism to make the southern order live up to the equality premised in *Plessy v. Ferguson*. For white southern reformers this was the right thing to do, especially given the inability of many of them to envision an integrated South. Southern white reformers began staking an alternative vision of the South that attempted to mitigate the worst of Jim Crow while bringing the South into rough alignment with American democratic ideals. White conservatives' limited and in many instances belated support of Jim Crow reform was a strategic move to inoculate the South from federal interference and to buttress their newly revived claims of states rights. As these conservatives would argue, claims for states rights could not be supported unless there was a concomitant assumption of state responsibility.[12]

For southern African Americans, the process of Jim Crow reform was an attempt to address the perceived servility and dead end of Booker T. Washington–style accommodationism while creating a pragmatic alternative to what they believed was the unrealistic approach of W. E. B. DuBois and others. It was not that southern black reformers did not believe that blacks should have first-class citizenship; rather they believed that the prospects for it were remote, while the immediate needs of the South's millions of impoverished and illiterate blacks had to be met.[13] Black reformers did not see themselves as passively accepting and adapting to the boundaries of the Jim Crow order. Instead they favored an attempt to shape that order through creating and exploiting opportunities for open, and for the time forceful, negotiations with that order. For these pragmatists Jim Crow reform offered tangible (albeit more limited) material as well political benefits. Indeed for some the vision of full citizenship based on integration that would become the cornerstone of NAACP strategy by the late 1940s was seen as undermining, if not destroying African American institutions and communities that were often the only bulwark against a hostile Jim Crow order.

For those in favor of immediate and unqualified citizenship, such as DuBois, Jim Crow reform underlined, and in some ways dangerously strengthened, the utter perversion of the American creed. Separate simply could not be equal; either one was a full citizen of the polity, or one was not. Anything in between was simply delusion and evasion of the fundamental essence of American democracy. While they offered a compelling alternative, blacks such as DuBois who pressed for an immediate fight for first-class citizenship faced a difficult battle for the hearts and minds of southern blacks, especially for the support of the region's black elites. Not all southern African Americans during the era of Jim Crow reform believed that a revolutionary change in the South was a viable possibility; indeed the periodic resurgence of lynching and white riots reminded the average black southerner about the physical and economic costs of challenging the Jim Crow order. A direct confrontation with the Jim Crow order was avoided in favor of reform, with its more tangible immediate benefits.

Jim Crow and Political Order

William Cash, one of the South's famous chroniclers, argued that although the South was "not quite a nation within a nation," it was "the next thing to it."[14] Like all orders, the Jim Crow order was based on a sense of shared or imposed (depending on one's perspective) understanding of as well acquiescence to the varied political, economic, and social elements that comprised the order. The Jim Crow order was seen by those both in and outside of it as a very real entity. Whites and blacks, southerners as well as outsiders, saw the South as an identifiable and durable political order.

Yet even during its height the Jim Crow order never experienced complete unanimity or support from whites, and especially from blacks. Despite a façade of harmony and stability, migration, unionization attempts, and postwar violence revealed the Jim Crow South to be periodically beset by multiple internal tensions, conflicts, and dissent.[15] This instability reflected the fact that the Jim Crow order was a complex and interconnected system of beliefs, laws, and state action. It was not a static entity existing outside of time or space. Nor was the Jim Crow order a purely instrumental belief system used to cloak or justify the actions of individuals or institutions.[16]

As C. Vann Woodward and V. O. Key each noted, there was no solid, monolithic South; there was in fact a variety of Jim Crow Souths, whose rise had been facilitated by the American federal system.[17] Each of these southern polities had its own variety of Jim Crow, and each consisted of a mixture of institutions, norms, and practices that were contested and protected, elaborated on and adapted to by whites and blacks. This multiplicity gave the Jim Crow order the ability to adapt to changing conditions. In the long run, however, the divergences between the multiple Souths and the extent to which each polity embraced reform or not would weaken the coherence of the whole and make it vulnerable to the multipronged attacks on it led by forces from above and below.

The complex belief system that both whites and blacks held under the Jim Crow order, as well as the order's own politics and institutions, were always subject to being reconstituted into new configurations. Indeed to sustain the Jim Crow order a constant process of creating and articulating meaning and legitimacy was needed not only to bind current members of the order to its political commitments, but also to draw in new members, attract sympathetic allies, or dissuade those hostile to the order. For example, the meaning and significance of the two World Wars, wars to protect democracy and freedom, had to be redefined and reinterpreted in order to fit, and not overturn, the legitimacy of the Jim Crow order. White politicians and white-dominated political institutions and organizations all engaged in an ongoing process of defining and shaping the Jim Crow order to preserve it and their place within it.

African Americans also played a part in this constant process of redefinition and legitimization. Although African Americans were forced to the margins of the South's political and economic spheres, they cast about for new ways to lay claim to forms of citizenship and political engagement that acknowledged the boundaries of the Jim Crow order. At the same time they sought the development of alternative strategies that could penetrate what they saw as the discordant fissures and spaces within the order and across the multiple political orders and traditions that made up the American polity. Southern blacks challenged the assumptions of whites that the Jim Crow order was a well-oiled, immutable, and seamless construct not only through reform, but also through organizations and institutions that made up southern black life "behind the veil," by transgressive acts, and and through the simple act of exiting the South in the Great Migration.[18]

These challenges to the Jim Crow order by African Americans as well as by sympathetic individual whites and organizations located outside of the South were by necessity small. The deployment of hard power through the use of terror and intimidation had created the Jim Crow order, while state-sponsored violence against African Americans in the form of tacit support for lynchings and direct state-sponsored mass incarceration for profit and social control made any ongoing challenges indirect and oblique.

Yet a political order based on oppression cannot rely solely on hard power. Soft power is also a useful and in the long term more cost-effective tool for maintaining power.[19] Those defending the Jim Crow order faced a constant and ongoing search for ways to repackage ideas that were seen as central to legitimizing the order's political commitments and to rearticulate and reshape the shifting and sometimes discordant elements that made up the order. The complex system of myth, law, and state action that supported the legitimacy and power of the Jim Crow order was based on the continual forging of a common understanding of the nature of the order. This understanding rested on both the creation of commitments and the securing of compliance. As I will show over the course of this book, over time the actors and institutions within the Jim Crow order would have to reshape that order in an ongoing quest to achieve their goals within its confines.

Citizenship and the Struggle for Order and Power

One of the ways that the understandings and commitments of the Jim Crow order were developed was through the redefinition of citizenship for whites and blacks, rich and poor, men and women. The multifaceted nature of the Jim Crow order was reflected in the multiple ways citizenship was defined and understood. I draw on the multiple definitions of citizenship offered by T. H. Marshall: political, civil, and social.[20] The Jim Crow order was an incomplete *Herrenvolk*, or racial democracy, in which social, civil, and political citizenship rested on racial status.[21]

The Jim Crow order had multiple kinds of civil rights citizenship for whites and blacks. Civil rights citizenship for whites approached the white supremacist ideal; for white males this included legal rights such as property rights and the right to jury trials, especially by a jury of one's peers, as well as the freedom from arbitrary and unjust arrest and imprisonment. Other rights, such as freedom of speech and assembly, were contingent upon observing the boundaries of the Jim Crow order.

Southern blacks had virtually no civil rights in the Jim Crow order. For them law enforcement was not a source of protection for life or property. From the end of Reconstruction until the 1920s southern whites used the legal system as a means of supplying convict labor to private firms. This arrangement generated enormous profits for the firms as well as state coffers. The thinnest layer of legality and profit motive separated the convict leasing system from slavery. Thus for southern African Americans interactions with the legal system were invariably negative, and contact with law enforcement was many times a bleak prospect. Because blacks could not serve on juries, their peers did not judge them. A biased trial leading to quasi-servitude was in many instances a positive outcome given the alternative: lynching. Lynching was the most visible aspect of the lack of blacks' civil rights citizenship. Between 1910 and 1954 196 blacks (men, women, and children) were murdered by lynching, an average of four people per year, with virtually no whites held accountable.[22]

As I explain in chapter 2, Jim Crow reform took on the problem of lynching and, by extension, the broader struggle over who would wield the power of the state. Reformers, especially white reformers, defined lynching as not simply a denial of the civil rights citizenship of blacks, but as a symptom of southern governments' inability to secure public order and the inability of elites to control the actions of lower class whites. The actions of the latter group were seen as tarnishing the South's reputation and its economic boosterism efforts, which touted the region's social harmony and stable group relations.[23] Without this basic control of the South's public sphere, all other attempts to wield the power of southern government would be endangered. Jim Crow reformers pursued a number of tactics, including strengthening central law enforcement powers by establishing state highway patrols. Coupled with the antilynching campaign conducted by the NAACP at the national level, Jim Crow reform was able to achieve two things: lynching was transformed from a socially acceptable form of black social control and mass white entertainment into an embarrassing exception, and by reasserting control over power and force, white elites beat back attempts by nonelite whites to control the color and class lines.

In chapter 3 I explore how Jim Crow reformers, energized by the New Deal and with access to its resources, attempted to further centralize government power in a political order that was characterized by a pervasive localism and general hostility toward government power. Although southern New Dealers played an important role in pushing for state-level administrative reform, university-based reformers and northern foundations also played a critical and largely overlooked role in this attempt to reshape and modernize southern state government. Their awkward position as critics of the state as well as state functionaries reflected the contradictory position in which many reformers found themselves. In the end reformers' attempts to reorient government power toward the needs of the South's have-nots faltered on the reformers' lack of political power and their inability as servants of the state to directly address issues of power and race.

As I show in chapter 4, the struggle to reshape the southern state would lead to a new struggle for political citizenship for whites. Guided by their belief that the root of the South's problems was economic inequality, southern New Dealers began a drive to reenfranchise the South's whites through an attack on the poll tax. Though not the most fundamental problem of the South's variety of discriminatory voting practices, the poll tax was the one that was most widespread, and strategically it was the one that seemed to harm whites the most. Some reformers embraced poll tax reform as a reflection of white privilege that was wrongfully withheld; others saw it as the means to other ends. For many New Deal southern liberals the goal of poll tax reform was the enfranchisement of a huge pool of have-not whites, who in turn would "naturally" support New Deal–friendly politicians in their struggle against the South's conservative elites.[24]

By emphasizing that this was a struggle for democracy for whites only, southern New Dealers sought to create a broad-based coalition at both the national and state level for electoral reforms. Indeed some white democratization supporters went even further, arguing that the disenfranchisement of large masses of whites threatened the survival of the Jim Crow order by exposing it to intervention and instability from below in the shape of demagogues like Huey Long. World War II and the emergence of a new wartime emphasis on democracy added even more fuel to the poll tax reformers' campaign. As the nation entered World War II in a fight to protect democracy, not only the Jim Crow order but the nation at large faced issues of legitimacy, as these taxes denied worthy white voters, and particularly white soldiers, the right to vote. The presence of the poll tax, at least for whites, became increasingly problematic and embarrassing. By 1953, with the exception of Mississippi, all of the southern states had either abolished the poll tax, reformed some aspects of it, or at least held a statewide referendum on the poll tax.

Social citizenship was the second form of citizenship that existed within the Jim Crow order. Social citizenship is defined by Marshall as the right to access certain social institutions and social services. In the South, despite the efforts of the most reactionary of the Redeemers to completely dismantle the public sector, both whites and blacks had limited social citizenship. A rudimentary and of course segregated and unequal social services sector existed for both races. Both had access to whatever charity hospitals and sanatoriums, old age homes, and mental institutions state and local governments supported. For some lucky whites there were old-age homes and pensions specifically for former Confederate soldiers.[25]

For most white and black southerners public education was their only experience of social citizenship. Ironically public education was one of the singular and lasting achievements of the Reconstruction era that whites in the Jim Crow order regularly demonized. For whites education also played a role in the securing of political citizenship. White southern education reformers overcame resistance to public education by linking white literacy to battles to restrict African American access to the ballot. Whites would be protected from the long-term effects of literacy tests by a public school system that would ensure that their children would be able to exercise their political citizenship. Over time, as the need to pass literacy tests faded (largely due to lax enforcement for whites on this rule), education came to be seen as a source of social mobility for the aspiring middle-class and, more important, as a marker of racial privilege.

Inequality in funding, which was reflected in gross disparities in building conditions, school supplies, and teachers salaries, was a visible sign of racial privilege. Inequalities of funding also led to real fiscal benefits for whites, as money that should have been spent on black schools were diverted to white schools instead. In the South's black belt counties where African Americans made up a huge proportion of the population, this meant that a tiny fraction of white children often received the lion's share of school education funds. Coupled with citizenship rights, the benefits conferred on whites as a result of segregated education were an important element of the South's racial democracy.

For southern blacks, as chapters 5, 6, and 7 will show, education was to play a pivotal role during the Jim Crow order. The right to education, however truncated and unequal, was the only form of citizenship for African Americans that remained under the order. The struggle for black education thus became a form of quasi-political organizing. In a political order that "decentered polls and parties" for African Americans, as the historian Glenda Gilmore argued,[26] the struggle to ensure adequate educational resources for black children, working-class youths and adults, and future professionals became a means for organizing within and across the different sectors of the black community. Education politics was also an arena in which blacks could have formal contact with a political establishment that had largely excised them from the southern polity. For southern reformers education provided a modest middle ground and starting point on which to ameliorate the worst aspects of the Jim Crow order.

Southern white reformers as well as large foundations such as the General Education Board and the Rosenwald Foundation played a key role in building and extending the South's segregated primary and higher education systems and the bureaucratic structures and professional networks that grew beside and entwined with the system.

The growth of black educational institutions at both the primary and higher education levels was the basis for the tremendous development of black social capital. The institutionalization of segregated education led to the establishment of a parallel set of institutions that were initially privately and later publicly funded. These institutions helped to establish and secure a black middle class whose members, mostly teachers but also social workers, doctors, lawyers, and others, would become the backbone of the NAACP's resurgence in the South, as well as the membership of dozens of local and national organizations that made up black Southern life "behind the veil."

In chapter 8 I explore how southern African Americans' quest for social citizenship dovetailed with their renewed insistence on the restoration of their political citizenship. Education politics and the managed race relations of Jim Crow reform had created and sustained a dense network of organizations and institutions, including civic groups and voters leagues, led by and for African Americans. The presence of these institutions and organizations did not presume unanimity; sharp disagreements remained within the African American community over tactics and goals.

During World War II African Americans noted the contradiction between American ideals and practices and used these contradictions to strengthen their own "Double V" campaign for freedom (and equality) at home and abroad. This renewed quest was also strengthened by the recognition of unions such as the CIO that organizing the South and increasing labor union membership was a critical battle that had to be won in order to secure the gains brought about by the New Deal. The fight to secure democracy for whites was accompanied by a renewed effort to regain the political citizenship of blacks. The NAACP reestablished a presence in the South and linked up, with varying degrees of success, with the political organizations that had been created by southern blacks.

Most accounts of political mobilization of African Americans in the pre–civil rights era focus on the important role that northern blacks played in influencing the strategy of the Democratic and Republican Parties. Partially obscured by the political activities of northern blacks was a massive increase in political mobilization by southern blacks. The number of blacks registered to vote in the South went from fewer that ten thousand in 1940 (out of a regionwide black voting age population of fifteen million) to more than a million registered voters by 1956. This massive mobilization was partially aided by individual state poll tax reforms and, even more critically, by *Smith v. Allwright*, a court case that struck down the white primary in 1944. Although these changes in electoral rules were important, the expansion in the South of not only the NAACP but the civic, professional, and social organizations that were nurtured by institutions created and supported by the Jim Crow order also played important roles in this mobilization.

As the extended discussion of southern citizenship throughout this book will show, the consolidation of the Jim Crow order in 1910 only began a process in which the South was engaged in a process of regime maintenance. In chapter 9 I trace the ending of Jim Crow reform during the late 1940s as the problem of regime maintenance became more transparent as the order become increasingly subjected not only to external challenges, but also to internal challenges posed by the different layers of discordant and sometimes conflicting commitments, aims, and understandings that underlay the maintenance of the order's legitimacy and power. While Jim Crow reform was one of the results of this process of regime maintenance, it also contributed to its ending. In the final chapter of the book I provide an analytic conclusion to this work, discussing how political scientists and historians have analyzed this era in southern and American politics and how a rethinking of this era along the lines presented in this book can help scholars understand the long and difficult road of democratic development.

Rosa Parks on the Bus

By the early 1950s, on any number of fronts, in small incidents and larger ones, the dissonance between the (il)logic of the Jim Crow order and the legacy of Jim Crow reform was increasingly visible. In South Carolina the end of the Jim Crow order began with a small request by black parents led by Rev. Joseph Delaine, principal of the black high school, for a school bus for the black schoolchildren of Clarendon County. Although 70 percent of the district's children were African American, white students had thirty buses available to transport them, while black children had none.

Clarendon County, like many rural counties in South Carolina and the South as a whole, had been the beneficiary of Jim Crow reform. The county had received school construction money from the Rosenwald Fund, one of the northern foundations that had funded Jim Crow reform. A total of $17,300 (about $200,000 in 2006 dollars) had been spent on three schools for blacks in the county. The county contributed 52 percent of the total cost, and the foundation contributed 16 percent. The already taxed and poor blacks of the county contributed 31 percent, or $5,400, for their three schools, which were built in the late 1920s. By 1949 these schools—massively overcrowded, with little or no money for modernization—were in terrible shape. The Spring Hill School adjacent to DeLaine's church was a two-story shack. Despite this, when presented with the request for a school bus, the chairman of the school board, R. W. Elliott, contemptuously dismissed the request: "We ain't got no money to buy a bus for your nigger children."[27]

What happened next became part of history. The legal case that blacks in Clarendon County brought against the school board, *Briggs v. Elliott*, was combined with other cases until, when it reached the Supreme Court, it became part of *Brown v. Board of Education of Topeka, Kansas*. Yet like Rosa Parks, the black high school principal Joseph Delaine had already been recruited by the NAACP as part of the new phase in America's "long civil rights movement."[28] He had a long career in education, having previously been principal of Rosenwald-funded schools. He was a member of the Clarendon County Citizens Committee, which had been in existence since the early 1940s. Once their struggle began, the African Americans of Clarendon County were aided by a network of local activists that had been established or strengthened by Jim Crow reform. Whites would also draw on the legacy of Jim Crow reform, pushing for a belated equalization of educational facilities and funding as a way to block increasingly frontal attacks on segregation.

The gradualism of Jim Crow reform, however, was now beside the point. To secure an adequate education for its children, the black community of Clarendon County had done all that it could, and indeed even what it should not have had to do, within the boundaries of Jim Crow reform. In the face of this struggle, and too many other discourtesies and simple wrongs, the ugly dismissiveness of school superintendent Henry Elliot was the final straw. The "quiet courtesy," carefully and necessarily cultivated during the years of Jim Crow, of Rosa Parks and the white and black southern reformers who preceded her had finally come to end.[29] Jim Crow reform had served its purpose, turning the Jim Crow order into a "place so wrong [that] it was right" for it to come to an end and for the civil rights movement to begin.

Chapter 1

The Problem of the South and the Beginning of Reform

The people of the south are best situated to understand the negro and his problem, and can and will do more for him in a practical way than theorists who live at a distance. It is a national burden which the whole nation must sympathetically bear, but the people of the South represent the direct remedial agent.

F. W. Blackmar, "Review: *Studies in the American Race Problem* by Alfred Holt Stone," 1909

The world of Jim Crow reform was complex and multifaceted. Reform was not, strictly speaking, the product of a tightly bound interest group or coalition but a movement, with a worldview shared by individuals and organizations over a period of time in a particular place. It was belief that the Jim Crow order in the South could be made to function more efficiently and more humanely. Many of the people and organizations identified in this chapter would remain a constant presence throughout this period, although there was some fluidity, with new individuals and groups entering and others leaving the world of Jim Crow reform.

Throughout its history Jim Crow reform was troubled by complexity and contradiction. For example, though the intellectual agenda of the movement was primarily set by native southerners, the reform movement received significant financial support from organizations from outside the South. This financial support was not neutral, and it critically shaped the intellectual agenda as well as strategies that reformers would embrace. From its beginning in the 1920s until its end in the early 1950s, Jim Crow reform reflected the belief of many southerners that the South was driven by a painful but necessary "reconciliation between progress and tradition." Southern reform was shaped by what the historian Dewey Grantham calls an emerging "regional imagination," a self-conscious approach to social and economic analysis and reform that rested on a highly articulated sense of identity and place.[1]

In its focus on revivifying state government from the constraints placed upon it by the Redeemers, Jim Crow reform was related to the southern "business [class] progressivism" of the 1920s. However, Jim Crow reform was distinctive from this business progressivism; these reformers argued that government action that did not involve any attempt to make the segregated order more equal or at least more efficient would undermine any hope for the South's true potential to be realized.[2] Jim Crow reform rested uneasily between two polar states, embracing the possibilities of "stateways," the ability of society to be positively shaped by state actions, and a sometimes wavering belief in the fixedness of "folkways." In the end Jim Crow reform fully embraced stateways, and in the process contributed to the changing of an order that many reformers had doubted (and some perhaps wished) would ever fundamentally change.

Many of the individuals and groups discussed in this chapter and throughout the book have been typically categorized as "southern liberals." A better way to categorize them is under the rubric of southern liberal reform. Southern liberalism has typically been identified with a small subset of white males. This identification has tended to ignore the southern black men and the southern women (black and white) who also played an important role during this period.[3] One reason for this exclusion is rooted in the early tactics adopted by these white male reformers, many of whom believed that the white South would accept their findings only if those findings were from white male southerners. Although they were not happy with this logic, many black male reformers accepted this exclusion as the price to be paid for moving Jim Crow reform forward. Individual women played important roles in reform; however, their activities as a coherent, recognizable group were largely invisible or more likely simply ignored by white male southern reformers. Unfortunately later researchers have not recognized that the strategic exclusion or casual minimization of the participation of blacks and women from the record left by white male reformers does not mean that blacks and women were absent from the reform movement. In this chapter I explore how and why these racial and gender divisions in the Jim Crow reform movement emerged and point out how these divisions in turn shaped Jim Crow reform.

The Meaning of Southern Liberalism

The label of "liberalism" in the context of the Jim Crow order does not capture one of the essential qualities of this period, which is that reformers, for a variety of reasons, accepted the boundaries of the Jim Crow order and worked for change within this order. Critics at the time and later routinely condemned these reformers for not openly challenging or condemning segregation. This criticism failed to appreciate that reformers almost by definition are not engaged in fundamental change. Calling the group of whites and blacks who grappled with the confines of the Jim Crow order "southern reformers" creates a more historically accurate and analytically useful category for analysis than "southern liberals."

Jim Crow reformers were reformers not only because they accepted and worked within the boundaries of the Jim Crow order to some degree; they were also reformers because their beliefs and actions fit squarely within America's newly emerging race relations paradigm, popularized by the University of Chicago sociologist Robert Park. Although the theory rejected biological racism as the justification for racial oppression, it masked and minimized racial oppression and exploitation with a more benign, cyclical theory of ethnic and racial interaction.[4] Jim Crow reformers were *southern* reformers in that they refined the race relations approach to reflect the open racial and social hierarchies of the South. They developed a more structured variant of the race relations model, which they called "interracialism."

Jim Crow reform first appeared in the wake of the dislocations created by World War I and its aftermath. The most prominent example of reform is the Commission on Interracial Cooperation (CIC). Although the founding of the CIC, its organization, and its activities will be discussed in more detail in the following chapter, a very brief discussion is offered here to illustrate the ideational as well as organizational boundaries of Jim Crow reform. From its beginning as a response to interracial violence after World War I, to its demise and then rebirth during World War II, the CIC exemplified the strengths and fundamental weakness of Jim Crow reform. The CIC's strength lay in its ability to create an alternative space for dissent to the Jim Crow order to be formulated and expressed and for concrete actions based on these dissents to be pursued. Its weakness lay in the fact that although the CIC and by extension Jim Crow reformers saw their indigenous roots as a source of strength as well as legitimacy, the movement was largely dependent on funding from organizations outside the South. In addition to funding, their inability to distance themselves from folkways, especially the maintenance of social inequality, led reformers to believe that they could be only a step ahead of southern public opinion, which made reform far more reactive than proactive in shaping the Jim Crow order. Indeed the formation of the CIC was fundamentally a reaction to confronting the change that war had brought to the South.

Through much of the 1920s a new breed of reformers and their organizations were ascendant; their beliefs as well as their organizations reflected racial, class, and gender differences within the Jim Crow order. Despite these differences, these reformers were animated by a "regional imagination," the belief that only certain kinds of southerners possessed the ability, the means, and the understanding to govern the New South. In deference to their belief in the strength of folkways, this process would take place through largely indirect attempts to restructure southern government, such as elite-led negotiations, bureaucratic restructuring, and incremental policy changes.

By the time of the New Deal this initial group of reformers was joined by the Southern Conference for Human Welfare and the Southern Policy Committee. These new reformers, like their predecessors, were self-conscious of and instrumental in using their southern identity to legitimize their positions. Like earlier reformers, these new reformers, now inspired by the New Deal, focused on ameliorating the dire economic and social conditions of the South through rational planning. But unlike the strategy of earlier reformers, the means of this amelioration would come through a direct assault on southern government and institutions. Stateways, not folkways, had contributed to the region's poverty, which in turn was the root cause of its racial inequality and oppression. Only a reconstruction of the southern state and its economy could lead to the emergence of a New South. For these southern reformers, under the benign apolitical and technocratic auspices of state planners, economic reform in the short run and the modernization of the southern economy in the long run would lead to greater prosperity. This prosperity in turn would reduce racial and class antagonism and competition. At that point, the democratization of the South could take place. Reformers realized that opening up the South's political sphere to what V. O. Key calls the South's have-nots would be the only way the secure economic reform.

Jim Crow reformers existed in a political order that was bounded by time and place. Many of the political, economic, and social elements of this order were structured by the ideational as well as institutional constraints and commitments made as the Jim Crow order emerged in the late nineteenth century and early twentieth. These ideational and institutional commitments, however, were not locked in; new understanding and new forms of legitimization of the Jim Crow order were constantly being reformed and rearticulated as the South faced the inevitable political, social, and economic changes that occur in every society. To understand the world of reformers and their choices, the policies they crafted and strategies they employed, we must first understand how they made what Ellen Condliffe Lagemann calls a "politics of knowledge" that would help these reformers both explain and then change the South.[5]

Stateways and Folkways: Southern Reform in Search of a Middle Ground

Most white southerners readily believed in William Graham Sumner's assertion that folkways were "one of the chief forces by which a society is made to be what it is." The origins of these folkways, Sumner argued, were lost in the mists of time and were structured by humans' most primitive emotions and impulses, hence the immutability of these folkways. Sumner characterized as "vain attempts" any efforts to address the violence and disorder, the visible inequality, or the lack of democracy in the South that could be attributed to folkways. The mores of the new Southern order, to the extent that they were detectable, could not be controlled by law. Blacks and whites in the Jim Crow South, he argued, were in a state of limbo, caught between the mores of the pre—Civil War era in which "peace and concord" reigned and a future in which the mores "which any one thinks ought to be are a dream." Sumner's solution to this state was for southerners to acknowledge that "legislation cannot make mores."[6] This advice was taken to heart by many conservatives, especially southern conservatives.

By the Progressive Era Sumner's dictums began to be questioned even by some southerners. Although reform-minded southerners did not doubt the durability of folkways, in keeping with their Progressive leanings they did not fully embrace Sumner's rejection of the state. Rather these reform-minded southerners believed that the rougher edges of folkways could be made to fit within the modern state. The turn away from Sumner and the hegemony of folkways was the result of two factors: the rise of southern Progressivism and the emergence of the race relations model.

Historians such as Jack Temple Kirby have argued that the triumph of southern Progressivism was the "great race settlement of 1890–1910—black disenfranchisement and segregation."[7] In the minds of many southern Progressives important reform could occur only once the political and social taint of blacks had been excised from the southern body politic. Yet the excising of blacks from the South's public sphere was not the sum total of southern Progressivism. Although many southern Progressives had openly and eagerly advocated black disenfranchisement as well as eugenics, still other southern Progressives prided themselves on speaking up for the forgotten South, for poor whites as well as oppressed blacks. The worldview of this latter group was shaped by what Frank Owlsey, a white reformer, called their "rather advanced standing on the race issue."[8] That is, unlike their contemporaries, these reformers' advanced understanding was based on acknowledging that the South's "race problem" could not be easily wished away by a nostalgic self-delusion or a belief in immutable folkways; neither could the race problem be permanently deflected through oppression, oligarchy, and misgovernment. For a complicated set of reasons ranging from paternalism and Christian obligation to fears about physical disease and moral contagion, some southern Progressives argued that the better elements, especially the new college-educated men of the South, had to confront the issue of race.

Willis D. Weatherford was one of these new college-educated men. His books on the southern race problem, *Negro Life in the South* (1910) and *Present Forces in Negro Progress* (1912), were part of a new wave of thinking emerging in the South that moved away from strictly Sumnerian analyses.[9] According to Weatherford and later white southern analysts, southern blacks were mired in poverty and degradation not just because of environmental or hereditary factors (which many white reformers still accepted as significant influences), but also because of factors rooted the structure of the southern economy and society. Weatherford argued in his early work that it was the responsibility of white southern "college men" to ameliorate the conditions of southern blacks. The reasons he gave ranged from white self-interest to Christian charity to a broad sense of duty to the American value of fair play. Weatherford's attempt to align reform inspired by social science with the white southern belief system was echoed in the meetings of the Southern Sociological Congress, which met annually from 1912 to 1920.

The first Southern Sociological Congress convened in Nashville, Tennessee, with more than seven hundred people in attendance. Many elements of the Congress were echoed in the Jim Crow reform organizations that followed it. The vast majority of the delegates were whites, with only a small number of handpicked blacks attending.[10] Although many of the attendees were men, a substantial number of attendees as well as conference presenters were women, reflecting the growing role of women in social and education reform. Many of the attendees were affiliated with religious organizations such as the YMCA (Weatherford's employer) and the Methodist Church. Others were members of the new professions of social work and public health. The conference addressed a range of topics: "child welfare, courts and prisons, Negro problems, enemies of the home (e.g., the problem of divorce and the money shark business)." The Congress also examined new solutions and new structures to address these problems, from the role of religious organizations and social workers to calls for better coordination and cooperation.[11]

The importance of the Sociological Congress lay in the fact that it was the first regionwide attempt to create a holistic understanding of the contours of the Jim Crow order. It was an attempt to craft a new basis for understanding the Jim Crow order as it existed and as reformers believed it ought to be. In this sense they were taking up Sumner's challenge to provide a useful, workable middle ground between the South's lost past and its unknown future.

The Southern Sociological Congress, as well as other groups that emerged at the time and were affiliated with it, such as the University Commission on Southern Race Questions and the Southern Publicity Committee, were all early though unsuccessful attempts at developing a coherent approach to reforming the Jim Crow order that addressed both the white and the black sides of the color line.[12] These early attempts established an important framework for, in the words of William Link, "a new basis of racial stability" that relied on a strategy to "educate whites about blacks and to encourage the spread of 'sympathetic,' that is to say paternalist, attitudes." The Sociological Congress, according to Link, also emphasized the need to create and sustain a "better class of Negroes." Contacts with this group would enable "cooperation in helping the negro in his struggle."[13] By 1919 attendance had dwindled, as first World War I erupted and then new organizations, particularly the Committee on Interracial Cooperation, emerged. War and its aftermath would sharpen and focus the initial efforts of those involved and turn it into Jim Crow reform.

War and the Turn to Organized Reform

World War I would come to mean different things for southern blacks and southern whites. For southern blacks it represented an upward path from the nadir of the Jim Crow consolidation era. A new generation, "vibrant with a new psychology," in the words of Alain Locke, emerged not only in the urban north but in the south as well.[14] Whites noticed the change. W. J. Cash observed that a new black southerner "was slowing lifting his head and beginning to grow perceptibly more assertive."[15] Whites traced this new assertiveness to the soldier citizenship experienced by southern blacks and the political, economic, and social dislocations created by the war.[16]

The immediate economic effect of the war was the spurring of black migration to the North as demand for industrial workers grew. The war started what would become the Great Migration of African Americans from the South to the North. Although the political impact of that migration would not be felt for another decade or so, when these black migrants would become northern voters, the immediate impact of this population movement threatened the economic and social basis of the Jim Crow order. The southern economy, in both rural and urban areas, still rested on the absolute exploitation of African American labor. Not only did blacks provide a source of cheap labor, but their very presence acted as a brake on demands from white workers. For southern political and economic elites, black migration critically threatened to reduce the pool of black labor, and thus the ability to impose low wages across the southern labor market.

The war era also came to symbolize different things for blacks and whites politically. The rise of the "New Negro" reflected not only the Harlem Renaissance, led by the black elite; the New Negro also reflected the impact of mass movements such as Garveyism among urban and rural northern and southern working-class blacks. These blacks saw in these mass movements a forceful and meaningful alternative to the submissive roles they were forced to assume.[17]

War-related migration also helped to create new possibilities for political awareness and action. Spurred on by black newspapers such as the Chicago *Defender* and by messages from friends and relatives extolling the financial, political, and social freedoms of the North, southern African Americans increasingly came to the conclusion that the South no longer held any opportunities for them.[18] These new northern residents would become the basis of a new political bloc, which would play a growing role in national politics from the New Deal onward.

For those who did not leave the South, even the urban areas offered slightly more freedom and certainly less overt social control than the repressive plantation counties. By 1920 southern blacks had begun a significant movement north or toward the urban South. The growth of the urban black population helped to spur the expansion of the region's small black middle class. This nascent middle class included teachers, doctors, journalists, and small business owners. The growth of this class would lead to a growing diversity in black political thought and leadership. Booker T. Washington's death in 1915 signaled the waning influence of the Redemption generation and the ability of whites to designate one person as the leader of all African Americans. The strategic accommodation adopted by Washington and his cohorts in the dark days of Redemption and the early days of the Jim Crow order would be replaced by a new generation of black southerners.

America's war for democracy had led to the enlistment of black soldiers in meaningful combat roles and the participation of blacks in war-related activities. The presence of armed and uniformed blacks was a direct challenge to the South's denial of citizenship rights to African Americans. Exacerbating and inflaming some white southerners were rumors that Europeans had treated black soldiers as equals; even more alarming were allegations that white French women had engaged in sexual relationships with African American soldiers. Whites feared that this behavior would lead to an increase in black assertiveness and a challenge to the Jim Crow order.[19] In addition to potential challenges from blacks, elite whites perceived other challenges to what had seemed to be a settled and peaceful order.

The war initiated political upheaval among whites as new voices struggled to be heard in the Jim Crow order. White women pressed for suffrage while lower- and middle-class men supported a newly resurgent Ku Klux Klan. As the Klan grew in Alabama and Georgia it openly threatened elites' control over the political and social bases of the Jim Crow order. While the Wilson administration had marked the high point of southern political power in a generation, the return of Republican administrations in the 1920s demonstrated the limits of southern power in the broader American political system.

By the end of the war the multiple challenges to white male supremacy posed by the display of black martial citizenship, coupled with economic stress, social tensions, and political competition, unleashed a furious torrent of hatred from whites toward blacks. This torrent resulted in the "Red Summer of 1919." Race riots erupted in large cities in the North and the South, in New York City, Philadelphia, Washington, D.C., Charleston, and the largest one in Chicago. There were also riots in smaller communities, such as Longview, Texas, and Elaine, Arkansas. In addition to the riots were the lynchings of black men in uniform, direct messages from whites to blacks that military service especially was a breaching of the Jim Crow order that would be severely dealt with. For some white southerners the riots served as a mechanism for reasserting control over the region's African Americans.[20] For blacks the riots served as a grim reminder of their second-class citizenship. Although some blacks met the riots and lynchings with resignation or acceptance, what shocked and dismayed many whites was the vigorous self-defense displayed by African American communities.

The violence and social disorder unleashed in the aftermath of World War I, coupled with the rise of a new Ku Klux Klan, dismayed and frightened upper- and middle-class white citizens, calling into question their belief that the great racial settlement of Jim Crow had ended the possibility of such violence and disorder. Not only did this violence damage the South's image, but it also challenged elite white southerners' belief in their ability to control blacks as well as lower-class whites.

The postwar violence revealed a number of shortcomings, tensions, and frictions in the Jim Crow order. Southern white Progressives began to craft an approach that emphasized "sane and sensible" solutions to this disorder. These early social scientists and reformers were joined by a small but influential number of white journalists who saw themselves as advocates for a new postwar South. This new coalition's focus on stability was not only a response to the current violence; it was also based on a widespread belief in the ever-present threat of violence and instability in the South.[21] For reform to truly work, they believed, whites and blacks would have to work together.

The violence unleashed by war and the real possibility of more political and economic uncertainty throughout the South convinced many white southerners that a more proactive stance was needed. The new politics of knowledge being created by these reformers was also shaped by the emergence of the race relations model for political reform and governance. This new model, which emerged out of the reform ethos of Charles Merriam and others at the University of Chicago, stressed that "modernization [was] a fundamentally rational political process prior to and absolutely determining of social and economic change."[22] Understanding this political process entailed engaging in a communal and collaborative search for understanding as a basis for action.[23]

Social Science, Race Relations, and Jim Crow Reform

The Great Migration of African Americans from the South to the North that began with the stimulus of World War I challenged the assumption of the geographic fixedness of the Negro problem. Whites, especially southerners, saw the movement of blacks out of their natural place as a challenge to their image of a stable racial order. The race relations model emerged out of a search for "more flexible ideologies and practices in order to preserve Jim Crow."[24] Robert Park, a former employee of Booker T. Washington and subsequently a sociologist based at the University of Chicago, provided a theoretical basis for the new race relations. In his view the problem of the American color line would be solved through gradual racial assimilation. Until that stage arrived, however, energy should be directed at achieving the earlier and necessary stages: the easing of tensions and the development of friendly relations and mutual interests.

According to Park's race relations theory, a dominant group and a minority group engaged in a cycle of conflict, competition, accommodation, and ultimately assimilation. Inequality was simply a function of where the minority group stood relative to the dominant group. Because this theory described a natural process, its proponents were skeptical about the need for and the efficacy of government intervention, believing that assimilation and thus equality would eventually arrive on their own.[25] For African Americans, however, just when assimilation and equality would arrive was less than clear. Race relations theorists thus had to develop a special American exception to make their theory work. The exception was based on a belief that, unlike other groups, African Americans were fundamentally a foreign entity that could not be absorbed into the American body.

Park's attempt to build a theory based on gradualism was somewhat flawed due to what he recognized was the uniqueness of the American racial system. Although his model distanced itself from biological racism, it still saw African Americans as culturally and biologically distinct. Assimilation for blacks could reach only a certain point, well short of any other group. The race relations approach assumed the permanency of a "biracial organization of society" in which the social segregation of Jim Crow was an "unfortunate evil that whites and blacks had to put up with as they [i.e., especially whites] learned to get along."[26] To solve the challenge of American racism and have it fit with his larger theory, Park decided that the race problem could be solved with a shift from horizontal segregation to vertical segregation.[27]

Park's theory perfectly fit the emerging ethos of Jim Crow reform. Although interracialism was important, it could not succeed without biracialism. In his article "The Bases of Race Prejudice" he explained that under vertical segregation, "biracial organizations preserve race distinction, but change their content. The distances which separate the races are maintained, but the attitudes involved are different. The races no longer look up and down: they look across." Indeed Park argued, "[Biracialism is a] unique product of the racial struggle in this country; [it does] not exist outside the United States."[28] Park's theory of vertical segregation purported to not only explain what could happen in the South, but to also provide a blueprint for the North. It also shifted the burden of racial inequality away from whites and placed it on blacks. Separate spheres would allow for separate and more equal development.

Vertical segregation won its first victory in Atlanta, the capital of the New South. In the 1920s Roland Hayes was one of America's most famous black classical singers; he had given concerts across Europe and the United States. In the United States, however, Hayes often refused to perform in front of segregated audiences. After months of delicate negotiations, prominent white and black Atlantans convinced Hayes to give a concert. The most important aspect of the event was that contrary to the *mores* and the folkways of the Jim Crow order, but not its laws, the audience would be segregated vertically rather than horizontally. That is, rather than relegating blacks to the upper balconies without regard to class or status, concert organizers split the hall with a line down the middle, top to bottom; whites were on one side of the line and blacks on the other. As a result wealthier or more elite concertgoers of both races could enjoy front-row seats. One can imagine the satisfaction these reformers felt as they gazed upon a real-life manifestation of vertical segregation.[29]

Coupled with the gradualism of race relations theory was southern interracialism. Interracialism was a mode of interaction, a process of cooperation and communication between the races that relied on education, appeals to religious sentiment, and the leadership of the better classes of both groups. Whites relied on these techniques because they not only distrusted and disdained the white masses, but they rarely possessed the power (political or otherwise) to act on their own. Blacks benefited from interracialism because white reformers often offered the only nonhostile and regularized conduit for the African American community to communicate its preferences and its grievances to white-dominated institutions. Interracialism thus provided the language as well as the tools for two groups that saw themselves as marginalized or oppressed by the South's political, economic, and social structure. Interracialism was not a static process; it drew on the reigning race relations paradigm as well as current trends in social scientific thought.

Gradualism and interracialism were central to the approach favored by the reformers as well as the foundations that supported them. Many believed that government action could not alter fundamentally organic processes; at best, it could offer "abstract empiricism, [a] bland presentation of race relation facts."[30] This approach avoided political sensitivities and fit well within an order in which race was increasingly managed through bureaucratic means.[31]

The development and elaboration of race relations theory and the techniques of interracialism were not simply the result of attempts by white southerners to search for and create order and meaning in a changing world. The new ways of thinking and dealing with race reflected the emergence of new kinds of nongovernmental organizations, primarily foundations that had their own interests in shaping not just southern society but American society at large. In their quest to manage the modernization of the American state, and by extension the South, foundations offered Jim Crow reformers critical financial support. But that support had a price, for the foundations insisted on having an important role in defining the boundaries of Jim Crow reform. Thus foundations provided not only monetary leadership, but the epistemological boundaries of race relations, based on their understanding of modern American social science.

Foundations and the Funding of Jim Crow Reform

Jim Crow reform was in many ways both created and supported by the actions of northern-based foundations. Reformers were highly dependent on and interlinked with these foundations, as they were involved in directly carrying out the foundations' wishes or received institutional or personal support in the shape of research and fellowship grants.

After the Civil War and throughout Reconstruction northern philanthropists set up schools and other institutions for southern blacks; they also set up foundations to support ongoing and future efforts. The largest of these Reconstruction-era foundations were the Peabody Education Fund (1882), the John F. Slater Fund (1882), and the Anna T. Jeanes Fund (1907).[32] By 1910 the abolitionist and religious sentiments that had established these earlier philanthropic efforts were replaced by a new kind organizational and approach: modern foundations supported by social science apparatus.[33]

Embodying this new approach was the Rockefeller Foundation, established in 1913 with an endowment of $35 million. With its new organizational structure and ethos, the foundation restructured its previously established General Education Board (GEB). Although it spent money on a variety of issues, including domestic and international issues such as public health and higher education, its contribution in the area of southern policy dwarfed that of other foundations.

The General Education Board was created in 1902 with a million-dollar pledge from the Rockefeller family. Created alongside the GEB was a sister organization, the Southern Education Board. The function of the latter was in the best tradition of Progressive practices, to collect and publicize statistics and other information about the dismal state of southern education to the citizens and press of the South in order to mobilize public opinion for needed reforms. The Southern Education Board was folded back into the GEB in 1914 with the establishment of the Rockefeller Foundation.

The other prime actor in Jim Crow reform was the Julius Rosenwald Fund, established in 1912 and later converted into a self-liquidating foundation in 1928. The Foundation was established by Julius Rosenwald, the founder of Sears, Roebuck, one of the nation's large retailers. The impetus for its creation came from the influence of Booker T. Washington, whose public stance of silent accommodationism was an uncomfortable legacy to black Jim Crow reformers. The Rosenwald Foundation would be the largest single funder of primary school education for southern black children in the Jim Crow era and would play an important role in the creation of black social citizenship.

By the 1920s these foundations formed an "interlocking directorate of northern philanthropy."[34] Indeed this was literally the case in 1937, when the Peabody, Slater, and Jeanes funds combined to form the Southern Education Foundation. Although the foundations played important roles in shaping various aspects of southern society and government, they rarely trumpeted their achievements due to white southerners' fears of outside involvement. These foundations were the silent partners of Jim Crow reform.

In the Jim Crow order many white southerners viewed northern foundations as potentially dangerous political outsiders. To weaken these suspicions, northern foundation leaders believed that they had to publicly profess their acceptance of the Jim Crow order. Indeed foundation leaders argued that southerners (meaning whites) were the only ones to understand the "peculiar" problems that faced the region. Thus the foundations' role was to support white southerners, not impose their own beliefs. Of course the reality was far more complicated. Far from having a subordinated role, given their monetary and intellectual influence foundations were in many ways equal partners in determining the shape of southern state institutions and in shaping how southern states conceived and delivered educational service in a segregated society.[35] Although they claimed and indeed felt themselves to be outside of politics, the foundations' shaping of state educational institutions and policies in fact created a political arena that whites and especially blacks would struggle to control.[36]

Foundations such as the Rockefeller Foundation and its subsidiary, the General Education Board, were central to the development of race relations science. Foundation leaders worked from the belief that the only possible approach was one that was "pragmatic" and "empirical." Thus foundation leaders believed that "rais[ing] the level of education in the South involved raising the level of both races, and to do this it was necessary to work through the race in power.... There was no alternative to this approach; there was no public opinion to support any other course. For those who were concerned with the development of Negro leadership thorough education this was the only route to follow."[37] Foundation officials argued that they simply followed the route that was set before them, a route that was determined by what they euphemistically called "the special circumstances of the South." Yet these special circumstances were not absolute; the foundations also played a not insignificant role in shaping that very route.

Southern Universities and the Regional Imagination

Southern universities were an important source of reform. During the 1920s southern universities and colleges began to slowly improve as a result of the nationwide growth and expansion of higher education, and partially through strategic donations made by northern foundations. By the 1930s and 1940s these universities provided a pool of individuals who were sympathetic to the aims of southern reform.[38] Animated by their regional imagination, many southern academics believed that they or their institutions could play a unique role in helping the South chart its own distinctive course, while also explaining the South to outsiders.

The ability of reform-minded academics to fulfill their reformist inclinations depended on their institution and their state. In Mississippi academic reformers had to proceed cautiously, with very little internal or external support; in North Carolina the reform ethos was to some extent embraced. Not only did the university's location matter to academics, but the type of institution mattered as well. Academics at state universities often found themselves unable to take a public stance on reform issues; instead their support for reform often had to be couched in oblique, objective language that limited their advocacy. And, as was the case in most things in the Jim Crow order, what side of the color line an institution lay on mattered for academic reformers as well. Activities that were acceptable for white academic reformers to engage in were in some instances not acceptable for black academic reformers. Although southern universities provided a space to support Jim Crow reform, they were still embedded within the larger Jim Crow order.

One of the southern universities noted for its role in the process of regional ideation was the University of North Carolina, home of Howard Odum, one of the South's leading social scientists. Odum arrived at North Carolina in 1920, having received a PhD from Clark University in folklore and a PhD in sociology from Columbia. The Columbia degree was under the supervision of Franklin Giddings, an eminent but highly conservative sociologist in the mold of William Sumner. Once at North Carolina Odum quickly established an academic infrastructure to support his vision of reform based on social science. He established the Department of Sociology and the School of Social Welfare in 1920 and later established the Institute for Research in Social Science. The Sociology Department and the Institute would train or provide a base for the white, mostly male social scientists, such as Guy Johnson, Rupert Vance, and Arthur Raper, who played important roles in providing the intellectual support for Jim Crow reform. Odum also started the *Journal of Social Forces*, which along with the School of Social Welfare—home to many of the women involved in the Jim Crow reform movement—would become an important link between the intellectuals and policy practitioners in the world of Jim Crow reform.[39] The academic entrepreneurialism of Odum would be copied and replicated by others, such as Roscoe Martin, a political scientist at the University of Alabama, and Charles Johnson at Fisk University.

Compared to southern white institutions southern black universities and colleges were absolutely unequal in terms of physical endowment and financial resources.[40] Yet despite these persistent inequalities, the 1920s ushered in a new period of improved higher education for blacks in the South. One of the most important changes was the shift to black leadership; major institutions such as Howard University and Fisk were now led by black presidents. The second shift was the waning grip of Washington's industrial model on white funders, which disdained the liberal arts in favor of vocational education. At the beginning of the Jim Crow order, under direct and indirect pressures from foundations and state legislatures, many black colleges were forced to jettison existing liberal arts curricula (or were not allowed to adopt these curricula in the first place) in favor of a curriculum that emphasized manual labor and domestic service. By the 1920s many black institutions of higher education were beginning to come out of the cramped box into which Washington accommodationism and white hostility had placed them.[41]

With this renewal, coupled with the influence of the Progressive ethos, black Jim Crow reformers began to emerge. Some were leaders of institutions, such as Benjamin Mays, the president of Morehouse College; Horace Mann Bond, the president of Ft. Valley State College; and Gordon Hancock, the president of Virginia Union College. Others were academics, such as the historian Luther Porter Jackson of Virginia College for Negroes and the sociologist Walter Chivers of Morehouse College. Like Odum, many saw these institutions as places to create a new infrastructure for social science–based reform. For example, with northern foundation money Hancock created and ran from 1931 to 1938 the Torrance School of Race Relations, the first of its kind.[42] Fisk University in particular would play an important organizational role in southern reform though the leadership of its president, Charles Johnson.[43]

Johnson was in many ways emblematic of the Jim Crow reformer; trained as a sociologist at the University of Chicago under Robert Park, he was heavily involved with the boards and personnel of the GEB and the Rosenwald Foundation, which funded Jim Crow organizations and institutions. He also played an important role within the African American community as head of the New York Urban League and as chair of the Sociology Department and later president of Fisk University.

During the New Deal Johnson worked with the Roosevelt administration on crafting policies that would aid the South, and especially poor southern farmworkers. His coauthored report for the CIC, *The Collapse of Cotton Tenancy*, was a key element in the enactment of the Bankhead-Jones Tenant Farm Act (1937). Later he worked with Gunnar Myrdal on *An American Dilemma*. Throughout his career Johnson grappled with the nation's race problem, which he defined as "the struggle on the one side, to improve status, and on the other side the resistance to this change."[44]

The emergence of black and white academics committed to southern reform did not erase the color line within the academic and reform communities in terms of their research agendas. For the northern foundations and other organizations that funded southern reform "empirical race relations studies" was considered a southern subject, best studied at white southern universities. Believing that only whites could be objective about race, foundations poured research money into white institutions. This made Odum and the University of North Carolina, not Fisk, the center of expertise on race relations.

By contrast, because they believed that African Americans were less likely to be objective and indeed more likely to be the object of government intervention, foundations developed Fisk University and other black colleges along different lines. Unlike white academicians, African American researchers were not pressured to be apolitical but were encouraged to become involved in local "social welfare agencies and organizations promoting interracial cooperation." Yet "given the etiquette of the racial caste system," African American social scientists and their departments did not "enjoy the political and social influence among local policy-making circles that the major administrators of the Chicago and Chapel Hill institutes [did]."[45]

Southern reformers emerged from both white- and black-controlled institutions, but their ability to shape Jim Crow reform varied. Because white reformers were seen as more objective and neutral, their policy advice was taken more seriously than that offered by blacks. Indeed in studies conducted by white and black teams the contributions of black researchers were largely minimized. This was reflected in the similar but perhaps even worse treatment of southern women, whether black or white. Shut out of public office and from higher education, southern women created an alternative, though no less significant, world of Jim Crow reform.

Women and Jim Crow Reform

Southern women, white and black, had to negotiate the boundaries of the Jim Crow order while also creating a place for themselves in the effort to shape the order. Despite these hurdles, southern women, both white and black, also played a significant role in shaping Jim Crow reform. Within each state a host of white and black local women's organizations were separately engaged in pushing for a wide variety of reform issues.[46] The richness and variety of women's groups reflected the smaller formal political role of white and black women in the Jim Crow order and their attempts to circumvent these limitations. For many women the spread of the women's suffrage movement, the emergence of new roles for women in the new profession of social work, and southern Progressivism had created a new, albeit limited, public role. For white and black women a significant element of their engagement with Jim Crow reform was based on their invocation of maternalist or domestic politics.[47] Yet despite these commonalities white and black women had distinctive reasons for participating in reform.

For white southern women religious organizations initially played an important role. Groups such as the Woman's Missionary Society of the Methodist Episcopal Church were active in early southern reform.[48] The rise of the southern women's social gospel movement also produced many reformers, such as Lily Hammond. The wife of the white president of Paine College, a black college, Hammond was head of the Southern Publicity Committee, whose goal was to encourage the press to publish "constructive-work in racial matters."[49]

These early forays into interracial reform took on more substance in the years leading up to and then following the passage of the Nineteenth Amendment. For individuals such as Jessie Daniel Ames, the suffrage campaign enabled the transition from southern ladies to citizens of a wider world.[50] For white women suffragists, the new networks and organizational capacities that the suffrage campaign had unleashed could not be put away. As it had for their northern counterparts, electoral pressure played a role in motivating white women's activism. In the decade after suffrage was won women's club culture flourished as women sought new ways to express their new citizenship rights. White women's groups included state and local chapters of organizations such as the General Federation of Women's Clubs, the League of Women Voters, the Business and Professional Women's Clubs, and the Association of American University Women.[51]

For black women the path to Jim Crow reform rested on what the historian Glenda Gilmore calls their distinctive difference from white women during the Progressive era: "White middle-class women lobbied to obtain services *from* their husbands, brothers and sons, black women lobbied to obtain services *for* their husbands, brothers, and sons."[52] Often leading southern black women reformers were the wives of prominent black men such as Margaret Murray Washington, wife of Booker T. Washington, and Jennie Booth Moton, the wife of Robert Moton, Washington's successor at Tuskegee. Although these two women were influential, some black women reformers saw them as too conservative.[53]

Lugenia Burns Hope was another prominent southern black woman leader. Although she was the wife of John Hope, president of Morehouse College and a CIC board member, Hope engaged in her own social reforms separate from her husband. For example, she led an unsuccessful attempt to persuade the YWCA to include black women. Despite this setback, she was successful in other areas. For example, she established in Atlanta the first black settlement house in the South, the Neighborhood Union. Hope was joined by other black women, such as Charlotte Hawkins Brown, who established and led the Palmer Memorial Institute, a preparatory school and junior college in the Tuskegee tradition.

Along with these prominent women were hundreds of less prominent, middle-class black women. Like their white counterparts, southern black women established state chapters of national organizations such as the National Association of Colored Women's Clubs, statewide federations of clubs, and local organizations such as Atlanta's Neighborhood Union.[54] Black women also organized within religious denominations such as the African Methodist Episcopal Church.

Though southern women were segregated on the basis of race and separated by class, some organizations created the possibility of cross-race and cross-class cooperation. For example, black and white women worked together on a regionwide basis under the auspices of national organizations such as the Women's Christian Temperance Union and the Young Women's Christian Association, as well as the Southern Methodist Church. Yet true to the now segregated mores of the nation, black and white women were separated into regular and "colored" branches or units. The CIC Women's Committee followed this pattern, placing white and black women in "parallel but separate committees"; in keeping with the gendered nature of southern and American reform, the subcommittees focused on "the home, the church and the school."[55]

The role of women's groups (both white and black) in Jim Crow reform reflected a long-standing gendered division of work in the American as well as southern reform movement. For "bureau" men, as the political scientist Camilla Stivers characterizes these male reformers, the goal of developing and extending the administrative capacity of government was achieved through the procedural reform of government structure, which in turn was based on a faith in science, "facts," objectivity, and expertise. By contrast, for female reformers and "settlement women," a comparative lack of access to state policymaking power meant reform was a bottom-up process based on coalition politics, buttressed by the "maternalist" rhetoric of women as "guardians of public virtue."[56]

The gendered differences in reform were reflected in how southern politics and history would later be put into practice and then interpreted. For example, southern white women resisted attempts by black women to make the case for suffrage for all women. Southern white southern suffragists, with the support of their northern white sisters, believed that explicitly rejecting the right of all blacks to vote would lessen resistance from conservative white men to their own desire for suffrage. Indeed southern suffragists argued that giving white women the vote would in fact strengthen political white supremacy.[57]

Despite their embrace of white supremacy, white female reformers would find themselves pushed to the margins of the southern reform movement. Reshaping the southern state was man's work.[58] At the time of the creation of the Commission on Interracial Cooperation, white male leaders were "somewhat skeptical of female participation" in organized reform for two reasons: the presence of black men on the CIC and the belief that women did not have the mental or physical stamina to engage in the delicate but hard work of racial reform.[59] In their belief that they could only stay one step ahead of southern public opinion, white male CIC leaders believed that having black men and white women serving on the same boards and perhaps working with each other violated the sexual etiquette of Jim Crow. Beyond fears about critics "howl[ing]" about possible racial intermarriage, the white male leaders of the CIC believed, "Not only would Southerners misunderstand women busying themselves with this thing, but emotionally women couldn't be trusted."[60]

Given the gendered division of labor of southern reform, it is not surprising that antilynching activity was first formally organized by the only quasi-political group left in the South: southern white women. In this sphere southern white women could link and subsequently subvert their identity as women and as guardians of southern purity and virtue to push for reforms such as child labor laws that were resisted by white male elites. The Association of Southern Women for the Prevention of Lynching and other women's groups were products of the intersection between race and gender in the era of Jim Crow reform from its CIC beginnings to the rise and fall of New Deal–inspired reform.

The Ideology of Jim Crow Reform

Jim Crow reform revealed the possibilities as well as the constraints of black southern life. As "members of the best classes" on the black side of the color line, some middle-class blacks became active participants in Jim Crow reform, while the majority of the urban professionals were beneficiaries in some way of the expansion and stabilization of the Jim Crow state.[61] Unlike their northern counterparts, who were beginning to be incorporated in northern political systems, many of these black southerners had been thoroughly schooled in the etiquette of the Jim Crow order: as children who had experienced the violence that had accompanied the emergence of the order and as adults whose daily interaction with the white-dominated public sphere was governed by the arbitrary rules that left them "living constantly at tiptoe stance."[62] Thus although black southerners were willing to seek out new pathways to freedom, they were still constrained by their physical and psychological location within the Jim Crow order. Black southerners in this postwar era saw themselves as pragmatic accommodationists working within an environment that was significantly different from that of their northern counterparts, who were at the beginning of their incorporation into the northern political system.[63]

Given the resistance of the Jim Crow order to the changes brought about by the war for democracy, southern blacks who became involved in the southern reform movement did not believe that the citizenship rights that had been almost wholly stripped from them could be easily or immediately regained through direct political confrontation or through the silent accommodation of the Washington approach. Instead southern black reformers believed that a cross-class but elite-led public campaign of moral and educational uplift and community building would create a new opportunity to reclaim citizenship. "Lifting as they were climbing," black elites would strive to make the Jim Crow order work better until it could be overturned.[64]

The black reformers viewed the Jim Crow order through a pragmatic as well as an accommodationist lens. They saw their actions as a "middle ground" between the "old politics [of Washington] and the new, between the timid politics of indirection and the undisguised use and organization [of African American political resources]."[65] If separate and equal was the law of the land, they argued, the South must live up to its obligations. This was important for moral reasons, but also for practical social and economic reasons as well. The Texas newspaper publisher Carter Wesley stated, "A realistic approach therefore requires that we take the problem as it is and seek to improve it as much as we may with the tools at hand and despite barriers."[66] Although pragmatic accommodationism would prove to be a limited though useful tactic given the contours of the Jim Crow order, ultimately it did not prove to be a clear path to the restoration of America's broken promise of full citizenship for African Americans. Nonetheless it provided a critical first step on this quest.

For whites the Jim Crow order and thus Jim Crow reform rested on their belief in white supremacy. On natural, political, and moral grounds whites believed that they had to assume the burden of caring for African Americans, whom they considered a "childlike" race. Although this assumption justified white dominance and control, it also vaguely obligated whites to aiding in the "uplift" of their wards, although to be sure, this uplifting was to the very minimal level that whites believed was appropriate for a permanently childlike race. Nonetheless southern whites shared with their black counterparts the strong belief that managed race relations were best left to the "better classes" of both races.[67]

The new race relations model and its focus on vertical segregation also contributed to this pragmatism. For some white reformers the demands of modern society meant that the old paternalism had to give way. African Americans had to be forced to take more responsibility for their own development. For example, Leonard Outhwaite, a Rockefeller Foundation staff member who led its race relations work, would declare that: "The black [must] get upon his own feet and take care of his own needs in schools, health, etc. by his own support either through taxes or personal contributions."

Indeed, Outhwaite went even further in making the claim for the development of self-sufficiency, though not equality, for African Americans:

> We are dealing with a group of people incorporated in our country for better or worse; that they are handicapped in many respects. There seems to be no way of getting rid of them even if we desire to do so.
>
> Our objective, then, probably is to bring them as early as possible to a state where they can develop their own leadership, and where they can finance their own welfare. The sooner that is done, the sooner the burden will be taken off the general welfare and the public administration of the rest of the country for their support.

Even Edwin Embree, who would head the Rosenwald Foundation and would later be a supporter of the modern civil rights movement, was moved to say, "Since they [African Americans] *are* here and likely to stay here, a sensible procedure would seem to be to educate them and keep them in robust health and give them an opportunity for expression. This will make them assets rather than liabilities economically and socially in the common society."[68] While some of these comments may have been made out of a belief in racial inferiority, many of these white reformers believed that they were taking a cool-minded, rational, pragmatic approach to what seemed to be the intractable problem of race in America.

Reducing the frictions caused by the workings of the Jim Crow order was essential for keeping social peace and encouraging economic development in the South. The ideational commitments and meanings that informed the Jim Crow order also shaped these reformers' response to the violence and uncertainty released by World War I. Jim Crow reform thus began when whites, for the first time since the establishment of the Jim Crow order, reached out to blacks and offered them a role, albeit very limited, in shaping the Jim Crow order. Thus did the first cracks appear in the South's whites-only public sphere.

State Power and the Jim Crow Order

As the Jim Crow order came to its end in the 1950s, southern liberals and, by extension, Jim Crow reformers had become objects of derision and scorn since the 1940s. During World War II Walter White famously quipped, "The highest casualty rate of the war to date seems to be that of Southern white liberals. For various reasons they are taking to cover at an alarming rate."[69] Black reformers also came in for criticism. One critic noted that despite their studies and conferences, direct political pressure, *not* the "best practices in race relations in the South," had produced improvements in life for southern blacks.[70] Despite these criticisms, which were to some degree accurate, Jim Crow reform had created something distinctive. Ralph Bunche, the preeminent black political scientist of that era, found in his analysis of southern politics in the late 1930s that the emergence of southern liberal reform lent "encouragement to the timid" and "unshackle[d] the large number of potential [white] liberals who could not face the prospect of isolation and martyrdom in the community for holding more progressive ideas." In addition to creating a small space for individuals who dared to dissent from parts of the Jim Crow order, the rise of organized reform offered these isolated individuals a "sense of solidarity and contact with each other."[71] Thus, even though these reformers were bounded by the limits of the Jim Crow order, their emergence served a valuable purpose in opening up the South's ideological and discursive space.

The space between the races and between fundamental change and stasis created by Jim Crow reform, however, was a space that was structured by two belief systems that ultimately ended up in conflict. The first belief system was that the Jim Crow order and in particular segregation was fixed and immovable. Segregation was based in folkways, in the age-old culture, customs, and habits. Thus change could occur only when folkways changed, and that was not any time soon. Virginius Dabney, a leading white southern liberal, epitomized this viewpoint when he asserted that only "within a century or so [would] the Negro...be much more nearly equal in his political and social status than is the case now."[72]

The second conflicting belief system of Jim Crow reform was structured by Progressives' belief in social science and a belief that the Jim Crow order could be perfected through an objective, neutral, and empirical approach that used the power of the state to modify folkways. Both white and black reformers believed that the race problem could be "scientifically analyzed" as a "social problem, that as such, [was] not essentially different from any other social problem...and by reason of this fact...respond[ed] to the same processes of adjustment or maladjustment."[73] The conflict at the root of Jim Crow reform occurred as reformers tried to disentangle where folkways ended and stateways began, as they were themselves confused about cause and effect.

As one of their first projects Jim Crow reformers focused on what seemed to be a key ailment of the Jim Crow order: government. The problem of the South was not just economic development or political exclusion and inequality; it was also bad government. To the extent that efficient and effective governmental structures did not exist, the distortions of economic backwardness and political factionalism were magnified. Good government would both cleanse and cauterize this ailing southern state and allow for the development of a more modern state. Reformers would, in their own words, "intelligently" and "scientifically" address the South's problems with homegrown southern solutions. However, to do this reformers would first have to confront one of the most pathological expressions of power in the Jim Crow South: lynching.

Chapter 2

Lynching, Legitimacy, and Order

> The lynching problem is of high national importance. Until America can discover and apply means to end these relapses to the law of the jungle, we have no assurance that ordered society will not at any moment be overthrown by the blind passion of a potentially ever-present mob.
> George Milton Fort, introduction to *The Tragedy of Lynching* by Arthur Raper

Violence was ever present in the Jim Crow order, from its roots in election-related voting intimidation and mob attacks during Redemption to its end with the bombings and beatings during the white South's massive resistance. It was state-sponsored or at the very least state-condoned violence and terror that had stripped civil rights and political and social citizenship from southern blacks, and it was violence and terror that maintained the color line that was subsequently established.

Some white southerners attributed this violence to white southern culture and its "savage ideal."[1] Many white southerners saw violence, especially lynching, as a grim but necessary technique to maintain white supremacy. With Redemption and the establishment of the Jim Crow order, only whites had a legitimate right to use violence if that violence was directed at African Americans whom whites believed violated the color line. In the case of lynching, all whites—those attached to the state or those acting at their own behest—had the power to use force against African Americans. Individual whites had the right to enforce the color line not because of folkways, but because the state gave that power to them. The historian C. Vann Woodward argued that the state delegated the power to enforce the color line to individual whites, the "streetcar conductor, the railway brakeman, the bus-driver, the theater-usher... [and] the hoodlum of the public parks and playgrounds."[2] Beyond this delegation of power was a de facto granting of power to whites based on immunity. With blacks excluded from juries and law enforcement, and indeed considered noncitizens, whites could be assured that they would not face any legal consequences or social sanctions for any violent act taken against an African American.

Lynching can thus be understood as a result of this delegation of power to individuals. Though some white southerners publicly objected to lynching, most of these objections were conditioned by the belief that lynching was the product of white mob violence, which local and state officials were at best helpless to stop. If officials did participate in these activities, it was seen as a regrettable though understandable result of their inability to resist the forces of folkways.[3] In this most basic of state tasks, and indeed central to the core commitments of the Jim Crow order—racial control and domination—southern governments seemingly did not possess a monopoly on the use of coercive power.

By the 1920s, however, southern states' control over coercive power became a larger issue. Throughout the early part of the century there had been periodic exposés of southern government's practices of convict leasing and convict labor. Many critics and reformers decried the brutality and violence of these practices, especially if they were applied to whites. However, some southerners, such as Woodrow Wilson, criticized these practices based on other concerns; for Wilson convict leasing was a "delega[tion] of sovereign capacities to private individuals."[4] The debate over whether lynching, like the leasing of convicts to private individuals, constituted a threat to state sovereignty could have remained simply an isolated, intellectual debate if not for the fact that the Jim Crow order was embedded within another political order. In the American political order, lynching had made it onto the congressional agenda. With that development and the perception that the rise of lynching was linked to the rise in lower-class white political mobilization, southern elites began to focus on the lynching issue.

After a decade of decline, the increase in the number of lynchings after the end of World War I seemed to belie the belief of white southern reformers that the South was making progress on race relations. Some white southerners argued that lynching should be addressed because it harmed not only the South's image but also the stability of the region's race relations. Other southerners took up the lynching issue for defensive reasons. Faced with the dreaded prospect of federal legislation that would interfere with the South's autonomy over race relations, some whites argued that a southern solution to this problem was needed.

Those interested in ending lynching in the South had to develop a justification for its cessation. This justification had to be translated into rhetoric that political and social leaders could communicate to other officials. In turn, these leaders would have to reverse course and withdraw the tacit approval that had been given to ordinary white citizens to personally enforce the Jim Crow order. In addition to rhetoric, actions that asserted that the states had sole power to punish serious transgressions of the color line had to be undertaken to reinforce the needed change. Jim Crow reformers, and in particular white women, became important actors in aiding the southern government's attempts to control the means of racial violence.

Southern reformers believed that both southern folkways and the stateways that sanctioned or at least excused lynching had to be reformed or overturned. For white women reformers, the folkways of southern chivalry that had been used to justify lynching had to be proven to be false and misguided. To do so, these female reformers would rely on the creation of networks of women from the "best classes" throughout the South who would use both informal and formal means of persuasion and social pressure to convince the men in their networks—husbands, brothers, and sons—to prevent and condemn lynching. Male reformers pursued a different strategy, resting on a neo-Progressive faith in science and expertise. They believed that a sober, objective, fact-based analysis of lynching would be more effective in changing white southern attitudes than appeals to sentiment. Given the regional and racial chauvinism of the time, the analysis and justification had to be seen as produced by and for white southerners.

Southern reformers, white and black, male and female, all played a role in challenging the acceptability of lynching and in creating a new justification for greater state power and control in the lives of white and black southerners. Lynching and lawlessness were two facets of a disease that threatened to weaken the legitimacy and authority of the Jim Crow order. Although southern political elites often favored minimal power for states, this did not mean that they endorsed a powerless state. Lynching was not only an expression of white social control over blacks; the persistence and growing public enthusiasm for it was also a reflection of white elites' inability to control lower-class whites and state political leaders' inability to control localities.

This chapter traces some, though certainly not all of the efforts of Jim Crow reformers to transform lynching from a heroic defense of white womanhood and white supremacy to a manifestation of bad government and social disorder that threatened the stability of the Jim Crow order. Pressure from above in the form of antilynching legislation being considered in Congress may have influenced (mostly elite) white southerners' attitudes toward lynching, but more influential were southern reformers whose framing of the issue allowed these elites to develop their own justifications for opposing lynching. By the 1930s southern politicians who, like Cole Blease and Theodore Bilbo, openly proclaimed on the national stage that lynching was justifiable were becomingly rare. Most nonsouthern elites and increasingly many southern elites were less willing to openly support lynching as an acceptable form of social control.[5]

The transformation of the minds, though not necessarily of the hearts of the white South was not only the result of pressure from above and outside the Jim Crow order; it came from the efforts of Jim Crow reformers to redefine and reject lynching in order to protect the order. This effort was spearheaded by one of the key organizations committed to Jim Crow reform, the Commission on Interracial Cooperation. In this chapter I trace the founding and development of the CIC to show how the antilynching campaign was central to the creation of Jim Crow reformers' identity and beliefs, how they defined what order and stability meant in the Jim Crow South. Jim Crow reformers, including the journalists in their midst, used the power of the press as well as moral pressure targeted though organized networks of respectable white women to end mob violence and public disorder. They also attempted to change and strengthen stateways, to shift power away from individuals and to the state, by encouraging the growth in state police forces and proposing new state antilynching laws.

The Return of Lynching

The end of World War I and the summer of 1919 had produced a surge in the number of lynchings (as well as race riots) after nearly a decade of decline (see figure 2–1). The lynchings that took place ranged from isolated instances of small groups of whites abducting blacks and working in secret, to large-scale spectacles where newspapers announced the lynching days in advance and whites from miles around came to see the killing.[6] The rise in lynchings and other racial violence was so noticeable that Woodrow Wilson, the symbol of the Jim Crow order's political ascendancy, was forced to issue a statement condemning lynchings.[7]

African American activists had mobilized against lynching from its very beginnings, with the most visible campaign led by Ida Wells-Barnett at the turn of the century.[8] After the war the antilynching crusade remobilized, this time with the enthusiastic support of the NAACP. Building on work done by the Tuskegee researcher Monroe Work, the NAACP also engaged in a public education campaign. One of the first steps in this campaign was the publication of *Thirty Years of Lynching in the United States, 1889–1918* in 1919. This

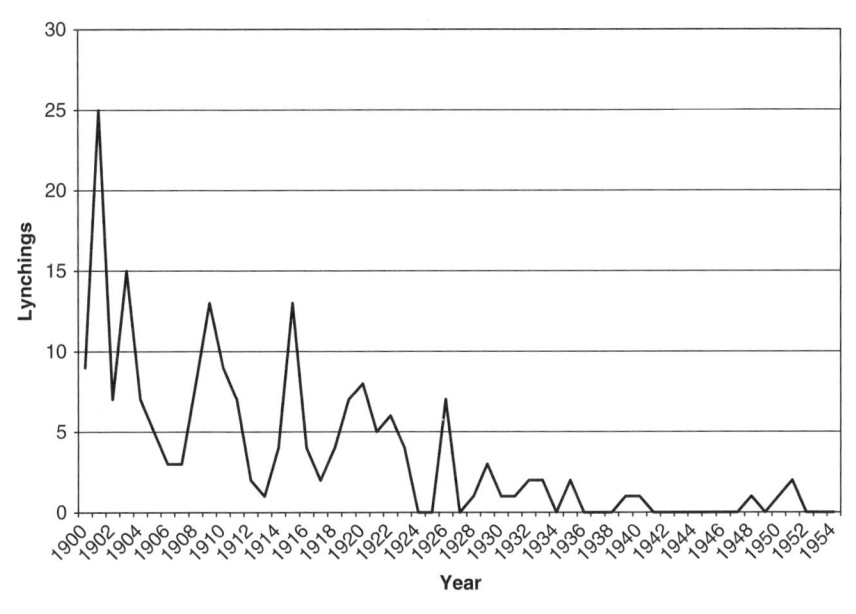

Figure 2–1 Lynching of African Americans in the South, 1900–1954
Source: Tolnay and Beck, *A Festival of Violence*, "Appendix, Table C-3: Time Series of Victims of Lynching in Ten States in the South, 1882–1930," 271–72; Project HAL: Historical American Lynching Data Collection Project, http://people.uncw.edu/hinese/HAL/HAL%20Web%20Page.htm.

report as well as others sponsored by the NAACP documented the extent of the lynching problem, but also the various reasons given by lynchers to justify their actions. What this report and others found was that lynchings were rarely if ever the result of white punishment of black male rapists (which was the white South's most cherished rationalization); rather lynching occurred when individual blacks or the black community in general was seen as violating (whether actually or not) the color line.

The focal point of this public campaign was to get federal action on this issue. In 1918, after intense lobbying and mobilization by the NAACP and other groups, an antilynching bill was introduced in the House by Leonidas Dyer, a Missouri Republican who represented a district with a significant African American population.[9] The Dyer bill "proposed to make mob murder or the failure to protect a federal prisoner a Federal offense and [would] levy fines against counties in which the offense occurred."[10] The bill was passed in the House by a 230–119 vote in January 1922. Resistance by southerners in Congress as well as the reluctance of Republican Party leaders meant that the bill did not make it to the Senate until after the 1922 midterm elections. The bill then made it out of the Senate Judiciary Committee, but southern senators proceeded to filibuster it. Although the attempt to pass a bill ultimately failed, the very fact that a bill had successfully passed that attacked racial practices of the South and challenged the white South's autonomy in that arena shocked many southerners.

The arguments deployed against the antilynching bill ranged from outright racist rants about African American sexuality and the sanctity of southern white womanhood to Calhounian arguments of states rights and fear of federal power. The argument regarding states rights was one with which that many southern elites were comfortable. Southern members of Congress argued that lynching was the South's problem and could therefore only be solved by southern action, although not necessarily even state action.

This call for southern action was taken up by other southerners. As one southern newspaper, the Macon, Georgia, *Daily Telegraph* argued, "We don't want any Federal laws to stop lynching. We have enough State laws for this purpose. All we need is an enlightened conscience, to be aroused to the seriousness of lynching."[11] The newspaper's assurance rested on dubious claims. First, where legislation existed it was patchy, but more important and fundamental the laws as such were never enforced. In addition, the *Telegraph*'s claims evaded the fact that with the two exceptions of the CIC and its sister organization, the Association of Southern Women for the Prevention of Lynching (ASWPL), organized responses by southern whites to stem the tide of lynching were almost entirely absent.

While the congressional antilynching bill and possible federal intrusion in southern race relations was one source of alarm for southern elites, southern white reformers looked on lynching from another perspective. Like other southern elites, they were alarmed by the revival of lynching in the postwar era, especially the more violent type of lynching characterized by its mass entertainment value. Unlike many conservative whites, they saw lynching through the lens of order, stability, and control. Lynching, they argued, was "a menace to private and public safety, and a deadly blow at our most sacred institutions. Instead of deterring irresponsible and criminal classes from further crime... lynching tends to destroy all respect for law and order."[12]

War and the Beginning of Organized Jim Crow Reform

Organized Jim Crow reform emerged as a result of the outbreaks in racial violence that occurred during and after the war. Thomas Jesse Jones of the Phelps-Stokes Foundation and Robert Moton of the Tuskegee Institute worked with Willis Weatherford and others to create a new network of reformers and organizations to deal with the violence and uncertainty. White men such as Will Alexander and M. Ashby Jones were recruited from organizations such as the YMCA and the Southern Methodist Church. The YMCA had already aggressively moved in the direction of setting up local interracial committees to address postwar racial tension; about eight hundred whites and five hundred blacks had been trained by Weatherford and Alexander (at racially separate institutions, of course) for the purpose.[13] The establishment of the CIC provided a focus for these disparate reform efforts.

The CIC was founded in 1919 to ease the "maladjustments" between the white and black worlds.[14] It was initially funded by the YMCA National War Work Council. The CIC quickly moved to establish local interracial committees throughout the South in communities with a population that was at least 10 percent black. In 1920 five hundred state and local committees were established, and by 1923 the number had risen to about eight hundred. Within each state the CIC paid one white and one black staff worker, who each worked to foster interracial dialogue. The CIC defined its role as bringing together the separate worlds of the Jim Crow order through a process of elite leadership, education, and persuasion. For example, the Texas CIC described itself as an organization that "establish[es] no schools, no hospitals, no playgrounds, but...works continuously to change attitudes so that the proper state or civic agency having such enterprises in hand may be interested in the welfare of all people who are touched by their work."[15] Although the CIC did not see itself as a direct service provider, it did aim to change attitudes. This limited role also fit with the organization's belief in the need to offer a factual and objective approach to the South's "race relations" problems.

The Limits of Interracial Membership

Both white reformers like Alexander and black reformers like Moton came to the conclusion that for interracialism to work, both whites and blacks would have to be involved. This biracialism had its limits, for whites dominated the movement and provided its most visible face. Yet this paternalism was not reflected in black membership. For both whites and blacks, blacks who did not embrace a Progressive ethos and new attitude were not welcomed. The "hat in hand Negro" was rejected, as was the "radical"; "educated and developed Negroes" need apply.[16] Initially only four African Americans were invited to join: Moton; Bishop Robert E. Jones of North Carolina, the only African American bishop of the Methodist Episcopal Church; John Hope, the president of Morehouse College; and Professor Isaac Fisher of Fisk University, editor of *Fisk University News*. The inclusion of Moton was not surprising;

not only had he been involved from the very beginning, but he also occupied a unique role. As the head of Tuskegee Moton had inherited the role of racial spokesman that whites had given to his predecessor. The inclusion of Fisher was also notable, as he was considered a conservative in the mold of Washington.

At the CIC's meeting in the summer of 1920 twenty-one southern blacks from a cross-section of professions participated. Many were educators, such as John Gandy, president of Petersburg Normal and Industrial Institute (later Virginia State), and Mary McCleod Bethune, the founder and head of Daytona Normal and Industrial Institute for Negro Girls (Bethune Cookman College). Despite this expansion the inclusion of blacks in the CIC was still limited and unequal. For example, although Moton played a key role in the establishment of the CIC, according to one historian, he let the "credit go to whites," stating that "a Negro who had persuaded white people to do what was right and fair for Negroes was wisest to give all credit to the whites."[17] Only one African American, Charles Johnson, would have a formal leadership role during the central organization's twenty-year existence, although a number of states (North Carolina, South Carolina, Kentucky, Louisiana, Oklahoma, and Tennessee) hired blacks as state secretaries.[18] The staff of the group's central office was all white and would largely remain so until the 1940s. Nonetheless, despite this inequality, the limited inclusion of blacks in the CIC marked a shift from whites "work[ing] *for* the Negro, to work[ing] *with* him."[19]

From the beginning, journalists were a critical element of the Jim Crow reform movement and critical to the CIC's success. Journalists and the papers they edited or owned played were important in communicating and garnering attention for the efforts of reform organizations like the CIC. Through their public support of interracialism as well as the other ideas and programs promoted by southern reform groups, journalists helped to nurture Jim Crow reform by offering an alternative, less reactionary view of southern life and by fostering a dialogue (however indirect) between the white and black worlds. Although there has been considerable focus on white journalists, such as Virginius Dabney of the Richmond *Times-Dispatch*, John Temple Graves of the Birmingham *Age-Herald*, and Ralph McDaniel of the *Atlanta Constitution*, there has been comparatively less attention to the role played by African American journalists in shaping southern reform, such as P. B. Young, editor and publisher of the *Journal and Guide* (Norfolk, VA), and Carter Wesley, editor and publisher of the *Houston Informer*, *Dallas Express*, and the *New Orleans Sentinel*.[20] Wesley was an important member of the Texas CIC, and Isaac Fisher was first the publisher of the *Southern Farmer*, which was read by thousands of southern blacks, and then the *Fisk University News*.

Leavening the "Lump": The Organizational Structure of Jim Crow Reform

The late 1920s to mid-1930s was a period of mixed success for the CIC and its affiliates. At first the main purpose of the nearly seven hundred local committees was to bring together "leaders of the two groups [blacks and whites] around some concrete situation which need[ed] attention." Organizers had hoped to have field workers or local committees established in all southern counties that had at least a 10 percent black population. In keeping with the race relations model, this would aid southern communities (e.g., white communities) to "leaven the lump," the indigestible foreign mass that blacks presented to a smoothly functional model.[21] As funding from the National War Work Council ended and tensions eased in the postwar period, many of these local committees would fade away. The CIC then largely became an organization based in Atlanta with a loose affiliation with individual state CIC committees.

The presence and strength of the CIC varied across the states during the 1920s. There were active state committees in seven states: Kentucky, Tennessee, North Carolina, Virginia, Georgia, Alabama, and Texas. The political and social context of individual states shaped CIC activities and strategies. For example, the presence of an active and increasingly politically powerful Ku Klux Klan in Alabama, Georgia, and Mississippi limited the effectiveness of the state committees. In Alabama and Georgia this meant that the CIC carried out its activities "as unobtrusively as possible" and "act[ed] with the utmost discretion." By contrast, in North Carolina and Virginia, two states that had early on embraced the managed race relations model, the state CIC committees were incorporated into the ruling elite. Governors sat on the boards of these state committees; this "semi-official" status in turn "greatly encouraged membership and general popular support."[22] This incorporation meant that these state CIC committees were extensions of the ruling elite and did not stray beyond or even mildly challenge the boundaries they set.

The state committees of Texas, Tennessee, and Kentucky were much more politically competitive and socially fluid (though still segregated and unequal) than in other Jim Crow states. Texas was exceptionally well-organized under the leadership of Mrs. Jessie Daniel Ames, who ensured that the state CIC was evenly represented by race as well as gender. In Tennessee and Kentucky a more competitive political structure (especially in Kentucky) enabled blacks to press for more concrete reforms. Indeed James Bond, an African American, would become the only nonwhite to become a state CIC chair and would help to forge the "Louisville way" of Jim Crow reform.[23]

Mississippi was in a class of its own. It was more or less resistant to Jim Crow reform attempts from the movement's beginning until its end.

Mississippi lacked a state CIC committee (although it had a women's subcommittee) as a result of the hostility of Mississippians to reform and the presence of the Klan. To the extent that Mississippi did enact some Jim Crow reforms in the 1940s, it was almost always after all the other southern states had already done so. The reforms that were adopted by the state were mostly on paper and lacked any fiscal support or policy substance.

The variety of state affiliates belied the CIC's fundamentally urban base. In Georgia, for example, the presence of the Klan restricted CIC activity to Atlanta and Savannah. In general, state CICs were intertwined with urban social welfare networks. Local community chest programs financed the CIC in Richmond, Norfolk, Atlanta, Savannah, Greensboro, Charleston, New Orleans, Houston, Louisville, and Memphis.

The headquarters of the CIC in Atlanta became the clearinghouse for interracialism. Thousands of pamphlets, news clippings, and reports were sent to newspapers and civic notables throughout the South, the rest of the nation, and a number of other countries. CIC members served on a variety of state and local commissions and organizations and worked with the northern foundations; all their efforts were attempts to impose rational governance on race relations.

Although the CIC and white southerners believed that the most effective way to reform the South was to show that it was developed and supported by southerners, the reality was quite different. Not only were there few philanthropic resources to tap in the South, but CIC leaders such as Alexander believed that simply engaging in a public campaign in to support reform would "arouse the most prejudiced...and subject the program to the control of general public sentiment in the section, thus hampering and modifying it to the point of emasculation." The CIC thus received the bulk of its early funding from four sources: the Phelps-Stokes Fund, the Carnegie Foundation, the International YMCA, and the Rockefeller-affiliated Laura Spelman Memorial Fund.[24]

Despite the CIC's preeminent role in southern reform, the early years of the Depression took its toll on the organization. In 1930 funds for the CIC headquarters dried up, many state and local affiliates became inactive, and fieldwork largely ceased in six states. There were two exceptions to this drop in activity: because of their connections to state government the affiliates in North Carolina and Virginia remained active.[25]

The CIC Confronts Lynching

During the 1920s the CIC took the lead in providing southern white organized opposition to lynching in the form of publicity as well as investigation. The CIC issued a series of pamphlets throughout the decade that condemned lynching and encouraged and then highlighted any condemnation of lynching made by southern white elites. Alexander and other whites affiliated with the CIC were dispatched around the South to avert lynchings, and more often to investigate lynchings after they had already taken place. The goal of these investigations was to publicize the lynching and the Commission's condemnation of it, shame "people of good will" in the South, and try to bring the perpetrators to justice. In this last purpose they almost always failed.

The CIC also focused on changing stateways. In a number of states they pressed for the adoption of state antilynching laws. They were successful in Kentucky, with an antilynching law enacted in 1920. The CIC was also influential in getting laws, though weak, enacted in South Carolina, Tennessee, and Virginia (see Table 2–1). Each of these laws had a variety of penalties or sanctions for those convicted of participating in a lynching, yet the laws essentially were meaningless, as the enforcement problem remained.[26] No one was ever prosecuted for violating these laws. Instead these laws were used by southern politicians such as Harry Byrd of Virginia to support their argument that a federal antilynching law was not needed. The CIC followed the instincts of its white leadership (and disregarded the wishes of its black members) by refusing to endorse the Dyer antilynching bill. For the CIC the crusade against lynching was fundamentally a search for law, order, and stability. The punishment of African Americans should be in the hands of the law, not the individual.

In addition to focusing on enacting laws, the CIC also worked to influence southern law enforcement to live up to its duties. As the CIC as well as other observers noted, sheriffs and other local law officials were elected officers; from the perspective of sheriffs confronting an angry mob of whites, stated Jessie Daniel Ames, behind the lynch mob stood voters, while behind the black person being lynched "stood nothing."[27] To address the electoral issue the CIC did not of course endorse political power for blacks, but rather attempted to persuade southern law officials that enforcing the law would be publicly acknowledged and celebrated. In 1925 the CIC decided to create an official award that would be given to a law enforcement officer who had averted a lynching. From 1925 to 1932 seventeen officials from eight states won the bronze medal.[28]

One of the troubling aspects of this early CIC work was its conflicted views on and semiofficial sanctioning of what would come to be known as "legal lynchings." Legal lynchings occurred when instead of a physical lynching, there was a swift and usually perfunctory trial that produced a predetermined execution sentence. Many white southern reformers believed that vanquishing the mob spirit and (re)imposing a veneer of law and order on southern society was the primary purpose of antilynching efforts, justice

Table 2–1 Southern State Legislative Sanctions against Lynching (as of 1935)

	Lynching	Aiding Lynching	Mob Violence	City/County Liability: Personal Injury	City/County Liability: Property Damage	Removal of Peace Officer who permits lynching? By?	Prisoner may be sent to another county? Under what authority?
Alabama	5 years – Death	1–21 yrs				Impeachment	
Arkansas							
Florida							Governor
Georgia	1 year –Death						Court
Kentucky	Life-Death	Life-Death	1–15 years		Yes		Court
Louisiana						Governor	Court
Maryland					Yes		
Mississippi							Court
North Carolina	2 – 15 years				Yes		
South Carolina					Yes	Conviction	
Tennessee						Conviction	Sheriff
Virginia	Death	Death	1 year - Death				

Source: "Legislative Enactments Against Lynchings," *The Book of the States* (Chicago: The Council of State Governments and the American Legislators' Association, 1935), p. 44.

was somewhat beside the point. This conflict would not be addressed by the CIC until the 1930s.

The CIC's activities in the 1920s on behalf of lynching masked what would soon be out in the open: the decades-long but mostly hidden tensions of southern reform between folkways and stateways and the conflict between men and women over the shape as well as the conduct of southern reform. From the late 1920s through the 1930s southern women, especially white women, understood lynching through the distinctive perspective of gender.

Women and Jim Crow Reform

The emergence of Jessie Daniel Ames and southern white women as the vanguard of the southern antilynching campaign during the 1930s was not a development that the men who created the CIC would have envisioned. Ames's emergence reflected two tensions within Jim Crow reform: between folkways and stateways and between men and women. Ames argued that while the "men were out making studies and surveys of lynchings...the women had to get busy and do what they could to stop lynchings."[29] Her comments reflected what would become the distinguishing characteristic of male-dominated southern reform: an obsession with form, procedure, and "facts" that was difficult to link to actual practice.

The campaign against lynching reflected the gendered structure of southern reform. Women relied on the creation of networks of women's groups, made up of the "best" people, who used investigation, persuasion, and social pressure on their husbands, brothers, and fathers. In furtherance of this gendered role, the women's campaign also rejected taking a clear political stance in favor of an antilynching law, whether at the national or state level.

The women's campaign also reflected the southern reformers' belief that the best way to influence other whites on a sensitive issue was to ensure that there would be no objectionable breaches of the color line. Thus the southern white women's campaign against lynching was notable for explicitly rejecting any open alliance with black antilynching groups, and in particular with black men.

The confluence between the gendered structure of southern reform, national politics, and antilynching activity had two phases. The first phase occurred during the 1920s as a movement among southern white church women and the CIC's Women's Section. The second phase occurred during the 1930s under the auspices of the ASWPL. Jesse Daniel Ames created the group in 1930. She was a Texan with a background in the woman's suffrage movement, a member of the Texas CIC since the 1920s, and the director of the Women's Section of the CIC. Ames was an important bridge between the different worlds of southern and white female reform. The women who joined her came from the League of Women Voters, the YWCA, the Federation of Women's Clubs, and the Parent and Teachers Associations.[30] The ASWPL was the center of a web of women's organizations that focused on antilynching efforts (see Figure 2–2). Reflecting the gendered boundaries of southern reform, most of the organizations affiliated with the ASWPL were religious ones.

The ASWPL followed the well-worn path of Progressive-type reform through a range of activities: investigation, data collection, education, personal persuasion, and publicity. With a small central committee controlled by Ames, the organization created a federated network of groups in each state, and within each state across cities whose population included 10 percent or more African Americans.

The women in these local areas were charged with focusing on the better class of people as well as local law enforcement officials as a means of changing southern elite attitudes toward lynching. The group's founding declaration, and key to its educational campaign and organizational strategy, was the argument that lynching was not a chivalrous act done "in their [white women's] name":

> Distressed by the recent upsurge of lynchings, and noting that people still condone such crimes on the grounds that they are necessary to the protection of womanhood, we, a group of white women representing eight southern states, desire publicly to repudiate and condemn such defense of lynching, and to put ourselves definitely on record as opposed to this crime in every form and under all circumstances.... It brings contempt upon America as the only country where such crimes occur, discredits our civilization, and discounts the Christian religion around the globe.[31]

This statement reflects the ASWPL's initial rejection of the biracial approach of Jim Crow reform.

Ames believed that the first barrier to biracial reform was southern folkways. Because folkways alleged that the sexual deviance of black men was the cause of lynchings, it would not do to have black men working directly with white southern women. Coupled with this reasoning was the everyday reality of the strict segregation of white women from black men. Given this reality, one would expect that black women would be the next best alternative as partners in the southern anti-lynching movement and members of the ASWPL. Yet this alternative was not pursued, although some thought was given to creating a biracial women's movement against lynching.[32] In addition to this strategic decision was the belief shared by many

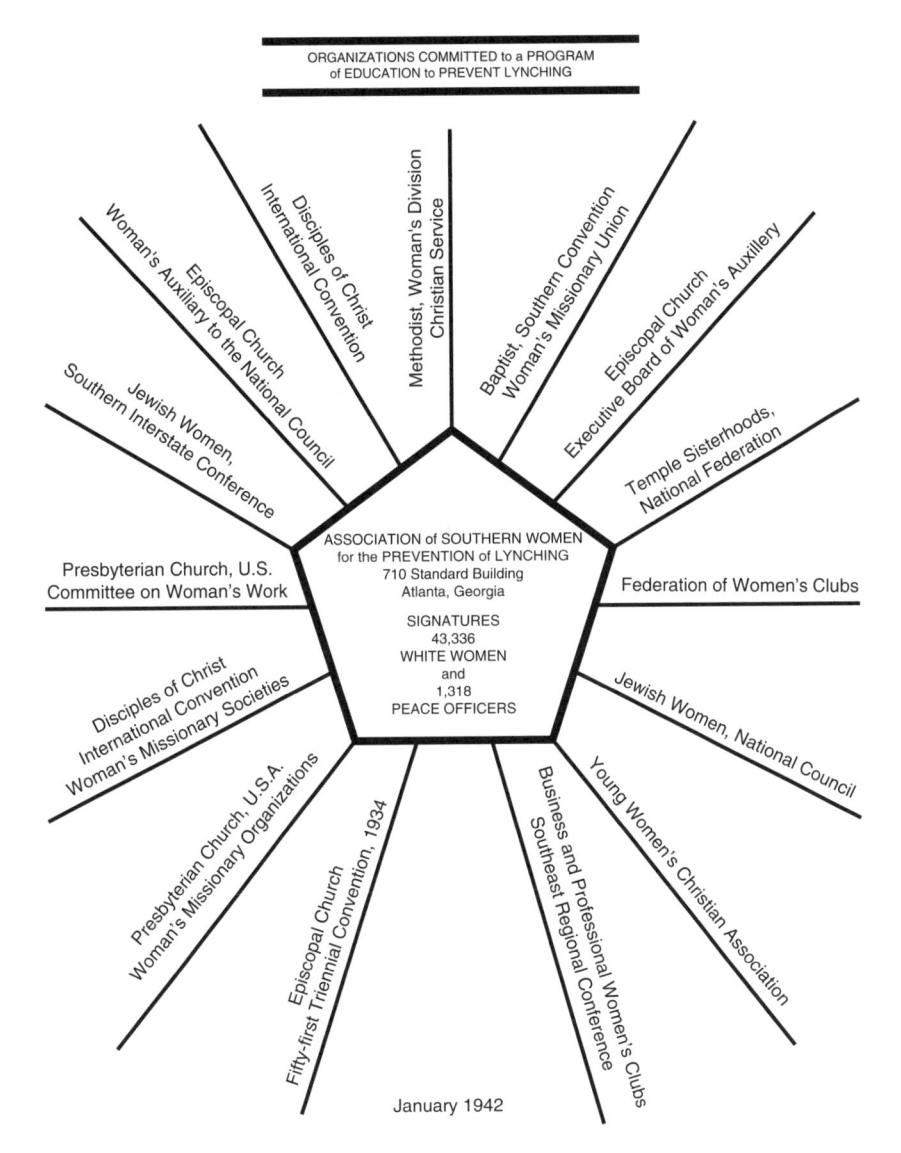

ORGANIZATIONS COMMITTED to a PROGRAM of EDUCATION to PREVENT LYNCHING

ASSOCIATION of SOUTHERN WOMEN for the PREVENTION of LYNCHING
710 Standard Building
Atlanta, Georgia

SIGNATURES
43,336
WHITE WOMEN
and
1,318
PEACE OFFICERS

- Woman's Auxiliary to the National Council
- Episcopal Church
- Disciples of Christ International Convention
- Methodist, Woman's Division Christian Service
- Baptist, Southern Convention Woman's Missionary Union
- Episcopal Church Executive Board of Woman's Auxiliary
- Temple Sisterhoods, National Federation
- Federation of Women's Clubs
- Jewish Women, National Council
- Young Women's Christian Association
- Business and Professional Women's Clubs Southeast Regional Conference
- Episcopal Church Fifty-first Triennial Convention, 1934
- Presbyterian Church, U.S.A. Woman's Missionary Organizations
- Disciples of Christ International Convention Woman's Missionary Societies
- Presbyterian Church, U.S. Committee on Woman's Work
- Jewish Women, Southern Interstate Conference

January 1942

Figure 2–2 ASWPL Network of Women's Organizations
Source: Ames, *Changing Character of Lynching*, 20.

white reformers that in the South reform was best undertaken by white reformers.

The lack of biracialism in the women's antilynching movement was the result of strategic choices made by white leaders such as Ames. In her quest to give the campaign as broad a base as possible in the white South, Ames decided to bar the formal involvement of African American women. She repeatedly stressed that the ASWPL was "not an interracial movement but a movement of Southern women interested in law observance and law enforcement." By restricting membership to white women, she hoped to draw women who would otherwise shun liberal reform. Indeed she argued that the boundaries of southern ideology made southern reform into a "little group of like-minded people, talking only to themselves."[33]

Ames's decision that the ASWPL would remain a whites-only organization was a disappointing development for southern black women. Black women activists such as Ida B. Wells, as well as African American clubwomen, had been focused on antilynching efforts since the turn of the century and were eager to forge links with the white women reformers on this issue. The black women had already begun establishing tentative links with white female reformers on health, education, and welfare issues.

Despite being rebuffed from white organizations, southern black women continued their antilynching activities, in some cases working quietly with local white women. The antilynching campaign was too vitally important for southern black women to deter them from continually making efforts to connect their cause with the campaign of southern white women. Although the Jim Crow order had stripped African American men and women of their political and civil rights, the impact was uneven. For black men to openly try to insist on the restoration of these rights would be physically dangerous at worst, and socially and economically dangerous at best. Although black women had the same restrictions, notions of gender protected at least some of these middle-class black women from immediate physical harm. More important, lingering claims to social citizenship as well as white paternalism gave black clubwomen the opportunity to engage in quasi-political activity. For black women lynching was an issue on which they could and had to intervene on behalf of their husbands and sons. Once inflamed, the lynch mob did not respect education, class, or sex.[34]

The black women's campaign was twofold. First, they aimed to persuade the national government to enforce its own laws and protect the life and liberty of its southern black citizens. The NAACP-affiliated Anti-Lynching Crusaders and the National Association of Colored Women were the two leading groups in this effort.[35] The second goal was to persuade southern white reformers to drop their reluctance to endorse federal legislation. In this latter campaign the women were somewhat successful; more white reformers began to openly endorse the antilynching legislation. However, by the late 1930s it was too late; the prospects for federal legislation had basically expired.

Politics and Pressure through Personal Networks

The approach of the southern white women emphasized the building of state and local networks that took advantage of personal relationships as well as the strong women's club movement. In the records kept by the ASWPL a glimpse of their approach can be seen. The ASWPL's strategy was to get pledges from southern whites that they condemned lynching. Reflecting the CIC's earlier strategy, the ASWPL actively sought the pledges of those who lived in counties that were at least 10 percent black. The campaign to gain pledges was aimed not only at the local notables but also at southern law enforcement officers. The pledge taken by these officers was straightforward: "Believing that lynching is a crime which should not be tolerated in any civilized country, I pledge my support as an officer of the law, to its eradication."[36] The pledge reflected the ASWPL's limited focus on law and order, not justice.

The organization believed that the act of signing the pledge would encourage southern whites to take a more active role in preventing lynchings in their communities. As respectable community insiders, pledge signers could put pressure on local officials to prevent lynchings or, if one happened anyway, to investigate it. By publishing the names of southern whites who signed the ASWPL antilynching pledge, the organization helped to decrease the isolation that southern moderates often felt within the orthodoxy of the Jim Crow order.

From 1931 to 1942 the ASWPL garnered more than forty-six thousand pledges; women signed the vast majority (96 percent; see Figure 2–3). In 1935 the association reported that 404 law enforcement officials had signed pledges. In 1936 the group reported that 2,686 pledges had been signed and by 1940 approximately 3,400 law enforcement officials had signed. Gaining the support of law officials was not a new tactic; in 1927 the CIC's Women's Section had started to give medals to police officials who had prevented lynchings.[37]

Notwithstanding these achievements, the organizational network that was the result of the ASWPL's and Ames's hostility toward public biracial cooperation on the issue lessened the organization's ability to win friends across the color line and to successfully attract younger southern women. In the face of Ames's intransigence on biracial cooperation and refusal to endorse federal legislation, the ASWPL lost its monopoly on the issue. Old allies as well as a younger generation of southern women, both white and black, became visible allies in the antilynching campaign, although by the late 1930s it was under the aegis of other organizations, such as the Southern

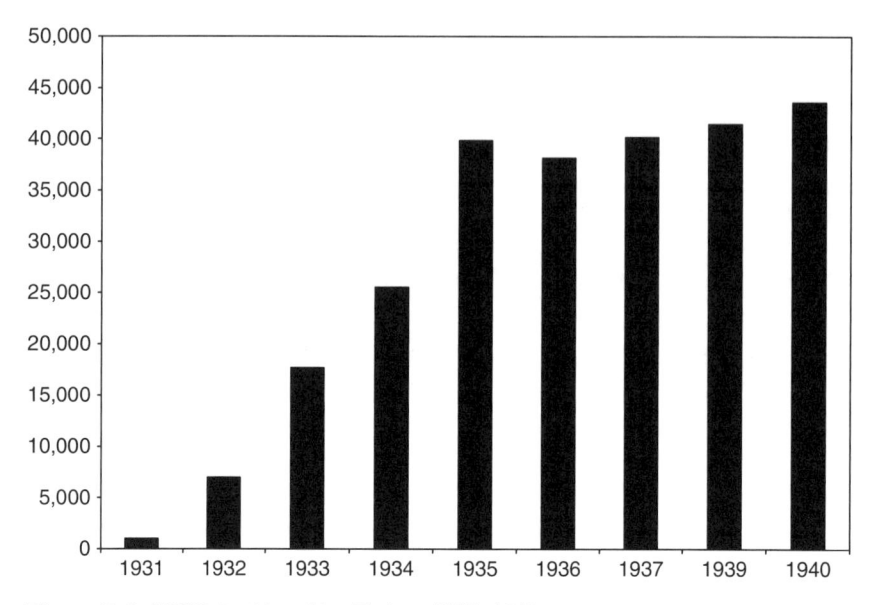

Figure 2–3 ASCPL Anti-Lynching Pledges, 1931–1940
Source: Jacqueline Dowd Hall, *Revolt against Chivalry*, "Table 3: Signature Pledges Against Lynching, Annual Totals" (180). Total sum calculated by author.

Conference for Human Welfare and the NAACP.[38] Increasingly southern reformers were forced to concede the limits of moral suasion as opposed to the benefits of electoral and judicial pressure.

Lynching and Social Science

The CIC's campaign against lynching reflected what primarily white male reformers believed was a pragmatic approach to the issue, given what it thought were the white South's heightened sensibilities on lynching. Compared to women, men, especially white men, did not have to grapple with the barriers of the southern gender line. As a result, the wing of the anti-lynching campaign dominated by male reformers was more political and more interracial. These reformers made the case that lynching was a reflection of the lack of political control. Yet their avoidance of direct political confrontation led to a clinical approach. For white male reformers lynching was the result of "baffling elements"; careful analysis would solve these puzzles and lead to the "diagnosis and prescription" of southern ailments, first of lynching and then of the southern state.[39] The CIC favored an analytical approach that emphasized letting the facts speak for themselves in order to persuade elites to assert greater social control not only over average white citizens, but also over local and state policing organizations, who at best stood by, and at worst were actively involved in (or colluded with) lynchings.

The antilynching efforts directly sponsored by the CIC involved the creation in 1929 of an all-male biracial committee, the Southern Commission on the Study of Lynching. The commission was chaired by George Fort Milton, who was a moderately liberal white journalist. The all-male commission included four African Americans who were part of the Jim Crow reform movement: John Hope of Atlanta University, Robert R. Moton of the Tuskegee Institute, Charles Johnson of Fisk University, and Benjamin Hubert of Georgia State College.[40]

This biracial committee oversaw the production of what it believed would be a definitive and objective analysis of lynching in the South. Arthur Raper, a sociologist trained at the University of North Carolina under Howard Odum, worked with Walter Chivers, an African American sociologist from Morehouse.[41] In keeping with the interracialism, each researcher investigated his side of the color line; the research was presented with Raper (the white) as lead investigator, while Chivers (the black) was relegated to assistant. Raper and Chivers's investigations resulted in the publication of *The Tragedy of Lynching* in 1933.[42] The work reported for a largely white audience what African American antilynching activists had known and argued all along: lynching was not the result of black male criminal activity (i.e., the rape of white women); rather most lynchings were the result of white efforts to control perceived black transgressions against the social or economic mores of the Jim Crow order.[43]

Although exposing the fallacies of lynching justifications was an important goal of the report, there was another, larger purpose, based on the reformers' belief that the "illness" of lynching lay in the weakness of southern government. To effectively combat the disease of lynching, "all elements of the population [had to be] provided opportunities for development." In general this meant that the elimination of the disease rested upon the "irresponsive and irresponsible population elements...be[ing] raised into a more abundant economic and cultural life." Whites, Raper argued, bore the brunt of the responsibility, especially the "white element which votes and thereby controls the collection and utilization of public funds."[44]

Presumably in the interest of appearing fair and objective, Raper argued that blacks also bore some responsibility in fighting the scourge of lynching by "demonstrating the ability, character and good citizenship of the race." This would entail "allay[ing] interracial fear and hostility...disavowing crime and the shelter[ing] of criminals;...reporting to officials and influential white friends when mob danger threatens; and...using their political influence wherever possible in the interest of honest and competent local government."[45]

Raper's analysis, which focused on exposing the myth of rape and the need for large-scale government economic and social intervention, also emphasized the role of the local press and the role of local and state officials in discouraging lynching. For example, Raper reported that although 714 people were lynched during an eighteen-year period, from 1914 to 1932, during that same period 704 lynchings were prevented as the result of enlightened attitudes and the assertion of official control. His point illustrates the CIC's emphasis on restoring government power.

State Police and State Power

The CIC and the ASWPL pushed for greater power as well as increased accountability on the part of local and state law enforcement officials. This focus dovetailed with the establishment and spread of state police departments though the 1930s.[46] Although state police departments had been established in other parts of the country since the early 1920s, the first southern state police department was not established until 1929, in North Carolina, the South's progressive leader, and in Tennessee (see Table 2–2). By 1939 all of the southern states had police forces; though their powers were quite varied, most were given the power to handle a "situation which threaten[ed] to become too difficult for the local police."[47]

The creation of state police forces, especially in the South, was one of the "most dramatic institutional innovation[s]" of the twentieth century; they were an "implied reproof for the manner in which rural police duties [had] been performed in the past."[48] Although this criticism of rural police could apply to most American states during the early twentieth century, it had a particular resonance with the South's lynching problem.

Reformers making the case for state police forces in the South drew on justifications for the police that were made elsewhere in the country (e.g., the greater mobility of criminals, the need for more sophisticated policing), but they also stressed the need for a state police force that had "no purpose save to execute the laws of the State" and that could thus ostensibly deter lynch mobs.[49] The governor of Missouri, Arthur M. Hyde, made this case in his annual message. He stated that the inability of state and local governments to prevent lawlessness and deter "riots, disorder and lynching" was not only due to the lack of professionalization among state and local officials, but was also due to their electoral vulnerability, as they were constrained by the "common desire of mankind to offend none of their constituents." A state police force, by contrast, argued Hyde, would have no "local, personal or political entanglements."[50]

Hence the creation of state police forces allowed local sheriffs and law officials a credible excuse for not participating in or allowing a lynching to

Table 2–2 Establishment of Southern State Police Agencies, 1939

State	Agency	Year Established	Total Personnel
Alabama	State Highway Patrol	1935	140
Arkansas	State Police	1935	54
Florida	Dept. of Public Safety	1939	60
Georgia	Dept. of Public Safety	1937	235
Kentucky	State Highway Patrol	1936	88
Louisiana	State Police	1936	150
Maryland	State Police	1935	120
Mississippi	Highway Safety Patrol	1938	61
North Carolina	State Highway Patrol	1929	123
South Carolina*	Highway Patrol	1930	118
	State Constabulary	1935	23
Tennessee**	Dept. of Safety	1929	129
Texas***	Dept. of Public Safety	1935	465
Virginia	State Police	1930	150

Source: Weldon Cooper, "The State Police Movement in the South," *Journal of Politics* (1939), 4: 414–33.
* The South Carolina Constabulary was established in 1893 and was reestablished in 1935.
**Agency renamed in 1939, from State Highway Patrol to Department of Public Safety.
*** Texas also had the state-wide Rangers, established in 1835 and given full power in 1874.

take place. The position of the state police was strengthened by the fact that all of the commanders and directors of these forces were gubernatorial appointments, whereas the rank and file were appointed through the merit system, unlike the bulk of state government personnel in the 1930s.

To be sure, state police and highway patrol departments in the South were certainly not friends of racial justice. Indeed sometimes they merely replaced the local police in committing racial abuses. Nonetheless an important source of regularized power had been put into the hands of the state. The state, not the lynch mob, would be the final arbiter of punishment for African Americans.

For southern African Americans state police forces were a mixed blessing; Myrdal notes in *The American Dilemma* that to blacks, the average policeman, no matter what his agency, was a "promoted poor white with a legal sanction to use a weapon."[51] Even for reformers the end of mob violence did not address the issue of "legal lynching" and racial repression in which these new forces could play a role. To the CIC's credit, the organization turned its attention to this issue, most notably in its financial support of the Scottsboro Boys in the 1930s and later its support for the hiring of black policemen in the South after World War II.[52]

The case of the Scottsboro Boys was an important evolutionary point for the CIC. The presence of the nonsouthern International Labor Defense League and NAACP in a policy domain that had previously belonged to the CIC ruffled some feathers. Beyond turf issues was the fact that southern reformers were being criticized for supporting what critics were now calling "legal lynching." Where Jim Crow reformers had hoped to divert mob violence through the court system, new critics saw this more formal use of state power as simply another form of lynching. Ames would come to the realization that allowing patently biased legal proceedings that guaranteed death was not equivalent to a lynching averted; instead, she argued, it led to a "the prostitution of the Courts" in which "the Constitution and the law become a hollow mockery."[53]

The injustice of the courts was not news to African Americans. In the case of legal lynching, as one critic wrote to George Fort Milton, the white Jim Crow reform journalist, "Your argument that 'the courts will convict Negroes' and that therefore Negroes need not be lynched, is a cold-blooded proposal to regularize lynching under legal forms."[54]

Lynching and the Transformation of Jim Crow Reform

With mounting pressure from above and from within its own organization, especially from its African American members, the CIC finally abandoned its earlier neutrality and in 1935 publicly endorsed federal antilynching legislation. By the early 1940s southern antilynching reformers were proudly declaring that the South was now "lynch free." Although the numbers vary, the South had recorded an unprecedented drop in the number of lynchings, and this state of affairs would largely be permanent. Widespread lynching was a phenomenon of the past.

A number of researchers have advanced explanations for the rapid decline in lynchings in the South, from mass migration of blacks to the North and to safer urban locations within the South, to the greater willingness of blacks to engage in individual as well as collective acts of self-defense. These analysts have largely discounted the activity of southern reformers in this area. Southern reformers are largely seen as offering too little and too late in terms of the antilynching campaign. Yet to dismiss their efforts as unquantifiable and thus empty rhetoric misses the role that ideas and organizations play in creating new political realities and justifications.

Jim Crow reformers played an important role in reasserting the power of government. By collecting and advertising the antilynching pledges of southern sheriffs and other law enforcement officials they sent an important signal about the new limits of the Jim Crow order. Southern reformers also parlayed their influence over the "best whites" into an influence over the press. No longer would the press play a key role in fomenting lynching as mass entertainment for whites through a terrifying and seductive mix of sex and violence. By according a voice, however limited, to "sane and sensible" southern African Americans in the southern antilynching campaign, white Jim Crow reformers were increasingly pushed to take a more visible political stand to buttress their belief in a workable world of separate and equal.

The greater visibility of southern reformers on the issue of lynching did not end the practice of lynching completely, although far fewer lynchings occurred. Neither did the antilynching campaign alter the fundamental power imbalance that lay at the heart at the Jim Crow order. Without civil rights, according to the black sociologist Oliver Cox, southern blacks were "extra-legal, extra-democratic objects, without the rights which white men are bound to respect." Without political rights, in the words of Jessie Daniel Ames, "Negroes, as a voteless people in a Democracy, [were] a helpless people."[55]

The mixed effectiveness of the antilynching campaign thus illustrated the limits of the Jim Crow order. Southern reformers continued their search for ways to make smooth the edges of this system. At the beginning of their antilynching crusade, few white reformers openly acknowledged that at its core, lynching was a dramatic symbol of the lack of civil rights citizenship for southern African Americans. Yet as the campaign progressed many white reformers were coming to the realization that only the restoration of political citizenship for southern African Americans would truly end lynching. Luckily this next step could be avoided, as the antilynching campaign of the early 1930s would overlap with the redefinition of the South and its problems. The New Deal would offer a new way to recast the southern race problem without confronting the color line that lay at its core.

The evolution of white southern reformers on the issue of lynching coincided with and reflected changes occurring within the CIC. The entry of southern liberal reformers into the Roosevelt administration, economic liberalism backed by government reform, and intervention would be the new solution to the South's ills.

Chapter 3

Southern Reform and the New Deal

> The south is our last frontier. In the development of its resources, human and natural, must be found the epoch of our national growth. That development, in turn, must in large measure depend on the contrivances of solutions to the region's political problems.
>
> V. O. Key, *Southern Politics in State and Nation*

When Jim Crow reformers confronted lynching during the 1920s, they took the first step in asserting the importance of stateways in shaping the Jim Crow order. As the Great Depression unfolded the South descended into greater economic misery and, in some states, political turbulence. To save the South, Jim Crow reformers, now joined by southern New Dealers, argued that the South's economic house had to be transformed, not just restored. Only the modernization of the southern economy could save the South from its current woes. But the creation of a new economic future for the South could occur only with a massive intervention of state power. Stateways, not folkways, would aid the South in its hour of need.

The question of who would wield that power and for what ends underlay the struggle to reshape the southern economy and, by extension, the southern political order. For the new coalition of Jim Crow reformers and New Deal technocrats the answer was simple: the modernization of the South would take place under the benign guidance of this new coalition. In this chapter I trace how a coalition to reshape the southern economy and the southern state first came together and then broke apart during the 1930s. The now established CIC-led Jim Crow reformers and the southern New Deal reformers, parallel though sometimes intersecting movements, would each try to change the nature of the southern political economy.

The path to transforming the stateways of the South first emerged during the Progressive era. By the end of the 1920s this Progressive impulse had waned in the South. As the 1930s unfolded a CIC-led coalition, backed by northern foundation money, emerged to provide New Deal policymakers with policy alternatives that were shaped by and for southerners. As the second New Deal unfolded, the CIC efforts to shape New Deal policy were challenged by the emergence of a second coalition, this one made up of southern New Dealers, who attempt to change southern stateways through continued efforts to enact national policy and through an effort to shape policymaking in the states. These reformers met varied levels of success. The most visible aspect of these New Dealers was the emergence of the Southern Conference for Human Welfare (SCHW), which would attempt to link together both older and newer groups of southern reformers. The emergence and the decline of this group as well as the CIC marked the end of a southern reform approach that relied on the power of social science and elite organizations as the sole means for influencing the Jim Crow order.

One of the founding myths of the Jim Crow order, that the South was a largely stateless region, lay at the heart of southern white reformers' inability to confront the intertwined issues of economic inequality and political disempowerment. The role of government—who controlled it and for what purposes—had always been, in the words of V. O. Key, "a deadly serious business."[1] By obscuring the role of the state, of southern government in determining who gets what, the architects of the Jim Crow order hoped to mask their own seizure of power. Progressive era reformers would take the first step in removing the façade of southern statelessness.

State Power, the Color Line, and the Jim Crow Order

In confronting lynching, early Jim Crow reformers confronted the heart of the Jim Crow order: the power of the state. Although some southerners had proclaimed the color line to be the central theme of southern history, an examination of southern history reveals otherwise. The central theme of southern history and politics was the struggle to control government.[2]

After Reconstruction the weakness of southern government acted as both crutch and barrier for reformers and conservatives alike. For reformers the alleged weaknesses of southern government explained their failed reform efforts. For conservatives the weakness of southern governments, deliberately cultivated, blocked attempts to increase the power of government. Small and strapped, controlled by shifting factions of politicians who largely acted at the bidding of powerful economic elites, these state and local governments existed more in name than in practice.

The picture of southern governments as powerless and passive nonentities was in fact a convenient fiction. The Redeemers justified their seizure of power on the basis that state governments had suffered corruption, debt, and incompetence under the biracial Reconstruction governments. The new rulers of the Jim Crow order created this fiction in an attempt to reestablish and justify what they saw as the South's tradition of, and their own interest in, a government of low taxes and minimal public services. Those interested in small government, however, needed justification or at least a diversion that would draw away the attention of those who envisioned a more positive role for government. The color line of the South proved to be an admirable distraction. Yet even this distraction was seen as one in which the hand of government was curiously absent. The enforcement of the color line was not the result of government action but rather the function of age-old folkways.

Though the overthrow of the Reconstruction governments created new state governments that were highly constrained in their powers, it did not end political competition between whites for control of these governments. In none of the states was the rule of the elites absolute. Periodically the little people, the "wool-hat boys" or the "Hills," would challenge the elites, the "Organization" or the "Big Mules," that tended to control southern governments. The South's emerging urban middle class also took part in these ongoing battles, constantly shifting support between the little people, from whom they emerged from, and the system, of which they were a part yet from which they were also excluded because of their class. The establishment of the Jim Crow order ensured that this political battle was solely a battle between whites.

The battle for political control of government was not only for the spoils of whatever faction gained power; it was also about the control over the size and scope of government as it impacted the class lines of whites, not the color line between whites and blacks. Although many of the elites who jockeyed for power in the post-Reconstruction era had hoped to constrain state governments for the foreseeable future, the pressure from other elites for services that would sustain greater economic development, as well as the ongoing challenges from nonelite whites, pushed southern state governments toward a slow expansion in size and scope. From 1902 to 1927 (see Table 3–1) there was a nearly sevenfold increase in government expenditures across the southern states.

This expansion in government was also based on the exclusion of southern blacks. Clear disparities in public services between whites and

Table 3–1 Revenue and Expenditures in Southern States, 1902–1927 (millions)

State	Revenue					Expenditures				
	1902	1915	1922	1926	1927	1902	1915	1922	1926	1927
Alabama	2.8	7.2	15.4	19.9	21.9	2.6	7.3	12.5	15.6	17.9
Arkansas	1.4	3.8	7.5	20.2	20.3	1.2	3.8	6.9	12.1	13.3
Delaware	.4	.8	4.8	7.8	7.8	.4	.7	3.8	4.8	5.1
Florida	1.8	3.1	10.5	28.7	27.4	1.0	2.6	8.9	10.8	14.7
Georgia	3.7	6.4	17.3	25.7	29.2	8.7	6.2	12.1	20.8	20.2
Kentucky	4.8	8.1	17.9	28.3	30.7	4.9	8.7	12.9	17.7	18.6
Louisiana	3.6	8.7	20.1	26.8	28.1	4.1	7.2	15.2	17.9	20.4
Maryland	2.8	7.5	18.4	23.2	24.4	2.8	6.7	13.5	18.6	19.7
Mississippi	1.9	4.9	11.1	17.1	16.4	2.5	4.9	10.5	12.8	13.0
Missouri	5.2	10.0	26.9	42.1	42.8	3.9	8.9	40.0	27.1	27.2
North Carolina	1.7	4.7	13.1	36.5	35.8	1.8	4.5	15.1	21.5	24.3
South Carolina	3.5	2.7	8.4	17.1	17.4	3.5	2.9	6.4	13.1	13.2
Tennessee	2.6	5.1	15.5	25.1	26.5	2.0	5.3	11.1	15.1	16.9
Texas	7.7	18.7	41.9	72.1	78.7	7.7	15.9	44.4	52.9	56.8
Virginia	3.9	9.4	26.5	33.7	38.9	4.2	8.4	19.7	22.3	24.5

Source: *Statistical Abstract of the United States* 1910, No. 308—Revenue Receipts and Expenditures, 222; *Statistical Abstract of the United States* 1930, No. 227—State Finances, 600.

African Americans reinforced whites' belief in their political and social dominance. In contrast with whites, southern African Americans were largely the objects of negative government. Government services were largely withheld from them: sidewalks and streets and streetlights stopped at the edge of black neighborhoods, and local governments did not plan or budget for libraries, parks, or other civic amenities for blacks. Exclusion was based on notions of white supremacy; it was also based on cold fiscal realities. With a small fiscal pie to begin with, fewer services for blacks translated into more for whites. Thus in addition to being pushed out of the electoral sphere, African Americans were seemingly going to be excluded from the southern administrative sphere as well.

The Progressive era coincided with a second wave of New South boosterism, a renewed push for southern economic development. Putting substance behind the claims that the New South was a region ready for industrial development meant demonstrating that the New South was peaceful and calm, that southern governments had the coercive power to control lynching mobs, union organizers, and striking workers. Controlling lynching was just one element of the modernization of the southern order. Encouraging economic development meant investing in hard infrastructure such as highways and dams; it also meant making an effort (no matter how token) toward substantiating the claim that the South had a contented, stable, and healthy workforce.

Southern Progressive reformers copied Progressive reformers from other parts of the country: they found an issue, researched the problem, and publicized the problem's potential danger to society and the possible solutions to this problem; then they encouraged local or state government to adopt the proposed reform.[3] Southern reformers then as well as later were highly dependent on outside support. In policy areas such as public health and education, foundations (mostly northern) provided significant funding for state and local governments to ensure that reforms were effectively carried out over the long time frames needed to ensure change. Through the examples provided by these demonstration projects, it was hoped that southern leaders would see the light and commit governments to adopt these services as part of the government's permanent responsibility. Although some of these reforms were adopted, other reforms, especially in the area of African American education, remained largely funded by northern foundations.[4]

Southern government reform was another focus of these Progressive reformers. Although many southern states were indifferent or hostile to government reform, some, such as Virginia and North Carolina, embraced government reform. Virginia saw reform as a means of centralizing and institutionalizing the power of the state's ruling faction, the Byrd machine.[5] But southern reform during the Progressive era resulted in mostly piecemeal results, as many southern elites resisted reforms that would challenge class, race, or gender hierarchies. More important, southern states lacked the capacity to support the institutionalization of these reforms within local or state governments. To the extent that Progressivism was embraced in the South, it was a Progressivism that was largely for the white middle class and that supported rather than threatened the political power of the ruling elite.[6] By the end of the 1920s the political and administrative structures of the Jim Crow order were largely unchallenged and unquestioned. The economic upheaval of the Great Depression and the wider debate over the role of government pushed a new generation of southerners into rethinking how the South's economic ills intersected with its political and administrative structures.

Jim Crow Reform and the Creation of a New Regionalism

The struggle to redefine the South's problems so they could be addressed through government action was given a boost during the New Deal. Franklin Roosevelt infamously proclaimed the American South to be the "nation's no. 1 economic problem." Stimulated by the National Emergency Council's *Report on Economic Conditions of the South* (1938), a burst of investigations and reports quickly followed.

A CIC-led Jim Crow reform axis was dominant at the start of the 1930s and through the first New Deal. CIC leaders such as Will Alexander joined the Roosevelt administration, and early Jim Crow reformers such as Howard Odum became more visible. Odum developed a theory of southern regionalism that attempted to provide a justification for southern reform and for the struggle to shape southern stateways, just as the race relations model and interracialism had done in the previous decade. Odum concluded that only a thorough assessment of the South's resources coupled with the guidance provided by a rational planning process would enable the South to stop wasting its resources and fulfill its potential.

This model of southern development was taken up by a smaller group of reformers, led by Roscoe Martin and other southern political scientists, who focused on reshaping southern government as a means to achieve this rational governance. First focusing on Alabama, and then examining the region as a whole, Martin and his colleagues attempted to change the "tone of government" in the South. Courthouse gangs, corruption, and incompetence would be replaced by a government in which "democratic society may be more completely realized" and where reform would be grounded in "concepts of justice, liberty, and fuller economic opportunity for human beings." Government reform would not be simply the piecemeal reform that had occurred during the Progressive era; it would be broader, more systematic, and more comprehensive; it would be "concerned with people, with ideas, with things."[7] Nonetheless, true to its origins, this attempt to transform the South through a transformation of stateways was a white elite-led movement. While purporting to speak for and represent southern blacks, the CIC-led coalition spoke largely to and for whites. In the end a small constituency, a narrow focus, and a reliance on northern foundation money ultimately led to the end of regionalism steeped in rational planning. Rather than transforming the state and the economy for the good of the South as a whole, the economic development of the South would occur under the control of southern political elites.

The CIC and the First New Deal

The designation of the South as the "nation's no. 1 economic problem" gave renewed vigor to a CIC that was groping for a role beyond its antilynching campaign. The election of Franklin Roosevelt revitalized some members of the CIC. Will Alexander of the CIC along with Edwin Embree of the Rosenwald Foundation met with Roosevelt in 1933; the goal of the meeting was to press Roosevelt to be more attentive to the needs of African Americans.[8] The New Deal could not immediately alter the Jim Crow order; standing in its way were southern members of Congress who were able to influence the broad contours of national policy to benefit the South. For example, as is well-documented, social welfare programs such as Social Security and Aid to Dependent Children were structured to exclude blacks completely by virtue of occupation or to allow for local administration, thus allowing southern governments to determine eligibility.[9] Southerners also created bureaucratic obstacles; for example, the Department of Agriculture was known as a bastion of white supremacy.[10]

The first New Deal was effectively hampered by Roosevelt's dependence on southern congressmen and his inability to maneuver around the institutional beachheads that southern white supremacists had created in the national government. Yet despite the limits placed on the first New Deal by southern politicians, the administrative agencies that carried out the policies that affected southern blacks the most—"the Farm Security Administration, the National Youth Administration, the Fair Employment Practices Committee, the Works Progress Administration and the Public Works Administration—would either be headed by a white southern liberal or strongly influenced by their presence in high positions."[11]

Will Alexander, the longtime head of the CIC, worked first with Rexford Tugwell at the Resettlement Administration, then headed the Farm Security

Administration. Clark Foreman, a white southerner who had worked for both the CIC and the Rosenwald Foundation, became "special advisor for Negro matters" to Secretary of the Interior Harold Ickes. In keeping with the long reach of the Jim Crow reform foundations, Foreman's salary was paid for by the Rosenwald Foundation, thus enabling Roosevelt to avert a confrontation with southern politicians on the issue. Yet in keeping with Jim Crow reform, a white man was appointed to speak on behalf of and for African Americans. Not surprisingly the NAACP and the northern black press were angry at this symbolism.

The influence of these white southerners on New Deal policymaking was on two levels. First, men like Alexander and Foreman were the first New Deal administrators to include blacks in substantive policymaking roles within the national government, thus bringing blacks into national policymaking circles to a degree that had not happened before in the U.S. government. Foreman, for example, hired (with funding provided by the Rosenwald Foundation) Robert Weaver, a Harvard-trained African American economist as his assistant, with the expectation that Weaver would eventually take over from Foreman. Weaver and other high-ranking blacks within and outside of the administration would come together to form a "black Cabinet" that pressed the Roosevelt administration to make the New Deal a fair deal for blacks. By contrast, the New Deal women's cabinet, as historian Linda Gordon notes, was not nearly as inclusive of non-white women.[12]

The second way that these southerners used their position to tilt at the color line was to use their administrative powers to press for blacks to get a greater share of New Deal—funded jobs in the Works Progress Administration and Civilian Conservation Corps and for greater access to New Deal services. As head of the Farm Security Administration Alexander "employed more black [field] supervisors than any other New Deal Agency."[13] These efforts were limited because it took sustained oversight and pressure from above to ensure that state and local administrators did not evade national directives. Given the scope of the New Deal and reformers' limited power, these attempts to create a fairer New Deal were sporadic.

The inclusion of blacks as junior partners in the New Deal was significant. Ralph Bunche called the doubling of African American federal employment and the creation of policymaking positions a "radical break from the past."[14] The black employees of the federal government located throughout the country and particularly in the South would strengthen a black middle class that had been ravaged by the Depression. More critically, those in the South protected by federal employment rules would have the freedom as well as the resources to help support the local organizations that would emerge over the next decade to challenge the Jim Crow order. Yet despite a greater willingness by the Roosevelt administration to grant more equitable treatment for blacks, there were limits to change within the national government. The first New Deal was open to white southerners advocating on behalf of blacks but hostile to direct black advocacy.[15]

Although individual members of the CIC helped to make New Deal policy more attentive to the needs of the South, the central CIC played a role a well. With the help of northern foundations the CIC began to sponsor additional reports about conditions in the South. In keeping with the color line of social science research, the reports focused on the black South. As Charles Johnson was the dominant black southern social scientist of the time, he directed almost all of these foundation studies, including *The Shadow of the Plantation* (1934), *The Collapse of the Cotton Tenancy* (1935), and *Growing Up in the Black Belt: Negro Youth in the Rural South* (1941). Howard Odum's research institute also produced a slew of studies, including Rupert Vance's *Human Geography of the South* (1932) and Arthur Raper's *Preface to Peasantry* (1936). Depending on the political sensitivity of the issue, sometimes foundations gave money openly; in the case of the lynching study, funding came from a secret $50,000 grant from the Rockefeller Foundation to the Rosenwald Foundation in 1934.[16] Legislation such as the Farm Security Act was significantly shaped by research conducted under the auspices of the CIC or Howard Odum's center at the University of North Carolina, with funding coming largely from the GEB and the Rosenwald Foundation.

A New Theory for the South

While the CIC focused on specific policy issues in response to national government policy, some reformers searched for a less reactive approach to the New Deal.[17] Howard Odum was one of those reformers. Although he too welcomed the New Deal and hoped to play a part in setting national policy for the South, Odum also firmly believed that the South should have its own approach to its development. He became the leading proponent of a new regionalism, an approach that he argued would dampen unproductive sectarian differences between the South and the rest of the United States. Like many white reformers he proposed a gradualist middle ground between what he believed was the durability of folkways, which both established and justified the separation of races, and a possibly heavy-handed stateways that could potentially impose a pace of change that would be too rapid for southern society to successfully adopt.[18]

Odum's partially formulated solution to the problems posed by these two extremes was "technicways," which he defined as "the habits and customs that develop as adjustments to the innovations of science and technology."[19] If recognized and handled properly technicways could give a "rational authority" to the state that folkways could not, while dampening any possibility of an overreaching of stateways.

This faith in technicways, in rational planning and empirical social science, would be the basis for Odum's southern regionalism. His opus, *Southern Regionalism,* laid out his belief that the South, based on objective social, economic, and physical criteria, constituted one of six regions of the United States. He thus rejected historical or romantic notions of regional identity in favor of an identity rooted in fact. In further rejection of mythology, Odum argue that the South comprised many Souths: "a black belt South, a piedmont south, a river delta south, a mountainous south, and a south of forests and piney woods."[20] All of these Souths, Odum argued, were suffering because the South's resources (natural and human) were not being adequately recognized, measured, and appropriately nurtured rather than wasted and exploited. Although Odum made a case for southern development based on fact and not fiction, it was a development that focused on white have-nots rather than all of the South's inhabitants, particularly blacks.

In the late 1930s Odum cast about for a forum in which to advance his southern regionalism. He saw the CIC, or a reconstituted version of it, as the perfect vehicle. The CIC had been weakened by the departure of longtime leaders such as Alexander, and its remaining staff had been sidelined by Ames's antilynching activities. Many CIC leaders, including Alexander, agreed with Odum that the CIC's time had passed. An organization that operated at the margins of the South using discretion and persuasion, while relying on the "good will" of the "best people of the South," was not an organization that could grapple with the clear economic and political needs of the South.

In 1944 the Southern Regional Council (SRC) was born out of the ashes on the CIC. Yet the imprint of the CIC and interracialism still remained, at least in the minds of white members of the SRC. An orderly, sane, and sensible management of race relations was still the primary goal, but the path to that goal was far different. Rather than piecemeal and highly local reforms that addressed current crises, the SRC advocated a program of explicit reforms. The SRC endorsed bringing African Americans back into the mainstream of southern life through a real equalization of schools and other public services, through protection of civil rights citizenship brought about by increased hiring of black policemen, and, most remarkably, through restoration (albeit slow) of political citizenship for African Americans. Yet for southern whites of the SRC, the color line of social segregation was still sacrosanct. On that matter, whites still expected absolute acquiescence on the part of southern blacks. Yet as World War II another war to protect democracy began, this mutual agreement began to be challenged, first by southern black SRC members and then, reluctantly, by southern whites.

Reforming within the States

Whereas Odum was interested in reducing racial animosities and promoting better understanding between the races, a new group of government reformers was more focused on the ability of social science to transform the exercise of power. The New Deal and the economic definition of the South were seen by government reformers as a chance to breaking a long-standing cycle of limited reform and reaction. Instead of putting "new wine in old administrative bottles," southern government reformers hoped to create a new consensus on the need to change southern government.[21] These reformers claimed, "Democracy [can] be more fully realized [only] if we can relate the resources of our region more closely and perpetually to the lives and living of more and more people."[22]

At the state level the traditional cycle of reform and reaction in southern state governments was seen as a fundamental stumbling block in the transformation of the South. The cyclical nature of government as well as measures that limited the reach of state government, either fiscally or administratively, were all seen as hindering the South's economic development and reintegration into the nation. The state constitutions and governments that were created by the post-Reconstruction Redeemers would have to reshaped in order for modern, New Deal—friendly politicians and their technocratic allies to exert more control. Unlike their fellow reformers at the national level, however, bringing African Americans back into the administrative state would remain out their grasp. For these reformers, the embrace of neutrality and a focus on "form and procedure," whether for strategic reasons, dictated by disciplinary dogma, or otherwise, led to neglect of the most fundamental constitutive element of the Jim Crow state: race.

Creating a New Government for Alabama

Academics and former New Dealers in Alabama took up the process of reshaping government. One of the leaders of this reform coalition was a quintessential "bureau man," Roscoe Martin, the chair of the Political Science Department at the University of Alabama and the founder and director of the university's Bureau of Public Administration. His bureau credentials came from the fact that he received his doctorate from the University of Chicago, where he had studied under Charles Merriam.[23] There he and his future southern government reform colleagues had imbued the Chicago School ethos, that "modernization [was] a fundamentally rational political process prior to and absolutely determining of social and economic change."

Understanding this political process entailed engaging in a communal and collaborative search for understanding as a basis for action.[24]

After graduate study Martin returned to his native Texas, where at the University of Texas he rebuilt its Bureau of Municipal Research, which he directed from 1933 to 1937.[25] Like many of his New Deal contemporaries in the social sciences, Martin worked for the federal government, spending a year as the chief research technician at the National Resources Planning Board. He was then hired to become the chair of the University of Alabama's Political Science Department.

Martin and most of the other southern state reformers were bound together by their common regional roots. This commonality of identity was to them a source of strength. They believed that only southerners could effectively communicate with local political officials, businessmen, and other civic elites.[26] Unspoken, perhaps not even recognized was the assumption that this was a conversation between and for *white* southerners. Along with their regional identity, this was an important characteristic that differentiated this set of reformers from other southern reformers: theirs was not a biracial alliance. Because African Americans had largely been excised from the public sphere, with the exception of education, the problem of government power did not seem to directly address them. This monoracial view of government meant that the southern state reformers' attempts to fundamentally transform government was ultimately futile, as they had no constituency that could mobilize or support their efforts to claim state power. They could not translate a desire for good government and rational planning into a coherent and sustained plan of government action.

Reform and Reaction in Alabama

The Brookings Institute had conducted an exhaustive five-volume study of Alabama government in 1932; the results of the study painted a largely abysmal picture that was for the most part ignored by Alabama's politicians.[27] Part of this neglect was due to the factionalism of Alabama politics. The state was politically and geographically divided between the largely white, Populist-leaning hill country of the north and the farmers of the south, and the "Big Mule" coalition of the state's black-belt plantation elite and the new industrialists of Birmingham and Mobile. Struggles between these factions resulted in a pattern of alternating cycles of reform and reaction that hindered the development of good government.[28]

Martin's arrival in Alabama in 1937 coincided with the height of the New Deal in the states. Even though the New Deal was experiencing growing opposition at the national level, the programs and funds that were emanating from Washington were beginning to be felt at the state and local levels.[29] Federal programs had introduced to the South long-opposed administrative reforms, such as the merit system and civil service retirement systems, as well as the modern "paraphernalia of management."[30] In addition to administrative reform was the other object of southern reform: state planning. As a result of funds from the Works Progress Administration and National Resources Planning Board and the influence of the Tennessee Valley Authority (TVA), almost all of the southern states had established or strengthened state planning boards by the late 1930s (see Table 3–2).

In addition to these administrative innovations, the New Deal had opened up a small political space between the elements within the Big Mule alliance and created alliances between elements of this group and the hill country. Pressure from outside the region, in the shape of new federal programs and policies, as well as their own self-interest prodded some elements of the Alabama political and business establishments to cautiously rethink the state of government in Alabama.

Martin quickly capitalized on this political opening by developing relationships with local and state politicians and bureaucrats, newspaper editors, and local (and influential) supporters of good government. He also established the Institute (later Bureau) of Public Administration, which began sponsoring meetings and local discussion groups. Through these contacts he proclaimed that there was a "state-wide clamor for improvement in the tone of [Alabama] public life."[31] Martin and the Bureau initially set to work on "improving the tone of government" through a project studying benefit levels and administrative practices for the Alabama Relief Administration. This project was followed by studies of county and municipal governments in Alabama and studies of state administration and the Alabama legislative process.[32]

The Bureau also benefited from the election of Frank Dixon as Alabama's governor in 1938. Dixon was part of Alabama's elite and a member of Birmingham's "good government" movement who ran on a traditional platform advocating efficient reforms in the state government.[33] Compared to the former occupant, Bibb Graves, a former Klansman but strong supporter of the New Deal, Dixon seemed to embody the old ideal of southern business Progressivism.[34] Nonetheless Dixon's administration offered an opening for Martin's new Bureau of Public Administration, allowing Martin to pursue the long-term goal of improving the tone of government in Alabama and, later, throughout the South.

Once elected Dixon appointed a council of advisors that included Roscoe Martin and introduced a number of reforms that were by and large drafted by Martin and his assistants. In the tradition of southern business Progressivism and in accordance with current public administration proscriptions, Dixon

Table 3-2 Southern State Planning Board/Commissions, 1935–1949

State	Number of Functions / List of Functions	Budget (1939–40)	New Deal Agency Year Terminated	Post–New Deal Agency Year Est.	Post–New Deal Agency Name
Alabama	4 / Land, forest resources, public works, recreation	5,000	Not Terminated	1943	State Planning Board
Arkansas	2 / Water, government and finance	30,000	1945	1945	Resources & Development Board
Florida	3 / Forest resources, public works, government & finance	10,000	1945	1945	State Improvement Commission
Georgia	12 / NA	15,000	1943	1943/1949†	Agricultural & Development Board / Dept. of Commerce
Louisiana	NA/NA	NA	1940	1942/1944	Dept. of Commerce & Industry
Mississippi	6 / Water, forest resources, population, public works,	77,000	1940	1944	Agricultural & Development Board
North Carolina	12 / Land, water, forest resources, population, transportation, education, recreation, health & welfare, housing,	2,000	1947	1947*	Division of Commerce & Industry / Dept. of Conservation & Development
South Carolina	6 / Water, forest resources, recreation, government & finance	12,500	1945	1945	Research, Planning & Development Board

(*continued*)

Table 3–2 (Continued)

State	Number of Functions / List of Functions	Budget (1939–40)	New Deal Agency Year Terminated	Post–New Deal Agency Year Est.	Post–New Deal Agency Name
Tennessee	12 / Land, water, conservation, population, transportation, public works, economic development & industry, education, recreation, health & welfare, government & finance	50,000		1935	State Planning Commission
Texas	NA / NA	NA	1939	1949**	
Virginia	10 / Land, forest resources, transportation, econ & industry, education, recreation, health & welfare, government & finance	24,000	Not Terminated	1948	Division of Planning & Economic Development

Source: Cobb, *Selling of the South*, 66; Lepawsky, *State Planning and Economic Development in the South* (1949); *The Book of the States*, various: 1939–1940, 1949–1950, 1951–1952).

† Department & Functions Reorganized.

* Board Abolished, Functions Split Between Agencies.

** Postwar Economic & Planning Commission liquidate.

centralized administrative power and eliminated "duplication and overlap."[35] A merit system was established, as was a state Legislative Reference Service. The state legislature was also "modernized"; the legislature changed its meetings from quadrennial sessions to biennial sessions, and the rates given for legislators increased from $4 to $10 per day.[36]

Due to the increasing credibility of the Bureau and its reputation for political neutrality, it was asked to assist in the transition of Governor-elect Chauncey Sparks in 1943. In fact the Bureau later opened up a Montgomery office that would assist Sparks's administration on a full-time basis. The role of the Bureau in both the Dixon (traditional good government advocate) and Sparks (conservative, former Klan member) administration underscored the studied neutrality of Martin and his fellow colleagues.

Sparks embodied the other extreme of Alabama politics. Primarily interested in agricultural issues, Sparks, like Dixon, was interested in good government but even more interested in protecting Alabama from what was seen as growing federal intrusion into race relations. The relatively liberal James "Big Jim" Folsom followed the reactionary Sparks as governor, and Folsom was followed by the conservative Gordon Persons. In short, Alabama's politics were driven by a pattern of action and reaction, whereby the pursuit of good government was readily cast aside in order to preserve the social order.

The Bureau of Public Administration and the TVA

In 1938 the Bureau undertook its first joint project with the Tennessee Valley Authority. The TVA's association with the Bureau was important for a number of reasons. The mandate of the Tennessee Valley Authority (created in 1933) was to develop the South, economically and socially. It relied on not only research and planning, but also cooperation with state and local governments to guide its activities.[37] The TVA made public administration and government reform not simply the domain of traditional neo-Progressive good government advocates, but also a critical element in the South's necessary economic and social development. It also provided an additional vital institutional locus for attracting other scholars and funding. The existence of the TVA underscored and strengthened a perceived need for a regional approach to government reform. Thus the Bureau's affiliation with the TVA helped to give further legitimacy to Martin's project among state politicians and, more important, northern foundations such as the Rockefeller Foundation.

With these local and regional links forged, and after several years of intermittent discussion, Martin and the University of Alabama formally approached the Rockefeller Foundation for support for a more ambitious regional approach. The Rockefeller Foundation was no stranger to the South, social science, or public administration. It had supported Charles Merriam's early attempts to strengthen the field and had been an early supporter of Howard Odum's regionalism studies centered at the University of North Carolina.[38] In their application to the Rockefeller Foundation for funding of the Public Administration Bureau Martin and the university argued, "There are vigorous progressive and intelligent groups of younger men in both houses of the state legislature who are vitally interested in effecting the improvement of government service and the public attitude towards government."[39] The Foundation agreed, envisioning the University of Alabama program as another way to extend Odum's regionalism approach. Although good government was an important issue to the Foundation, it was not nearly as motivating as creating institutional capacity within the South that could address the South's most pressing issues and as a means to make a strategic investment in a state that was not known for its progressive government.[40] Indeed later, in an internal discussion of extending funding throughout the South, Rockefeller officials would argue that external funding would enable researchers to have "enough strength to insure care in the approach to rather delicate public questions."[41] The Rockefeller Foundation decided that because the Bureau was located in the South, and in keeping with the Foundation's desire to achieve a focused approach to southern issues, the General Education Board would be the vehicle to provide support to the Bureau.

The Bureau's expansion was thus helped by the timely support of the GEB; from 1937 to 1948 the GEB granted $82,500 to the Bureau, about 38 percent of its budget. After this initial support Martin persuaded the GEB to commit to funding the creation or strengthening of similar organizations at the universities of Kentucky, Tennessee, South Carolina, Georgia, and Mississippi. In short, the Bureau's carefully cultivated image of political neutrality as well as its political connections helped to persuade reluctant funders like the GEB that investing in Alabama's program was not simply a parochial dead end but a matter of regional significance. Indeed GEB funds supported a range of work done by various southern bureaus: Tennessee's bureau worked on the state's constitutional revision committee, and in the early 1950s South Carolina's bureau would work with Governor James Byrne on the state's ambitious plan to equalize its school system in an attempt to avert litigation pressing for school integration.

As a result of its growing association with the TVA, the financial support of the GEB, and Martin's own interest in regionalism and the South, in 1943 the Bureau under Martin's leadership began to shift its focus away from Alabama and individual states to a broader regional focus. The study of southern problems in government and the development of solutions were still important activities, but even more important was changing the nature of governing. In addition to legislative and administrative reform, there was the need for a new type of administrator for state government. Although the introduction of the merit system had improved the situation in Alabama and elsewhere, what was needed was a cadre of appropriately trained and motivated individuals who could work within southern state governments to improve southern governance.

Administering the South: The Southern Regional Training Program

Martin approached the GEB for additional support for a one-year training program in public administration for master's degree students.[42] The Southern Regional Training Program, as the program was called, was to be a joint endeavor between Alabama, Tennessee, and Kentucky.[43] The rationale for the program was the need for "administrators and researchers whose training will facilitate their understanding of the regional nature of the southern economy and their appreciation of the common strengths and weaknesses of governmental and administrative practices and institutions in the region."[44] The program thus lay at the heart of the state reformers' efforts. As a friendly editorial in the Birmingham, Alabama, *Post* opined in 1944, "Efficient public administration is all important.... Politics is not a field to be left wholly to the politician." Southern reformers argued that public administrators were some of the few people in the South who could provide a rational, dispassionate, and measured response to the vast changes that had arisen in the wake of the New Deal and World War II. There was no reason that the methods used in science or business could not be used in the South. Given this rationale, again the GEB agreed to fund a program that would influence southern state capacity.

The GEB committed $25,000 to the program over a three-year period. Although the fellowship was open to all applicants, the fellowship description noted that applicants from the South would be favored, though not to exclusion.[45] Thus most of the students who applied for the ten fellowships were either from the South or were attending southern institutions. After a brief orientation the fellows would intern either in state government, at a participating university, or at the TVA.[46]

Despite the program's aim of training future administrators who were sensitive to the region, the program itself was run on an apolitical basis. A memorandum from a conference sponsored by the Bureau in 1944 underscores this apolitical approach: "Questions of policy...should be subordinated, and should be treated only where they are inseparable from problems of administration proper."⁴⁷ Individuals who knew implicitly the boundaries of the Jim Crow order would run the order. In this instance, the circular nature of the Jim Crow order remained intact: folkways would shape stateways, while stateways, through day-to-day policy decision making, would reinforce the folkways of Jim Crow.

After completion of the program most of the fellows accepted positions in local and state southern governments. For example, a graduate of the program's first year accepted a position in Kentucky's Department of Finance, and another worked in Tennessee's Department of Welfare.⁴⁸ As agreed upon, the GEB slowly ended its funding for the program by the early 1950s.

The Rise and Fall of Southern State Planning

Martin's partnership with the TVA reflected the belief of southern government reformers in the power of planning. Part of this belief was the sense that only an outside force could impose needed changes on a South that was as unwilling to change as it was unaware of the necessary techniques for this transformation. Martin's solution was to strengthen and expand the power of state planning departments. Although his communication with the GEB stressed the independence of state bureaus, a later assessment of the southern bureau movement as well as extant reports highlight the important linkages between the university bureaus and state planning departments.

Led by Martin but bound together though disciplinary as well as funding linkages, these departments, bureaus, and boards produced exhaustive (and in many cases mind-numbing) studies of the South's resources. Many of these studies were in what one historian called "the Odum tradition," thick descriptions of various aspects of the South presenting an overwhelming yet clear picture of the condition under consideration, while adhering to the belief that good science entailed that information be presented neutrally and objectively. The facts would speak for themselves for those ready to undertake "intelligent political action."

The case of Georgia is instructive. Governor Ellis Arnall, Georgia's second New Deal governor, approached Martin for advice on restructuring Georgia's government.⁴⁹ Part of Arnall's concern was related to his belief in good government practice. Just as important was the reality that Arnall and his allies were locked in a bitter political struggle with conservative politicians, led by Eugene Talmadge.

Talmadge's constant interference in state administration during his time in office during the 1930s reflected the politics of a government run by a spoils system; it also reflected emerging southern conservative anger over the impact of the New Deal on the Jim Crow order.⁵⁰ Talmadge's anger toward the Roosevelt administration and his refusal to comply with regulations led to the temporary suspension of the state's relief funds. In the case of higher education, Talmadge accused state university officials of not wholeheartedly endorsing or supporting his extreme views on segregation. His attempt to oust university administrators led accrediting agencies to temporarily strip the state's colleges and universities of their accreditation. For Georgia's aspiring white middle class (one of the main sources of voters in Georgia's restricted political system, before the poll tax was removed), the threat to their upward mobility, not the threat to the Jim Crow order, was one of the reasons for Arnall's defeat of Talmadge. By reinforcing his administration's good government credentials as well as blunting the impact of politics on administration, Arnall could strengthen the appeal of his political faction in future elections.

With Arnall's support, as well as the assistance of Martin, the GEB funded the establishment of a bureau at the University of Georgia in 1943. At the same time Arnall also established the Georgia Agricultural and Development Board. The Board, composed of leading white citizens, would focus on seven areas: education; trade, commerce, and business; agriculture; health; public works; government; and industry. The Board was financed by special funds allocated by Arnall, who hoped that funding from the GEB would also be forthcoming.[51] According to Arnall, the purpose of the Board was to act as a "laboratory" to demonstrate "how a progressive approach to state reorganization and sound development can be worked out."[52] The GEB was disinclined to be involved in what ultimately turned out to be an organization that was the child of politics. The GEB preferred to focus its funds on the university bureau as a way to protect its and the bureau's long-term interests.[53]

The actions of the GEB were prescient. Arnall's designated successor narrowly lost the following election, and the Talmadge forces, under the direction of his son, fundamentally changed the nature of the Georgia Board, which they associated with the previous administration. In 1949 Arnall's Board was stripped of its funds and authority, while the Department of Commerce took over the state planning functions as well as new economic development activities.

Although the transformation of the Georgia Board was linked to state politics, the decline in state planning was part of a regional as well as nationwide shift to state-sponsored business development. Mississippi, long the region's laggard in many areas, proved to be its leader. In 1935 it established its Balance Agriculture with Industry program, which used a mix of policy and tax incentives to attract new industry to the state. With the war winding down, other states, in and outside of the south, looked at Mississippi's experience as a means to weather an expected postwar economic downturn.

Given these fears, civic and economic boosterism, long a feature of American political and economic policy, experienced a resurgence in the postwar period that state planners were largely helpless to resist. By 1950 almost all of the southern states had established new state planning departments that largely focused on economic development, narrowly conceived of as luring manufacturing businesses to the state (see Table 3–2, pp. 79–80).[54]

A Southern New Deal for the Jim Crow Order

As the second New Deal unfolded, a new group of southern reformers emerged. Although the New Deal was a national response to a national crisis, southerners saw the crisis as well as the solution through their particular lens of southern identity. The Southern Policy Committee was set up in Washington, D.C., to focus more attention on the South. The group first met on an informal basis. Southern politicians such as Lister Hill and John Sparkman were attendees, as were New Deal officials such as Clifford Durr (Rosa Parks's employer and later her lawyer), Abe Fortas, and occasionally Lyndon Johnson. Members of the Southern Policy Committee were instrumental in setting up and staffing the Conference on Economic Conditions in the South, which would issue the National Resource Council's *Report on Economic Conditions in the South*. The publication of this report in 1938 provided the southern New Dealers a template for action.[55]

While this report was being prepared the Southern Policy Committee began to meet on a more formal basis. The all-white delegation to the first meeting included traditional reformers such as Will Alexander and "southern liberal" journalists such as Virginius Dabney and Julian Harris. In a break with the past it also included representatives from labor, albeit from the conservative American Federation of Labor. Later the Southern Policy Committee included Brooks Hays, who would become a House Representative.[56] This group spawned a number of others at the state level in Arkansas, Alabama, Georgia, and Virginia. The reports of these state policy committees on issues such as voting, administrative, and economic reform were an important element in opening up the policy discourse in these states. More concretely, as a result of New Deal policies southern reformers were able to develop more permanent bases within state government.

Jim Crow reform during the New Deal was, as before, shaped by the desire to avoid issues of race and to avert what reformers saw as an ever-present threat of racial violence. When and where race was confronted, it was usually by conservatives, who worked to ensure that the New Deal's social welfare policies did not threaten racial hierarchies. For southern New

Deal policy activists race was secondary; to them the South's problems were fundamentally economic in nature. Once these problems were solved, other problems (e.g., the race problem) would also be solved.[57] According to Supreme Court Justice Hugo Black, one of the most visible of these southern reformers, "The core of the problem is economic." Solve those problems, Black said, and the "race problem will work itself out." Yet Black's economic liberalism was still tinged by the reformers' overall elitism; neither blacks nor average whites were ready to "vote intelligently," making them "ready game for corrupt and demagogic politicians." Southern elites, including reformers, still feared undiluted democracy. Even more critically for those who lament the South's "lost alternatives," southern liberal reformers' fear of the masses seeped into their fear of the labor movement.

The belief of these southern New Deal policy activists that only economic equality could set the stage for later transformation of the South was widely held. However, outside of federal programs this belief was not really put into practice. The emergence of the Southern Conference on Human Welfare provided a focal point for southern New Deal activism; for many historians it symbolizes the height of southern liberalism. For the first time the limited efforts of Jim Crow reformers were united with organizations such as the Congress of Industrial Organizations. Ironically the SCHW was convened both as a protest against the dismal picture painted by reports on the South and as a starting point for those interested in improving the South.[58]

This initial cooperation was the basis for a new attack on the poll tax, both at the national level and later at the state level, given the obstructionism of southern members of Congress. Even the slightly more liberal poll tax reformers were able to create an alliance with white Jim Crow reformers only by arguing that the health of the Jim Crow order and its white members was at stake.

Although the SCHW initially made connections with Jim Crow reformers, in the long run they were not durable. White Jim Crow reformers were put off by the perceived radicalism of the SCHW's agenda, which did not accommodate itself to the Jim Crow order. African American reformers were dismayed by the lack of organization within the SCHW and its multiple targets. By the late 1940s and the beginning of the cold war, the SCHW was increasingly under attack; it would eventually crumble under its association (alleged and otherwise) with the left and communism.

The demise of the SCHW occurred only a little later than the demise of southern New Deal policy activism. The end of the 1940s in some ways marked the end of organized Jim Crow reform outside of the auspices of the Southern Regional Council. Southern reform was weakened by the slow disappearance of prominent politicians like the senators Frank Porter

Graham and later Claude Pepper and Governor Ellis Arnall, who were sympathetic to the New Deal and to moderation on race relations. The Dixiecrat revolt in 1948 would force politicians like Senator Lister Hill of Alabama, who had previously been sympathetic to southern reform, to toe a far more conservative line. As a result of the passing of this brief political opening in the South, some of the New Deal policy activists would find a new organizational home in the SRC or retreat back to academia. Others, like Arthur Raper and some of their predecessors, would leave the South. Still others, like Clifford and Virginia Durr, would become inside agitators, while other former Jim Crow reformers like Virginius Dabney and John Temple Graves would become vociferous defenders of the Jim Crow order.[59]

Conclusion

By the time of the New Deal, Jim Crow reform had changed in terms of individual participation and organizational form. White southern reformers had split into three camps: agrarian romantics, regional sociologists, and southern New Dealers.[60] Nonetheless, overall Jim Crow reform did not stray far from its essential limitation; it was still bounded reform, aiming to reconcile and smooth over the stresses and strains within the disparate elements of the Jim Crow order and between the Jim Crow order and other existing orders within the American state. Although individual members of the reform movement may have wished to do so, Jim Crow reform did not exist to directly challenge the order within which it was located and from which it drew its identity and purpose. Southern reformers coupled their Progressivism to the planning rhetoric of the New Deal, arguing that the South could not advance if a significant portion of its human resources remained underdeveloped, and the potential for social instability as a result of this underdevelopment remained.

The limitations of the government reform approach can be seen in the ending of Roscoe Martin's state reform efforts, as well as the demise in general of southern planning. Although the historical strength of southern civic boosterism played a role in the demise of New Deal–style planning, other factors also contributed to its disappearance. With the decline of the New Deal the active search for answers and solutions to New Deal–defined problems decreased. In turn, the technique that Jim Crow reformers had embraced from the beginning—statistical portraiture—increasingly spoke to no one and changed nothing. Southern state reformers lost their bid to shape the path of southern economic development control. In some ways this was not surprising; historically the United States had always been somewhat hostile to planning and the South was no exception. The end of the National Resources Planning Board and the New Deal in general took away much of the financial and ideological support for state planners.[61]

In states where the reformers had received critical support from sympathetic state politicians, their project became embroiled in and ultimately the victim of state politics. The state of Georgia was an example of this phenomenon. The notion that the South could plan its destiny gave way to a vision of the South that continued to tout its main assets: cheap, nonunionized labor and business-friendly government. The development of the South was once again directed by elites, although with the influence of the state reformers this direction was more systemic and bureaucratic than before. The South's development was dependent on outside forces, the benefits of which would accrue primarily to the elites and only secondarily to the common people.

At their height southern state reformers produced dozens of studies, reports, and monographs on the state of southern government and its institutions. Bureaus were created in numerous southern states to spread and nurture the gospel of southern state reform. These studies and activities strengthened the South's intellectual and administrative integration into the nation by relegitimating government in the South and introducing to a new generation of southerners the notion that a government by and for the people was not antithetical to notions of efficiency and effectiveness.

The New Deal expanded the horizons of individual southerners and stimulated the formation of new groups who worked with established southern reform groups. The New Deal policy activists, with their belief in economic liberalism, were open to transforming rather than reforming the Jim Crow order. Yet their activities were highly constrained. They did not have the types of linkages to state governments possessed by other groups of Jim Crow reformers, such as educators; therefore their policy recommendations were rarely put into practice. They were also highly dependent on a favorable national political environment as well as the continued electoral success of southern politicians such as Brooks Hays and Claude Pepper. As these politicians were defeated and left office, the power of these southern policy activists weaned as well. Nonetheless, like the Jim Crow reformers of the 1920s, these policy activists further eroded the notion of a solid white South. Their focus on overturning southern poll tax laws, which had played a critical role in stripping political citizenship from lower-class whites as well as blacks, would create a fundamental change in the southern political structure by opening up the political order to the white have-nots and by placing the lack of political citizenship for African Americans back on the nation's political agenda for the first time since the turn of the twentieth century.

The New Deal Progressive ethos that had animated many of the southern public administrationists was quietly dismissed as an "innocent, bright-eyes faith...in government, cooperatives and planning."[62] For southern state reformers a technocratic, nonconfrontational approach to changing southern politics and society that was born in the Progressive era and nourished in the New Deal was dismissed as outdated. Yet the democratic promise of the CIC and the southern New Deal activists could not be contained. The next chapter traces how the democratization of the white South unfolded.

Chapter 4

Democratization for the White South

> If you were going to make real basic changes, you had to do something about the electorate.
>
> Robert Weaver, quoted in Patricia Sullivan, *Days of Hope*

The political, economic, and social changes stimulated by the New Deal and World War II posed new challenges and threats to the dominance of southern elites, and to the Jim Crow order at large. The existence of these potential threats offered southern reformers a two-pronged opportunity to develop new strategies for advancing Jim Crow reform. First, they would make the argument that southern leadership had to expand the southern (white) electorate in order for southern Democrats to continue to have an important influence on the national Democratic Party. Second, by expanding the electorate to the south's (white) have-nots, southern reformers hoped to create an important new source of support for southern politicians loyal to the New Deal. Protecting the New Deal meant the protection of the economic liberalism that would modernize the South. In the late 1930s southern reformers realized that a small dose of democratization was needed now, rather than later, to achieve this goal. To advance these arguments an older cadre of southern reformers would develop alliances with the new southern New Deal reformers. Together these groups would develop a network of state-based and national organizations that would push for poll tax reform at the state and national levels. In keeping with their reformist traditions they would draw on their belief in social science to develop a rationale for poll tax reform that emphasized how poll tax reform would maintain the Jim Crow order rather than fundamentally transform it. In keeping with the New Deal reform consensus, the need for reform was couched in the belief in economic liberalism, that the South's problems were fundamentally economic in nature.

Of all the aspects of the Jim Crow order, in retrospect it is not surprising that the poll tax emerged as one of the organizing issues around which southern white reformers would coalesce and to which southern black reformers would give limited support. As white supporters of poll tax reform would repeatedly argue, the tax affected more whites than blacks. Thus, although some blacks would benefit from the abolition or liberalization of the poll tax, southern white reformers repeatedly emphasized that all whites, in an absolute sense, would benefit from ending the tax. For black reformers, given the boundaries of the Jim Crow order, poll tax reform "as such represent[ed] progress."[1] For Jim Crow reformers, given their boundaries, the poll tax issue was the "ideal meeting point" for reconciling the Jim Crow order with the rest of the United States.[2]

The Organization of Poll Tax Reform

The Southern Conference for Human Welfare was the most visible of the groups pressing for poll tax reform during the 1930s and 1940s. The role of the SCHW is notable because under its umbrella the organization was able to briefly, for the first time, bring together a variety of groups that had rarely found common ground, from traditional southern reformers to groups such as the CIO.[3] Unlike the Commission on Interracial Cooperation, the SCHW was willing to publicly challenge the Jim Crow social order, most famously by not abiding by segregation ordinances in its meetings. Aided by its relationship with First Lady Eleanor Roosevelt, the SCHW became one of the first southern groups to openly press for poll tax reform. Other state and national groups involved in poll tax reform were the National Committee to Abolish the Poll Tax (NCAPT) and the Southern Electoral Reform League. Because the number of southern liberals was relatively small, both groups had substantial overlap in membership. The NCAPT was based in Washington, D.C., and was closely allied with congressional strategy, while the Southern Electoral League was largely a loose collection of state groups. These anti–poll tax groups would sponsor a number of studies designed to persuade southern opinion leaders as well as average southerners of the benefits of repeal for the white electorate.

Despite being more democratic and inclusive, the SCHW's premise for poll tax reform still rested on the basis of economic liberalism. White (both southern and northern) supporters would make and indeed emphasize the following nonracial arguments about the need for poll tax reform. First, far from purifying southern politics from corruption, the poll tax was seen as largely contributing to growing corruption. Critics cited repeated instances of the buying and manipulating of votes via the payment of poll taxes.[4] Second, reformers argued that the tax was antidemocratic and that the abolition of the poll tax would upend the notion that southern government ought to be under the control of the "better classes of people" and out of the hands of "the corrupt, the illiterate, the ignorant, the disinterested, and the trifling."[5] Democracy should be for the masses (of whites), not a small elite.

Although African Americans did not approach poll tax reform with the same level of ardor as white reformers did, reform was not unimportant to them. But unlike whites, blacks saw the effect of the poll tax through the lens of strategic accommodation. For example, although most African American leaders opposed the poll tax, there was support for the tax from people in states such as Arkansas, where voting restrictions were not as harsh as in other areas. In some areas the poll tax was the only significant hurdle, and a small number of black Arkansans were able to vote. These leaders feared that repeal of the poll tax could lead to the imposition of even more restrictive registration procedures.[6] These small exceptions aside, poll tax reform was strategically important to African Americans on a number of levels. For example, as the African American newspaper the Chicago *Defender* argued, poll tax reform would "hasten the advent of certain white progressives to power ... [who would] implement state laws as to usher in a new era of justice and quality to a mass of inarticulate whites and Negroes."[7] Although the chances were slight of obtaining poll tax reform through congressional legislation or judicial decision, a victory in one of these arenas would provide a valuable tool in the overall fight for African American political rights by establishing a precedent, for the first time since Reconstruction, for federal government intervention into southern political institutions.

Southern white women were another group that was visibly mobilized in opposition to the poll tax. As Sarah Wilkerson-Freeman argues, southern women increasingly viewed the poll tax as a gender and class issue that undercut the promise of the Nineteenth Amendment. Especially in lower-income families, gender roles ensured that if a choice had to be made based on the money available, the male's right to vote would almost invariably win out.[8]

Working at the state level, through the Women's Committee of the national Democratic Party, and their personal contact with Eleanor Roosevelt, these southern women used the crisis of the Great Depression to focus attention on the disproportionate effect it had on (white) women. The insistence of some southern feminists on the primacy of gender as opposed to race would later infuriate leading southern liberals such as Virginia Durr.[9] Despite these differences, southern white women played an important role in developing a network of supporters in different states to push for either reforming or ultimately abolishing the poll tax.

The role of southern white women and African Americans was downplayed when the later history of the poll tax reform movement was told by political scientists such as V. O. Key and his students. Jim Crow reform coupled with New Deal liberalism would strategically minimize these contributions in order to support a struggle for a democracy for (white) men.[10]

The Poll Tax and Southern Politics

In the post-Reconstruction era the poll tax in the South emerged as one of the elements used by whites to secure the Jim Crow order.[11] Along with other disenfranchising techniques, such as literacy tests and understanding clauses, the poll tax was designed to evade the reach of the Fifteenth Amendment and any other federal intervention. In the aftermath of the political upheaval of Populism in the late 1890s the poll tax also became one of the key instruments used by the southern political elite to decrease if not entirely negate the influence of lower-class whites on southern politics. By 1910 the poll tax had been reframed as an instrument of racial solidarity. For southern political elites support for the poll tax was first and foremost an important rhetorical device used to uphold white supremacy by creating solidarity across (white) class lines. Despite this solidarity with lower-class whites, the tax was also seen by elites as a way to purify southern politics of the influences of these lower-class people and to ensure only the participation of the "better elements." By diminishing the white electorate the South's small political and economic elite was able to perpetuate its power at both the national and state levels and protect its interests from challenges from within or outside of the Jim Crow order.

By 1908 all of the southern states had enacted a poll tax. Along with the white primary the tax was seen as an important tool that secured and maintained political power for the southern political and business elite. Paradoxically, for poor whites the poll tax provided an important symbol of their privileged white standing.[12] These privileges notwithstanding, by the 1930s, as a result of the poll tax, it was estimated that white electoral participation dropped to less than a third of the total white voting age population.

Each state administered the poll tax differently (see Table 4–1). Most states made very little effort to collect the taxes, which were typically due anywhere from three months to almost a year prior to an election. A typical state poll tax was one dollar (about $24 in 2005). In a desperately poor region with low cash incomes this was a significant outlay. In addition to the administrative and financial hurdle of the taxes, six states had cumulative measures imposed on residents who failed to pay taxes. Alabama and Georgia had the most punitive measures, requiring payments ranging from $36 to $47 in order to vote. In Alabama a voter who failed to pay poll taxes potentially had to pay up to the equivalent of $865 (in 2005 dollars) in order to vote, and a delinquent voter in Georgia faced a potential poll tax bill of $1,128 (in 2005 dollars). As a result of the financial and administrative barriers of the poll tax, by the time the Jim Crow order was fully established voting by both blacks and whites plummeted, although the means by which black disenfranchisement and white de-incorporation came about differed.

Nonetheless, despite this diminishment of political power, many lower-class whites did not initially believe that the poll tax was directed at them,[13] even though white elites put forth a restrictive definition of white southern democracy to justify the new order. This version framed white democracy as an issue of individual moral fitness. The ability to pay a poll tax defined those worthy enough to engage in politics. If a white person was

Table 4–1 Poll Tax in the South

State	Poll Tax Enacted	Rate	Cumulative Feature?	Poll Tax Action Taken: Abolish/Reform?
Alabama	1901	$1.50	To $36.00	1944 (R); 1953 (R)
Arkansas	1893	$1.00		1938(A)*; 1941 (R); 1949 (R); 1956 (A)*
Florida	1889	$1.00	To $ 2.00	1937 (A)
Georgia	1908		To $47.00	1945 (A)
Louisiana	1898	$1.00	To $ 2.00	1934 (A)
Mississippi	1890	$2.00	To $ 4.00	No Action
North Carolina	1900	$1.43		1920 (A)
South Carolina	1895	$1.00		1951 (A)
Tennessee	1890	$1.00		1943 (A)*; 1949 (R); 1951 (A)
Texas	1902	$1.50		1949 (A)*
Virginia	1902	$1.50	To $ 4.50	1949 (A)*

Source: Key, *Southern Politics*, 599–618; Kousser, *Shaping of Southern Politics*, 62–83; Ogden, *Poll Tax in the South*.
Note: A= Abolish; R=Reform; * = Failed to Pass; Current Value: $1 (1940) = $14.49 (2005).

unwilling to sacrifice a dollar for democracy, that nonpayment was evidence that he or she lacked the worthiness needed for citizenship and was certainly not ready to participate in politics.

The New Deal and the Emergence of an Anti–Poll Tax Coalition

At the start of the New Deal southern members of Congress, who comprised and also represented this elite, initially welcomed the material benefits of the New Deal. By the middle of the 1930s, however, some members of the South's elite and its political representatives were increasingly alarmed at the economic and social upheavals that the New Deal began to pose for the Jim Crow order. They began to turn against Roosevelt and the New Deal, blocking the enactment of important legislation.[14] By the end of the New Deal Jim Crow reformers were uneasily straddling the increasing divisions between traditional southern Democrats and the national Democratic Party organization. The first clear strain occurred in 1936, when the party at its National Convention voted to abolish the two-thirds rule for nominating candidates in favor of a simple majority vote. This rule was used by the South to ensure that Democratic candidates would be beholden to southern interests. Coupled with this rule change were the growing criticisms from liberal Democrats about the South's "rotten districts" in which there were few voters because of exclusionary practices. These voters and their representatives had the same electoral impact as districts with more voters but exercised disproportionate power over national policymaking.[15] Some activists suggested threatening the South with actually enforcing the provisions of the Fourteenth Amendment, which "reduced a state's representation by the proportion of citizens over 21 that were denied the right to vote in federal elections." This would mean that the South's representation in the House would decrease from sixty-nine to nine members.[16]

In 1938 Roosevelt dramatically signaled his frustration with southern conservatives by supporting attempts to unseat incumbent southern Democrats and proclaiming his support for abolishing the poll tax. To take advantage of this new (and, as it turned out, temporary) national stance against the South, a new group, the Southern Conference on Human Welfare, emerged.

Despite this broad base of southern and nonsouthern support, the poll tax issue was seen by the majority of southerners (including some white southern liberals) as an issue created, fomented, and thrust upon the South by outsiders, who were not sympathetic to what southerners called "the South's special problems." The SCHW was not unaware of this dynamic. In the 1942 congressional elections Jennings Perry, a southern member of the SCHW and the Southern League for Electoral Reform, suggested that the organizations downplay the poll tax issue to avoid harming the reelection prospects of the few remaining southern liberals still in office.[17]

Poll Tax Reform at the National level During the New Deal

In 1939 Representative Lee Geyer (D-CA) introduced a poll tax reform bill (H.R. 7534) in the House. Although the bill went nowhere, it provided the impetus for further national-level organizing around the issue. In 1941 Senator Claude Pepper of Florida, one of the last staunch southern New Dealers, introduced another poll tax bill, the Geyer-Pepper Bill (S. 1280). This attempt to enact poll tax reform in Congress was successful in the House, passing on a vote of 254 to 84. The bill, however, was filibustered by southern senators. Although Roosevelt had raised the issue of poll tax reform in his brief attack against southern Democrats, he declined to expend anymore of his political capital on the issue. The poll tax issue was also weakened by the perception that it was not only an intraparty dispute, but fundamentally a southern issue.

Although poll tax reform ran into the implacable opposition of southern members of Congress, at the state level campaigns for abolishing or reforming the poll state were initiated or reenergized. The most visible of this New Deal–inspired reform was in Florida, where Senator Pepper led efforts to repeal the state's tax in 1937. In Arkansas a coalition of forces managed to get a referendum on the ballot in 1938 to abolish the poll tax; however, Roosevelt's open support for poll tax reform was cited as one of the reasons that the referendum was defeated. Although Louisiana's repeal of the poll tax occurred under different political conditions, southern reformers gave qualified approval to the reform as it demonstrated how New Deal economic liberalism could be supported. By 1940 four of the eleven southern states had either abolished the poll tax, enacted limited reform, or held a state constitutional referendum on the tax (see Table 4–1).

Despite these state reforms, in some ways the poll tax issue at the national level seemed to be headed in the same direction as the efforts to pass a federal antilynching law; it was considered a regional and racial issue that merited sympathetic hearing but no significant support from other political actors.[18] Indeed a brief and not very in-depth overview of poll tax legislation at the national level would reveal a pattern familiar to American reformers: legislation would be passed by an attentive House over a period of years, largely for symbolic reasons, then the Senate, usually at the behest of a small group of opponents, would stymie this legislation until the issue lost its potency and

Table 4–2 Success at the National Level: House Votes, 1942–1949

	Geyer Bill 1942	Marcantonio Bill 1943	Marcantonio 1945	Bender Bill 1947	Norton Bill 1949
Vote	254–84	265–110	251–105	290–112	273–116
Southerners For (%)	8.8	4.8	4.8	5.7	6.7
Southerners Against (%)	71.6	79.0	75.2	85.7	81.0
Southerners in House	102	105	105	105	105

Source: adapted from Frederic Ogden, *The Poll Tax in the South* (University: University of Alabama Press, 1958), "Table 19: Analysis of Vote in House of Representatives on Final Passage of Anti-Poll Tax Bills," 253.

energy and supporters moved on to another new issue. Indeed in all five poll tax bills that were passed by the House (from 1942 to 1949) southern representatives were remarkably united; in no instance did less than 70 percent of southerners vote against any particular bill (see Table 4–2).[19]

The South and America's War for Democracy

The beginnings of World War II transformed this internal and regional issue into a national one and shook up a stalled legislative dynamic. In the words of one historian, World War II provoked a remarkable "democratic revival."[20] As the war in Europe expanded and many democratic countries fell to Nazism and fascism, a growing consensus emerged that these countries were defeated because of the weakness of their democratic spirit and institutions. The United States could withstand this threat and save the world only if its own democratic house was in order. The country could not fight for democracy if it was not able to confidently believe that the American creed was matched in its execution.

As a result the emphasis of Jim Crow reformers on economic liberalism and democratic gradualism during the New Deal was challenged and then pushed aside. America's entry into the war effectively spelled the end of the New Deal and sent many of the white southerners that had been working in Washington back to the South. These return migrants would form part of the state-based reform movements that operated during the 1940s. More important, the democratic rhetoric of World War II pressed Jim Crow reformers to directly address the South's "democratic deficit." Unlike the aftermath of World War I, nearly two decades of organizational activity and institution building prior to Word War II provided a means of translating the rhetoric, limited reforms, and slim political openings created by a war for democracy into action.

A war-driven emphasis on asserting that the American creed was strong and unsullied turned the spotlight on some, though certainly not all, of America's undemocratic practices.[21] By virtue of its own assertion of separateness the South came under new scrutiny. But whereas during the New Deal attention had been focused on the South's economic impoverishment and underdevelopment, this new scrutiny focused on the region's democratic deficit. Critics looked at the South as the country's weak link. How could the American creed be used as part of the war effort if it is suffered from a fundamental internal weakness? The South's defenders sought to come up with answers to questions like this.[22]

The South and, by extension, many of its white southern reformers was put into an ideological and political quandary. Both fearful of and lacking the capacity to imagine a fundamental transformation of the Jim Crow order, they attempted to square the American creed with what Howard Odum, a leading southern sociologist, regionalist, and white southern liberal reformer, called the "southern credo": a political, institutional, and cultural commitment to white supremacy.[23] To align these belief systems, white southern reformers would have to reinvent and reshape the meaning of democracy into an idea that could easily fit into their capacity for creating change, but that would also support the essential antidemocratic nature of southern political institutions. This complex restructuring entailed redefining the poll tax issue as an issue of *white* democracy. By writing out or eliminating race from the issue, they could square the American democratic revival with the Jim Crow order. Abolishing the poll tax became a way of reclaiming and reasserting the South's adherence to democratic norms (albeit for whites only).

Although my discussion has focused on the reframing of poll tax reform as an issue of white democracy and on the role of white reformers, this does not mean that African Americans, particularly southerners, were missing from the story. Despite the way the poll tax issue had been framed the existence of a device that locked out not only millions of blacks but also millions of whites from American democracy supported African Americans' contentions that America failed to live up to its democratic premises. The fight for poll tax reform was also another means by which African American civic groups could extend the process of citizenship training that had begun during World War II. It helped southern African American leaders focus their efforts on a device that could bring tangible results. That is, while the poll tax could be shown to be antidemocratic, efforts to mobilize protest against it could be used as a means to develop and exploit a limited range of political influence. It was a campaign based on contradictions, alongside of campaigns to support the elimination of the poll tax were campaigns to encourage the paying of poll taxes. In states such as Virginia and Arkansas, where other barriers to participation such as literacy and understanding clauses were absent, encouraging the payment of poll taxes provided a way to develop new African American voters.[24]

Fighting and Voting for Democracy: The Soldier's Vote Bill

The South's opposition to federal action on the poll tax was breached by the effective coupling of the rhetoric of democracy with that of military duty and sacrifice. America could not deny the right to vote to millions of military personnel who were fighting to protect American democracy. This coupling led to the enactment of the Soldier's Vote Act of 1942 (PL 712) and the first clear linkage between the war's democratic revival and the poll tax. The law provided an absentee "war ballot" for military personnel so that they could vote for candidates for federal office, provided that these individuals satisfied the registration and suffrage requirements of their state of residence.[25] What worried southerners, however, were proposed amendments to the legislation that would have exempted military personnel from paying a poll tax in order to vote for state offices. Even though two poll tax states, Mississippi and South Carolina, exempted active service members from the poll tax, representatives from these states as well as other southern states saw this law as yet one more assault on the South. Although southerners were able to amend the legislation so that states controlled the distribution of ballots, the first legislative linkage between the war for democracy abroad and the war for democracy at home had been created. As a result of the timing of the legislation, the actual turnout of military voters was small, less than 2 percent of the estimated 5.5 million active duty military personnel.

In 1943 the Green-Lucas bill (S. 1285) was introduced to amend and strengthen the Soldier's Vote Act by creating a bipartisan War Ballot Commission. Among other features of the bill, the Commission would replace the largely ineffectual system of state-supplied ballots that southerners had been successfully inserting into the original legislation. In addition the bill would have set aside all state poll tax requirements. Roosevelt announced his support for this bill in 1944. This attempt to amend the legislation created even more southern congressional anger. Senator James Eastland of Mississippi direly predicted that the bill would "send carpetbaggers into the South to control elections."[26] Again showing their unity and the growing cooperation with Republicans, southerners were able to block the Green-Lucas bill and other proposals, substituting instead an act that essentially protected the status quo established by the 1942 Act. Although a War Ballot Commission was created, states still retained the right to control who had access to the war ballot.

Given their reluctant acquiescence to the Soldier's Vote Act, southerners were in no mood to compromise on the poll tax bills introduced afterward. Southerners repeatedly and openly declared that national anti–poll tax bills were part of a plot to "enfranchise the Negro in the South."[27] To ward off the possibility of this federal interference into southern affairs, the South sought a "southern solution to its problems"; poll tax reform at the state level would be the solution out of the impasse created by changing national political configurations as well as changing ideas about the meaning of democracy. By championing state-level poll tax reform southerners could define and control the tenor of democratization in the South in a way that lessened pressure from above in the form of national legislation and minimized the dissonance between America's competing racial orders.

Social Science and Rational Democratic Reform

Social science became one of the solutions for one of the most stubborn problems facing reformers: how to advance legislation in state political systems that were, by the whole, hostile to the very notion of the equal inclusion of blacks in the political sphere. The answer lay in turning the issue into an issue of white democracy, sanitizing and buttressing the issue through scientific evidence, and then presenting it as a southern solution. The administration of Ellis Arnall, the last New Deal governor of Georgia, is an example of how southern reformers allied themselves with sympathetic politicians in order to develop a new rationale for southern democracy that would be acceptable to the reformers' goals of creating politically viable solutions that in their view rested on minimizing the role of race in the Jim Crow political order.

Ellis Arnall and Southern New Deal Liberalism

The election of Ellis Arnall in 1942 marked the brief ascendancy of New Deal liberalism in Georgia.[28] Arnall ran for office on a platform that emphasized good government and helping Georgia recover from the upheavals of the Talmadge administration. One of the key issues of the campaign was that the state university system had recently lost its accreditation due to Talmadge's political interference. In the end the pro-reform spirit of Arnall, as well as considerable help from college students (and their parents) angered by the possible loss of their college credits, helped Arnall overcome Talmadge's deep political roots in rural Georgia.

What is noteworthy about Arnall's election is the role that race played in the final stretches. Sensing that the tide was about to turn, Talmadge turned to the classic race-baiting strategy of the South. He claimed that Arnall's reform proposals would lead to, among other things, the desegregation of Georgia's universities. Arnall responded in classic turn by trumpeting his own southern heritage and reassuring voters of his commitment to segregation. Talmadge was roundly criticized by the state's leading newspapers for "manufacturing a racial issue where none existed before."[29] In the end Talmadge's appeal to race and racism, which had come to his aid before, failed him. The corruption and inefficiency of his administration, not the maintenance of white supremacy, was foremost on the minds of Georgia voters.

Once elected Arnall quickly showed his reformist zeal.[30] The state university system was reorganized, as were several aspects of state government; a teachers' retirement system and a state merit system were created; and the state penal system was reformed. The high point of his administration was the reform of Georgia's 1877 Constitution. Constitutional reform was an issue that had been advocated by Georgia government reformers since 1901. The constitutional revision committee created by Arnall is where the role of social scientists and the articulation of a new southern political style can be seen.

A New Constitution for Georgia

Since 1901 a variety of politicians, reformers, and academics had called for or created committees to draft a new state constitution for Georgia. The latest of these calls had been issued in 1940 and was spearheaded by a group calling itself the Citizens' Fact Finding Movement of Georgia. This was an alliance of the Rotary Club, the League of Women Voters, and other groups that agued that a new constitution was "imperative" if the state was to "progress as she should" and democracy be saved in Georgia.[31]

Despite the efforts of these citizens, constitutional reform did not play a role in the Arnall-Talmadge campaign. Instead "good government" was the broad platform on which Arnall ran. After his first legislative session ended, Arnall in 1943 called for the establishment of a constitutional revision committee so that a constitution for a "modern government and suited to the needs and conditions of the people of the State" could be produced.[32] The committee would meet from 1943 to 1944.

In addition to its mandate to streamline and rationalize state government, the committee addressed two important voting issues: the status of the white primary, which was included in Georgia's 1877 Constitution, and the poll tax. In April 1944, in the midst of the constitutional committee's deliberations, the U.S. Supreme Court ruled against the white primary system in Texas in *Smith* v. *Allwright*. The decision jolted the southern political establishment, and politicians scrambled to assess its implications. Within Georgia's constitutional committee there was disagreement over whether, in an attempt to save the white primary, to delete all references to (and thus all state control over) primary elections, or to acquiesce to the Court's decision and find some other way to maintain control over the electoral process. Groups such as the Atlanta League of Women Voters argued that without government oversight the possibilities of voting fraud and corruption were increased. Arnall, however, supported the conservatives on this issue, stating that he was against "any regulation of primaries in the Constitution or on the statute books of this state."[33]

Arnall's dissimulation on this displayed the essence of southern liberalism. On the issue of exclusion he cited existing statutory exemptions based on age (those between eighteen and twenty-one and over sixty), military service, and gender (the exclusion of first-time women voters) and stated, "I have sometimes wondered who was left to pay the poll tax."[34] Who was left, and remained unnamed, was the state's African American population. While the ending the white primary would have opened up new political opportunities for African Americans, ending the poll tax would largely benefit whites, who presumably could be convinced that it was only a small psychic price to pay. In short, the racial implications of the poll tax were deliberately downplayed in favor of an approach that emphasized that repeal of the poll tax was simply a nonpolitical, technocratic fix of the system.

Despite earlier efforts by anti–poll tax supporters to convince Arnall to publicly support the elimination of the poll tax, the governor refused to take a stance, declaring that "the Chair [Arnall] had no deep-seated convictions on it." With this neutral stance, the rest of the commission, with two exceptions, voted to retain the poll tax.[35] A slightly revised constitution, retaining the poll tax, was completed in time to be submitted to the 1945 legislature. To take effect it would have to gain the support of the state legislature and be submitted directly to the voters for ratification. Given that a December 1944 Associated Press survey found that most state legislators favored keeping the poll tax, it would not have been surprising if legislators and voters approved the new constitution, including retaining the poll tax.

But despite the recommendation of the committee, as well as Arnall's stance, the prospects for eliminating the poll tax were better than ever before. Georgia's political leadership was against keeping the tax even though there was resistance from rank-and-file state legislators. Both the Georgia State House speaker and the State Senate president were against the retention of the tax, and Georgia's U.S. senators, Walter George and Richard Russell, also favored repeal. For the U.S. senators, the appeal of poll tax elimination could be traced to ongoing attempts at the congressional level to enact anti–poll tax legislation.[36]

Arnall thus faced a choice: he could shore up support among Georgia's conservative voters by supporting the retention of the poll tax, or he could potentially change the face of the Georgia electorate by endorsing poll tax reform. Arnall made the latter choice. It was a choice partially based on electoral calculation—new voters could help the future electoral prospects of his reform faction—and his worsening relationship with the Georgia Democratic Party balanced against his relationship to southern New Deal liberalism and Jim Crow reform.

Social Science and the Development of a Democratic South

In keeping with his stance, in December 1944 and early 1945 Arnall called for a study of the poll tax in order to guide his and the legislature's decisions. This move has been a largely unexplored aspect of Georgia's poll tax struggle. Arnall's main biographer mentions his call in an aside, and Frederic Ogden's work on the poll tax (the most comprehensive contemporary work on the issue) only briefly mentions Arnall's proposed study. Arnall gave the following reasons for the study:

> [It is] time to take stock [of the poll tax] and find out for ourselves what practical effects the poll tax had. To that end a factual, careful study of the poll tax is needed and should be made. So far most of the agitation for and against the poll tax and most of the discussion about it have been based on prejudice and emotion rather than an impartial analysis of concrete facts. In simple truth, not much is known about the poll tax, beyond what casual observation teaches, for no careful study of that tax in operation has been made. It is this lack of an adequate factual basis for consideration of the poll tax that the proposed study is designed to remedy.[37]

This statement, made in 1944, gives no hint of the fact that Arnall had discussed the poll tax issue with other southern reformers as governor-elect in 1942.

Arnall's call for a study reflects how Jim Crow reformers were able to find common cause with sympathetic politicians. In general these reformers and political allies embraced social science as a means of creating and justifying a new southern alternative. They believed that individuals were, on the whole, rational actors. Racial animosity was not inherent in the southern (white) character, but a result of political demagoguery that exacerbated the tensions caused by economic distress and competition. Once given the facts, and with their self-interest pointed out, Jim Crow reformers believed, the average white southerner would support their limited view of southern democracy. White Jim Crow reformers believed the promise of this new southern state would be equally attractive to southern African Americans. As Arnall argued in his autobiography, "Fundamentally, the problem of the Negro in the South is a problem of economics. In a prosperous South, in a South that did not suffer from colonialism and exploitation, the Negro would prosper and would be able to obtain most of the things that he desires."[38]

Implicit in Arnall's evaluation was the belief that values such as democracy and citizenship, and more important equality, were easily traded in favor of material well-being. But he was mistaken: African Americans in the late 1940s were not willing to accept the trade-off that he and his reform allies were offering, and white southerners were not willing to embrace reform.

The End of the Georgia Poll Tax

A variety of motives have been assigned to Governor Arnall's decision to ultimately openly support the repeal of the poll tax. According to Frederic Ogden, Arnall did so after a personal appeal by Franklin Roosevelt, a claim that Arnall later denied.[39] Others have argued that Arnall's support was part of his ongoing battle with Talmadge and his supporters. Indeed in the battle over ratification of the proposed constitution, Talmadge campaigned against it (and by association Arnall) as an "anti-democratic," "pro-New Deal" scheme to "centralize power" and undermine, if not end, white supremacy in Georgia.[40] In short, the fallout from the *Smith* decision forced Arnall to take an unequivocal stand on the issue.

In the end, however, what may have motivated Arnall, in addition to political calculation, was the essence of Jim Crow reform. Some of his biographers, as well as Arnall himself, argue that his evolving stance on race was a balance of political strategizing and a growing sense that some (not all) aspects of the Jim Crow system harmed the South both morally and economically.

Like other southern reformers, Arnall also argued that the South's racial problems were in fact due to economics. The exploitation and domination of the southern economy restricted economic opportunities for all, and thus led to competition and hostility between the races. Arnall also uneasily acknowledged that Jim Crow's separate but equal doctrine had not lived up to its implicit trade-off; while saddled with segregation, blacks received less than equal facilities and services. Finally, the broad effects of the country's fight for democracy in World War II had unleashed doubts about the fit of the South within American democracy.

Describing himself as a "democrat; with a small 'd' please," Arnall would later state, "What the hell difference does it make if you sit down and eat with Negroes, visit with them in their homes, talk with them?" Coupled with his claim that blacks ought to have some political rights, this statement was wildly radical for a southern politician.[41] Yet this radicalism was leavened with pragmatism. Openly and consistently advocating for racial equality and refusing to engage in race baiting would not have gotten Arnall, in his words, "elected door keeper."[42]

Southern chauvinism also played a role in Arnall's stance. His support for repeal of the poll tax reflected the growing pressure from outside the South. Arnall said, "[I am] tired of seeing my state...kicked about in Congress." He then added that there was no danger of blacks voting as long as the white primary was retained.[43] For Arnall the southern politician, as well as for southern conservatives, better a southern solution—that is, repeal of the poll tax—than allow federal intervention in such a crucially important area and open the door to further intrusions.

Yet what was revealing about Arnall's stance and that of the rest of the Georgia political leadership was that support for the elimination of the poll tax was couched in terms of democracy for whites. Eugene Talmadge, Arnall's bitter foe, echoed the arguments of liberal anti–poll taxers in his claim that on the whole the poll tax harmed more whites than blacks. The rest of Talmadge's argument was the unspoken aspect of the anti–poll tax crusade: that despite the poll tax, the path to the ballot for blacks was blocked not only by the now threatened white primary but by extralegal means as well.[44] With this widespread support, the Atlanta *Journal* stated, "the days of the poll tax in Georgia are numbered."[45]

Arnall ultimately called for the repeal of the tax in his 1945 legislative agenda. He backed his decision by stating that if the legislature did not repeal it, the state government would refuse to collect it. This statement drew widespread condemnation, as it was this type of autocratic behavior that was indulged in by Talmadge and against which Arnall had run. He furthered his threat by privately telling legislators that if they refused to repeal the tax he would get rid of it by executive order. If they wanted to reinstate the poll tax, legislators would be in the difficult position of asking newly enfranchised white voters to become disenfranchised.[46]

In January the Georgia Senate voted 31 to 19 to repeal the tax, with a provision for biennial registration. The House passed the bill on January 31, but with a provision of permanent registration. The latter provision was adopted into the final version and was signed into law by Arnall in March 1945. Georgia had become the fourth southern state to repeal the poll tax. Arnall was immediately lionized by liberals (both southern and northern) as a harbinger of a better, more democratic South.[47]

Arnall further cemented his liberal credentials by taking the next daring step: allowing African Americans to vote in the 1946 primary elections. In the wake of the *Smith* decision Rev. Primus King unsuccessfully attempted to vote in the 1944 Georgia primary. He then filed suit against the state (*King v. Chapman et al.*, 62 F. Supp. 639 (1945)). In October 1945 the Federal District Court found in King's favor, ruling that the Georgia primary was unconstitutional. A Federal Appeals Court upheld the decision in March 1946, and the U.S. Supreme Court refused to review the decision. However, because of the nature of the ruling, all was not lost for defenders of the racial status quo. The wording of the decision was such that if the Georgia Democratic Party was converted into a private organization, white control over access to the ballot could be maintained. Arnall refused to call a special session of the legislature so that a way could be found to evade the Court's decision. The Democratic Party was forced to amend its rules and allow African Americans to vote.

The response of the African American community to Arnall's decision was immediate; by the end of the year 150,000 African Americans had registered, second only to Texas and far above the rest of the South, where the number of registered black voters was in the low thousands. But Arnall's call to fellow white Georgians to "uphold the courts, the Constitution and laws of our land" fell on deaf ears as Talmadge seized on Arnall's stance as a betrayal of white Georgia. This last step of Arnall's, coinciding with a region-wide conservative backlash, ousted him and other southern liberals from office and ended the South's brief flirtation with racial moderation. By 1947 the window of opportunity had seemingly closed, as the Georgia state legislature repealed its primary laws in order to circumvent the *King* decision.[48] For Georgia an era of massive resistance and mobilization, on the part of whites and blacks, was about to begin.

Democracy for the White South

By framing poll tax reform as a way to redeem white democracy, southern reformers accomplished a number of things. First, they took the issue away from national actors and interests and placed it in the hands of regional actors and interests. Thus pressure at the national level could be recalibrated to adjust to the shifting needs of the various actors, interests, and institutions that composed the Jim Crow order. Southern members of Congress could delay poll tax reform legislation at the national level by claiming that the South was making a credible internal effort to address the issue. Reformers at the state level could make use of ongoing national attention to the South's democratic deficit as a means of putting poll tax reform on the southern public and legislative agenda.

Second, the campaign to redeem white democracy eroded the political and social power of southern political elites. To maintain the Jim Crow order southern democracy itself had to be redefined. A democracy for all (whites) could not be based on economic distinctions. The ability to vote was the right and the privilege of all (white) Americans, not simply the "better class." Indeed such distinctions among whites was dangerous given that the *Smith v. Allwright* decision in 1944 invalidating the white primary was allowing southern African Americans a partial opening into southern politics.

The expansion of poll tax reform as an issue of white democracy caught the eyes of southern politicians at the state level. The South's one-party system, with its varied levels of factionalism, had led to a perennial condition of political "ins" and "outs."[49] Manipulation of electoral rules, among other political institutions, was one of the favorite instruments used to gain power. If restricting the white franchise had worked to benefit one group, why couldn't extending the white franchise be used to benefit another group? By framing poll tax reform as an issue of white democracy and not, as its supporters claimed, a threat to white supremacy opponents of reform could not credibly argue against the expansion of the white electorate. Furthermore politicians could not resist the possibility of creating a new and more potent electoral coalition from these new votes. As Eugene Talmadge, a quintessential Jim Crow politician, sagely noted, "When you control the machine you want as few voters as possible so that the machine's proportion will be as big as possible. But when somebody else's machine controls, you need some new voters...to swamp it."[50] The "inexorable law of American politics," Ralph Bunche observed, "is to get the vote, and once vote hungry candidates taste a helpful vote...it is relished."[51]

Other practical considerations, such as the rising cost of corruption, also came into play. For example, poll tax reform garnered labor support not only because it was consistent with democratic practice and values, but also because reform would make it easier for white, and in some cases black, union members to vote. For most unions the accepted practice of paying poll tax bills in exchange for votes was an expensive risk given the uncertain outcomes of southern elections. Even state politicians realized that winning elections meant facing the ever higher costs inherent in poll tax receipt buying.

Thus by reframing poll tax reform as an issue of white democracy, southern reformers were able to build a much broader coalition at both the national and the state level. The coalition built at the national level became the genesis of the coalition of groups that would later support the modern civil rights movement. While each state had a different configuration of groups that were pressing for poll tax reform, what is remarkable about each coalition is that they featured groups that would become the elements of the "new" New South: business moderates, suburban voters, and urban "good government" advocates. By 1948 these coalitions had picked up an important new source of support: returning World War II veterans who realized that their fight for democracy was now a domestic one. These veteran groups played important roles in leading the fight for state-level reform in Arkansas, Georgia, Tennessee, and Texas.[52] In the poll tax reform campaign many of these groups saw a way to clean up the South's image and position southern government on a more responsive, orderly, and businesslike path.

The reenergized state-level campaigns proceeded along different paths. Of the eight remaining states that still had poll tax laws, Georgia and Tennessee (albeit temporarily) abolished them during the 1940s (see Table 4–1). Georgia abolished its poll tax in 1945. Tennessee's legislature, under pressure from a variety of reform groups and led by the journalist Jennings Perry, abolished the poll tax in 1943.[53] This action was overturned, however, by the state's supreme court, whose justices were beholden to the Crump machine, which relied on poll tax fraud. Nonetheless supporters of reform were able to get significant changes in the tax enacted in 1949, leading to its effective abolishment in 1951.

In the remaining states poll tax reform came in much more limited steps. In Arkansas, despite the defeat of the referendum in 1938, significant reforms were enacted in 1941 and 1949. In 1956 supporters were able to get a referendum on abolishing the tax on the ballot; however, it failed to pass. In Texas and Virginia poll tax referenda were on the ballot in 1949. In Texas support for poll tax reform was led by traditional southern reform groups as well as leading liberal figures such as the former congressman and San Antonio mayor Maury Maverick. Maverick's involvement was ironic as he was indicted and then acquitted of the common but illegal practice of paying poll taxes for individuals. These liberals and reform groups were also joined by state legislators who represented heavily Mexican American districts, which were being mobilized by returning Mexican American World War II veterans.[54] Yet despite the support of these groups, the referendum failed to pass, getting only 44 percent of the vote. Given the tremendous impact made by the *Smith v. Allwright* case, which had originated in Texas, and the pending *Sweatt* case, which threatened segregated higher education in Texas, this result was not surprising.

In Virginia a long campaign by a disparate alliance of opponents of the Byrd machine, ranging from Democratic Party outsiders to the state's small

Republican Party, battled the state's poll tax in both the judicial and legislative arenas. By the late 1940s the Byrd machine was forced to beat back surprisingly tough challenges for control of the governor's office. Coupled with these electoral challenges was a new headache: largely true allegations of massive poll tax fraud that endangered the machine's grip on power. To dampen the furor caused by these allegations and to outmaneuver the ongoing campaign against the poll tax led by the Virginia Electoral Reform League, the Byrd machine craftily put forward a poll tax reform measure that would have substituted even more restrictive suffrage requirements in place of a tax. Thus instead of mobilizing voters to vote for the measure, reformers found themselves mobilizing voters to vote against the machine's version of reform. The measure failed to pass when 75 percent of voters voted against it.[55]

After exhausting its appeals against the *Smith v. Allwright* decision, South Carolina abolished its poll tax in 1951. In 1953 Alabama became the next to last southern state to address the poll tax issue. Although outright repeal failed, the tax's cumulative feature was significantly decreased to allow for many new (white) Alabamians to participate in the political system. The battle for poll tax reform was largely led by a coalition of seven state women's groups, including the Business and Federated Women's Clubs, which had a combined membership of 150,000. Working as members but also as allies of these organizations were female academics affiliated with Alabama's state government reform group, such as Professor Hallie Farmer of Alabama State College for Women. These women used a blend of objective research and emotional appeals to southern ideals to press for an expansion of democracy for southern white women.[56]

That left Mississippi. Although a number of the state's governors had supported some type of reform, and the state's most liberal governor, James Folsom, had pressed for outright abolition, the Black Belt–dominated legislature refused to allow any consideration of the issue to make it onto the legislative agenda. Mississippi remained the only state where poll tax reform failed to have a significant public or legislative debate.

The democratization of the white South, with the exception of Mississippi, Texas, and Virginia, had begun. Although their actual success in reforming or abolishing the poll tax in the South was mixed, southern reformers were remarkably successful in helping to change the South's level of support for the tax (see Figure 4–1). In 1941 only 35 percent of southerners were in favor of abolishing the poll tax, compared to 63 percent outside of the South. By 1953 opinion on the issue had moved. First, the percentage of southerners in favor of abolishing the poll tax increased to 59 percent of those surveyed. Second, the gap between the South and the rest of the nation narrowed; whereas in 1941 there was a gap of nearly 30 percentage points, by 1953 this gap narrowed to 12 percentage points.[57]

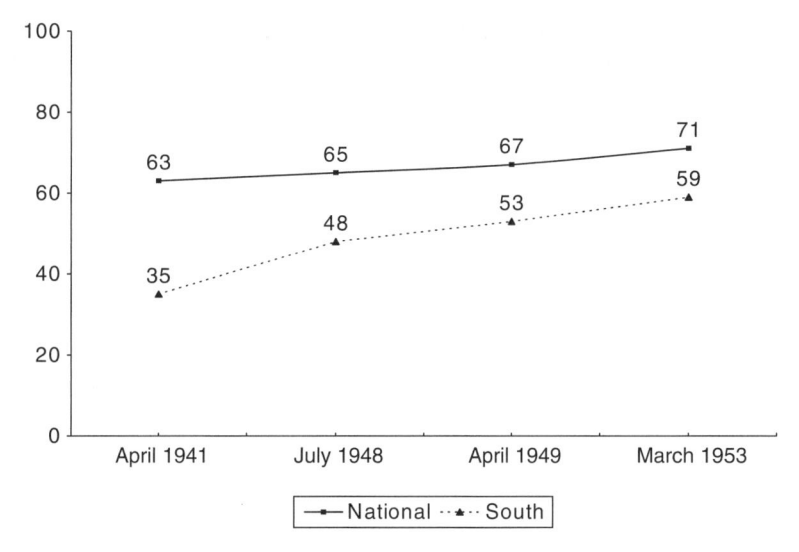

Figure 4–1 Public Support for Poll Tax Reform
Source: "Gallup and Fortune Poll," *Public Opinion Quarterly* 5 (1941): 470; "The Quarter's Polls," *Public Opinion Quarterly* 12 (1948): 567; "The Quarter's Polls," *Public Opinion Quarterly* 13 (1949): 557; Ogden (1958): 252.

Many of the supporters (as well as the critics) of poll tax reform worked from a New Deal assumption that the South would experience a liberal democratic revival because of the inclusion of the white have-nots. The growing public support in the South for poll tax reform during the 1940s shows that democratic rhetoric had some influence on southern public opinion.

Although contemporary analysts of the poll tax such as V. O. Key and his student Frederic Ogden were correct in their assertion that the repeal of poll taxes would not bring in the tens of millions of voters claimed by anti–poll tax advocates, these researchers also acknowledged that they could not at the time of their analysis predict the long-term effects of this democratic reform.[58] The long-term effects were startling. From 1932 to 1960 the voter turnout gap between the South and the rest of the nation narrowed. The total number of popular votes cast in all presidential elections in the southern states nearly tripled, from 3.7 million in the 1932 election to 10.3 million in the 1960 election, a 172 percent increase (see Figure 4–2). By contrast, during this same period the number of popular votes cast for president for the country as a whole increased by only 73 percent. Although the South increased the number of voters in presidential elections, there were important differences between the southern states. States that retained the poll tax through 1960 increased the number of presidential votes by a factor of 1.3, whereas states that abolished the poll tax increased the number of presidential votes by a factor of 2. Even excluding Florida, which experienced spectacular population growth, the number of votes in states without a poll tax increased more than in states that retained the poll tax.

In keeping with the rest of the nation, almost all of the southern states had an increase in the number of voters between 1948 and 1952 (see Figure 4–2). For the South this was the period of the rise and fall of the Dixiecrat revolt, whose significance lay in the fact that it was the first formal political break of some of the southern states from the Democratic Party.[59] On average, Dixiecrats received only 22 percent of the vote in states that had either abolished the poll tax (Florida, Georgia, Louisiana) or substantially reformed it (Arkansas and Tennessee) at the time of the 1948 election (see Figure 4–3). Excluding Louisiana, where Dixiecrats captured 49 percent of the vote, the average Dixiecrat vote in reform or non–poll tax states decreased to about 16 percent. In states that retained the poll tax—Alabama, Mississippi, South Carolina, Texas, and Virginia—Dixiecrats won on average 47 percent of the vote. Yet both Texas and Virginia had relatively strong poll tax reform movements during 1948, and supporters managed to get their respective state legislatures to place the issue on the 1949 ballot. Dixiecrats averaged only about 10 percent of the vote in these two states.

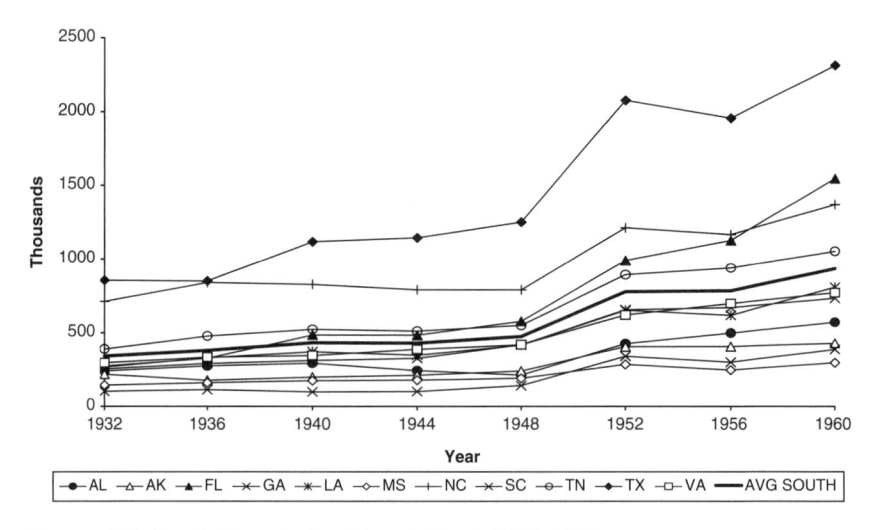

Figure 4–2 Popular Vote for President in South, 1932–1960
Source: United States Bureau of the Census, *Historical Statistics of the United States, Colonial Times to 1970.* Washington, DC: Government Printing Office (1975), Series Y135–186.

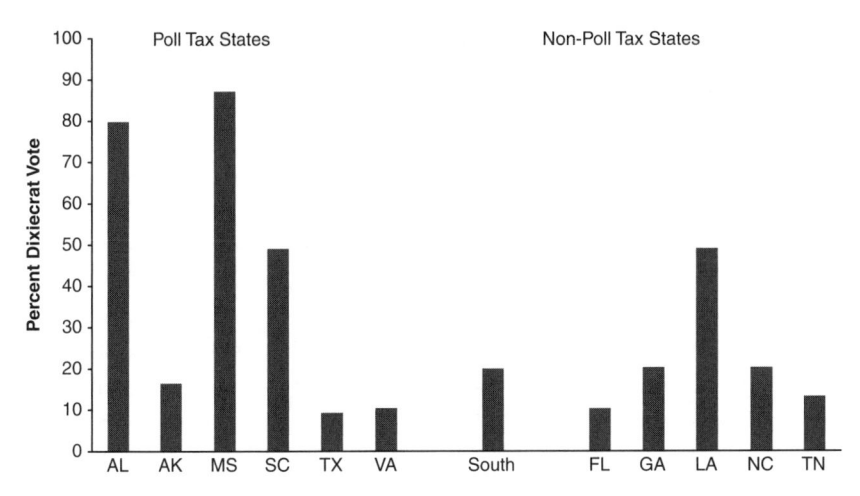

Figure 4–3 Dixiecrat Vote
Source: Popular Vote Cast for President, by State and Political Party: 1836–1968, series Y 135–186, U.S. Bureau of the Census, *Historical Statistics of the United States from Colonial Times to 1970* (GPO: Washington, DC, 1976), 1077–78.

Dixiecrats ran strongest in the three states—Alabama, Mississippi, and South Carolina—that still retained poll taxes and had not yet had significant public debate about the tax. In these states Dixiecrats won 72 percent of the vote. This pattern of support suggests that although the significant presence of blacks may have been a source of support for the Dixiecrats, as some analysts have argued, the absence of a poll tax and the increase in the size (and possible heterogeneity) of this new white electorate may have in fact played a role in the Dixiecrats' inability to garner more significant support.

Conclusion

With the exception of Mississippi, Texas, and Virginia, the democratization of the white south had begun. Although Key and Ogden and other contemporary analysts of the poll tax were correct in their assertion that the repeal of poll taxes would not bring in the tens of millions of voters that supporters of reform claimed, they were wrong in their understanding of how these millions of new voters would be incorporated into the political system and the problems this reframing would pose in destabilizing the "Solid South."

For the masses of southern whites, widespread democratization was a resounding success. The long-standing elite notion of a democracy restricted to a better class of whites was publicly discredited. As a result millions of whites (re)gained the franchise. Indeed this forgotten revolution created a new white electorate that responded to the broader pressures from below and above in ways not anticipated, or desired, by southern liberals. The democratization efforts of the Jim Crow reformers brought in millions of newly enfranchised white voters and opened up the political terrain in many states to new voices and new opportunities for political entrepreneurs. Higher levels of education and income coupled with greater urbanization and new patterns of suburbanization meant that these new voters lay outside the control of traditional white elites.[60]

These new white voters, who held no automatic allegiance to traditional political elites, proved open to the appeals of southern politicians who themselves were not members of the traditional political elite and were in many ways creatures of a "new" New South. These new politicians would help pave the way for the eventual entry of these voters into the Republican Party. They used the possibilities opened up by Jim Crow reform, and later the civil rights movement, to incorporate new white voters.[61] Thus, although most analyses point to race, and in particular the Democrats' support of civil rights, as driving working-class whites out of the party and into the welcoming arms of the Republicans, the path to this destination was not as clear-cut or straightforward as the conventional narrative has it.

With poll tax reform reframed as an issue of reconstitution or reinvigoration of *white* democracy, the extension of political and economic rights and benefits to blacks became even more problematic. How could white southern politicians promise newly incorporated white voters that the foundation of the new white democracy was safe in the face of rising African American political mobilization and increasing national attention to civil rights issue? By the early 1950s, before the *Brown* decision, on the heels of increasing white democratization would come mounting attempts to limit the spread of this democratization to blacks. Thus Alabama enacted its infamous (and later overturned) Boswell Amendment in 1946, which strengthened the discretionary and arbitrary powers of local voter registrars. Georgia, with the Talmadge forces back in charge, changed its voting laws in the late 1940s to allow the massive purging of newly registered African American voters.[62] Poll tax reform had allowed the South to begin to rejoin the United States. However, like their forebears of the late nineteenth century and early twentieth, many white southerners still defined democracy as a privilege restricted to and enjoyed only by whites.

Although state-level poll tax reform had started off as a movement "with the endorsement of the best leadership and thought of the South" and as the "most forward political step there since the Civil War," by the 1950s it was an issue whose time had come and gone.[63] In light of the deeper, bitter struggle for civil rights that followed, the poll tax seemed to be a narrow technical issue, like lynching, that history had largely bypassed. Yet it left a significant impact on southern and national politics.

The story of 1940s campaign for poll tax reform and democratization of the South challenges much of the conventional wisdom about the South and about the shaping of modern American politics. In terms of understanding how the democratization of the United States has unfolded, poll tax reform points out the significance not only of region, but also of ideas. Democratization is not only the achievement of new mechanisms of political inclusion but also the development of new ideas that undergird and justify these democratic extensions. The democratization of the white South showed that by 1954 the "Solid South" was not quite so solid. For a political order that had seemed resistant to electoral pressure and was only beginning to be subject to significant judicial assaults in the 1940s, it is surprising that these political reforms occurred. It almost certainly contradicts common assumptions about the impregnability of the Jim Crow order in the pre-*Brown* era. The varieties of Souths and their varied paths to democratization created a multiplicity of openings for the civil rights activists who would take the place of southern reformers in shaping and ultimately ending the Jim Crow Order.

The next part of the book looks at another decades-long struggle on the part of reformers: the attempt to make the southern educational system more equal while still keeping it separate. This quest would strengthen the rationale of Jim Crow reform: that a more rational, better governed order was good for whites and blacks. But at the same time, the quest to perfect the Jim Crow order would strengthen African Americans' claims to social citizenship and reenergize their fight for political citizenship. From the 1920s to the 1940s whites and blacks attempted to create a world in which the worst aspects of the Jim Crow order could be softened. For whites, this softening would lead to and ensure a sane and safe path toward stable race relations, a world in which blacks and whites could live apart yet be equal. For blacks, the Sisyphean struggle to at least reach parity in educational resources would strengthen the moral, political, and legal basis for ending Jim Crow, first in schools and universities, and then in all parts of the Jim Crow order.

Chapter 5

The Natural Way: Education in the Jim Crow Order

> To educate the Negro, you must have the whites of the South with you. If the poor white sees the son of a Negro neighbor enjoying through your munificence benefits denied to his boy, it raises in him a feeling that will render futile all your work. You must lift up the "poor white" and the Negro together if you would approach success.
>
> General Education Board, Review and Final Report, 1964

Reforming the Jim Crow order meant not only harnessing the power of the states; it also meant using state power to invest in the South's human resources through public health and education. Although New South boosters made a point of advertising the region's cheap and nonunionized labor, this did not mean that the labor force offered could be wholly illiterate, unhealthy, and incapable of operating in a modern industrial setting. Education of some sort was necessary for industrial development; it was also necessary to secure lower-class whites' participation in and black acquiescence to the ruling coalition of the Jim Crow order. Jim Crow reformers would play a leading role in creating the educational infrastructure that they hoped would perfect the Jim Crow order.

The emergence of Jim Crow reform in the 1920s stimulated the emergence of what Jim Crow reformers would call the "golden age" of segregated education. In particular the activities of northern foundations as well as the growing acceptance by many states of a minimal responsibility toward black public education led to this modernization of segregated education. This golden age rested on a mix of white paternalism, black pragmatism, and the institutionalization of state racial management structures. White paternalism derived from a very specific sort: the "cooperation of the best white citizens of the South."[1] To advance their objectives of modernizing segregated education, foundations in particular would deploy a leveraging strategy: they would provide funds to southern state and local governments, and in return these governments would agree to permanently fund new educational activities for African Americans. Although African Americans were part of this leveraging strategy through their own financial contributions or through their implementing of the strategy as teachers and low-level bureaucrats, they were never the architects or equal partners in the shaping of southern education policy.

By the end of the decade this paternalism was institutionalized in state education departments, and small but growing numbers of white education professionals saw the provision of black education as less of a novel and delicate undertaking that had to take into account white sensibilities and more of a routine task. Although some white educators believed that the provision of education to whites and blacks should be in accordance with the latest educational best practices, the reality was that overt equalization would have most likely led to their dismissal.[2] African American teachers were the beneficiaries as well as the creation of this golden age. Yet as their numbers grew, so too did their self-interest as professionals and their role as community leaders clash within the confines of Jim Crow reform.

Education, Inequality, and the Making of a Political Order

During the Jim Crow order's ascension the imposition of electoral devices such as literacy tests and understanding clauses threatened the white electorate. For many southern whites education was "key to the maintenance of the new white democracy...[the] solid guarantee to poor whites of their future ascendancy"[3] and of their continued political inclusion. With the consolidation of the Jim Crow order, this threat to political exclusion lessened. Education was increasingly seen as a means of individual social mobility, but also as a valuable and visible marker of caste status. For many whites segregated education was integral to the meaning and practice of Jim Crow. It was in this arena that white supremacy and its obverse, white paternalism, could be most visibly displayed, and the rewards of race and class could be distributed accordingly. Segregated and unequal education was designed to visibly reflect and maintain the subordinated status of African

Americans. This was a view shared by elites and nonelites, reformers as well as reactionaries.

For white reformers, the maintenance of visible inequality was necessary to secure any expansion. As Henry Lee Tucker, the president of Washington and Lee University, warned northern philanthropists, no progress toward the education of blacks could occur without first and visibly addressing the needs of whites. White reactionaries did not even support this visible inequality. To them, not only did education "ruin a good field hand," as Senator James K. Vardaman of Mississippi exclaimed, but it also put dangerous ideas about social and political equality into the heads of blacks, inspiring them to "demand equality."[4]

Yet the Vardamans of the South could not stand in the way of capitalism. By the 1940s most southern white elites embraced the necessity of more education for African Americans. Even members of the white southern Delta elite—reactionaries, if any group was to be called that term—embraced improvements in African American education. Although the mechanical cotton picker was almost a reality, these planters remained years away from being fully mechanized and thus still needed a reliable and inexpensive labor pool as well as a consumer base for the small-town merchants that made up the Delta elite.[5]

For southern blacks, education would be the last vestige of the citizenship rights that had been stripped from them with the rise of the Jim Crow order. Yet how to exercise this power would be an issue of contention among southern blacks and between those living with the Jim Crow order and those living outside of it. Many African Americans, both northern and southern, viewed Booker T. Washington's Atlanta Compromise as a misguided strategy of accommodation at best, and at worst a craven surrender of citizenship, made worse as the surrender was made on behalf of a group without their consent. Yet for southern African Americans, accommodating and adapting to the Jim Crow order, whether through the Washington machine or otherwise, made a sort of sense in an environment that seemed to be closed to any alternatives other than exit. John Gandy, president of Virginia State Normal Institute (later Virginia State University), stated in 1920, "At present there is no hope for Negro people to share directly in determining the educational policies of this country."[6]

In the face of political and institutional resistance as well as personal resignation and despair, southern African Americans faced a difficult task: the maintenance of public education in a political and social order that not only devalued black education, but in some ways saw it as a dangerous and useless practice. To the extent that white schools remained in disarray, little to no attention was paid to black schools. Due to the loss of political and civil rights during Redemption, African American gains in education made during Reconstruction were disappearing. One example of this linkage between loss of political power and educational inequality was the case of Alabama. According to Horace Mann Bond's research (funded by the Rosenwald Foundation), in 1898 black and white children in Alabama were more or less funded equally out of the $168,000 spent by the state on education. By 1929, nineteen years after the adoption of the Alabama constitution, which formally established the state's political Jim Crow order, that funding was massively unequal. Black schools received only 35 percent of the funding they were entitled to if separate was in fact equal.[7] This inequality in funding was reflected in the quality of school facilities. By the beginning of the twentieth century most schools for African Americans were literally shacks. The Spring Hill School in South Carolina, where Rev. Joseph DeLaine was the principal, was on the verge of collapse, as were thousands of other black public schools in the South.

Accommodating to and at times subverting Jim Crow education gave southern African Americans the possibility of creating valuable sources of physical and social capital. In an era that had "decentered polls and parties" for African Americans, bargaining with whites over education involved the exercise of quasi-political activity that would be necessary to preserve a sense of agency and possibility for the future.[8] Racial management and educational policy would serve as the distinguishing hallmarks of the Jim Crow governance and the main battleground from Reconstruction to *Brown* and beyond.

Dollars for Education: Building Jim Crow Education

In 1923 Howard Odum's *Journal of Social Forces* published an article written by Isaac Fisher, a black CIC board member (and Tuskegee sympathizer). The article, "Multiplying Dollars for Negro Education," proclaimed a new orthodoxy of Jim Crow education: "*Formula*: Race Relations + Good Will = x Dollars Now Available for Negro Education. Is not this the natural way?"[9] This equation was based on the complexity and contradictions of the "layered orders" that rested within and alongside of the Jim Crow order. In this formulation race relations meant the that "best men" of both races would together spend northern foundation money on a program of education that would aid southern blacks but not threaten what was considered a given for ordinary whites: the provision of publicly financed education. Yet public education occupied a curious role in the Jim Crow order. It reflected the need to respond to the external pressure (whether real or imagined) of the federal order and the inability of southern governments, for a range of political and economic reasons, to fully jettison Reconstruction-era educational policy commitments. Thus because of the demands of the Jim Crow order, education—at all levels—was one of the few, if not the only, significant public service offered by southern states, and it was the only public service with any kind of continuity offered to southern African Americans.[10]

During the brief flowering of transformative egalitarianism that at times characterized the Reconstruction South (and elsewhere), public education for whites and blacks was established in the "constitutional moment" of Reconstruction.[11] In the Redemption era white "exclusionists" attempted to repeal this commitment. For these exclusionists the principle of equality of funding between the races went too far. Not only did they believe that African Americans could never be equal to whites, but they also believed that spending public funds on blacks was misguided, dangerous, and inherently unfair to whites. Exclusionists thus challenged African Americans' legitimate, though minimal and tenuous claim to the public purse and to the social rights that education conferred. In a number of states, including North Carolina and Alabama, exclusionists backed constitutional amendments to separate funding educational streams (i.e., taxes) between the races. In North Carolina this came in the shape of a proposal that would "limit black school expenditures to the amount paid by Negroes in taxes"; Alabama's exclusionists urged the state's constitutional convention then meeting to set up a separate taxing system.[12]

Despite their best efforts, when the Jim Crow order was initially established white exclusionists failed in their attempt to sever this obligation to public education for southern blacks. One reason for the failure lay in the pattern of intraracial politics. The mass disenfranchisement of blacks meant that control over government was a battle between whites for control over resources. In Alabama Horace Mann Bond found that the state's "battles over exclusion reflected battles between white factions, usually the majority white hill counties versus the planter dominated black-belt counties. While majority-white counties had nothing to lose [fiscally] from exclusion, counties with larger black populations including black-belt counties, under exclusion, faced the prospect of dividing up revenues in a way that could disadvantage whites."[13]

While political friction within the Jim Crow order was one reason for the exclusionists' failure, another was fear over political forces outside of the order. Southern elites had an ever-present fear that the federal government would intervene in southern politics. Indeed an attempt by white exclusionists in North Carolina's legislature to amend the state's constitution was beaten back on the grounds that not only would the specific amendment invite a challenge in federal court, but related legislation critical to securing the Jim Crow order such as the literacy test could also be challenged in court, leaving open the possibility that "both amendments [the literacy test and racial separation of taxes] would fall together."[14]

Although the fear of order-challenging federal intervention proved largely unfounded until after World War II, the establishment and maintenance of the Jim Crow order demanded that threats be taken seriously and dealt with immediately. Thus rather than explicitly limiting or barring blacks from public education, which could bring about federal intervention, politicians such as North Carolina's "Progressive" governor Charles B. Aycock favored techniques of "quiet management." Aycock argued that the day-to-day administration of education be left in the hands of local officials, whose good sense and understanding of local needs would ensure inequality of funding between the races.[15]

The constitutional moment of Reconstruction also created a template for government service provision to which southern state governments largely adhered. Not only was the concept of free schools enshrined; also created was the outline of a legal and bureaucratic structure that was more modern and centralized than had ever existed in the South. All of the southern states created the position of state superintendent of education, and all provided for some means of state taxation for funding public schools as a means of supplementing county and local taxation (see Table 5–1). Not surprisingly, educational battles then (and now) would revolve around educational funding.

Where the southern states differed was in the area of school terms and compulsory attendance laws. Only 60 percent of the states had a mandated minimum school term, and only 50 percent had attendance laws. In the latter case, having a law on the books did not mean that it was enforced, as opponents of child labor discovered. This lack of enforcement was particularly

Table 5–1 State Constitutional Provisions for Education

Provisions	% of States
Requirement of state free school system	100
Provision for state superintendent	100
Provision for state board of education	60
Provision for county superintendents	40
Provision for common school fund	90
Provision for county or local taxation	50
Provision for state taxation	100
Minimum school term prescribed for state aid	60
Clauses concerning compulsory attendance	50
Clauses concerning federal land grants	80
Clauses forbidding aid to sectarian schools	40

Source: David Tyack and Robert Lowe. "The Constitutional Moment: Reconstruction and Black Education in the South." *American Journal of Education* 94, no. 2 (1986): 236–56, "Table 1: Educational Provisions in the Reconstruction Constitutions (1868–1870) of Ten Former Confederate States." Note: Table excludes Tennessee.

true in the case of southern black children, whose education was largely ignored by southern white administrators. The needs of the southern agricultural economy, the small budgets for instruction, and the quiet management style of white school officials added up to a persistent gap in instructional days offered and student attendance between black and white children that would not be closed until well into the 1940s.[16] Despite this constitutional foundation, to a large degree the legal and bureaucratic structure it created existed solely in name; a state department of education often "consisted of a single room in the farthest corner of the ornate capitol, with a deserving Democrat, who might or might not have finished high school, serving both as superintendent and as the entire staff."[17]

The physical conditions of southern primary schools mirrored this vagueness. According to one report, most southerners (black and white) lived in rural areas whose schools were "miserably supported, poorly attended, wretchedly taught, and wholly inadequate for the education of the people." Within this sea of failure there was still inequality; schools for African Americans were "so-called by courtesy only" since the "resources [were] not sufficient to take care of the white schools."[18] Although black public schools were separate and inferior, there was wide variation across the region. Part of this inequality reflected the fact that the consolidation of the Jim Crow order happened across a number of decades and within different state and local conditions. In Birmingham, for example, one study found that black schools benefited from a shift during the 1880s to a "centralized, bureaucratized, and professionalized urban school system that was able to isolate itself somewhat from electoral politics. And the professionalization and political independence of schools were supported and intensified by municipal and state reform efforts that have typically been labeled 'progressive.'" These positive developments were tempered by a finding that despite this limited support for black education among "urban, white, professional educators," these individuals still believed in inequality, which "strictly delimited the absolute educational gains and the educational thresholds that they prescribed for blacks."[19] Despite these gains, blacks in Birmingham as well as elsewhere in the South lost access to the state as the long-term effects of disenfranchisement began to be felt.

Although public education in the South was given the outlines of a modern system during Reconstruction, later reformers would have to fill in this vague sketch within the limits of the Jim Crow order. To do so they had to reconcile their quest for efficiency and economy with the emerging and sometimes conflicting political, economic, and social aspects of the Jim Crow order. Indeed according to the historian William Link, the challenge for Progressive reformers was developing a "formula for black progress that would reconcile [their] white supremacist views with a program of purposeful development."[20]

Progressive white reformers achieved this goal by assuming race as an immutable fact and the southern caste system as not only an inevitable but a rational response to the manifest shortcomings of African Americans and the tragic legacy of a misguided Reconstruction policy. They were able to institutionalize this belief with the assistance of northern foundations, which increasingly viewed their Reconstruction efforts to aid the education of former slaves through the triumphal revisionist prism of the Jim Crow order.

By the time Jim Crow reformers emerged, this viewpoint had transformed into a belief that they performed a special function and invaluable role within the South: furthering the development of the segregated education system (euphemistically referred to as "dual education"). Their function was not to analyze or critique the system:

> [The] bi-racial population [of the South] and the resultant dual system of schools are undeniable facts.... To argue the presence of peculiar educational problems in the South would be to evade the issue. To deny their existence would be to ignore the facts. To face the facts and to be concerned about the development of means of solution of the existent problems is to give thought to a question which the South must face and solve intelligently before her fairest destiny may be attained.[21]

These reformers believed that the "educational problems growing out of this situation" could be addressed only through "fair-minded recognition and scientific study."[22] Ultimately this was a presentation of facts without context and certainly without any theorizing or questioning of the status quo. This stance fit their professional and personal reluctance to take a clear position on the Jim Crow order; it also reflected the leanings of the northern foundations that shaped southern education.

Institutionalizing Primary Education

One of the key strategies used by the GEB but also by the other southern educational foundations in their request to create a modern educational system for the South was to create and subsidize the development and institutionalization of an administrative as well as a physical infrastructure. To create an educational administrative structure the foundations drew on a new organizational technique, called the "agent" approach. Emerging in the late nineteenth century, this technique placed individuals in state institutions to advance a particular policy goal, such as farming methods. These agents were subsidized through federal or private funds.[23]

Foundation-funded agents led campaigns to increase state support for teacher training, the creation of high schools, and the building of school facilities. For example, to mobilize public opinion in support of the creation of high schools, the GEB funded and assigned to the white state university "a trained specialist in secondary education—a man [they were all men] who could inform, cultivate, and guide professional, public and legislative opinion" and lobby states to repeal laws that blocked these initiatives.[24] There were also efforts to increase the analytical capacity of these departments. During the 1920s the GEB extended its support of quasi-state education officials in five additional areas: schoolhouse planning and construction (particularly to aid rural communities), information and statistical divisions, school libraries, teacher training and certification, and county administration and supervision.[25]

Although these functions were new to the South, they were very much in the mainstream of current thinking about state organizational structure. Rational planning and analysis conducted by trained, objective personnel was the vital link that produced good policy outcomes. Pragmatic reasons also drove these decisions. Because this education analysis would be developed and produced in-house, foundation officials believed that state political leaders would be more likely to accept their recommendations.

Given the ideology of white supremacy, increasing the educational administrative capacity for black schools came later. However, at least at the foundation level there was roughly the same amount spent on white public education (approximately $6.5 million) as on black public education ($7.9 million).[26] Of course, given the massive underfunding of black public education by public agencies, in many ways GEB funding did not even begin to equalize this systemic inequality. Nevertheless African Americans cautiously welcomed these foundation initiatives and the resources they additionally generated. Although self-help was often the only recourse left to them, most southern African Americans had a fundamental understanding that there were limits to this approach. School facilities could be created through a combination of cash, contributed labor, and other resources, but the training of qualified teachers and the paying of their salaries had to be a burden that was supported by the state.[27]

The power asymmetry between blacks and whites in the Jim Crow order reflected southern blacks' limited ability to access the resources of the state. White administrators, for a variety of reasons, engaged in the silent management advocated by Governor Aycock and instituted increasingly unequal patterns of finance and administration. Foundation resources, although burdened at times with the racist expectations and limitations of the period, provided African Americans with a critical source of support for accessing these additional state resources. Although the funds were often supplied to create a passive yet more productive workforce, black communities were at times able to subvert these foundation goals. Northern philanthropy money could act as a "'Trojan horse' allowing blacks to 'sneak past' the normal barriers erected to their political influence and use the state itself to help achieve their goals."[28]

The foundation-leveraged improvements were important, but public education for blacks remained the product of white paternalism, subjected to the vagaries of bureaucratic structure and power. Thus, as one researcher has noted, black leaders were forced to ask for services in ways that did not directly confront the political status quo. Instead of asking for educational equity as a matter of justice or fair play, black school officials and leaders asked for marginal improvements that did not signal an attempt on their part to obtain equal status with whites.[29]

Despite the disparities between the races in terms of foundation support, there were important initiatives funded by the foundations that did reflect the distinctive needs of southern African Americans. These initiatives were the extension of the state agent model to cover black education and the Jeanes Teachers Programs. Reformers hoped that these programs would lead to an indirect method of institutionalizing black education that could bypass the general white hostility toward education for blacks.

The Bureaucratic Foundations of Jim Crow Education

Although Jim Crow laws mandated the separation of black and white students (as well as textbooks, buses, desks, and other educational accoutrements), they did not specify how this separate or dual system was to be administered. This was of course in keeping with Aycock's theory of silent management, that educational inequality was best delivered through unstated though clearly understood means. Jim Crow reformers in the education field, their foundation allies such as the GEB, and others realized that silent management often led to silent, if not willful, neglect. Without any kind of accountability, especially the kind provided by African American voters, school administrators had nothing (other their conscience) to prod them into making provisions for black public education. Through the efforts of the local and state CIC as well as the foundations the development and institutionalization of a formal and positive role for black public education was created.

Given this situation, the GEB proposed extending its state agent model to black public education. From 1912 to 1914 six states accepted the GEB offer: Alabama, Arkansas, Georgia, Kentucky, North Carolina, and Tennessee; by 1919 all southern states with dual systems employed state agents.[30] All of the agents were white men. Eventually the GEB and the states would fund an additional position for an assistant state agent for Negro education, which was often filled by an African American.[31] This often happened with the lobbying and support of African American teachers. For example, Missouri's teachers were able to pry open the state's education bureaucracy by successfully having an African American named as the state inspector of Negro schools. By 1936 five states would have Negro supervisors.

The role of state agents was largely administrative; they developed and ran teacher training programs and supervised the Jeanes Teachers Program. In addition they worked to extend modern educational practices to local districts by encouraging districts to close overcrowded one-room schools and build larger, more efficient and modern consolidated schools. Their most important activity, however, was to act as a permanent voice for African American education within state government; the agents lobbied for "normal school appropriations" and "agitat[ed] constantly to convince influential whites of the value of at least elementary education for their colored neighbors, so that the public purse be opened a little wider."[32]

The Division of Negro Education in North Carolina was probably the preeminent example of this new institutionalized state racial management structure. The Division "offered [blacks]…a channel for formal redress in matters of education[;] it also offered new—if circumscribed—opportunities for direct representation in state policy-making…open[ing] new doors to black representation within an otherwise lily-white world of state policymaking." Though these offices were concerned with the administration of African American education, in their structure they had separate and unequal divisions. North Carolina's African American staff, for example, worked in a building separate from their fellow white staff members.[33]

For whites these new black departments of education served as a means to co-opt and constrain African American leadership and to persuade ordinary African Americans that whites were fulfilling their paternalist obligations to them. This discharging of obligations was meant to dissuade blacks from more militant alternatives such as litigation and to stem the growing tide of blacks that were leaving the South in search of better economic and educational opportunities. The more informal means of administrative control as well as traditional patterns of interracial dialogue that existed in the rural South were no longer workable in the more urbanized South.

Gender and Jim Crow Education

The bureaucratization of the Jim Crow education was shaped by color and by gender, as the experience of black women teachers reveals. The Jeanes Fund was one of the smaller northern education philanthropies that focused on black education. Created in 1907 with funding from a Philadelphia Quaker heiress, the foundation focused on rural black education and the issue of teacher training.[34] The employment of black women was central to the Jeanes strategy, which revealed the race and gendered contours of Jim Crow reform. Because these teachers were directly employed by government in a quasi-supervisory capacity, they could not be seen as threatening that political and bureaucratic structure. Black women were seen as far less threatening to whites than black men.[35]

The signature program of the Jeanes Foundation was the funding of African American women teachers who would aid black schools in their mission of creating better domestic and manual workers for the white South. At the same time the foundation was also influenced by the county agent model then sweeping the United States. In 1908 these two influences came together. The foundation funded a network of women who organized and supervised rural schools. In keeping with the emerging leverage strategy of these foundations, it was hoped that the success of these teachers would be recognized by local school districts and state governments, which in turn would gradually assume the funding for these teachers.

In 1908 Jackson Davis, then a county superintendent in North Carolina and later a long-time employee of the GEB, hired the first Jeanes supervising industrial teacher, Virginia Randolph. The association of the GEB with the Jeanes Program would grow stronger over the next four decades. The GEB would take over the Jeanes Fund role, as money from the fund was exhausted; the program employed more than five hundred teachers from 1914 to 1949 for an approximate cost of $1.35 million. As the GEB had hoped, increasingly the role of these teachers became more institutionalized as many counties started to fund their positions; in some cases the Jeanes teachers became assistant county superintendents of Negro schools and thus were part of the local administrative structure.[36]

By and large whites saw the activities of these teachers through the prism of white supremacy. The Jeanes teachers, these whites noted approvingly, were "carrying the gospel of 'learning by doing.'"[37] A number of historians have shown that in fact many Jeanes teachers were deeply subversive of the program's intent.[38] For example, although Jeanes teachers were supposed to be providing industrial education, they often used this approach as a cloak to hide their intention to provide a traditional academic education to their students. Beyond pedagogical objectives, the activities of these often remarkable women served another purpose. The school improvement campaigns led by Jeanes teachers became a focal point for community organizing. These school improvement campaigns ran the gamut, from sanitation and health issues to fundraising for new supplies and facilities. In Mississippi in the midst of the Depression Jeanes teachers raised approximately $64,000 in private sources, and teachers in North Carolina raised about $36,000 during the same period.[39] These school improvement campaigns were less overtly threatening than direct political activity, but they still involved politics. They demonstrated to whites and to blacks the investment African American communities continued to make in education, and they provided a space for community involvement that crossed class as well as sectarian barriers within the African American community.[40]

The Building of Black Schools

Foundations donated money to build much of the South's educational institutions, from the elementary to the collegiate level. This donation of funds was rarely made without any strings attached; states and localities often had to promise to incorporate these buildings into the overall system. The provisions of agents and buildings was part of a leveraging strategy that "use[d] private funds to directly establish services *in the public sector*, sometimes with or in combination with partial public funding," which then "secure[d] the institutionalization of the services as a routine matter of state policy."[41]

The emergence of high schools for blacks is one example of this leveraging strategy. The growth of black high schools was shaped by the limitations of the Jim Crow order, and in particular the hegemony of the Tuskegee model; high schools with an academic curriculum were seen as unnecessary for blacks, whose primary purpose was to provide simple industrial, agricultural, or domestic labor. The irony of the Tuskegee industrial training model, or rather the unspoken (by whites) reality that the Tuskegee model rested upon, was that the white establishment never funded industrial schools adequately enough so that actual industrial training could take place.[42] Nevertheless nearly a decade after public high schools for whites were established, the philanthropic and educational communities increasingly believed that black high schools provided a critical link between the newly strengthened (though still weak and underfunded) primary education system for blacks and the private and public black colleges and universities that were also in the process of being strengthened by northern foundation money. Not only would these schools supply industrial or vocational training, but they would also act as a temporary and intermediate source of further training for black elementary school teachers, who themselves often possessed only an elementary education.[43]

To get around lingering white resistance to higher academic education for blacks, supporters of secondary schools for blacks labeled them "county training schools" in order to highlight the vocational aspect.[44] This also made the new schools eligible for federal funds, specifically those provided through the Smith Hughes Vocational Training Act (1917). With outside (nonstate or local) sources of funding, foundation officials and African Americans could leverage additional funds and commitments from state and local officials. In keeping with the foundations' leveraging strategy, the funding for the schools was contingent on several conditions being satisfied: state and local governments would fund at least $750 in salaries and offer at least eight years of schooling, and the schools would be owned and maintained by the public school system.[45] Thus funded by the Slater Fund, the GEB, and federal vocational training funds (per the Smith Hughes Act), approximately six hundred county training schools were built by 1933. By 1937 all of the high schools had been formally incorporated into local public school systems.[46]

Rosenwald Schools: The Building Block of Primary Education

The clearest manifestation of the ability of northern foundations to shape the southern educational system was the Rosenwald school building program. Julius Rosenwald, one of the founders of Sears Roebuck, created the Rosenwald Foundation. The Rosenwald school building program began in 1912, after Booker T. Washington approached Rosenwald for aid for rural schools. Rosenwald granted Washington $25,000 to build six schools. From 1913 to 1917 the money was directly distributed by Rosenwald.

After Washington's death, and with the emergence of organized Jim Crow reform in the 1920s, the focus of the Rosenwald Foundation became broader. Rosenwald's goal was to help southern blacks most in need of support: those in the rural South. The objective of the Foundation was to "stimulate public agencies to take a larger share of social responsibility."[47] In 1917 the Foundation was incorporated to oversee the funding and construction of schools and state and local compliance with the Foundation's requirements. To ensure compliance with its objectives, the Foundation "mandat[ed] that funding requests go through state departments of education and by establishing and paying the salaries of both white and black assistants to the white 'Negro Agents' within state bureaucracies. These actions contributed to the establishment of a competent network of administrators, including some African Americans, who would continue to advocate for increased state funding for public schools long after the Rosenwald initiative ended."[48] The Rosenwald Foundation also strongly believed in self-help and community ownership; African Americans could not just ask for money for a new school, they had to lobby and persuade local officials to endorse their proposal, and even more significantly they themselves had to donate money toward the construction of their school.[49]

The school building program was immediately popular. Although the Rosenwald funding formula disregarded the fact that blacks were paying for a public good that whites received for free, southern black communities responded enthusiastically to the offer. From six schools the program grew to one hundred schools in 1914, and then three hundred schools were planned for in 1918.[50] In 1928 the Rosenwald Foundation shifted its priorities; it would fund schools only where it had not previously constructed schools. By 1932 the school building program came to an end; by then the Fund had been responsible for the construction of "4,977 public schools, 163 vocational shops [and] 217 teacher's homes in 883 counties throughout 15 southern states."[51]

Of the 22,294 rural schools for blacks in the fourteen southern states, about 20 percent had been leveraged, that is, funded by contributions from southern blacks, state and local governments, and Rosenwald funds. These schools had a capacity of 556,730 students, or about 26 percent of all black children in rural areas. Still, the leveraging strategy pursued by Rosenwald must be considered a success. In 1916, when the first wave of schools were planned and constructed, state and local governments contributed only about 16 percent of the total costs (see Table 5–1). By 1923 state and local governments were contributing around 50 percent of the cost, and by 1930 these governments were contributing nearly 63 percent of the cost. Contributions from individual whites remained small (around 4 to 6 percent of the total funding), and the Rosenwald Fund's contribution remained at around 18 percent of the total cost for much of the program's duration. The contribution from black communities significantly decreased during the history of the program, from 45 percent in 1916 to around 18 percent in 1930. Though blacks were still required to contribute, white-controlled state and local governments began taking on more of their responsibility, albeit only with the inducement of Rosenwald funding.

Although the Rosenwald schools served a significant part of the southern rural black school population, the valuation of the schools also displayed the clear inequity of the system. For example, the value of all black rural schools in 1926 was approximately $25.6 million; Rosenwald schools, which in that year served a quarter of the students, were valued at $15 million. By 1928 the valuation of these schools had increased to about $23 million, again with a large proportion of these schools funded by Rosenwald monies.[52] In short, Rosenwald schools, which served a minority of the South's black children, were beneficiaries of a majority of the capital spent on rural primary education.

These are impressive numbers, yet a closer look at the funding distribution reveals the structure of Jim Crow education as well as the variance

Table 5-2 Contribution to Rosenwald School Buildings by State, 1912–1930

State	Total Buildings	Total Cost	Rosenwald %	Black %	White %	Public %
Alabama	370	979,401	21	38	8	33
Arkansas	289	1,367,076	16	9	3	72
Florida	62	657,809	9	6	7	79
Georgia	192	863,426	18	23	7	51
Kentucky	121	524,270	14	12	2	72
Louisiana	376	1,397,827	21	27	4	48
Maryland	120	573,385	14	12	1	73
Mississippi	529	2,328,544	19	32	12	37
North Carolina	704	3,94,996	15	15	2	68
Oklahoma	152		14	3	0	82
South Carolina	416	2,421,462	16	18	8	58
Tennessee	315	1,506,983	15	17	1	66
Texas	382	1,543,796	18	16	3	63
Virginia	326	1,450,004	15	24	1	59
Total/Avg	4,354	18,458,324	16%	18%	4%	62

Source: N. C. Newbold, "Common Schools for Negroes in the South," *Annals of the American Academy of Political and Social Science* 140 (1928): 222; and J. Scott McCormick, "The Julius Rosenwald Fund," *Journal of Negro Education* 3, no. 4 (1934): 605–26. Note: Calculations by author.

within the multiple Souths of the Jim Crow order. Jim Crow education in the South was not only unequal and unfair, it also varied significantly by state. Table 5–2 shows the breakdown of funding sources for Rosenwald schools from 1912 to 1930. Of the $3.98 million spent on these buildings, the Rosenwald Foundation donated about 19 percent. Southern African Americans contributed about $1.13 million, or about 28 percent of the total amount, and state governments contributed $1.83 million, or 46 percent of the total amount. In no state did the Rosenwald Fund contribute more than 30 percent of the total funding. The lowest amount of funding occurred in the border states, such as Kentucky and Maryland. This is not surprising as the Rosenwald fund was conceived of as an instrument to aid blacks in the most educationally impoverished areas of the South.

The Rosenwald Fund's commitment to the areas with the least public commitment to African American education was tempered by its insistence on black self-help and state involvement. African Americans in Georgia, for example, contributed about 47 percent of their schools' total cost. However, blacks in an even poorer state, Alabama, contributed 40 percent of the total amount, and in the case of Mississippi, blacks contributed 35 percent of the funds. Despite a high level of support from black Georgians, one report found that Georgia lagged behind other states. Nearly a quarter of the 193 counties in the South that were eligible for at least one Rosenwald school were located in Georgia.[53]

This uneven coverage reflected not only African American financial and social capacity; it also reflected a widespread variation in state government spending on African American education. While a state such as Arkansas contributed 66 percent of funding, Mississippi, its Deep South neighbor, contributed only 39 percent of the funds for Rosenwald schools in the state. This brief analysis suggests that the goal of creating a state government commitment to African American education was not completely successful. A closer examination of differences between states as opposed to an overall average suggests important differences that shaped the kinds of citizenship capital that African Americans were able to develop and reflects the influence of white reformers in resolving the frictions of the Jim Crow order.

African American Schoolteachers in the Golden Age

One of the results of the foundation-stimulated expansion in black education in the South was the rapid increase in the number of African American teachers. Not only did their numbers increase, but, like their white counterparts, these teachers also became increasingly professionalized. Part of this professionalization came from rising levels of education that was provided by black normal schools (i.e., teacher training colleges), colleges, and universities that were part of the South's segregated higher education system. As the number of teachers increased, again like their counterparts on the other side of the racial divide, African Americans began to organize professional educational associations.[54] Almost all southern states had these organizations, and membership included most, though not all, of the state's African American teachers (see Table 5–3).

Most African American educational groups, such as state teachers associations, were founded in the late nineteenth century, and a transformation swept over these groups in the 1930s.[55] By the mid-1930s these organizations had begun publishing regular journals or newsletters that covered pedagogical issues but also other issues that the leadership deemed important to its membership. Given the limits on overt political activity, these other issues were camouflaged as education-related, but "self-interest and social reform converged as [teachers] engaged in a cluster of issues centered on racial equality."[56] Although their focus was putatively on education reform, teachers and other community members increasingly saw education and social citizenship linked to democratic citizenship.

Because they were part of, but separate from, the white state, these teachers were able to use the structure of segregated education to create social as well as increasingly political linkages among themselves, first at the local level and then at the state level. In the 1930s and 1940s teachers groups stepped into the civic organizational void left by the absence of the NAACP in the South and the remoteness of Jim Crow reform organizations like the CIC, which were controlled by white elites. The activities of the teachers would in turn create the "communications network required for civil rights activism." In Texas teachers even provided the financial support necessary for legal challenges to the Jim Crow order.

The ability of these state and local teachers associations to play a role in either instigating or supporting policy changes in the Jim Crow education order was dependent on their organizational strength and effectiveness as well as the political structures in which they were embedded. Teachers organizations in Texas, Kentucky, and Virginia displayed remarkable levels of organizational effectiveness; other teachers groups did not. The weakness of some teachers organizations often reflected the political and economic context within which they operated. For example, the Mississippi Association of Teachers in Colored Schools was founded in 1906, relatively late compared to the organizations in the other segregated states. Its membership was small, composing only 13 percent of the state's African American teachers. Although it would work with the few white reformers in the state, in general the Mississippi political establishment was largely resistant to any of their overtures.[57]

Table 5–3 African American Teachers Associations in States with Segregated Public Education

State	Founding Year	Name(s) of Association	Total Black Teachers in State (1931)	Membership percent	Dues	Journal? Start date?
Alabama	1881	Alabama State Teacher's Association & American Teachers Association	3637*			Yes, NA
Arkansas	1886	Association of Teachers of Negro Youth	2000	35%	$1.50	Yes, 1930
Florida	1891	Florida State Teacher's Association	2700	32		Yes, NA
Georgia		Georgia Teachers and Education Association				Yes, 1941
Kentucky	1877	Kentucky Negro Education Association	1525	92	$1.00	Yes, 1930
Louisiana	1901	Louisiana Colored Teachers Association (Louisiana Education Association, 1947)	3800	53		Yes, 1925
Maryland	1914	Maryland State Teachers Association	1850	60		
Mississippi	1906	Mississippi Association of Teachers in Colored Schools	5972	13	$0.50	Yes

Missouri	1884	Missouri State Association of Negro Teachers & two other independent regional associations	1218	63	Yes, 1935
North Carolina	1881	North Carolina Teacher's Association	1400	89	Yes
Oklahoma	NA, pre-1917	Oklahoma Association of Negro Teachers			
South Carolina		Palmetto State Teachers Association			
Tennessee	1923	Tennessee State Association of Teachers in Colored Schools & 3 other independent regional associations	2800	36	$0.50 Yes, 1928
Texas	1884	Colored Teacher's State Association of Texas & 3 other independent bodies	3100	68	$1.75 Yes
Virginia	1882	Virginia Teachers Association	2000		Yes

Source: Walter G. Daniel, "Current Trends and State Activities." *Journal of Negro Education* 6, no. 4 (1937): 661–72.

By contrast, the success of some teachers groups reflected their ability to shape reform policies that to modern eyes are problematic, but that were in fact consistent with the ethos of equalization and pragmatic accommodation that surrounded these groups. For example, the Kentucky Negro Education Association boasted a membership of over 90 percent of the state's African American teachers. With their support and the aid of Charles Anderson, the first African American elected to the Kentucky House of Representatives since Reconstruction, the state passed the Anderson-Mayer Bill in 1935. The bill established an out-of-state tuition grant program for postgraduate study for African Americans, who were unable to undertake graduate education within state because the state's institutions for blacks did not offer these programs and its white institutions did not admit them as students. This legislation provided an example for other southern states to copy. In the wake of Supreme Court decisions such as *Gaines v. Canada* that began the slow legal process of pressuring southern states to equalize higher education funding (or face the prospect of integrating state higher education institutions), out-of-state tuition aid bills would become an important strategy.

The Texas Colored Teacher's Association also had an active educational and political agenda. Texas teachers worked closely with a variety of groups supporting litigation fighting the state's white primary; their association also worked on its own and with its white counterpart on a number of education reform efforts. The association successfully lobbied for the establishment of a retirement fund, a lengthening of the school day, the raising of high school standards, and the raising of minimum wages for teachers. Like their colleagues in Kentucky, teachers in Texas also supported the establishment of an out-of-state tuition grant program, given the lack of opportunities for graduate study within the state. In 1935 and 1936 the association urged the Texas state legislature to adopt out-of-state scholarships, as had been done in Oklahoma.[58] In 1939 the Texas state legislature appropriated $50,000 for the program.

The Virginia Teachers Association was typical of the stronger organizations. In the 1920s it attempted to "move beyond the innocuous formalities of the annual meeting...[and] tried to sustain communications with rural teachers, expose them to current issues, and upgrade their training throughout the year.... It linked professionalization and educational reform, challenging a racist status quo built upon limited opportunities for black children and discrimination against black teachers."[59] The activities of the association reflected the attempt of these organizations to move beyond a narrow professional focus to broader advocacy; thus in addition to creating an employment bureau, a teacher recruitment week, and a teachers institute staffed by college faculty, the Virginia association also created a fund for impoverished schools in rural counties.

From 1930 to 1954 the Virginia Teachers Association transformed itself from educational booster to professional advocacy group. Working with the Virginia Voters Leagues, the group encouraged black teachers to pay their poll tax bill to set an example for the African American community and in particular their students. This poll tax payment campaign expanded the political capabilities of the association and created an important network for information to be transmitted outside of the control of whites.

Politics, Education, and the End of Paternalism

The golden age of segregated institution building was drawing to its end in the 1930s. Although black public education had improved since the 1920s, it still lagged behind where it should have been, if separate had in fact been equal. For example, the increase in the number of schools had outstripped the demand for qualified teachers. Several important studies at the time estimated that although nearly six thousand new teachers would be needed to fill existing vacancies, only two thousand were graduating from teacher training colleges. Besides the problem of demand was the issue of the quality of the South's existing pool of African American teachers: the report claimed that twenty-seven thousand of the African American teachers in the South were undertrained: two-thirds had less than a high school education, and the remaining third had less than two years of college (or normal school) education.[60]

There were clear fiscal limits to the GEB and Rosenwald system. One limit was the Great Depression; as its fiscal impact spread, foundation officials (especially those in the South rather than in the northern main offices) were right to be suspicious of southern governments' commitment to education. State officials looking for ways to cut state budgets began focusing on what they saw as unnecessary frills in education departments. The GEB shifted its funding focus away from new initiatives to simply supporting existing program commitments. From 1924 to 1938 the GEB spent about $1.3 million to create and maintain the state educational administrative functions that it had developed in order to change the "whole tone of public school education in the South."[61] Although the Great Depression posed a challenge for maintaining these administrative and fiscal commitments, once again the white South was not able to completely turn back the clock and reverse its policy commitments.

For African American teachers, the impact of the Great Depression highlighted the inequity of Jim Crow education. The salaries of all teachers in the South were cut. Virginia's public teachers saw their average monthly salary ($69.72 in 1928–29) drop by $21 between 1931 and 1937.[62] For black teachers, whose salaries were a fraction of whites, ' this was proof, if they needed any, of the expendability of black public education. Like white teachers organizations during the same period, the Virginia Teachers Association began to embrace the "'labor union idea,' relinquishing the preoccupation with pedagogical issues."[63] Given the limitations and long-term aspects of this approach, Virginia's African American teachers as well those in other states looked for more immediate relief from the courts.

Foundation-stimulated growth had also pushed black educators to the limit. Foundation-supported initiatives to increase the quality of white teachers meant that pressure was placed on improving the quality of black teachers as well. This pressure to improve the standards of black teachers was not based on altruism; rather in the face of newly filed salary equalization cases, this concern for African American teacher standards increasingly reflected southern governments' realization that race-based salary iniquities would have to cloaked under "objective" measures.[64] Yet even as these new requirements were imposed by state and local governments, the ability of black teachers to financially keep up with whites did not match their ability to access higher education.

By the end of the 1930s southern African Americans were increasingly impatient with a system that required them to pay again for public services for which they had already paid through the tax system. The democratic rhetoric of World War II also helped shape the black critique of education funding. Although they were discussing high schools, North Carolina parents' argument about public education reflected a more overtly political aspect to education: "Education for citizenship must be supported, controlled and administered by that same government which has its being in the hearts and minds of citizens who give it governmental powers."[65] Charles Thompson of Howard University and editor of the *Journal of Negro Education* summed up this new mood:

> Negroes have little or no voice in the administration of school funds, either directly or indirectly; neither do they have the opportunity to hold any offices which have any direct relation to policy-making; nor are they allowed to participate in any appreciable extent in the selection of school officials.... The entire educational establishment is controlled and run *by* the white people and mainly *for* the white people.[66]

In his view and increasingly in the view of the NAACP, mass revolt was "suicide," migration was an option that did not produce systemic change, and "race relations" was a worthless approach that had not produced anything. The courts were the only solution. There was some dissension to this view. For example, W. T. B. Allen, the African American field agent for the GEB, argued that such action would create a white backlash and that "public opinion [was] more effective than court action."[67] Indeed Allen's argument against direct confrontation would remain the stance of white Jim Crow reformers for the next two decades.[68]

Equalization and Institutionalization

The unintentional consequences of Jim Crow reform and public school equalization were the emergence of legal challenges to the Jim Crow order. Between 1935 and 1945 twenty-five teacher salary equalization cases were filed across the South (see Table 5–4). Some cases were filed with the encouragement of the NAACP; others were filed by teachers acting on their own. These suits were difficult for African Americans to bring. White school officials often fired the plaintiff(s), thus removing the basis of a suit. In states where it was more difficult to summarily fire a teacher, school officials used intimidation, bribery, or a combination of both to divide teachers and dissuade them from filing lawsuits. The Buckingham County Teachers Association in Virginia led that state's first organized meeting to challenge salary inequality. Although the salary equalization drive was aborted when the president of the association was dismissed, it helped launch the NAACP's salary equalization drive in

Table 5–4 Salary Equalization Cases Filed and Teacher Salary Ratios

State	Equalization Cases Filed: 1936–1945	Black–White Teacher Salary Ratio, 1939
Alabama	2	0.47
Arkansas	1	0.59
Florida	7	0.51
Georgia	2	0.44
Louisiana	3	0.43
Mississippi	0	0.29
North Carolina	0	0.72
South Carolina	2	0.39
Tennessee	3	0.64
Texas	1	0.62
Virginia	4	0.61
Total/Mean	25	0.52

Source: Teacher salary information from Leander Boykin, "The Status and Trend Differentials between White and Negro Teachers' Salaries in the Southern States, 1900–1946." *Journal of Negro Education* 18, no. 1 (1949): 40–47. Information on salary equalization cases comes from Thurgood Marshall, "Teacher's Salary Cases," *The Negro Yearbook*, ed. Florence Murray (New York: Current Books), 49. Note: Teacher salary ratio calculated by author.

Table 5–5 Impact of Institutionalization on Teacher Salary Ratio

Variable	Model 1	Model 2
Dependent variable: Teacher Salary Ratio		
Public Contribution	.666***	
	(2.700)	
Black Contribution		−.733
		(1.760)
Salary Cases	−.017	−.010
	(.953)	(.496)
Constant	.172	.692***
	(1.260)	(6.040)
Adj. R^2	.347	.098

* $p \leq .10$ ** $p \leq .05$ *** $p \leq .001$

N = 11 states; t values in parentheses.

1936.[69] Despite subtle and not so subtle opposition, salary cases continued to be filed and threats were made to file cases in order to force state and local governments to abolish the blatant salary discrepancies between white and black teachers.

By 1939 black teachers made approximately half the salary of white teachers. There were variations, of course; in North Carolina African Americans made 70 percent of the salary of whites, while in Mississippi black teachers made only 30 percent of white teachers' salaries. Although these were disheartening figures, they were an improvement from figures at the turn of the century, thanks to education reform, specifically the institutionalization of black education, and the professional and community mobilization effects of Rosenwald funding, which in turn was linked to blacks' greater willingness to engage in litigation.

Using the statistical technique of ordinary least squares regression, we can estimate the relationship between Rosenwald funding (as a measure of institutionalization) and teacher salary ratios (see Table 5–5). By controlling for the effect of the number of salary cases filed, the impact of Rosenwald funding, and thus institutionalization, can be measured. The impact of state and local participation (PUBLIC CONTRIBUTION) on salary equalization was statistically significant and positive. The more public funds contributed to Rosenwald schools, the higher the black-white salary ratio would be for that state. On the other hand, the relationship between African American funding of Rosenwald schools and teacher salary equalization was negative. The greater percentage contributed by blacks toward school construction resulted in a smaller salary ratio. Thus state and local government willingness to contribute to public education for blacks was followed by the greater equalization of teacher salaries.

The turn to the courts to reform Jim Crow education is probably the most fully explored aspect of the civil rights movement. Yet the path to the courts was shaped by Jim Crow reform, which offered the opportunity for indirect challenge, for the chance (to use an often overused term) of black agency. Education was probably one of the few arenas left to southern blacks for semi-open, semipolitical mobilization. Raising money for school buildings, supplies, and teachers' salaries provided a way to bring together communities that were not only separated by the usual differences over personality and other issues, but also by a political, social, and economic order that often purposely divided and weakened black communities.

Southern paternalism allowed for expressions of African American community uplift, as long as these efforts did not challenge the Jim Crow order. Indeed whites were more than willing to support, or at least not discourage, African Americans' quest for better educational opportunities if that meant that the community bore much of the expense itself. However, the process of mobilization for education was fraught with contradictions, dilemmas, and ambiguities. By and large white reformers opposed the turn to the courts. They argued that such a strategy alienated sympathetic white allies and did not recognize the limited ability of stateways to reshape southern folkways.

Although white reformers opposed litigation, they were not able to develop a viable strategy after the unfulfilled promise of foundation-led equalization. One reason for the lack of new policy alternatives was that the end of the golden age coincided with, and perhaps was exacerbated by, the gradual withdrawal of the foundations from the field of primary education in the South.

Northern foundations such as the GEB had begun planning for their "own obsolescence" in the 1920s because they feared that the southern states would become too dependent on their presence; they believed "the education of Negro children [should be] thought of as part of the regular job of States and counties."[70] The withdrawal of the Rosenwald Foundation was in keeping with Julius Rosenwald's wishes that the foundation self-liquidate in order to force its administrators to engage with immediate problems rather than focus on organizational continuity. Many of the northern foundations believed that they had effectively served their functions: the seeds had been planted; now it was time to let the system grow. In accordance with its founder's wishes, the Rosenwald Fund closed its doors and liquidated its assets in 1948. The GEB did not finally shut down until 1960, but by 1952 its goals and funding reflected a winding down of activity.[71]

Generational change also hastened this change in focus and attention. By the late 1930s the foundation personnel and the education reformers who had begun or supported these programs had either retired or died. New personnel were eager to spend the remaining foundation monies and time on new initiatives. Shifting policy commitments and declining institutional resources left white Jim Crow reformers few policy alternatives to avert the growing clash within the Jim Crow order between challengers and defenders.

Observing the rising frustrations of African Americans as well as their willingness to directly engage in citizenship politics, white reformers sensed that something had changed. Although Will Alexander was speaking of African Americans, he could also be speaking of liberal whites:

> In subjecting Negroes to American education we have made them Americans. So completely American are they that they will not submit passively to being pushed around as they are under segregation. Educational opportunity for the common man is part of the American way of life. In giving it to Negroes, we have let them in on the meaning of democracy. Their unrest under their special limitations is the result not of sinister influence from the outside, but of our education, which, for all its faults, is the best thing in our democracy. The education of Negroes in America has not been a mistake. Here we see American faith and American idealism at their best. Segregation on the other hand, is rooted in fear and in doubt as to whether or not our faith in democracy is strong enough to overcome our fears as to what may be some of its consequences.[72]

Conclusion

By the 1940s Jim Crow reformers were able to modernize southern education according to a highly restrictive definition of modernity. Within state education departments a visitor could find

> corridors...lined with specialists whose salaries are paid without protest by taxpayers no longer suspicious of public education. One door may be labeled "Division of Teacher Training and Certification," another may [say] "School Libraries." Behind other doors basic statistics and information about the school system are compiled and kept up to date. Behind still others modern and efficient building plans are drawn and made available to localities that fifty years ago did not even have outhouses for their schools.[73]

This quest for modernity did not fully translate into a system of harmonious racial management. The gap between education provided for whites and for blacks remained. In some cases racial disparity seemed to be gaining speed as the post—World War II era of prosperity sent new educational resources flowing in a one-way direction: toward white schools. Unlike the early decades of the Jim Crow order, blacks were no longer content to find ways to work around or within this institutionalized inequality. Despite the best efforts of Jim Crow reformers, education did not ameliorate the worst effects of the order; rather, the continued inequality highlighted its contradictions. The harder blacks ran, paying for the educational services and funds that local governments seemed ever reluctant to provide, the further educational equity seemed to be from their grasp. Yet for blacks the limited fruits of Jim Crow reform would provide the ammunition to confront these contradictions.

The professionalization of the South's dual system of education, including a hesitant and reluctant movement toward equalization, had created some important benefits for African Americans. Racial management had solidified African Americans' tenuous claim to social citizenship that remained at the end of Reconstruction. The necessity of maintaining, at least in a nominal sense, a dual system, along with the support of northern foundation money, had enabled African Americans to leverage the state at all levels of the educational system. This leverage helped to create or support a parallel though separate set of organizations and institutions that would indirectly provide critical resources for the African American communities and would become the foundation on which the modern civil rights movement would build.

The quest for equalization, for the full assertion of social rights, would be transformed and extended into a quest for political and civil rights. The black elementary schools and high schools, colleges and universities of the South built with the aid of northern foundation money and the support of southern reformers would provide the leadership as well as the ordinary people of the civil rights movement and destroy the very order that reformers and foundations were trying to stabilize.

White reformers faced their own dilemma as African Americans increasingly and openly defined education as not simply a quest for social citizenship, but also as a movement for political and civil rights. While white school administrators attempted to defuse to defuse the "desegregation crisis" through new variations on their tradition of quiet management, many politicians and ordinary citizens were not content to address the issue through bureaucratic channels. Massive resistance meant protecting and reinforcing the critical role that education played in the creation and maintenance of the Jim Crow order. The next chapter discusses how these dilemmas and conflict over the role of education played out in the field of higher education as Jim Crow reformers attempted to adapt the order to new challenges from within and outside the South.

Chapter 6

Higher Education for Blacks in the South: Pragmatism and Principle?

> To you who are discouraged, citizenship is not in constitutions, but in the mind.
>
> James Shepard, quoted in Thuesen, "Classes of Citizenship"

In their quest to modernize the South and to stabilize race relations, Jim Crow reformers turned their attention to higher education for southern blacks. In the case of higher education, like primary education, Jim Crow reformers also had to respond to pressures from outside and within the Jim Crow order. White reformers along with their foundation allies began the era with a vision of a higher education system—shaped by rational planning and elite leadership—that would lead the way in transforming the South. Much as they had done with primary education, reformers and foundations saw the neglect of black higher education as an important opportunity. For southern white and black educators, northern foundation support could be used to leverage the South's weak support for higher education into more resources that could be used to stabilize and expand existing institutions, create more professional opportunities, and, for some academics, encourage the opening up of the South's intellectual and political discourse. The South provided northern foundations with an ideal laboratory in which to test their belief that foundations could have a more systematic and deep-seated effect on society.

In this chapter I explore the shaping of higher education for blacks by focusing on the role of Jim Crow reformers, foundations, individual whites, black educational leaders and administrators, and especially state government. At the heart of the struggle was the question of whether and how southern states could be encouraged or forced into supporting a system of genuinely separate *and* equal higher education for blacks in the South. Just as reformers sought to rationalize primary education in the South, they sought to create a similar pattern of rationalization and centralization of higher education. The goal of the GEB, for example, was the creation of an "orderly and comprehensive *system*" that was "territorially comprehensive, harmoniously related [and] individually complete." This new system would "discourage unnecessary duplication and waste and & encourage economy and efficiency."[1] In keeping with the emerging race relations model, black colleges and universities were an inevitable part of this new rationalization.

With the settlement of the Jim Crow order seemingly assured, whites could more readily embrace a new role in black higher education. This role was to develop and provide, despite inequalities, a parallel world that would decrease the frictions within the Jim Crow order. Not only was creating a professional class good for managed race relations and the stability of the order, but it would be good for whites. For example, training black doctors was considered important for "humanity" but also for "self-protection" because "fundamental work in hygiene and disease prevention must be done by the colored practitioner."[2]

As in many aspects of Jim Crow reform, whites wanted to control the timing and pacing of these changes, while blacks were focused on achieving and exercising a degree of autonomy and social citizenship. In the 1940s the question of equalization itself was highly contested within the southern black community as it raised the prospect of whether this strategy would in fact further legitimize and entrench the Jim Crow order. The distinction between pragmatism (Washington) and principle (DuBois) had historically divided the African American community. In the area of black higher education it reflected the internal divisions within the African American community that would have to be mended in order to develop an effective collective strategy. Thus although it was easy to see the equalization struggle as part of a larger plan to essentially bankrupt southern governments into dismantling Jim Crow education, the actual contours of how equalization played out across the South was more complex than its architects or its detractors acknowledged.

Jim Crow reformers operated within a political and social order that was bound by time and place. It is important to keep at the center of analysis the reality that in the 1920s, 1930s, and even the 1940s the possibility that the U.S. Supreme Court would end segregated education within the foreseeable future was for the average southerner, black or white, unlikely. Although NAACP lawyers were beginning a slow, methodical fight against de jure segregation, the uncertainty over the outcome of this venture was massive. Indeed many white Jim Crow reformers throughout this period (and some even beyond) were hostile to the NAACP and saw the intrusion of the group into the higher education policy domain as not only unwarranted but disastrous. They repeatedly proclaimed that NAACP activities would set back the slow and careful work of modernizing and equalizing higher education for blacks in the South. Although the NAACP, with the assistance of an increasingly friendly federal court, would later emerge to decisively reshape higher education in the South for blacks, during the era of Jim Crow reform existing institutions and political alliances created the possibility for incremental but achievable reforms to be realized.[3]

To understand the politics of education, and of southern politics in general, during the Jim Crow reform era, we need to keep in mind the limits of the Jim Crow order. For example, given the seeming unlikelihood that southern higher education would be integrated in the near future, the average white and African American educator, student, and ordinary citizen had to frame an individual as well as a communal response to the order. Southern whites and blacks attempted to create and perfect separate and equal worlds within the realm of higher education, a strategy that would be tested in the aftermath of the *Gaines v. Canada* decision, which constituted the first blow against segregated education and the plan for a rational dual university system. The road to challenging segregation in higher education has been seen as fairly straightforward: the NAACP used the lever of equalization to force southern states into desegregating white institutions. However, this historical account largely glosses over the ways the Jim Crow order had already structured the actions and beliefs of both white and black university administrators, foundation personnel, education reformers, and ordinary people by the 1930s. Before the struggle for equalization could begin, a more fundamental struggle over the right to higher education had to be waged first.

Southern Black Colleges and Universities: The Last Redoubt of Social Citizenship

Primary education was not the only arena in which the Jim Crow order had to accommodate to a broader political order. The federal government established an institutional commitment to higher education for blacks with the enactment of the Second Morrill Act in 1891, which specifically provided federal funds for public colleges and universities for blacks.

Although white-controlled state governments gave African American institutions only a fraction of the monies to which they were entitled, they were not able to completely exclude African Americans from publicly financed higher education. As a result of this outside institutional commitment, there was an ongoing struggle to control higher education for blacks in the South. This struggle reflected the ongoing struggle for power between and among whites and blacks within the Jim Crow order.

The South's publicly supported black colleges and universities were some of the most visible vestiges of the political, civil, and social citizenship that had been stripped from African Americans in the wake of the rise of the Jim Crow order. Because the federal government and private foundations supplied much of the funding for the maintenance of these colleges, state governments could not simply erase them, as they had done with so many other aspects of black citizenship. Because of the independence (albeit highly constrained) of black colleges, perhaps more so than the primary education system, these institutions became important sites of inter- and intraracial cooperation and organization as well as conflict.

In Texas the state's constitution promised, "One university [i.e., the University of Texas] was to serve the major needs of all the citizens of the state" and would "include an agricultural and mechanical department or branch for Negroes [i.e., Prairie View] and a branch university for colored."[4] Although Prairie View A&M had been established in 1879 as a "normal and industrial college," many black educators did not believe that it was the equivalent of the first-class university promised to them in the state's constitution. Black teachers, black civic organizations led by Carter Wesley, the black journalist and publisher, and the Texas CIC pursued an equalization strategy that coalesced around a long-standing constitutional commitment on the part of the state of Texas.

For many African American leaders who had been stripped of political power during the long ascendancy of the Jim Crow order, these institutions provided an important organizational and intellectual base to retreat to and regroup. One of these new educational leaders was James Shepard, originally a Reconstruction politician and later president of North Carolina College for Negroes. Despite the criticism of African American social scientists such as E. Franklin Frazier and Ralph Bunche, who derided these institutions as bastions of an overly cautious, small-minded, materialistic petit bourgeoisie, the institutions allowed for the development of a range of groups, from fraternal organizations to professional associations, that could exist outside of white control and oversight.[5]

Many whites took steps to curb this limited sphere of black independence. Because they could not erase publicly supported colleges, white governments attempted to limit the independence and influence of these institutions by fiscally starving them and by controlling the individuals (students, faculty, and administrators) who worked and studied at them. White officials monitored everything from whether the curricula was "too academic" to ensuring that college events open to the public offered only segregated seating. White officials also worked to ensure that the leadership of these institutions was under their control. The president of Georgia State Industrial College was forbidden to leave the campus grounds; John Gandy, the president of Virginia State University, was pressured to resign from his fraternal organization, as education officials feared he would use unofficial contacts with other whites to exert political pressure on them.[6]

The Waning Shadow of Tuskegee

Coinciding with and complementing these attempts to control higher education for blacks was the dominance of the Tuskegee model. Until his death in 1915, the dominant model of higher education for blacks was Booker T. Washington's Tuskegee industrial education model, in which training in trades such as farming, blacksmithing, and domestic service was put forward as not only adequate but the limit for black higher education. The dominance of the Tuskegee model reflected the large degree of unanimity, at least among whites, about the scope and purpose of higher education for blacks. Such was the strength of Tuskegee model that in many cases black educational leaders staked the survival of their institutions on embracing it (with varying degrees of sincerity). The insistence of funders, both foundations and state legislatures, on this model had starved private and public institutions for blacks of funds needed to maintain or expand academic standards. The dominance of the Tuskegee model had forced African American administrators to maintain an exhausting pretence that they were adhering to the vocational model that had been imposed upon them. Although many southern black educational leaders probably sincerely believed in the Tuskegee model, many embraced it for largely strategic reasons. This compliance was less prominent in the private sector. Private institutions controlled by the African Methodist Church consistently refused to abandon liberal arts curricula for blacks in favor of the Tuskegee model.

By 1920, however, most reform-minded whites were slowly accepting what many African Americans privately believed but less publicly dared to declare: the Tuskegee model could not be called higher education, especially in a modern society. The GEB led this emerging consensus among whites, arguing that although institutions for black higher education in the South had "kept alive the spark of learning in a bleak and barren period," they were not prepared to meet the current educational needs of blacks in the

South, especially the need to train "those who will lead the race in its efforts to educate and improve itself."[7] Not only were these institutions failing African Americans; they were failing the standards of modern higher education in America. This failure, as well as the lack of "systematic planning in the creation of these institutions" and of "consideration of regional needs," offended the GEB's Progressive sensibilities.[8]

Coupled with the diminishing power of the Tuskegee model was the growing financial crisis of southern black higher education. As their Reconstruction supporters died out, the northern religious organizations that had built and supported private higher education for blacks during Reconstruction and the early Jim Crow era were increasingly cutting back on or ending their financial assistance. As the Great Depression deepened, many of these religious bodies no longer had the financial ability or the interest in maintaining close control of these colleges. For example, the American Baptist Home Mission Society founded Jackson College in Mississippi in 1877. In 1934, in the midst of the Depression, the society announced that it no longer had any funds to support the college. To save one of the four higher education institutions available to blacks in a state that had the highest population of blacks in the South, the GEB facilitated the transfer of Jackson College to state control.[9]

The turn away from the Tuskegee model was also due to generational change and changes occurring in the racial composition of college leadership. The crisis of survival that had characterized the state of black higher education in the South during the early dark days of the Jim Crow order had passed, and the educational leadership that managed the transition of these institutions—white presidents of black institutions—and a governance style that was paternalistic at best were fast disappearing. In 1926 Mordecai Johnson became Howard University's first black president. During the 1920s Fisk University, at that time the South's preeminent private institution for blacks, went though a period of considerable turmoil as students and faculty wrested control away from a white-dominated board of trustees and put it into the hands of a more responsive and professional president and a more representative board.

The leadership of public and private colleges was passing into the hands of new education leaders who foundation officials praised as "represent[ing] a new generation of leadership among the Negroes, new in the sense that it was more dynamic and more sharply defined."[10] In many ways these leaders were far different from the former politicians and religious leaders who had initially governed these institutions. They were individuals who saw their leadership not simply as a vocation but also as a profession. John Hope, who became president of Atlanta University in 1929, was one of the new leaders singled out by white reformers. Hope's attractiveness lay in his "patience, sanity and zeal" and his willingness to help "in the slow solution of one of the great problems of our time." But despite this generational and racial transition, the new leadership remained with few exceptions within the boundaries of the Jim Crow order, and in the case of a number of black college presidents became members of Jim Crow reform organizations such as the CIC.

The Status of Black Higher Education in the South

Although the 1920s ushered in a new approach on the part of foundations toward black higher education as well as a change in institutional leadership, the reality of black higher education remained problematic. There were still vast disparities in funding between white and black institutions. In the case of publicly supported institutions, these disparities in funding led to inequalities in physical plants and curriculum offerings. As in primary and secondary education, African American taxpayers were given separate and unequal access to higher education. In general no southern state fully funded black institutions to the extent that they were entitled to under the Morrill Act (see Table 6–1). Southern states gave black public institutions on average only 43 percent of the state funding they were entitled to if there had been a real equalization policy. Like primary education, however, this regional average masked substantial and surprising interstate variation. For example, while Mississippi was among the worst in adequately funding primary education, its 53 percent funding for black higher education was among the region's highest.[11] By contrast, North Carolina and Virginia, states in which white reformers prided themselves on their "advanced attitudes," each gave black higher educational institutions only 33 percent of the funding to which they were entitled.

This inequality in funding was reflected in the curricula of these institutions. On the whole the academic offerings of these institutions were limited to agriculture, mechanical arts, home economics, arts and sciences, and education. Only one school offered a collegiate-level science program, only four offered business studies, and only two offered a nursing program. The fine arts were practically nonexistent at these institutions, underscoring the vocational legacy of the Tuskegee model.

Nevertheless despite the rhetoric extolling the South's new era of race relations, interracialism, and vertical segregation, southern whites did not offer southern blacks a viable and separate world within this order. Thus outside of Howard University, no other law schools for blacks existed in the South. Aside from a few spots offered outside of the South, African Americans interested in medicine were confined to Howard University and Meharry

Table 6-1 Funding and Programs of Black Land Grant Colleges

State	State Percent Funding Received	Science	Business	Nursing	Fine Arts & Music
Alabama	0.43				
Arkansas	0.29				
Delaware	0.20				X
Florida	0.50			X	
Georgia	0.33				
Kentucky	0.15				
Louisiana	0.39				
Mississippi	0.53				X
Missouri	0.06				
N. Carolina	0.33	X	X	X	
Oklahoma	0.10		X	X	
S. Carolina	0.50		X		
Tennessee	0.24		X		
Texas	0.25			X	
Virginia	0.33			X	
W. Virginia	0.20		X	X	
Total/Mean	0.43				

Source: Davis, "The Negro Land Grant College," 327. Funding received under Morrill Act, 1930–31.

Medical School. Even outside of the rarified air of professional studies, the golden age of segregated education meant more demand for advanced teacher training; many black students left the South for this training, but many students could not. Then there was the simple issue of justice. If white teachers did not have to leave the state for training, why did African Americans?

As a result of this disparity between white expectations and reality, southern African Americans working through their own local and state organizations, and at times with the NAACP, found a weapon with which to attack the soft underbelly of the Jim Crow order: separate was not equal. To make separate equal would force the various elements of the order to square an impossible circle. That circle was white supremacy, which demanded not only horizontal separation but also vertical difference: whites were not only separate *from* blacks, they were also *over* blacks.

The Multiple Roads to Equalization

Unlike in the struggle for primary education, white Jim Crow reformers largely stood outside the struggle to equalize black higher education. To the extent that they did participate it was largely to direct criticism and warnings to blacks whom they felt were moving too fast for southern (white) folkways to adapt. Blacks would play a central role in this equalization, although there was no dominant black group setting the agenda. Teachers early on established the groundwork for initial education policies that mitigated but did not solve the inequality that existed between white and black institutions. African American teachers were highly dependent on the Jim Crow order for their economic well-being. At the same time, the social capital that derived from their income and occupation enabled to them to have a limited form of strategic engagement with the order. Thus teachers in Kentucky and Texas were able to extract limited concessions (e.g., out-of-state tuition grants and summer institutes at black public colleges and universities) from white authorities that advanced their professional goals. Many within and outside of the black community were ready to defend these hard-won concessions, especially in the face of the NAACP's untried and uncertain litigation strategy.

Black college administrators, especially those at publicly funded institutions, composed a second group of black reformers. As southern governments responded to more aggressive attempts at equalization, black administrators were forced to accede to largely flimsy attempts at equalization concocted by white policymakers in order to evade the court's reach. Yet while some black administrators saw these state-sponsored equalization attempts as simply legitimating the Jim Crow order, other administrators saw these policies as a means by which to strengthen the fragile fiscal and academic status of black institutions. The state of Texas, with the aid of Prairie View A&M's president, would use this institution as a means of delaying the fulfillment of the state's constitutional commitment. Only when the judicial tide began turning did Texas state officials seriously begin to plan for a separate and equal university for blacks. However, by then it was too late.[12]

The third group involved in this equalization struggle was the NAACP. During the 1930s the NAACP increasingly shed its reformist approach to the Jim Crow order and embraced a transformational role. Working from a central decision to focus on the South's Achilles' heel—that separate was not equal—the NAACP looked for test cases. While it worked with local and state organizations, its focus was on setting precedent rather than on implementation. This organizational focus put it at odds with local people, who saw in the NAACP strategy an uncertain possibility of change that lay in some distant, unknown future, not the immediate possibility of achieving real though incremental change that litigation (or the threat of it) had brought about. The tensions between these groups—the teachers and students on the ground; the NAACP, which used a long-term strategy; and the middle ground, occupied by state educational and political leaders—would shape the equalization struggle in the 1930s and 1940s.

Putting Teeth into *Plessy: Gaines v. Canada*

In 1938 the U.S. Supreme Court in *Gaines v. Canada* ruled that in the area of graduate education, states operating segregated educational systems had to provide substantively equal facilities. The path to *Gaines* began in the early 1930s, when the NAACP developed a long-term strategy that focused on the Achilles' heel of *Plessy v. Ferguson*: that although southern states had wholeheartedly embraced separation, they had not in any way lived up to its constitutional complement, equality. The southern educational system was not only separate, but also cruelly unequal, with African American students at all levels (primary, secondary, and collegiate) receiving pennies for every dollar allocated to white students. Of course this number varied across time and location, but the main point is that nowhere in the South did funding for African American education even come close to funding for whites.[13] By focusing on graduate education, the NAACP could focus on an area that, unlike primary education, was not shrouded by the cloak of quiet management and was not complicated by being decentralized into thousands of different school districts and thus different circumstances. Furthermore the NAACP could ally itself with the largest, most educated and organized group in the southern black community: teachers.

By focusing on this clear inequality of higher education, the NAACP hoped that southern states would be forced to choose between the creation of a separate—and probably ruinously expensive—equal system of graduate education or the desegregation of the white state university. From that point on other parts of the Jim Crow order would also become vulnerable. The first success in this strategy was the case of *Murray v. Maryland* (1936). Donald Murray, an African American graduate of Amherst College and a Maryland resident, wished to attend the University of Maryland Law School. However, Maryland did not admit African Americans to the state's law school, and it also did not offer a separate law school for African Americans and others excluded from the state university. In 1936 the Maryland Court of Appeals ruled that the lack of alternatives for Murray essentially meant that *Plessy* was being violated, and it ruled for Murray's admission to the state law school. Because the case did not go to the Supreme Court, the *Murray* decision was binding only on Maryland. Murray entered the law school the following year, making the University of Maryland Law School the first southern institution in modern times to be integrated.

On the heels of *Murray* came the case of Lloyd Gaines, a graduate of Lincoln University, Missouri's only public institution for African Americans. As he stated in his court testimony, Gaines desired entrance into the University of Missouri's law school rather than accept an out-of-state tuition scholarship because the state school was less expensive, closer to home, and would enable him to more successfully practice law in Missouri.[14] To avert the unimaginable possibility of integration, Missouri officials proposed that Gaines attend a new law school (which had just been proposed and did not actually exist) established as part of Lincoln University. In its court challenge, among other points the NAACP endeavored to convince the court that this attempt at equalization and the state's system of out-of-state tuition grants for African American graduate students were both inherently unequal. The only remedy to this inequality was integration. The Supreme Court did not agree to go that far, ruling simply that the state had to provide equality of opportunity for all students within its boundaries. Thus out-of-state tuition grants could not substitute for the provision of equal, in-state facilities.

Although important in creating the first Supreme Court precedent for equalization, the impact on Lloyd Gaines was less significant. Gaines did not enroll in law school; instead he vanished.[15] Nevertheless an important precedent had been set: in the area of graduate education, separate had to be equal, and it had to be provided in-state. What "equality" meant was to be an object of contention for the next decade.

The *Gaines* decision marked a temporary pause in the NAACP's equalization strategy as the ongoing effects of the Great Depression added further strain to the organization's finances. With the onset of World War II the NAACP decided to expend its limited resources in other areas. But though attention shifted at the national level, local activists and educators continued their struggle to force southern state governments to comply with the *Gaines* decision.

Pragmatism versus Principle

One choice facing southern blacks in the wake of the *Gaines* decision was pragmatic accommodationism: forcing southern states to fulfill the spirit as well as the letter of the law and continuing the long-standing tradition of leveraging new resources and status for black higher education. This choice offered both individual and institutional advancement. Faced with the prospect of integration, many (but not all) southern state governments provided more (though not massive) amounts of aid to often fiscally beleaguered black institutions. As more pressure mounted—through increased enrollments and the threat of more lawsuits—a number of southern states created new graduate schools, which offered new or potentially better opportunities for administrators and academics. Thus in the immediate moment the leverage provided by *Gaines* could enable black institutions, educators, and students the opportunity to make significant institutional and individual advances.

Yet this pragmatic approach did not come without costs. By acquiescing in essentially the structural and fiscal elaboration of Jim Crow, leaders as well as critics of black colleges and universities would be providing a form of political, intellectual, and institutional support for the Jim Crow system. Even more problematic was the fact that these new resources did not automatically translate into better facilities or schools. Thurgood Marshall, arguably one of the lawyers most responsible for equalization suits in the wake of *Gaines*, denounced these new institutions as merely "Jim Crow schools" and the administrators and professors who staffed them as people who were damaging the struggle for integration.[16]

Foundation officials certainly feared that a disastrous diversion of resources would be the result of *Gaines*. Jackson Davis, speaking for himself and perhaps for the GEB and the Jim Crow reform establishment, argued that although the *Gaines* decision was important, it was perhaps a "pyrrhic" victory: "[Southern states] may set up a whole series of separate schools, with small enrollments and inadequate support. This would undoubtedly create institutional interests which would be hard to break. The very purpose to do away with separation might thus work to prolong it."[17] Yet, as was usual with white Jim Crow reformers like Davis, while there was no clear denunciation of segregation, there was also no constructive alternative offered.

Against this backdrop the other choice was principled opposition coupled with reluctant accommodation, a stance embraced by the NAACP and its allies, most notably Charles Thompson, the editor of the *Journal of Negro Education*. According to Thompson, the *Gaines* decision put African Americans in a difficult situation: they had to "strain every nerve to improve their situation within the framework of segregation and at the same time be unceasing in their efforts to abolish it." In Thompson's opinion, to combat both opportunism as well as the South's tried and true strategy of divide and conquer, African Americans needed to constantly "distinguish clearly between sound strategy and effective tactics."[18] With black newspapers such as the *Pittsburgh Courier* stating that *Gaines* was the "greatest decision on that court since the grandfather clause was declared unconstitutional," southern blacks began the *Gaines* era with a mixture of skepticism and hope.[19]

The Question of Institutional Advancement

In addition to grant programs and the expansion of graduate programs, the *Gaines* decision handed African American administrators a new tool in their efforts to extract more resources from tight-fisted southern legislatures. How they handled this tool reflected the growing dilemma of Jim Crow reform that southern black reformers would have to face: the need to choose between principled opposition and pragmatic accommodation.

Dr. James Shepard, the president of North Carolina College for Negroes, was one administrator who attempted to leverage this new opportunity. Shepard bitterly opposed any overt effort to force the state to equalize resources that involved integration. In his opinion, such tactics would set off a white backlash that would seriously weaken the state's support for black higher education. Shepard had some basis for his concern. His institution had only recently gained its status as a four-year baccalaureate degree-granting institution. Financially the college (as well as other black higher education institutions) was still reeling from the economic effects of the Great Depression. Never enthusiastic supporters of black education, state legislatures imposed massive budgets on black higher education during this period. Thus Shepard's cautiousness on the issue was not unusual. Most black colleges and institutions in the late 1930s were in precarious financial and academic shape, dependent on the goodwill of often indifferent, if not hostile, state legislatures.

In 1933 Shepard believed that this precarious state of black higher education was threatened by a lawsuit filed by Thomas Hocutt, who sought admission to the University of North Carolina's School of Pharmacy. Although Hocutt lost, Shepard offered North Carolina legislators an alternative to the risks of further litigation. By establishing graduate programs at his college, more radical demands could be managed by Shepard, and the "friendly relations between the races [would not be] in any way disturbed at the present time."[20] The 1923 appropriation for North Carolina College was $23,000; by 1939 it was $128,000, and by 1944 it was $171,000.[21] Of course even this was still a fraction of what the state was spending on its white university system. Yet other black higher education institutions would soon draw on the people who administered or were trained at North Carolina's graduate programs.

Even administrators who did not seek accommodation with southern whites realized the leverage afforded to them by the *Gaines* decision. Dr. Sherman Scruggs, the president of Missouri's Lincoln University, explained his request for a $291,000 increase in funding: "[Lincoln is] constantly faced with the mandate to offer a quality of administrative and instructional services that are equally comparable with that of the University of Missouri in all the offerings that it provides."[22]

Evading Equalization: The Persistence of Out-of State Tuition Grant Programs

One of the key victories of *Gaines* was that the early response of southern governments to the equalization problem—out-of-state tuition grants—was ruled unconstitutional. Yet despite this ruling, one of the first dilemmas of *Gaines* quickly emerged: the persistence and indeed expansion of these programs. Despite their unconstitutionality, twelve more southern states would enact these programs, most within five years of the decision (see Table 6–2). Even though there was presumably no constitutional basis for them, southern states had a number of reasons for creating or expanding these programs. The attractiveness of these graduate grant programs lay in their function as a temporary pressure valve. For example, states may have used these programs as a short-term way to evade the daunting logistical and fiscal barriers of creating a meaningfully equal separate system. States may also have used the programs as a way to defuse more pressing demands for fundamental change in the southern higher education system, and the Jim Crow order at large. By offering the most ambitious and presumably most restive individuals the opportunity to pursue higher education, state officials hoped to minimize the chances of their own African American citizens bringing a *Gaines*-type suit.

In addition, by proposing a grant program state officials could potentially divide local African American groups into warring, and ineffective, factions. Taking note of ongoing state-level battles over the equalization of teachers' salaries, government officials knew that many in the African American community were willing to accept some concrete though limited advances in the face of a long, protracted struggle to an uncertain victory. South Carolina's experience with this is instructive. African American leaders successfully resisted the state's attempt to create a tuition grant program before a substantive legal challenge could be brought and a legal precedent could be secured. When a legal challenge did emerge, the state responded with not only a tuition program, but also a new graduate program, including a law school.[23] Finally, some states could point to earlier support from African American teachers for these programs as justification for their expansion, rather than truly addressing institutional inequality. By creating individual benefits, white southern officials could undermine the basis for the creation of collective action within the African American community. Indeed there was the danger that these programs would allow states to not only evade the issue of creating comparable graduate facilities, as required by the *Gaines* decision, but also potentially divert attention and resources away from the larger question of desegregation.

Opposition produced its own set of issues. The first was the limited range of options available to African American educators at state-controlled institutions. As employees of the states, most educators were unable to refuse direct orders from state government. While principled opposition to the grants program would undoubtedly have given some people a sense of moral satisfaction, others contended that southern legislators would have used public opposition as an opportunity to rid the state of even this minimal obligation. Thus outright opposition to the out-of-state tuition programs by African Americans could have limited opportunities for higher education for the hundreds of African Americans who had no other alternative.

Table 6–2 Establishment of Out-of-State Tuition Grants

State	Established	Equalization Suit?
Alabama	1945[a]	
Arkansas	1943	
Delaware	1947	
Florida	1945	
Georgia	1944[a]	
Kentucky	1936	Eubanks v. University of Kentucky (1941)
Louisiana	1946	Hatfield v. Louisiana State University (1946)
Maryland	1935	Murray v. University of Maryland (1935)
Mississippi	1948	
Missouri	1929	Gaines v. Canada (1938), Bluford v. University of Missouri (1942)
North Carolina	1939	Hocutt v. Wilson (1933)
Oklahoma	1941[b]	Sipuel v. Oklahoma State Board of Regents (1948)
South Carolina	1946	Wrighten v. Board of Trustees University of South Carolina (1947)
Tennessee	1940 [a, c]	Redmond v. University of Tennessee (1937); Michael et al. v. University of Tennessee (1939)
Texas	1939	Sweatt v. Painter (1950)
Virginia	1936[d]	
West Virginia	1927	

[a] In-state tuition grants to private black college or university (BCU).
[b] State began appropriation before formal legislative approval.
[c] Out-of-state grants taken from public BCU's regular appropriations.
[d] Alice Jackson unsuccessfully applies to University of Virginia (1935).

Given the dilemmas posed by these grant programs as well as the strategic considerations behind their creation or expansion, a brief examination of the tuition grant programs during their height will help to better illustrate the changing landscape of higher education and the limitations of reform in the pre-*Brown* South.

The Development of Out-of-State Tuition Grants for Graduate Study

In 1927 West Virginia created the first out-of-state tuition grant program. With only one state-funded institution for African Americans, and that a teacher's college, the state decided to create a program through which it would award grants for its African American students to gain higher education outside of the state (see Table 6–2). Only one other state, Missouri, followed West Virginia's early lead, creating its own grant program in 1929. Three states, two in response to pending equalization cases, also created tuition grant programs prior to the *Gaines* decision: Maryland (1935), Kentucky (1936), and Virginia (1936). After the *Gaines* decision, and before the full impact of World War II, five more states created programs. Only Tennessee created the program in response to an equalization suit.

Seven southern states created grant programs between 1945 and 1948. Only two of the programs, Louisiana's and South Carolina's, were in immediate response to an equalization suit. Some of these later programs were essentially last-ditch attempts to stave off desegregation. For example, Mississippi was the last to enact a program, although it was never fully funded or functional.[24] This may have been a reflection of Mississippi's official intransigence and the weakness of the Mississippi black educational community.

Most of the tuition grants could be used for courses that were not available at the state's black institutions but were available within the state's white university system. The tuition grant programs, like other aspects of the Jim Crow system, were manifestly inadequate and unfair (see Table 6–3).[25] Most of the programs paid for just the difference in tuition costs between the state system and the out-of-state system; only a few states paid for tuition differentials or travel. Even fewer paid for living expenses.

Complicating these programs was the role of private black colleges and universities. Three states—Tennessee, Georgia, and Alabama—offered in-state tuition grants to these private institutions for students interested in programs not offered at the black public institution or within the white university system. Virginia and a few other states entered into contracts with Meharry Medical College and later Tuskegee Institute to provide a set number of slots in their programs for state residents.[26]

The states varied in terms of funding for the programs (see Table 6–3). For example, in 1944 Delaware and West Virginia had the lowest appropriations among the states that offered the program: $5,000 and $9,000, respectively. By contrast, Missouri appropriated $30,000, Maryland $35,000, and Virginia $40,000. By 1949 the average appropriation was about $35,000, a figure dwarfed by the millions of dollars spent on in-state higher education for whites.[27]

The administration of the grant program demonstrated another aspect of the *Gaines* dilemma. While many of the states vested control over the grant approval process within the state (and white-controlled) board of education, other states placed the administration in the hands of the board of trustees of the black public institutions (see Table 6–3). This latter action thus opened the possibility of some black control over educational funding. Indeed in

Table 6–3 Southern Out-of-State Tuition Grant Programs

State	Appropriation ($) 1944	1949	Grant Scope	Administration
Alabama		25,000	1[a]	DOE
Arkansas	5,000	35,000	1	DOE
Delaware		3,600	1	DOE
Florida		40,000	1/2	DOE
Georgia		35,000	[a]	DOE
Kentucky	10,000	40,000	1	DOE/BCU
Louisiana		50,000	1/2/3[a]	DOE
Maryland	25,000	40,000	1/2/3	BCU
Mississippi		NA		DOE
Missouri	30,000	20,000	1	BCU
North Carolina	15,000	32,625	1/3	BCU
Oklahoma	15,000	50,000	1/3	DOE
South Carolina		10,000	[b]	DOE
Tennessee		NA	1/3[a]	DOE/ Coordinator Negro Higher Education Committee
Texas	25,000	NA	1/2/3	
Virginia	40,000	95,000	1/2/3[c]	BCU
West Virginia	9,000	7,500	1	DOE/Supervisor of Negro Schools

1 = tuition; 2 = transportation; 3 = living expenses; DOE = Department of Education; BCU = black college or university.
[a] In-state tuition grants to private BCU.
[b] Limited to medical and dental students.
[c] Requires 20 grants to be applied to Meharry Medical College (1944).

Missouri and Virginia direct control was placed in the hands of administrators of a designated black public institution. In Tennessee, although direct control was given to African Americans (at Tennessee A&I), administrators had to take grants out of the institution's annual appropriation. As one observer noted, "Needless to say, few scholarships are actually available for Negroes in Tennessee."[28]

Making the situation even more problematic was that in most cases grants were not automatically given; students had to apply for them. This meant that whites could limit access to higher education to "safe" students. For example, Kentucky students were required to "sign a 'waiver' of any rights to equal education in the State of Kentucky" in order to receive any funds.[29] In the few cases where African American administrators had gained a means of control over access to higher education, this meant that frustration over limited access to graduate education was deflected and directed onto the shoulders of black administrators rather than onto the system that set up the inequities in the first place. Given these circumstances, the African Americans administering these programs undertook a "yeoman's assignment" in trying to fairly administer a program that was inherently unfair and inadequate.[30]

Whether for in- or out-of-state use, most grants were small, sometimes not paying for the full academic year. The majority of grants were for graduate training in education, medicine, and law. Indeed given the high costs of creating separate institutions for the latter two professions, some states began to restrict grants to just those professional programs. None of the programs paid the true cost of attending school out of state. And of course none of these programs could compensate for the lost opportunity cost of developing local professional networks or access to local employment markets. Indeed it is these latter points that the U.S. Supreme Court would use in *Sweatt v. Painter* (1950), a case that ultimately ended the constitutional basis for separate and equal graduate and professional education.

The Case of Virginia

Virginia is one of the few states where administrative records of the out-of-state tuition grant program still exist. This section briefly presents some aspects of the Virginia program as a way of further highlighting the complex role that black higher educational institutions and local politics played in the struggle against segregation.

Virginia State College (now university) was founded in 1882 as Virginia Normal and Collegiate Institute. In keeping with the growing conservatism of the early Jim Crow era, in 1902 the state stripped the school of its status as a baccalaureate degree–granting institution.[31] Its status was restored in 1922, when it also became the recipient of land grant status; it was the only public institution for African Americans in Virginia. Compared to the ten other public institutions for whites in Virginia, it was massively underfunded. From 1920 to 1930 the average per capita spending on higher education for African Americans was $.56 ($6.54 in 2005 dollars), while the average per capita spending on whites was $4.64 ($54.20).[32]

In 1935, on the heels of the *Murray* decision, one African American attempted to change this unequal system. Alice C. Jackson applied to and was subsequently rejected from the all-white University of Virginia.[33] The possibility that Jackson's rejected application could lead to lawsuits prompted the state of Virginia to enact the Educational Equality Act (1936), which provided "equal educational facilities for certain persons denied admission to Virginia state colleges and universities and institutions of higher learning."[34] The act created a graduate program at Virginia State

College and an out-of-state tuition grant program. The act also did what the white leadership wanted and black leadership feared: the decision, by thirty students and Jackson herself, to accept out-of-state tuition grants left the NAACP without a plaintiff to contest Jackson's rejection from the University of Virginia. One African American at the time likened the students who accepted the grants to Judas and criticized the African American leaders who accepted Virginia's "sop."[35] Thus for the moment the state of Virginia had put off a *Gaines*-type lawsuit and had effectively split African American leadership.

The creation of these programs was not imposed on a wholly unwilling Virginia State. Its president, John Gandy, allegedly lobbied numerous states to designate his institution as a regional institution for African Americans. Although Gandy was not successful in that endeavor, he was successful in lobbying for the creation of the tuition grant program. In 1940 control over the grant program was handed to Virginia State.[36]

The Structure of Virginia's Program

One of the most interesting characteristics of the Virginia grant program was its relatively long duration; it ran from 1936 to 1967. In the first year 128 students received grants (see Figure 6–1). The program would reach its pre-*Brown* height of 647 students in 1949. The program's largest expansion came in 1958, four years after *Brown*, with 695 students receiving grants. By 1967 there had been a steady decline in the number of students applying for grants. Although there was no discussion of this in the Virginia records, this decline perhaps reflects the increased opportunities and funding available for graduate work in Virginia and elsewhere for African Americans. The program began with $9,357 ($133,280 in 2005 dollars) in funding (see Figure 6–2). Funding eventually plateaued at around $190,000 (about $1.1 million in 2005 dollars) per year until 1967. This was of course a fraction of the money spent on graduate education for whites in Virginia.

The second characteristic of the Virginia program was that it was part of another southern strategy—the creation of regional programs—to avoid the cost of setting up expensive professional schools, especially in the medical field.[37] Under the auspices of the Southern Regional Education Board (discussed in the next chapter) in 1945 Virginia contracted with Meharry Medical College to provide medical education for nineteen doctors and dentists at a total cost of $9,100. In 1950 the program was expanded to include Tuskegee's veterinary program. Like the general graduate fund, much of the growth in the number of students served and in funding available occurred *after* 1954.[38]

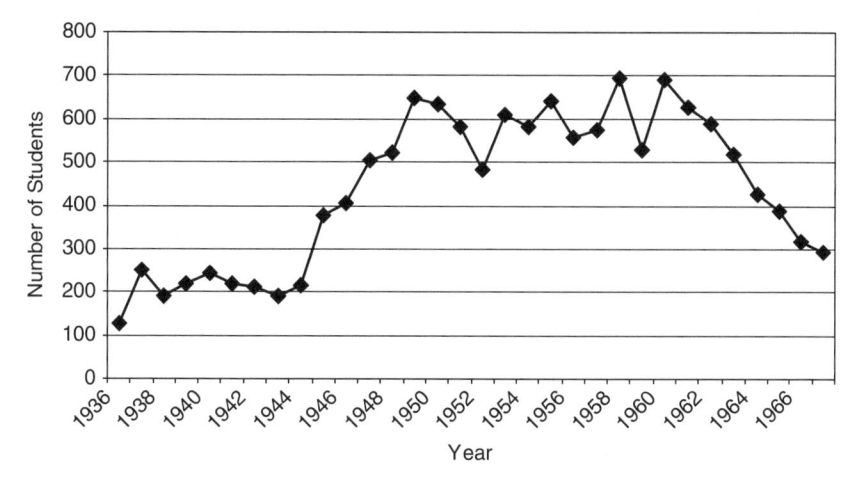

Figure 6–1 Virginia Students Granted Out-of-State Tuition Grants
Source: Capps, "Virginia Out-of-State," 29; and Virginia State College, *Annual Report, Graduate Aid Fund*, 1945 through 1967.

The strange dualism of Virginia medical education reached its height in 1961, when the state medical college enrolled twenty-five African American students, while the Aid Fund also supported twenty-five students. From 1945 to 1967 the program funded the education of approximately 130 doctors and dentists. In a state where only 248 of Virginia's 2,400 physicians were African Americans (in 1948), this was an important development.[39]

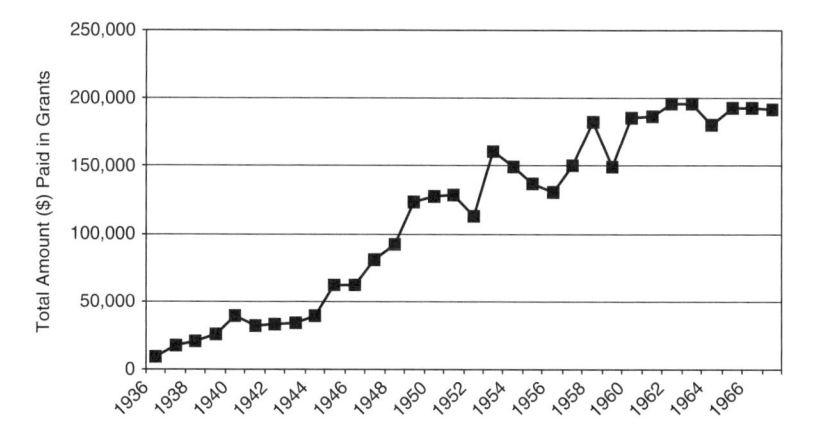

Figure 6–2 Virginia Students Granted Out-of-State Tuition Grants
Source: Capps, "Virginia Out-of-State," 29; and Virginia State College, *Annual Report, Graduate Aid Fund*, 1945 through 1967.

The growth in numbers of students and funding reflected the growing demand for professional education among African Americans. The program's persistence reflected the continued existence of a dual system of higher education in Virginia, with the bulk of African American graduate students still going out of state despite, or perhaps because of the token creation of a graduate program at Virginia State and the token admittance of one or two African American students at Virginia's white institutions.

The End of Equalization and the Beginning of Integration

Many African Americans had greeted the higher education equalization cases as a significant victory in the battle against Jim Crow. Charles Houston, the lead lawyer on the *Gaines* case, said that it "'completely knocked out as a permanent policy' the practice of paying Negro students' tuition in other States in place of giving them schooling in their home States."[40] Others were less optimistic about the overall transformative impact of *Gaines* on southern higher education. Within activist and elite circles the response was tempered and even dismissive. For example, Ralph Bunche dismissed the decision as merely one of the NAACP's "pyrrhic victories."[41]

The most consistent coverage of the impact of *Gaines* on African American higher education was in the *Journal of Negro Education.* Charles Thompson, the editor of the *Journal* and a professor at Howard University, voiced the uneasiness and dissatisfaction of the African American educational community over the state governments' response to *Gaines*. According to Thompson, "[African Americans] have been divided on the questions; some quite honestly and others because of vested interest."[42] In particular the traditional groups of college presidents that were part of the Jim Crow reform coalition quietly disagreed over "the question," as some of their institutions, such as Fisk and Atlanta University, clearly benefited from state-sponsored equalization.

Efforts by African American administrators to work within the system created by *Gaines* were increasingly condemned by African American educational leadership. For example, the *Journal of Negro Education* reprinted the "Recommendation of an Out-of State Scholarship Fund for Negroes in Florida," drafted by William H. Gray, the president of Florida A&M College, and adopted by the state of Florida in 1945. According to the editor's note, the report was published "as an illustration of how these things happen, of the basic premises from which one proceeds in making them, and of *the part some Negro educators play in their making*" (emphasis added).[43]

However, the *Journal* editor was not totally unsympathetic, acknowledging, "[The] president of a Negro publicly-controlled college…finds himself in a delicate position." But he added, "While we do not expect any president of a Negro college to talk himself out of a job; neither do we expect (nor can we allow) him to cut the ground out from under our fight by irresponsible talk or ill advised action."[44]

Most critics focused on what they called the "makeshift" character of these graduate programs and their schools. One argued that if not for the "intelligent and skilled leadership of these institutions," a much larger crisis in black higher education would have developed.[45] For Horace Mann Bond, *Gaines* "telescop[ed] within a decade a development that was fifty years overdue." As a result, according to Bond, there was a "'bull market' in formerly despised Negro teachers; [a] frantic effort to assemble faculties studded with Ph.D.'s; [and a] skyrocketing of salaries for Negro teachers on all levels; these have their seriocomic aspects as well as their heartening values." His criticism of these programs is even more damning, likening them to "mushroom growths, unencumbered by the usual impedimenta of the higher and graduate learning, such as books and laboratories and learned research scholars, to assume the stature of 'graduate school.'"[46]

Other critics were even less generous. Mojdeska Simkins, a South Carolina NAACP leader, heaped scorn on what she dubbed the "so-called '*Graduate School*'" of South Carolina; in her view, "administrative officials at the college consort[ed] with legislative and education department officials in hoodwinking the few shortsighted Negroes who fall victim to the asinine scheme."[47]

Thus by 1950 the cautious endorsement of the *Gaines* approach to higher education for African Americans—equalization—came to end. The *Gaines* decision, hailed as a decisive victory in 1938, was dismissed as a "fiasco" twelve years later as the modern civil rights movement emerged and the boundaries of the Jim Crow order were no longer as the end of change but the begining.[48] Despite the efforts of southern governments, the contradictions of *Gaines* as well as the simple injustice of the South's response to it—creating a class of exiled students—would prove be a motivating force in creating a more cohesive approach within the African American higher education community. The NAACP announced a full frontal assault on *Plessy* and on segregation. The *Gaines* model, developed in an earlier political, social, and economic time and place, was seen as completely unsuited for the demands of the new movement.

By 1949 five southern border states (Arkansas, Delaware, Kentucky, Oklahoma, and West Virginia) had given up the *Gaines* equalization approach. Faced with the reality of creating equal facilities for relatively small African American populations and with the prospect of more litigation (and in the case of Oklahoma, two lawsuits lost by the state), it was easier to allow limited quiet desegregation of graduate schools to begin.

Other states continued to pursue a *Gaines* approach, with the exception of Mississippi, which refused to provide anything for its African American citizens.

The Collapse of Equalization Reform

The mixed response of southern black educational leaders and civil rights activists to the dilemmas of *Gaines* reflected the rapidly apparent limitations of Jim Crow reform. For African Americans, publicly embracing *Gaines* could send multiple and sometimes conflicting signals. Was support of *Gaines* a signal that black educators and other citizens endorsed the Jim Crow system, or was it simply a case of shortsighted opportunism? Or was the embrace of *Gaines* a sign that these administrators were eager to use the case as a strategic means to subvert the Jim Crow system?

Making it even harder to discern motives and understand actions is the fact that each state presented its own set of political, social, and institutional arrangements. Thus both Virginia's and North Carolina's early embrace of these limited equalization programs reflected each state's "managed race relations" approach. Mississippi, Alabama, and Georgia, which had refused to develop any meaningful equalization programs, would repeat this pattern with their intransigence toward integration of white higher educational institutions.

In the end, for some states timing and, as the NAACP hoped, logistics made the *Gaines* equalization approach to black higher education increasingly unfeasible by the end of the 1940s. With the availability of the G.I. bill, African Americans by the thousands attempted to enter graduate (and undergraduate) programs. No state was willing or able to meet that demand under the *Gaines* equalization program. In 1950 those southern states that had not already done so faced the issue that *Gaines* had allowed them to evade: integration.

The politics of massive resistance halted any further attempts to desegregate Virginia's higher education system. Virginia's tuition grant program continued to function despite the *Brown v. Board of Education* (1954) decision and despite rulings in 1955 by the state supreme court and by the state's attorney general that it was unconstitutional for the state to use public funds to pay private school tuition.[49] The grant program remained in operation until *Green v. County School Board of New Kent County* (1968), which ended Virginia's refusal to meaningfully desegregate its higher education institutions.

The long duration of the tuition grant program in Virginia was just one of the tools that the state used to engage in its campaign of massive resistance. The roots of this ability to defy the meaningful desegregation of higher education in Virginia lay partially in the Gandy administration in the 1930s and its willingness to first support the creation of the program, and its later acceptance of administrative responsibility. To be fair, as a publicly supported institution Virginia State did not really have a choice. The state of Virginia bears most of the responsibility for the lack of desegregation. With those most likely to benefit from desegregation shipped out of state, and given all the other battlefronts in the civil rights struggle, the meaningful desegregation of all of the state's higher education institutions could be put off.

Whatever the reasons given for embracing or resisting the possible benefits of *Gaines*, the impact on individual African American students was significant. As seen in the case of Virginia, hundreds of African American students were able to access graduate school. The majority of these students became teachers; others became doctors, lawyers, and other professionals. Indeed the law schools were critically important in developing a new generation of southern African American lawyers, a group that had almost completely disappeared in the Jim Crow South. However, by not pressing southern governments to make good on these early equalization rulings, the NAACP and its allies hoped to use the continued inequality of black education as leverage in their ongoing struggle to overturn the Jim Crow order. The costs of this struggle would be born by African American students and communities. Some, such as Lloyd Gaines, Charles Bailey, and Thomas Hocutt, would see dreams remain unfilled. Gaines disappeared under mysterious circumstances before his appeal. Bailey, who had threatened a lawsuit against South Carolina in 1938, gave up his quest to become admitted to the state's law school (where his grandfather had graduated in 1876) and accepted a position with the U.S. Post Office. In 1933 Thomas Hocutt, who filed one of the first higher education equalization lawsuits against a southern state, gave up plans for a career as a pharmacist, moved to New York City, and worked in its subway system as a motorman.[50]

Despite the African American educational leadership's disavowal of *Gaines*, the case's legacies remain. Black higher education institutions at the beginning of the *Brown* era found themselves on a much firmer fiscal, academic, and institutional footing, partly as a result of the equalization efforts spurred on by *Gaines* and southern governments' fear of impending change. The time, effort, and resources put into the building up of these institutions would not easily disappear with the onset of the end of de jure segregation. Southern governments used these institutions as bulwarks to delay meaningful desegregation. Black colleges and universities were loath to give up a special identity in favor of a one-way desegregation that negated the very real role that these institutions played in the African American community. The next chapter examines the efforts by white Jim Crow reformers to reshape higher education in the South against the backdrop of change occurring both within and outside of the Jim Crow order. Unlike the past, these changes and challenges created new pressures to which white Jim Crow reformers were increasingly unable to accommodate and adapt.

Chapter 7

Building the Jim Crow University System

> For the life of me, I can't see why, if the Negroes in Texas refuse to accept a $100,000 law school in a three and a half million dollar university that the Negroes in South Carolina would accept a $10,000 law school in a $1.50 university.
>
> Thurgood Marshall, quoted in Burke and Hine, "The School of Law at South Carolina State College"

Jim Crow reformers were deeply interested in strengthening southern institutions of higher education. In many ways education was central to their vision of stabilizing and elaborating the Jim Crow order, and these institutions played an important role in this. Not only did southern universities and colleges provide intellectual space and financial resources for individual reformers; these institutions were also important sources of legitimacy and authority that reformers would collectively draw on and use to advance their agenda. Using southern universities Jim Crow reformers created a new southern ideology of race relations and interracialism, which preached that reform inspired by social science coupled with mutual tolerance could create a harmoniously segregated order. Black colleges and universities would provide the middle-class leadership necessary to help govern a new vertical segregation, which would be more just for southern blacks but still secure for southern whites. During the New Deal university-based reformers led a movement to mobilize the South's human resources under the aegis of government reinvigorated by efficient and rational planning.

During the late 1940s there was a shifting in the ideological and political terrain on which a foundation-led restructuring of the southern higher education system had rested. Yet even as attempts to strengthen southern higher education proceeded, Jim Crow reformers were losing whatever cohesiveness they had once possessed on the issue of education. African Americans were increasing unwilling to play a deferential role in education reform. The strengthening of southern black social capital and social citizenship, which had emerged as a result of earlier foundation funding of primary and undergraduate education, began to be increasingly felt. African American teachers organizations and administrators began to more openly lobby and then litigate for the meaningful equalization of education at all levels. They then allied themselves with the NAACP, which many white Jim Crow reformers were either deeply suspicious of, if not hostile toward. Outside of the Jim Crow order the New Deal and later World War II led to a variety of political and ideological changes at the national level: the federal judiciary began to look more sympathetically at these equalization claims, the white liberal establishment began to more openly embrace racial equality, and groups such as the NAACP began in the late 1940s to openly reject equalization approaches in favor of a more radical integrationist approach.

Both southern whites and blacks were forced to grapple with equalization and the role it would play in the survival of the Jim Crow order. For southern blacks this meant a bitter struggle over tactics and strategies. Could equalization be a viable strategy alongside of integration, or did equalization further legitimize an order that was increasingly under open attack? There were white southerners, admittedly few, who for a variety of reasons felt that the South had to live up to the separate and equal provisions of *Plessy*. Making segregation more equal was important not only because they believed it was the right thing to do in the context of the Jim Crow order, but because they hoped it would prevent further attacks on the system by demonstrating the South's own good faith efforts. In his 1938 report to the Board of Regents of the University System of Georgia, Dean Walter D. Cocking (who would later be attacked by Eugene Talmadge for being soft on segregation) stated that although "no facilities for graduate work [would] be provided in the public Negro colleges in the near future...it [was] fair and just that the State should provide higher educational advantages to all citizens."[1]

In the late 1940s, among conservative whites especially, the reluctance to support any higher education for blacks and whites was influenced by their desire to encourage the economic boom that had begun to transform the

South during the war. Adding to the pressure of economic development was the new G.I. Bill, which sent hundreds of thousands of southern whites and blacks into the region's underfinanced and physically antiquated institutions. The pressure was particularly acute at the graduate and professional school levels, where there were not nearly enough spaces given the demand. Developing adequate graduate programs for whites, let alone blacks, was cumbersome and expensive. Yet if southern universities did not address this demand, students would go elsewhere. Policymakers feared that this would result in a massive brain drain and that the South's postwar economic transformation would be threatened.

White southern politicians cast about for ways to address the needs of the vast number of new students while at the same time stave off increasingly effective claims for equalization of funding between white and black institutions. The solution politicians settled on was a proposal that Jim Crow reformers and their foundation allies had been advocating for at least two decades: the creation of a regional university system that was still separate but more rational and efficient. Yet the alignment of political will with the wishes of Jim Crow reformers was too late. The educational technocrats were making their apolitical attempts to rationalize the Jim Crow order in the middle of increasingly bitter political and moral battles over the survival of the Jim Crow order itself.

The struggle to reshape higher education in the South reflected tensions between whites over the future of the Jim Crow order; it also reflected emerging tensions within the African American community about which strategy was best to overturn the order. For southern blacks, largely led by black Jim Crow reformers, equalization was a critical first step toward developing greater opportunities for blacks within the order. Many educational leaders acknowledged that equalization initially strengthened the order, yet black reformers also believed that it provided the means by which to slowly assault the order from within. This stance would come into conflict with the stance of other southern blacks who were increasingly and publicly cynical about white reformers' promises to get the white South to meet them halfway. The gradualist approach would also come into conflict with the changing strategy of an increasingly effective NAACP, which was aggressively regrouping in the South in terms of membership and organizational strength. The rise of the NAACP posed an immediate challenge to the older black Jim Crow reformers, who had shaped higher education policy for blacks in the south. The longer challenge was between two different strategies to confront the Jim Crow order: one, espoused by Jim Crow reformers, largely worked within the order, while the other strategy attacked the order itself.

Restructuring Southern Higher Education

The rise of the Jim Crow order coincided with a period of intense debate and rising tensions over the mission of higher education for whites and blacks in the South. These tensions cut across the region's white political and social elites. Some saw the university's central constituency as the traditional southern white elite and believed that the focus of the university should be the traditional liberal arts. Others saw the new modern university as a resource for the region's emerging urban middle classes, or the state itself, with a curriculum focused on the applied sciences. Unlike the debate over higher education for blacks, the debate over higher education for whites was more complex and considered. To the extent that a similar argument over black higher education took place among whites, it was based on the degree to which higher education for blacks should perfect the Jim Crow order by supplying suitable blacks versed in managing the order's race relations.

In the late 1920s these tensions were abating. A division of academic labor was emerging in the world of white higher education. Aided in part by targeted northern foundation funding, a small group of southern public and private universities (the University of Virginia, the University of North Carolina, Duke and Emory Universities) were drawing closer—though not equal—to the elite institutions of the Northeast. Outside of this elite circle were the bulk of the South's public and private higher education institutions for whites. These institutions were arrayed along a spectrum of adequate to abysmal in terms of quality and resources. Resources available to these institutions (measured by value of the physical plant, numbers of qualified faculty, and availability of student services) remained limited. Public institutions were highly dependent on state legislatures, which had historically exhibited weak political as well as fiscal support for higher education, especially for education that was not perceived as increasing the economic capacity of the state.[2]

Beginning in the 1920s the GEB pursued a two-pronged approach that directly addressed what foundations and others felt was a chronic underinvestment in higher education in the South. The South's best and brightest, which implied mostly whites but also included blacks, were forced to leave the South for adequate graduate education and professional training. Once these individuals left, they were unlikely to return, resulting in a regional brain drain that would hamper the South's development efforts.[3]

Led by the GEB but with the involvement of the Rockefeller-created Laura Spelman Rockefeller Memorial, the Kellogg Foundation, and the Carnegie Corporation, the first step in solving the South's higher education deficit was a targeted focus on individual institutions. The South would be best served through the creation of flagship universities. These "centers of excellence" would be the beacon for the rest of the South and stand as symbols of the South's untapped capacities. It was a given that there would be separate universities: an elite circle of schools such as the University of Virginia, the University of North Carolina, and Duke University for whites; and for blacks Howard, Fisk, Atlanta, and Dillard.[4] Howard Odum was one of the champions of this approach. In his classic work, *Southern Regions*, he argued that the South needed "at least five [superior] universities for whites and one for Negroes."[5] Despite his focus on institutional excellence, Odum's allotment of universities reflected the hierarchy of the Jim Crow order. There still existed two distinct and significantly unequal institutions: those for whites and those for blacks. The final report of the GEB reflected this by now unsurprising inequality: approximately $208 million was spent on white higher education institutions, while only $56 million was spent on black institutions.

The second foundation-led approach viewed southern higher education as an organic whole. Unlike other areas of the country, such as the Northeast, foundation personnel saw in the South a chance to create a higher education system that would be more in tune with the needs of an expanding nation. The crown jewel of this rationalized system would be the centers of excellence, the white and black flagship universities of the South. Later the vision would embed these centers within a comprehensive regional university system.[6]

The development of foundation-created and -supported southern centers of excellence as well as a regional university system would gradually intersect with another unanticipated consequence of foundation efforts. In addition to the overall strengthening of southern higher education, northern foundations had earlier made a commitment to professional education for blacks. However, efforts to improve graduate education for blacks was increasingly out of the hands of white Jim Crow reformers as African Americans began to press southern state governments to improve access to graduate education. As was seen in the previous chapter, lobbying by African American teachers and educators and litigation such as the *Gaines v. Canada* case made efforts to rationalize southern higher education along the lines and the timing preferred by white Jim Crow reformers increasingly difficult. As the focus of these equalization efforts turned to the establishment of graduate and professional schools, the conflict with the foundations' goals became even starker, while the rift between whites' and blacks' (and between conservatives' and more activist blacks') understandings of the boundaries of Jim Crow reform became even wider.

Problematic Victories: The Development of Graduate Programs

The black Jim Crow reform leadership and the NAACP shared the goal of establishing graduate programs and especially professional schools for blacks. The support of many southern blacks for the establishment of these professional schools was straightforward: out-of-state tuition grants simply could not cover the true cost of attending school out of state and could serve only a fraction of the demand, which was increasing every year due to the upgrading of black undergraduate programs and the impact of the G.I. Bill. The establishment of these programs was in direct response to *Gaines* and other equalization suits that were still being filed, despite the NAACP's limited involvement. As seen in the previous chapter, the range of these programs was fairly narrow. Most states that offered graduate programs did so in the area of education, reflecting demand from the South's largest group of African American professionals. The provision of education programs also reflected state government attempts to create better-qualified African American teachers. These qualified (but never quite equal) teachers would buttress white southerners' arguments that the states were eager and able to provide better educational opportunities to black students in a segregated system.[7]

Although the NAACP strategy was also focused on using equalization as a means of undermining the Jim Crow order, in the late 1940s the organization's strategy shifted to a direct attack on the order. By focusing on forcing the South into the establishment of comparable graduate programs for African Americans at public institutions, the NAACP hoped to maneuver southern states into one of two choices: they could either make massive, unaffordable, and in the long run unsustainable investments in separate institutions, or they could integrate. As the NAACP anticipated, at least in the case of law schools, states that attempted to create separate and plausibly equal institutions would largely fail in their attempts. These failures would hand the NAACP even more ammunition to eventually argue that separate *could never be* equal. To make this argument, however, the organization would have to convince southern blacks that equalization was a flawed strategy, while also encouraging blacks to attend these schools in order to sustain the financial pressure. As Charles Thompson argued, southern blacks were caught on the edge of two strategies. In the absence of a social movement, they were also asked to forgo what was normal for American society: the chance for individual progress and achievement and possibilities for institutional advancement with only a vague hope that conditions would change and a new political window would one day open up. *Brown* still lay in the future; before them lay the reality of the Jim Crow order.

Jim Crow Law Schools

On the heels of the *Gaines* decision, Missouri state officials attempted to head off any more attempts at integration. The state legislature introduced and passed the Taylor Bill in 1939, authorizing Lincoln University, the state's sole black land grant university, to "establish whatever graduate and professional schools [were] necessary to make Lincoln University the equivalent of the University of Missouri" and appropriated $200,000 out of special funds to accomplish this purpose.[8] Lincoln University was then told to create a school for Lloyd Gaines to enroll in the following fall. Beyond the actions of the state legislature, many within the state's black community expressed deep skepticism that any of those monies would actually appear.

The skepticism was not wholly misplaced. The Lincoln University Law School created to accommodate Gaines was established in a rented room in St. Louis and furnished with a recently bought ten-thousand-volume law library. Five individuals were hired: a dean from Howard University and four faculty members. Lincoln University's law school, called by one critic "the smallest law school in the world," was clearly a second-class institution compared to the University of Missouri Law School.[9] Reflecting its shortcomings, the law school proved relatively short-lived; it briefly closed in 1943 due to a lack of "properly accredited students," reopened in 1944, and then closed for good in 1955.[10] In 1950 the University of Missouri was integrated under court order, seriously weakening the more makeshift graduate programs at Lincoln.

For William E. Taylor, who served as the first dean of the Lincoln University Law School, and the other faculty, the dilemma of *Gaines* must have been painfully obvious. For ambitious legal scholars and administrators, outside of the limited and extremely competitive opportunities offered by Howard University and the practically nonexistent opportunities available in white universities, there was no other comparable academic position than that offered by Lincoln and the other Jim Crow law schools.[11] At the same time, as Texas was creating its law for blacks, administrators there looked to Lincoln faculty and graduates to staff the new law school.

The drive to expand graduate and professional education for African Americans was gingerly grasped by some African American administrators. James Shepard used the threat of litigation (such as the *Hocutt* case) as well as real cases such as *Gaines* to expand the offerings at North Carolina College for Negroes. In 1939 he succeeded in creating the North Carolina College of Law. Its makeshift character was similar to Missouri's. It was a two-room operation located in the college's administration building; one room housed the law school library, which remained partially unpacked due to lack of space, and also functioned as its classroom, and the second room was an office for the Law School dean.[12]

South Carolina state officials fared somewhat better in their attempts to create a separate law school at the South Carolina State College for Negroes (SCSCN). For much of the institution's history it had provided mostly industrial education and teaching certificates. Only in 1924 did it gain the right to grant baccalaureate degrees. The Depression hid the college hard, as it did other black educational institutions. In 1932 the president of the college reported that the school was virtually penniless.[13] Despite this weak educational foundation, in 1939, in response to the *Gaines* suit, state legislators proposed an out-of-state tuition program and the creation of a law chair at SCSCN.[14] In 1945 the state legislature finally authorized but did not fund a tuition grant program; it did, however, authorize $60,000 for the establishment of a graduate school and a law school at SCSCN.[15]

The state's hand was forced when John Wrighten III, a graduate of South Carolina State and a World War II veteran, sued the University of South Carolina Law School for admittance. Lawyers for the NAACP, including Thurgood Marshall, argued Wrighten's case. As had other states, it was clear that South Carolina would attempt to create a separate law school rather than integrate. The result of this exercise could potentially be a law school that existed in name only. Miller Whittaker, the president of SCSCN, emphasized as much, testifying in court that a law school could not be set up in less than six months and that it would not be the "full and complete equal of the law school at the University of South Carolina."[16] Despite this resistance from South Carolina blacks to the establishment of a makeshift law school, the desire of the state to quash any attempts at integration was upheld by Judge J. Waties Waring. Although he had a growing reputation a racial moderate and even declared that it was "almost impossible to intellectually compare" the proposed new law school with the USC law school, Waring ruled that the state via SCSCN be given the chance to try.[17]

South Carolina's Negro law school opened in 1947 with a dean hired from the relatively newly established black North Carolina Central College of Law. Two other professors were hired, one doubling as the law librarian. The law school and its library were located in one classroom of the SCSCN college library. Nine students (five full time and four part time) were enrolled.[18] Although blacks in South Carolina had not been united in the support of any of these programs, once these schools started operation they offered new opportunities for both students and educators. Open support by blacks of the new graduate programs reportedly infuriated Thurgood Marshall, who could not see why South Carolina's blacks were willing to support the barebones "$1.50" law school created at SCSCN by the state. Despite Marshall's condemnation, Wrighten, who had sued for admission to *a* law school, enrolled in 1949 and graduated three years later. He became one of the state's leading civil rights lawyers.[19]

Louisiana's law school, established at Southern University, was also small and woefully underfunded. According to the historian Richard Kluger, the state's Jim Crow law school was "missing a few things, like a library." The law school also lacked a faculty member "qualified to teach the Napoleonic legal code, peculiar to Louisiana, so that no black graduate of Southern would be able to practice in the state."[20]

The situation in Oklahoma was in some ways similar to Missouri's. Ada Sipuel was a graduate of Langston University, the state's black public land grant institution.[21] Like Gaines, for personal, professional, and financial reasons and in the absence of a separate law school for blacks, Sipuel wanted to attend the University of Oklahoma law school. She was denied admission due to her race, and with the aid of the NAACP (who considered her an ideal plaintiff) filed suit.[22] The state's response to Sipuel's application and the ruling by the state supreme court, which supported the university's position, was to create the Langston University College of Law, which was to be established in a separate section of the state capitol building. In this roped-off area were three instructors, three classrooms, and separate access to the state capital's law library. It closed within a year after it was opened as a result of the Supreme Court's decision that the Langston school did not offer Sipuel an education equivalent to that offered to whites, and thus she was entitled to attend the University of Oklahoma law school.[23]

As a result of the ruling Sipuel was allowed to enter the University of Oklahoma under a highly constrained manner: she was forced to sit at separate tables in the classroom, library, and cafeteria and was accompanied by guards who ensured that neither she nor white students transgressed the boundaries. This roped-off strategy of segregation came to an end with another court ruling, *McLaurin v. Oklahoma State Regents for Higher Education* (339 U.S. 637, 1950). George McLaurin successfully challenged the University of Oklahoma's attempt to segregate within a doctoral education program, requiring him to sit at a separate section in the classroom and at a separate table in the library and cafeteria. The U.S. Supreme Court rejected Oklahoma's approach in 1950. What made the impact of these suits even stronger was the university's slow realization that providing a separate comprehensive graduate program for Oklahoma's relatively small African American population would be ruinously expensive and administratively unfeasible and that most of the students at the university were not overly resistant to limited graduate school integration.

The *McLaurin* ruling came on the same day as *Sweatt v. Painter*, which cleared the way for the NAACP to develop a clear line of attack on *Plessy*, and subsequently on the Jim Crow order. The *Sweatt v. Painter* case came as a result of a decades-long attempt by Texas African American teachers, black civic groups, and white reformer allies to force the state to live up to one of the provisions of its constitution: the provision of a university comparable to the University of Texas for the state's black population.

The Case of Texas: The Beginning of the End of Equalization

The Texas CIC, originally headed by Jessie Daniel Ames, took an early interest in higher education for blacks. Like other state CICs and individual southern reformers, it did not advocate for racial integration. Rather, in the words of Carter Wesley, the African American newspaper publisher, he and the other Jim Crow reformers took a "realistic approach": "[We did not] concern ourselves with the elimination of segregation in Texas schools."[24] The CIC's efforts were paralleled by the Texas Colored Teachers Association (CTA), which would lobby with the CIC for educational reforms.

The CIC advocated for higher state spending for Prairie View A&M, which was then considered an adjunct of, and decidedly subordinate to, Texas A&M University. When Texas state legislators attempted to turn the presidency of the institution into a political spoil, the CIC, along with black educators, were able to beat back this attempt and have the presidency remain in the hands of an educational administrator. The CIC also credited itself with influencing Texas legislators to make the first appropriation for graduate aid for blacks in 1923. In 1935 and 1936 the CIC and the CTA lobbied the state legislature to create a permanent appropriation for out-of state aid, as had been done in neighboring Oklahoma. In 1939, with an eye on the *Gaines* decision but partly at the behest of the CIC and with the clear support of the Texas CTA, the legislature appropriated $50,000 for the program.[25]

Despite these initial gains, attempts to increase educational appropriations for higher education for blacks and for the establishment of real in-state graduate facilities for blacks were repeatedly rebuffed by the state legislature and governor. In their view, in the midst of first a depression and then a war, the needs of white schools had to come before the needs of black schools. By 1942 the CIC and educational groups had grown increasingly frustrated with this resistance; the CIC stated, "The problem of higher education of Negroes in Texas is too large to be dealt with in an adequate manner by this Commission." A more politically inclusive stance was suggested by the CIC, which recommended that the state establish a "[biracial] conference of outstanding educators, lawyers, statesmen, ministers and public spirited citizens...to agree upon a wise program and course of action." The state did appoint a five-member commission. One of the two African Americans on the commission was Dr. W. R. Banks, the principal emeritus of Prairie View and a member of the Texas CIC. Not surprisingly the report issued by the commission suggested a continuation of the scholarship program, the establishment of graduate and professional schools at Prairie View, and making more funds available to Prairie View in order for the institution to attract grants from the GEB, Carnegie, and Rosenwald Funds.[26]

By the early 1940s, however, the struggle for equalization was beginning to shift. African Americans were loath to relieve the state of its long-standing constitutional commitment to the creation of a superior university for its African American citizens. The state's white university officials kept a watchful eye on how other southern states grappled with the *Gaines* decision.[27] In 1945 the state legislature directed the University of Texas, in conjunction with Prairie View, to establish programs not offered at the University of Texas if a request for enrollment in a program was made.

In 1946 Heman Sweatt, with the support of the NAACP, filed a court case that would change the contours of the equalization debate for the whole South and initiate the end of white reformers' prominent role in shaping black higher education. The state's reaction to the threat posed by the *Sweatt* litigation was rapid, given its earlier reluctance to seriously address efforts to equalize higher education and to create a state university for blacks. After decades of lobbying, white officials rushed to set up the Texas State University for Negroes in Houston, which would house, in addition to a law school, a medical school for blacks. In the meantime a temporary law school funded by an emergency appropriation of $100,000 was set up in Austin, and a much larger and more permanent school established in Houston. The temporary law school, set up in six months, was small and clearly inadequate; it was located in a converted residence in Austin, the state capital. Its facilities consisted of two classrooms, a library stocked with ten thousand books on loan from the University of Texas law library, and three instructors also on loan from the University of Texas Law School. Plans were being made to recruit black faculty from graduates of northern law schools as well as from Howard and Lincoln Universities.

Despite this attempt to create a separate and somewhat equal law school, the black community of Texas—with some exceptions—decided to support the NAACP's attempt to essentially bring an end to equalization strategies. The role of Texas's African American teachers in the fight against the white primary and the subsequent *Smith v. Allwright* decision is well known to historians; less well known is the role of these teachers in supporting one of the key court cases in the pre-*Brown* era, *Sweatt v. Painter*. The path to *Sweatt* was coordinated and funded by three groups: the Texas Council on Negro Organizations (an umbrella group), the NAACP, and, the Texas Commission on Democracy in Education (TCDE), which was formed by the Texas CTA in 1941.[28] The objective of the TCDE was the "equalization of educational opportunity and participation [of blacks] in local state and federal agencies."

Teachers raised $5,000 to support the TCDE, and would later raise $12,000 for the Sweatt Victory Trust.[29] The U.S. Supreme Court decision in 1950, which rejected the separate but equal approach for graduate education, vindicated this support.

White Southerners and the Dilemmas of *Gaines*

Southern states deployed a number of strategies to respond to the increasing internal and external political pressure (and litigation) to make segregation more equal. Out-of-state tuition, bare-bones graduate programs, and nominal professional schools were used strategically to co-opt students, divide the African American community, and forestall future court cases. Yet even as they deployed these tactics, white politicians were coming to the realization that white reformers had already reached: institutional equalization between the races would be nearly impossible for perpetually poor states in the South to achieve. In search of other alternatives that did not involve integration, white policymakers grasped a policy alternative that had been at least a decade or so in the making: a proposal to create a system of regional education wherein the costs of funding modern higher education, for both whites and blacks, could be shared across the region. With great fanfare policymakers announced their support for the proposal at the Southern Governors Conference in 1945. Despite its focus on both white and black graduate education, civil rights activists immediately attacked the proposal as an attempt to create an end run around *Gaines*.

The regional higher education program rested on at least a decade's worth of analysis and planning supported by the GEB, the most influential of the foundations that shaped Jim Crow reform.[30] The reformers' problem, however, was that their rational approach was quickly overtaken by events. What had begun as an exercise in creating the next best solution within the confines of the Jim Crow order had lost its apolitical gloss. Defenders of the Jim Crow order saw the regional program as a way to defend that order by creating a new standard of legitimacy. Opponents of the Jim Crow order saw regional education as a symbol of the South's unwillingness to live up to the credo of separate and equal.

Cooperation and Co-optation: The Creation of the Southern Regional Education Board

The creation of a regional system of higher education was a topic that southern educational reform groups as well as the GEB had periodically turned their attention to. Organizations such as Southern Association of

Colleges and Secondary Schools, the Conferences of Deans of Southern Graduate Schools, and the Southern University Conference had from the 1920s periodically organized conferences on the idea. In the midst of the Depression education policymakers argued that regional cooperation was a way to "avoid duplication and sheer waste of money [while] working together to build formative centers of Education and Culture." Specific cooperative arrangements on both sides of the color line were held up as examples of how southern universities could get around the limitations imposed on them due to their small size and relatively weak financial position.[31]

The limitations of southern universities became even more apparent with the end of the war and the establishment of the G.I. Bill. Thousands of veterans, white and black, attempted to enroll in these institutions. White veterans encountered a higher education system that had been battered by the Depression and then had stagnated during the war. Facilities were overstretched, and spaces in some professional programs did not match the demand. The situation was dire for black veterans, as most states had underinvested in black institutions for decades; by and large these institutions lacked the facilities and space necessary to provide education. By 1945, seven years after the *Gaines* decision, there had been only piecemeal and largely cosmetic efforts at equalization at the graduate level.

Despite these drawbacks, specific examples of regional approaches to higher education had been developed. As discussed earlier in the book, with GEB support, political scientists at the University of Alabama created a Southern Regional Training Program, in which a group of southern universities together ran a master's degree program in public administration. By dint of location and interest, students in this program focused on the problems of the South. The political scientists who created the program were also involved in helping Governor Chauncey Sparks reform Alabama government along more efficient lines. They also were heavily involved in elaborating on the TVA ideal, the coupling of a belief that problems of the South could be addressed through rational (i.e., government) planning and cooperation.

The GEB-sponsored plan of creating a regional network of centers of excellence also influenced the crafting of this policy. In the 1930s support for the targeted strengthening of individual institutions expanded into more explicit support for a comprehensive regional university system. Supporters of this regional system generally made their case based on a newly revived sense of southern regionalism and on efficiency grounds.[32] Howard Odum, who was one of the most conservative of the Jim Crow reformers, not only supported the creation of a regional system of flagship universities but also suggested that "a special development would provide for inter-institutional education of Negroes in three or four of these institutions."[33] Odum's support for these flagship universities as well as an unspecified form of interracial, interinstitutional arrangement reflected the emerging belief that the South's problems could be addressed only by regional solutions.[34]

In 1945 both southern educators and southern politicians examined the issue of graduate education in the South. The GEB sponsored a series of regional conferences during the year to consider the issue of graduate education for African Americans in the South. Both white and black educators attended these meetings. At the Conference of Deans of Southern Graduate Schools white educators and foundation personnel learned that although southern blacks were "realistic in their approach...and [were] willing to...temporary expediencies," on the whole the black educators in attendance unanimously rejected regional approaches to solving the graduate school issue.[35]

Southern politicians, however, seized the spotlight and the initiative on the issue of equalization and regional cooperation. Not only would regional cooperation help to redistribute the region's white students, it would also be useful as a way of staving off further efforts at equalization, or even worse, integration. The Southern Governors Convention met on December 7 and 8 of that year. At the meeting Governor Chauncey Sparks would advocate a "treaty arrangement" among the southern states, whereby students could use a scholarship to go to other states that offered a program that was not offered in their home state. Sparks's idea was based on a similar arrangement that had been created in Alabama only a few years earlier.

These intermittent discussions, as well as real examples of regional cooperation in higher education, were influences when the Southern Governors Conference convened. Despite these reformist origins, race played a large role in the crafting of a new regional strategy for higher education in the South, though the racial implications of the plan were largely left unspoken or couched in careful language. The educators invited to the conference mostly spoke in generalities. For example, one of the speakers at the 1947 conference, Doak S. Campbell, the president of the University of Florida, stated that it was the "obligation of the state to provide or purchase those education services that are necessary for the education of a sufficient number of its citizens to maintain the agencies and services essential to the public welfare."[36] The University of Florida was one of the institutions that had pressured William Gray, the president of Florida A&M University, into writing a report (which was roundly criticized by other blacks at the time of its issuance in 1947) that seemed to endorse the creation of a piecemeal graduate program at that institution.

The following year the Governors Conference held more discussions on the issue. Certainly pending equalization cases at the state level influenced their discussion.[37] Indeed some of the governors in attendance would be the vanguard of the South's political rebellion of 1948: Millard Caldwell of Florida, Strom Thurmond of North Carolina, Chauncy Sparks of Alabama, and Fielding Wright of Mississippi. The governors were aided in their plan by Meharry Medical College's sudden announcement that it would close at the end of the 1947–48 academic year if it did not receive a significant infusion of funds. Meharry was one of two black medical schools in the South; along with Howard University, it trained almost all of the nation's African American physicians. Given that Meharry was under the control of whites, it was not problematic for its administrators to offer the college to the South as a joint venture.[38] Once Meharry indicated its willingness to be the linchpin of the proposed compact system, the Southern Regional Education Board (SREB) quickly came into being and its racial impetus was made explicit. The governors agreed, "The purpose of this Conference [is] to be the provision, either within the several states or without, of adequate facilities for higher education for whites and Negroes."[39]

Thus at the end of the Governors Conference the Southern Regional Education Board was created. It would bear the marks of its dual parentage: neo-Progressive reform on the one hand, and southern conservative reaction on the other. A Regional Education Compact was signed by nine southern governors in February 1948 and would take effect once six state legislatures ratified it. In contrast with their slow decade-in-the-making support in equalizing black universities, South Carolina, Mississippi, and Louisiana ratified the compact within months of signing. When the other southern state legislatures met, they too quickly ratified the compact: Georgia first, then North Carolina and Arkansas, followed by Tennessee, Oklahoma, and Florida. A new southern administrative manifesto had been issued, only this one was to protect the sanctity of segregated institutions. Indeed the somewhat inexplicable quest for congressional approval of the compact, which in fact was not really necessary, was seen by opponents as an attempt to gain congressional endorsement of administrative segregation.[40]

Almost as soon as the SREB was created a new controversy would engulf the organization. The controversy lay in the roots of its creation, its role in stabilizing segregation and providing the white South with a new way to delay substantive equalization as well as integration. The furor over the SREB's involvement with Meharry Medical College, a black institution, would signal the end of the ability of white Jim Crow reformers to take the lead in shaping southern higher education. In their place new actors and interests emerged.

Meharry Medical College: Rational Planning Meets Politics

The roots of the SREB controversy lay in the decision by the GEB to support medical education in the South for blacks by focusing its attention on Meharry Medical College. Meharry, however, was fundamentally a creature of the GEB and of the Jim Crow South. It was a private institution founded during Reconstruction by the Freedmen's Aid Society of the Methodist Episcopal Church. A white president as well as a white board of trustees led it. With fervor and funds waning for support of black education in the South, the Freedmen's Society, like other northern religious organizations, gave up control of Meharry in 1915.[41]

Meharry's position was precarious since it was not, unlike other medical schools, affiliated with a university. Its natural affiliation would have been with Fisk University, one of the top institutions for blacks in the South, which was also located in Nashville. However, whereas in the 1920s Fisk was increasingly controlled by blacks, whites controlled Meharry, and each group was suspicious of and unwilling to cooperate with the other.[42] Meharry received the bulk of GEB funding for black medical education from 1916 to 1960, but despite this financial support, Meharry's institutional configuration saddled it with fundamental problems. In 1936 these institutional issues led to the loss of its AMA "A" rating. The GEB reversed this loss by directing the hiring of a new president and new instructors, all of whom were white.

Unlike other higher education institutions for blacks, the administration and faculty of Meharry was still controlled by whites. This, and the knowledge that Meharry was fundamentally a creature of the GEB and not an organic part of the black higher education community (despite its student body), contributed to the hostility that was directed toward the institution as it became part of the South's strategy to avoid attempts by African Americans to equalize professional education in the South.

The GEB also saw Meharry as a creature of the foundation and as part of a larger strategy to rationalize and improve higher education in the South. As part of its initial decision to focus on southern education, the GEB had made an earlier commitment to graduate education for African Americans, specifically medical education. The GEB-sponsored Flexner Report (1909), which evaluated the state of American medical school education, found only two black medical schools that were "worth developing": Howard University and Meharry Medical College.[43] Based on the report's findings, the GEB decided to support and develop both institutions, as well as establish other medical facilities for African Americans in the North and South. Due to Howard's public status, the GEB gave that school $600,000 between 1920 and 1936, at which point Congress began appropriating more money for its support. The bulk of GEB support for professional education, however, went to Meharry Medical College, which received about $8.7 million between 1916 and 1960.[44] Of all the foundation-supported schools, Meharry and Dillard University were most closely creatures of the foundations.[45] As a result when the foundations' separate strategies for developing southern higher education began to converge in the 1930s and 1940s, Meharry would more often than not be at the center of these conflicts.

Thus GEB decisions regarding the school were made in the context of its strategy of focusing on key regional institutions regardless of race.[46] In keeping with this strategy the GEB began debating making a significant grant to Meharry's endowment in 1933, although the actual amount of the grant ($4 million) and the announcement of it would not occur until 1944.[47] By that time the context of black higher education had significantly shifted, not only as the result of the *Gaines* decision and the southern states' myriad attempts to evade responsibility, but also because of the democratic revival of World War II, which stimulated increased black political activism and impatience with Jim Crow inequality.

GEB officials were alarmed when both white and black southerners seized on their apolitical support of Meharry. White state officials saw in Meharry a relatively easy way to avoid creating a costly medical school for African Americans in their state. Existing or new grant programs could be extended to an actual contractual arrangement with Meharry. In 1944 Alabama approached the GEB with a proposal for the foundation to fund a contract between the state and Meharry for the training of black Alabamans who wanted to attend medical or dental school. The GEB's counsel advised against supporting Alabama or any other state in this manner.[48] Despite this warning, and reflecting the waning control foundations could exert on their client institutions, Meharry entered into the SREB contract as well as separate contracts with southern states. The southern black press blasted the creation of the SREB as "an unabashed, shameful and effective way for the General Education Board to enable the southern states to avoid their plain duty to their Negro citizens."[49]

Despite its very roots being intertwined with the segregation issue, the SREB quickly attempted to distance itself from controversy. It was difficult for this to occur as its first director, John E. Ivey, was a sociologist trained at Odum's Institute for Research in the Social Sciences at the University of North Carolina. Nevertheless the SREB would take the following position: "It shall make regional arrangements to supplement educational facilities within the States. It is not the purpose of the Board that the Regional Compact and the contracts for educational service there under shall serve any State as a legal defense for avoiding responsibilities established or defined under the existing state and federal laws and court decisions."[50] This of course was completely disingenuous on the part of the SREB. As Table 7–1 shows,

Table 7-1 The Southern Regional Education Plan, 1949–1950

State	Black Students	Cost	White Students	Cost	Total Students	Total Cost
Alabama	20	$22,500	0		20	$22,500
Arkansas	23	$33,750	69	$86,250	92	$120,000
Florida	22	$26,250	0		22	$26,250
Georgia	18	$15,000	0		18	$15,000
Louisiana	7	$15,000	7	$9,000	14	$24,000
Mississippi	13	$21,000	23	$47,000	36	$68,000
N. Carolina	23	$31,500	30	$23,000	53	$54,500
S. Carolina	0	$1,500	0		0	$1,500
Tennessee	9	$9,000	24	$21,500	33	$30,500
Texas	31	$27,000	10	$10,000	41	$37,000
Virginia	12	$31,500	12	$12,000	24	$43,500
Total	178	$234,000	175	$208,750	353	$442,750

Source: Amy Wells, "Mischief Making on the Eve of *Brown v. Board of Education*," 5.

roughly the same number of white and black students participated in the program.[51] White students, however, were not nearly as equally distributed across the participating states, but were from only seven states, and nearly 40 percent came from Arkansas alone. Nonetheless the SREB followed the lead of earlier co-optive programs by appointing blacks to the board and only later to its administrative staff.

Even more telling about the role of the SREB in supporting segregation is the case of Virginia, as discussed earlier in the book. The state continued to use the regional arrangement for its black students until the late 1960s. The continued participation of Virginia also reflected the cautious support given to the program by some black administrators, much as had happened with out-of-state tuition grants. Again this support, as in earlier years, was vigorously condemned in editorials in the *Journal of Negro Education*. Charles Thompson's editorial "Why Negroes Are Opposed to Segregated Regional Schools," blasted the regional planners and their naïveté:

> [It is] inconceivable...that a group of the most intelligent white educators in the South...could or would sit around a conference table on more than one occasion and arrive at the conclusion that segregated education is none of their business; or come to the conclusion that even if it is their business they are powerless to do anything about it, except to make an ineffective attempt to improve the situation within the segregated framework....Negroes and their friends had thought that the South had arrived at a point...where it could face all of the issues involved and demonstrate that it has the statesmanship and the

courage which are necessary to make a forward social step.... But in this hope Negroes have been disappointed and aggrieved.[52]

Now dubbed "deluxe regional Jim Crow," the regional plan forced southern black university administrators to publicly take a side on the regional education plan, and by extension on the embrace of integration-first strategies.

The efforts of white politicians did not avoid organized opposition. In Atlanta a group calling itself the Atlanta All Citizens Committee on the Southern Regional Education Plan convened a meeting, the Southwide Conference on the Regional College Plan, in May 1948. The committee brought together sixty civic groups. Educators of course played a role, with invitations sent to heads of black colleges and universities, including two that were under heavy criticism, Meharry and Atlanta University. Both institutions were partners in the SREB plan.

The makeup of the committee reflected the fact that the late 1940s was a transitional moment in the Jim Crow order. Some of the groups participating were part of the Jim Crow reform coalition, such as the National Council of Negro Women, the Georgia Interracial Committee, the Georgia Council for Methodist Women, and the Tuskegee influenced-National Negro Business League. Other groups reflected the new interracialism of the South: the Georgia Civil Liberties Committee, the American Veteran's Committee, and the Southern Regional Council, the CIC's heir. Allied with these organizations was the Southern Conference Education Fund, which took the SCHW's place in the more liberal wings of southern reform. A third part of this committee represented the emerging black-controlled groups that would form the modern civil rights movement: more established groups such as the NAACP, the Urban League, and the Atlanta Civic and Political League, and new civic religious groups such as the Atlanta Baptist Ministers Union and the Interdenominational Ministers Union.

The findings of this conference reflected the newly strengthened civil rights approach. The group summarized their objections in a pamphlet listing "ten reasons why the regional plan is opposed." The group blasted the plan for not being an "honest answer to an educational problem." The plan was "discriminatory and constitutional" and "formulated in an undemocratic manner." Not only was it "uneconomic and unreasonable," but it acted as a "brake on the present trend toward integration" that made "legal redress more difficult."[53] The conference reported nearly unanimous endorsement of opposition to the plan. The one exception was the representative from Meharry.

Although Meharry's representative, Dr. D. T. Rolfe, was the only exception to this opposition physically present, he was not the only one present in spirit. Stetson Kennedy, a white journalist, reported that "some of the most 'prominent' Negro educators in the South were conspicuously absent," suggesting that they were "perhaps blinded by the prospect of big jobs at the proposed regional colleges."[54] Kennedy's observation noted a process that had already started to take place: the co-optation (reluctant or not) of many education leaders by the expansion of segregated higher education. The position would put many of the more cautious educators in an increasingly uncomfortable position; though many would later be vilified as opportunists, some were victims who were unable to escape from the framework of gradualism and accommodation that had shaped them.[55]

The End of Equalization

The uneasy coalition and consensus on the status and scope of southern higher education, which had been carefully forged by Jim Crow reformers, lay in shreds as the SREB controversy exposed the widening rifts between and among whites and blacks over the future of the Jim Crow order.

The attempt to reform the Jim Crow order or create roadblocks in the face of change through the development of a "deluxe Jim Crow" university system would expose the contradictions and weaknesses of the order. As Horace Mann Bond noted, by sending African American students out of state, and often to the North, the white South planted the seeds for its eventual downfall. Most white southerners involved in higher education either received their training at mediocre white southern institutions or taught or administered at these institutions. The known universe for them was quite small, and they were content. By contrast, for the hundreds of African Americans who had received higher education in comparatively better northern graduate programs, new possibilities, political and intellectual, had been opened up. They often returned to the South unwilling to be content with the political status quo or the status quo of mediocrity that plagued both white and black higher education.

The immediate effect of the Jim Crow law schools, and perhaps unintended by whites, was that they vastly increased the presence of African American lawyers in the South. For example, when Southern University School of Law graduated its first two graduates in 1950, it *doubled* the number of African American lawyers practicing in Louisiana.[56] In a final irony, in South Carolina, among other states, a number of these law school graduates, such as John Wrighten and Matthew Perry, would become local counsels for the NAACP as the modern civil rights movement unfolded in the late 1950s and then expanded through the 1960s.[57]

Increasingly whites and blacks saw that equalization was no longer just a means to perfect the Jim Crow order; instead both whites and blacks saw it as a tool to delay more serious challenges to an increasingly besieged Jim

Crow order. Southern state universities responded to this challenge in different ways. Some states, primarily outside of the Deep South, had begun limited desegregation at the graduate level, though they still remained firmly segregated at the undergraduate level. In the lower South, as the 1950s unfolded, resistance to integration hardened, while equalization came to a standstill.

The end of equalization and the rise of integration-based challenges to higher education signaled the waning of Jim Crow reform and the rise of a new challenge to the Jim Crow order. That challenge was the reemergence of black political citizenship. White reformers had been pushed aside by white politicians who now increasingly believed that reform was by extension a threat to the Jim Crow order. Southern blacks saw in the SREB controversy the last vestiges of managed race relations being stripped away. Black Jim Crow reformers were increasingly forced by the rising tide of black political activism to move away from the world of Jim Crow reform and its focus on social citizenship, toward the a new world where the struggle for political and civil rights citizenship for blacks would come together to form the civil rights movement.

Chapter 8

Jim Crow Reform and the Rebirth of Black Political Citizenship

> The Negro's status in Southern politics is dark as hell and smells like cheese.
>
> Ralph Bunche, *The Political Status of the Negro*

Through a process of bargaining and other forms of indirect politics, Jim Crow reformers attempted to perfect the Jim Crow order. The path toward stabilizing and then modernizing the Jim Crow order had led white reformers toward redemocratization of the white South. With aid from the white have-nots, they and their New Deal reform allies hoped to create a more equal but still segregated South. For African Americans the path to democratization and political citizenship was more circuitous. The reformers' struggles to expand the boundaries of African American social citizenship intersected with, and ultimately became intertwined with, the rise of political citizenship among southern blacks. For southern African Americans Jim Crow reform politics was the connective tissue that would eventually link ideas, interests, and institutions surrounding social and political citizenship into a transformative racial order that would reshape the South and American politics. The successes and failures that African Americans experienced in the political arena during the 1940s changed their relationship to the Jim Crow order that they were trying to reform. Jim Crow reform politics created the strategic and institutional bases for the modern civil rights movement.

Jim Crow reform was one of the foundations on which the reemergence of black citizenship politics was built. The educational campaigns of the 1920s and 1930s, from the community organizing around Rosenwald schools to battles over higher education equalization, created a new sense of political identity and efficacy among many (though not all) of the South's African Americans. The strengthening of social citizenship among southern African Americans was further developed through a rich network of local professional, civic, and fraternal groups. These networks were based on earlier activism around education, social welfare, and economic justice issues. This activism was given a boost with the enactment and spread of the New Deal, which symbolically (more than materially) boosted southern blacks' social citizenship claims. The New Deal also helped to strengthen and in some places expand the black middle class where they were hired to help administer or implement New Deal programs for blacks. The groups and networks involved in strengthening black social citizenship overlapped with, but also were independent from, the newly revitalized southern wing of the NAACP, which reemerged in the 1940s. These groups and networks, made up of ordinary citizens, both middle class and working class, helped to reconnect blacks to the political system.

The reclamation of southern blacks' lost political citizenship was also nourished by political transformations occurring in the South during the 1930s and 1940s. One of the important influences of this rebirth of citizenship was the anti–poll tax campaigns that had emerged in almost every southern state during the 1940s and the poll tax abolition bills that were introduced, debated, and voted on in Congress through much of the decade. Where poll tax reform was accomplished, there was one less barrier in the way of black political participation. Equally important were the organizational structures and linkages built up during these campaigns between white moderate, good government groups like the League of Women Voters and newly established black civic groups. The emergence of unions, especially the CIO, as a political force during the 1930s and 1940s also began to change the southern political landscape. Many of the individuals and organizations who were involved in the anti–poll tax movement, people like Virginia Durr and Luther Jackson and organizations like the SCHW, allied themselves with the organizing drive led by progressive unions in the late 1930s and through the 1940s. The high point of this union movement was the CIO's Operation Dixie, the goal of which was to organize workers and create new voters. Although Operation Dixie did not achieve the goals of its organizers, the individuals and organizations associated with this campaign contributed important political, organizational, and financial resources that came from their broader connections to the world outside the Jim Crow order.[1] All of these resources helped to nourish the quest to regain African American political citizenship.

In this chapter I trace the emergence of black political citizenship during the 1930s and 1940s. I examine one of the most critical efforts in this early pre–civil rights era, the struggle to overturn the white primary, one of the most significant institutional barriers that thwarted black political participation. The fight against the white primary reveals the growing impact of the NAACP in capturing a leadership role in the black South and displacing the black Jim Crow reform agenda. The fight coincided with the growth of state and local civic leagues and voter organizations that would emerge all across the South and in most of the region's major cities. These organizations linked the social capital that had emerged from Jim Crow reform with a new, more assertive attitude toward reclaiming black political citizenship. The growth in the NAACP during the 1940s reflects this flowering of black political citizenship. An analysis of the impact of institutional change, political competition, and black political and social capital shows how political citizenship emerged in the pre-*Brown* South.

Redefining and Reclaiming Political Citizenship

The reclaiming of political citizenship rested on the right to vote. In order to vote, one had to be registered. The question of whether voter registration as opposed to voting is a meaningful measure of political mobilization must be addressed. In the context of the Jim Crow order, given the barriers to registration—legal, social, psychological—the act of registering to vote was an important part of African Americans' public reclamation of their civic identity.

This claim, it must be noted, rests on some empirical limitations. First, prior to 1950 the numbers of African Americans registered to vote are based on estimates given by newspaper editors, civic groups, and political figures.[2] Only three states (Louisiana, Florida, and Virginia) collected voter registration data by race. Second, it is not clear whether African Americans who registered to vote in the pre-*Brown* era actually did vote and whether or not their votes were manipulated or coerced. The evidence for this is very scanty and largely inconclusive.[3] Despite this uncertainty, voter registration numbers provided a tangible way for both supporters and opponents of the Jim Crow order to measure how successful they were in opposing or defending the order.

I use the term "political consciousness" rather than the more familiar "political mobilization" because, in addition to overcoming legal and institutional barriers to registration, southern blacks had to confront the etiquette of Jim Crow. Registering to vote was a political act; not only did it assert a claim to political citizenship, but it violated the mores of the Jim Crow order. As a number of contemporary researchers noted, the process of registering to vote often crossed the many lines of Jim Crow etiquette. In rural areas, going to the voter registrar's office may have involved going to a private home. Going into a white home, not as a servant or tradesperson but as a political equal, violated the etiquette of Jim Crow.[4]

In the context of the South, the act of registering to vote was an important part of African Americans' public reclamation of their civic identity. Thus registering to vote was a sign that an individual had decided to exercise, even if in a limited way, claims of political citizenship.

The reclaiming of political citizenship was "cognitive liberation" of the most practical kind.[5] It was directly linked to the policies and institutions created by Jim Crow reformers. In their quest to secure their fair share of public goods (paved streets, better schools, black policemen, and more) the South's black citizens developed a newfound political identity and a new sense of efficacy.

The quest for material benefits was important, but the development of citizenship politics was just as important; that is, while getting a street paved or a school built was important, so too was creating new norms and values within the African American community that encouraged and celebrated the expression of political citizenship. Jim Crow reform was linked to early attempts to reclaim political citizenship. Both were important parts of a much longer process that aimed to convert from nonvoters to voters a generation of African American southerners that had been inculcated with one of the key ideologies of the Jim Crow order: the belief that politics was "white folks'" business.

The Establishment of the Jim Crow Order and the End of Mass Black Politics in the South

To most observers, by 1912 the political universe of the South was as fixed as the stars in the sky. The redemption of the South and the threat of Populism had led to a wave of constitution writing and other political machinations that excluded as thoroughly as possible most African Americans and many lower-class whites. Southern democracy in the Jim Crow order was a democracy of the privileged and the few. As Figure 8–1 shows, black voter registration in the South declined from a range of 60 to 70 percent to less than 5 percent by 1912. In Virginia African American political participation, which was at a high of 96,000 registered voters in the 1880s, fell to 21,000 (out of 147,000 of voting age) in 1902.[6] In Louisiana

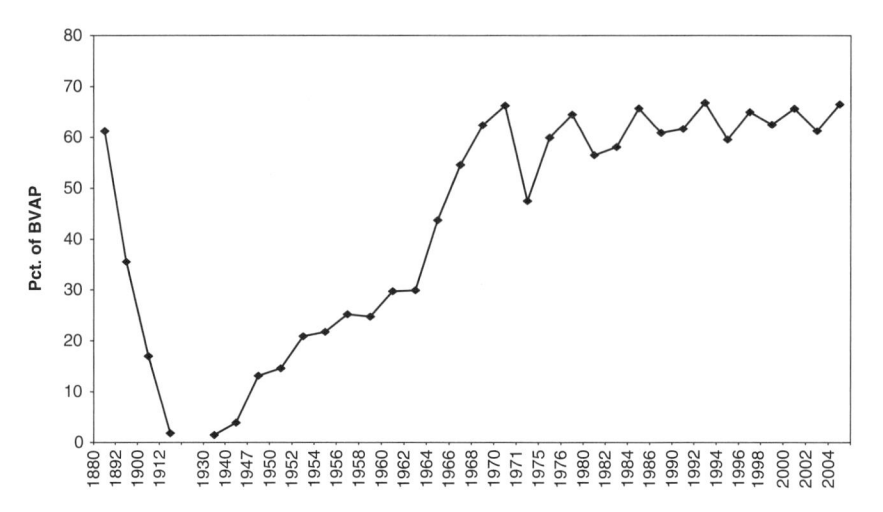

Figure 8–1 Black Voting in South, 1880–2004
Sources: For 1880–1912, see Kent Redding and David R. James, "Estimating Levels and Modeling Determinants of Black and White Voter Turnout in the South: 1880–1912," *Historical Methods* 34 (4): 141–58; Lawson, *Black Ballots*, 134; Lewinson, *Race, Class and Party* App. II, Various Registration Statistics, 214–20; Price, *The Negro Voter in the South* 5; Bureau of the Census, *Statistical Abstract of the United States, 1973*, Table 701: White and Negro Voter Registration in 11 Southern States: 1960 to 1971 (Washington, DC: GPO), 436; Bureau of the Census, *Statistical Abstract of the United States, 1976*, Table 747: White and Negro Voter Registration in 11 Southern States: 1960 to 1971 (Washington, DC: GPO), 466; Bureau of the Census, *Statistical Abstract of the United States, 1977*, Table 812: Voter Registration in 11 Southern States, by Race: 1960 to 1976 (Washington, DC: GPO), 507; Bureau of the Census, *Statistical Abstract of the United States, 1986*, Table 421: Voter Registration in 11 Southern States, by Race: 1980 to 1986 (Washington, DC: GPO), 507; Bureau of the Census, *Statistical Abstract of the United States, 1999*, Table 486: Resident Population of Voting Age and Percent Casting Votes—States: 1988 to 1996 (Washington, DC: GPO), 1998; Bureau of the Census, *Statistical Abstract of the United States, 1998*, Table 490: Resident Population of Voting Age and Percent Casting Votes—States: 1988 to1996 (Washington, DC: GPO), 1998; Bureau of the Census, Table 4a. Reported Voting and Registration of the Total Voting-Age Population, by Sex, Race and Hispanic Origin, for States: Nov. 2000, 2002, and 2004.

the number of black (male) registered voters fell from 81 percent in 1879 to about 3 percent in 1900.

The impact of this new political order on the broader American political order was significant. Southern (white) members of Congress were able to amass enormous institutional power as they were repeatedly returned to Congress as a result of uncompetitive elections. Democratic presidents of the United States were beholden to the white southern elite due to party rules and the disproportionate effect of southern delegates. The Republican Party periodically engaged in "lily-whitism" campaigns: attempts to purge African

Table 8–1 Black Voter Registration in the South by State, 1930

Deep South	Total Registered	Percent BVAP	Other South	Total Registered	Percent BVAP
Alabama	3,500	0.7	Arkansas	5,100	2.0
Georgia	10,000	1.9	Florida	2,200	0.8
Louisiana	1,723	0.4	North Carolina	2,000	0.5
Mississippi	850	0.2	Tennessee	4,550	1.7
South Carolina	1,200	0.3	Texas	15,000	2.9
			Virginia	14,000	4.5
Total	17,273		Total	42,850	2.1
Total Black Voting Age Population (BVAP)	2,276,500	0.7	Total Black Voting Age Population (BVAP)	1,997,961	

Source: Registrations: Paul Lewinson, *Race Class, and Party*, 218–20. Note: Black voting age population calculated by author, from census data.

Americans from participating in party politics in order to create a politically viable "white man's party" in the South.[7] The Republicans' lack of success left the South and the rest of the Democratic Party in the tight grip of the southern Democrats. The Republican Party, to which Frederick Douglass had urged blacks to give their devotion, walked away from their southern supporters. The result of this bifurcation of politics and the strength of the Dixie wing was the "imposition" of southern interests on public policy.[8]

By 1930, the number of African American eligible to vote in the South was abysmal, and voting participation was negligible.[9] In most states less than 1 percent of the black voting-age population was registered to vote (see Table 8–1). This meant that out of a regional voting population of 4.2 million African Americans, only sixty thousand had the right to vote. In this dismal universe of electoral lockout, some states were more thorough than others in their exclusion of blacks from the political sphere. In the deep, or core, South only the tiniest fraction of African Americans was registered to vote. One early study estimated that only 850 African Americans in Mississippi were registered voters, out of a voting-age population of slightly less than a half million people. Georgia stood out as the Deep South's anomaly, with ten thousand African Americans registered to vote. The rest of the South (outside of the core) did slightly better in this age of exclusion, allowing 42,850 African Americans to register, or about 2.1 percent of the voting-age population.

The "right to vote" existed more in name than in practice, however. Some African Americans remained on the voting rolls because they had registered in earlier, more politically inclusive days. By 1930 those still on the rolls were either dead, had moved up North, or knew better than to mess with white folks' business. Those who didn't know better, who managed to get registered as a result of the intervention of powerful local whites, had the honor of voting in the general elections but were by definition excluded from the white Democratic primary.[10]

Confronting the Barriers to Political Citizenship

A number of barriers stood in the way of broader African American political participation in this age of political exclusion. Institutional barriers were foremost, with the poll tax and the white primary as the most visible. What the poll tax and primary did not accomplish, literacy and understanding clauses and other arcane registration rules took care of. With the vast majority of blacks working in either the low-wage agricultural or domestic sector, little extra money could be found, let alone spared, for the privilege of voting in the general elections since the real decisions were made at the primary stage. Registration rules made the prospect of trying to get on the rolls a humiliating task at best. Trying to vote meant risking severe economic punishment through loss of employment or credit; at worst, trying to vote could be a death wish. As the early studies on lynching documented, attempting to vote was considered an offense punishable by death.

Attempts to attack the poll tax had mixed success. One early defeat was the U.S. Supreme Court's 1937 ruling in *Breedlove v. Suttles* (302 U.S. 277) which upheld Georgia's poll tax law. As a result, poll tax reform was pursued through a national and a state-by-state legislative strategy. For southern blacks, this meant that they were dependent on the ability and desire of whites to abolish or reform the poll tax system.

But the poll tax was only one of the institutional barriers that stood in the way of African Americans reclaiming political citizenship. Voter registration laws such as understanding, literacy, and residency rules were also difficult to challenge in court as the federal court system was inclined to view these regulations as local and political matters that fell outside of its jurisdiction. Challenging the white primary offered another route to reclaiming political citizenship.

Attitudes also stood in the way of political participation. For white elites, politics was a serious business that only the "best people," the best educated and the most civically aware, should be involved in. For nonelite whites, blacks' political noncitizenship reaffirmed their special citizenship and status within the Jim Crow order. Even though this stance was, in the views of liberal critics, completely counterproductive, a kind of "false consciousness," it was meaningful.[11] Although lower-status whites had considerable difficulty exercising formal political citizenship, this barrier was not as rigid as it was for blacks. Unlike their behavior toward blacks, most registrars rarely imposed the full array of registration rules on whites. Even when whites did not (or could not) exercise political rights by voting, whites automatically possessed a degree of political citizenship denied to blacks, and their opinions, no matter how latent, were still part of the political calculations made by southern leaders.

The hearts and minds of black southerners comprised another set of barriers. Removing blacks from electoral politics was one of the most successful results of the southern campaign of violence and lynching during the Redemption period. With the dying-off of the Reconstruction generation, those former slaves that had actively participated in politics, a generational void emerged. Most contemporary observers believe that among southern African Americans, especially the most rural and the least educated, was inertia, a sort of fatal resignation. Politics was by and large white folks' business. As one respondent to an early political participation study exclaimed, "Votin' is fo' the white folk's.... We ain't got nothing to do with that." The ongoing economic depression contributed to this fatalism. Another respondent to the same study said, "Boy, I ain't worked in two years, and I hardly enough to eat in so long, I can't even remembah. I just got no money to be payin' poll taxes."[12]

This resignation, though regrettable, was not irrational. It was eminently rational to decide that a vote in the general election would not make a difference in an election that had been de facto settled in the primary. It was a rational decision that one lone vote might not be worth a livelihood or a life. The southern black remnant of the Republican Party was mostly oriented around the capture of the few crumbs of political spoils allotted to the region and to their race. The NAACP, seen by most modern observers as one of the engines of cognitive liberation and political mobilization during the early civil rights movement, had virtually collapsed in the South after World War I and would not reemerge until World War II.[13] Indeed given the lack of a regional or national organizational or political infrastructure to support black political participation, the decision of most African Americans to not participate in politics was understandable.

Nevertheless, although there was some resignation there was not an absence of political consciousness. Recent research has shown that during the 1920s the Garvey movement was very popular in the South, leading some researchers to argue that Garveyism sustained a political focus for African Americans during a period in which their prospects for formal political inclusion were at the worst.[14] Jim Crow reform also provided an alternative venue for political action. Organizing for better schools allowed African American communities to engage in quasi-political activities without openly threatening the Jim Crow order.

Thus although the Jim Crow order was in many respects authoritarian, it was not totalitarian. As in many political orders, political openings existed caused by friction between and among the institutional and ideological features of the order. Jim Crow reform existed within these spaces, and African Americans took advantage of these small political openings, most of which lay in the urban South.

Blacks, Urban Politics, and Policy in the Pre-*Brown* South

Despite the best efforts of the white architects of the Jim Crow order, African Americans were not completely eliminated from the South's political landscape. Blacks held on to a vestige of their former political citizenship due to the lack of institutional coherence and alignment within the Jim Crow order. The Jim Crow order existed within the broader American federal order; thus within the order were multiple political jurisdictions, each of which had its own set of formal and informal electoral rules and norms.

For example, although the white primary rule covered state and federal elections, in many instances it did not cover local municipal elections. In these elections blacks could participate in politics in a very minor way if they were well organized and if local politicians found their votes politically advantageous. In cities with a city commission and a city manager, such as those common in Virginia and in Texas, blacks also had the potential to participate in elections. In some cities where state and federal elections were covered by the white primary, blacks could (theoretically) vote in the main election Although this blocked off direct political action it sometimes offered indirect political influence for blacks. Where blacks were blocked from voting in local primary elections, they could vote on bond referenda and in similar kinds of special elections. In some cases election rules made it a requirement that a certain percentage of registered voters vote in a bond referendum; if not, the measure would automatically fail.[15] African American civic leagues could thus register voters and threaten to not encourage actual voting in order to put pressure on the white political system.

Unlike in the rural South, cities offered a political opening and fostered a safer political space, a "protective anonymity." In this urban space there existed a rich array of social capital networks that served to stabilize remnants of political citizenship from the Reconstruction era and provided the resources for the slow rebuilding of black political citizenship.[16] In any large southern city there was a

> Negro fraternal building, in which might be found all the offices and leading spirits of Elks, Masons, Pythians, etc.; all active centers of welfare work and discussion, and often closely linked with the Negro Republican committee. In the same building or separately was the professional quarter of the negro community...; the regional headquarters of one or more of the substantial Negro insurance companies; several real estate firms; a branch of the Urban League or the [NAACP].

This urban-based social capital often had policy outcomes. Paul Lewinson argued that the "city community was endowed with a better school system than the broken-down shack which often served a rural community.... There might be a...private or even public hospital for Negroes."[17]

Ralph Bunche's view of the possibilities of black urban politics was far more critical than Lewinson's assessment. According to Bunche, black political participation in urban politics had not "derived local benefits on a pro-rata basis as a result of...participation in any city....More logical is the deduction that, with or without the political participation, negroes receive only that amount which is necessary, not to satisfy their equitable claims, but merely to soften their demands for 'just deserts.' "[18]

Though Bunche was highly critical of the prospects for black engagement in urban politics, he and others saw a promising new age of black political participation emerging in the urban South, particularly in Arkansas, Florida, Georgia, Tennessee, Texas, and Virginia.

Memphis and Atlanta: Possibilities and Limitations of Urban Politics

The cities of Atlanta and Memphis offer a glimpse of the possibilities as well as the limitations of black urban politics in the pre-*Brown* South. Compared to the rural South, blacks in both cities contributed to and benefited from the social capital that was created as part of urban life. In each city there were commercial and civic areas that were the center of African American life; in Atlanta it was "Sweet" Auburn Avenue and in Memphis it was Beale Street. Both cities were examples of the possibilities of urban life; each had a large (for the Jim Crow era) population of middle-class blacks, and a substantial (for the South) black-controlled business community. Atlanta was more of an anomaly because of its concentration of black colleges and universities. Despite their similarities, blacks in each city faced a different set of institutional barriers, partly based on their location within the Jim Crow order. Atlanta was located in a Deep South state with a closed political system dominated by rural interests, whereas Memphis was located in an Upper South state with relatively more political openness and competitiveness.

Blacks in Atlanta faced a political system that was entirely closed to them. In Georgia the white primary covered not only primary elections for state and federal office, but also, since 1892, the Atlanta municipal election. In addition, Georgia had a $1 cumulative poll tax. As a result of this political exclusion and institutional barriers, Atlanta's white political establishment had no need for black votes and more or less refused to negotiate with the black community on municipal issues. In response to this white intransigence, and perhaps because of the extraordinary level of social capital infrastructure within the black community, Atlanta's black community leadership became increasingly unified and attempted to present a cohesive approach to dealing with the white power structure.[19]

By contrast, although Tennessee had a white primary, this rule did not cover Memphis elections. The continued and (for the South) significant presence of the Republican Party in the state meant that the wholesale purging of black voters that had occurred in other parts of South had not occurred in Tennessee, at least in its cities. The competitive nature of Memphis elections and the continued political activity of black Republicans resulted in Memphis blacks having a very limited and highly subordinated incorporation into Memphis city politics. This in turn created opportunities for individual political advancement and thus repeatedly opened up fissures within the city's African American leadership.[20]

A comparison of public school funding in Atlanta and Memphis provides a mixed picture of the impact of black political participation. Atlanta is the most cited case of African Americans taking advantage of the temporary and small openings of the political system. These openings were caused by a provision in the city's election laws requiring that a majority of the city's registered voters participate in an election. Although only a few hundred blacks could vote, this was a large enough bloc that their failure to vote would disqualify the election. In 1919 two school bond issues were defeated (including one for $4 million) with the aid of black voters. Faced with this threat, in 1921 Atlanta's mayor agreed to devote part of the funding to black schools. This pledge resulted in the building of Atlanta's first high school for blacks. In 1926 another bond issue was proposed, and again promises were extracted from the school board. The promises in this case were not kept.

The constant refusal of white Atlantans to engage in any kind of political dialogue coupled with the enormous social and economic resources of the black community strengthened the position of black civic organizations, particularly the NAACP, the Atlanta Urban League, and the Atlanta Civic and Political League. Despite the presence of the CIC and other interracial organizations, black leadership in Atlanta increasingly turned to community organizing. During the 1930s these organizations began to embrace direct action such as boycotts and protest marches, as well continuing to encourage voter registration to increase the ability of black voters to engage in strategic political action.

In Memphis educational politics and outcomes followed a different path. Black politics, though still weak, remained vibrant in Memphis. For example, black voters played an important role in establishing the political machine of E. H. "Boss" Crump, who ruled the city for nearly five decades. In 1927 the competition between two mayoral candidates (one of whom was backed by Crump) sparked a massive voter registration drive within the Memphis black community led by Roscoe Conkling Simmons, Booker T. Washington's nephew. As a result of the drive Memphis blacks temporarily composed 40 percent of the city's registered voters. Among the rewards that Memphis blacks received for this political support were an additional two high schools, one in 1927 and another in 1936.[21]

This subordinated incorporation, which had led to some limited results, shaped black political mobilization in the city as well city and state policy responses. Because black teachers were beneficiaries of the Crump political machine, unlike in other cities there were no organized efforts among Memphis blacks for the equalization of teacher salaries and school facilities.

Unlike in Atlanta, there was no formal salary differential rule for Memphis white and black teachers. Unofficially salary inequalities existed; by 1944 black teachers made only 44 percent of white teachers' salaries. In 1947 the state of Tennessee formally equalized black and white teacher salaries. This move toward formal equalization perhaps reflects pressure on the state that had arisen in the shape of higher education equalization suits filed in 1937 and 1939; it also reflects a policy consistent with the state's own out-of-state-tuition grant program, which was established in 1940. More important the lack of organized effort reflects the ongoing, though sporadic engagement in local politics that did not exist for Atlanta's blacks.[22]

These two cities are evidence that with enough resources and opportunity, the Jim Crow order had not entirely eliminated political participation, and thus the political citizenship, of southern blacks. Yet these political successes were mixed and to a large extent represented extraordinary efforts to gain relatively small rewards. Despite black Atlanta's resources, a public high school for blacks (the Booker T. Washington High School) did not open until 1924, and a second one did not open until 1947. Limited inclusion in Crump's political machine enabled blacks in Memphis to have a high school in 1887. Nonetheless political exclusion, and its policy effects, were by and large the rule, not the exception. Ralph Bunche, for example, argued that blacks in Memphis received a "pitifully small" number of patronage spots of the "most menial work."[23]

This brief analysis reveals that political participation, no matter how limited or compromised, had its uses, for blacks and for whites. Although considered a dirty secret, in places where African American voting still occurred white politicians in tight political races would often make quiet pitches for support. This was a risky proposition, for an opponent could use the attempt to solicit black votes as evidence that the candidate was insufficiently firm in defending the political color line.[24] One example of this occurred in the closely fought congressional races in 1936 and 1938 between Colgate Darden, Virginia's "Organization" candidate (and future governor of Virginia and president of the University of Virginia), and Norman Hamilton, the editor of the *Portsmouth Star*. Hamilton defeat Darden in 1936 by a margin of 2,000 votes in a district where approximately 1,300 African Americans were registered. In 1938 Darden used the fact that Hamilton had established a campaign office in a black neighborhood against him; the campaign sent out pictures of the office with claims that Hamilton favored blacks over whites. At the same time Darden made a pitch for African American votes.[25]

The temptation to get votes, no matter where they came from, was one that few politicians could resist. Thus one appeal of the white primary was that it removed the ability of blacks to offer their votes to candidates eager to seek an electoral edge. As Ralph Bunche noted, white political power was dependent on a "gentleman's agreement whereby the candidates [were] to abide by the decision rendered in the primary." The weakness of the system was that it was not enough to deter reneging on this agreement: "There is a growing conviction in the South that whenever and wherever the Negro is registered in any significant numbers, the whole primary system will collapse from its own inherent weaknesses, since narrowly defeated primary candidates will be attracted by the possibility of stealing the election with the aid of the Negro vote."[26] Since Reconstruction and then the Populist insurgencies of the late nineteenth century, the Democratic Party of the white South had feared and hated black votes. The presence of black voters undermined one of the key linchpins of the Jim Crow order: separate and unequal rested on the powerlessness of blacks and lower-class whites, who together could be tempted into an alliance that could overthrow the power of the elites.

The political opening offered by urban politics was just one of the factors that contributed to the maintenance of a minimal level of political citizenship for urban blacks. Another important factor during the 1920s and 1930s was the mobilization around education that Jim Crow reform and Rosenwald funding had stimulated.

Education and the Emergence of Political Consciousness

Education reforms and Rosenwald funding had led to increases in the number of teachers and school buildings, and also to growing organizational capacity within black communities. This capacity was displayed in a number of ways, from the increasingly political activities of teachers associations to the growing and increasingly louder demands from African American parents for equalization of funding and facilities. One of the results of this organizational agitation was the increase in the number of salary equalization cases, whether actually filed or simply threatened. Between 1936 and 1945 twenty-five cases were filed across the South (see Table 5–4).

Salary equalization cases were not entirely driven by the NAACP. As discussed in chapter 5, the impetus for litigation often came from local teachers, such as the case of the Buckingham Teachers Association in Virginia and the suit brought by the Little Rock Colored Teachers Association. Not only did the impetus come from local teachers, but local support was in fact necessary to success. As Mark Tushnet notes in his study of the NAACP, successful civil rights litigation required a strong community base as well as grassroots support.[27]

Although salary equalization cases did not end of the Jim Crow order, they were important steps toward ending it. In the short run, however, the results of this litigation strategy, as well as the lobbying from African American teachers associations and their allies among the white education reform movement, led to more states approaching—though not achieving—the equalization of white and black teachers' salaries.

Education politics and reform had an effect on African American political consciousness; my statistical analysis confirms this. African American political consciousness was measured as the change in the percentage of African Americans registered to vote between 1930 and 1940. Education reform was measured in two ways; the first education reform measure used is the black-to-white teacher salary ratio in each southern state in 1939 (see Table 5–4). The second education reform measure is based on the type and scope of Rosenwald participation: the percentage of the total cost of the Rosenwald schools in a state contributed by African Americans (BLACK CONTRIBUTION) compared to the percentage of the total cost contributed by state and local governments (PUBLIC CONTRIBUTION). There was an inverse relationship between the two types of contributions (see Contribution Ratio in Figure 8–2). States that

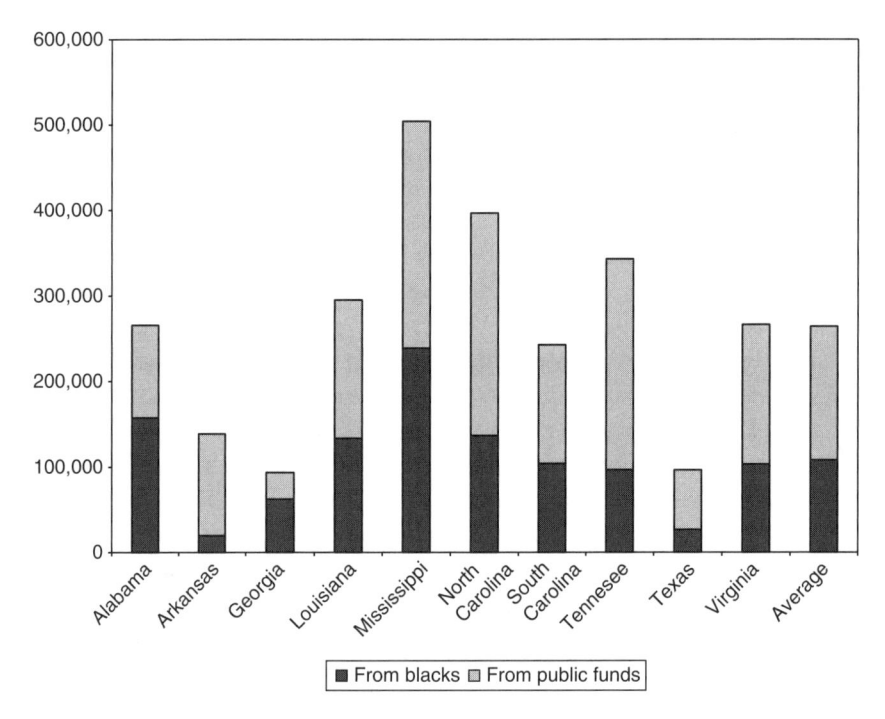

Figure 8–2 Contribution to Rosenwald Schools: African American and State/Local Governments
Source: N.C. Newbold, "Common Schools for Negroes in the South," *Annals of the American Academy of Political and Social Science* 140 (Nov. 1928), 222. Calculations by author.

contributed more in state and local public funds tended to be states wherein African Americans contributed less, percentage-wise. States where African Americans contributed higher than average amounts also tended to states wherein the public sector contributed fewer funds. The Rosenwald contribution was fairly even across all states, so it was not compared.

Using a technique called ordinary least squares regression, I estimated the effect of the type of Rosenwald funding as well as teacher salary equalization on African American voter registration rates in the eleven core southern states (see Table 8–2). The type of participation in Rosenwald schools was significant in explaining variation in voter registration rates. In the first model, the analysis shows a negative relationship between African American contributions to Rosenwald schools and voter registration rates. The higher the percentage that African Americans in a particular state contributed toward the building of Rosenwald schools, the less likely there would be an increase in the voter registration rates between 1930 and 1940. Overall this was a strong and negative relationship. States where African Americans supported the building of Rosenwald schools largely through the efforts of their communities as well as through the monies contributed by the Rosenwald Foundation were also states that had abandoned their responsibilities, in a so-called dual system, toward these children. This abandonment reflected these states' lack of support for African American claims of social citizenship. In turn this rejection of claims to social citizenship was mirrored by the resistance of these states toward any exercise of political citizenship by African Americans.

Thus although African Americans in Alabama and Mississippi contributed, percentage-wise, more than any other state to their schools, this contribution did not translate into increased levels of voter registration. In these states political receptivity to equalization, and thus to some form of social and political citizenship, was very weak. The local and state governments of Alabama and Mississippi contributed the least amount of funds to the Rosenwald schools compared to other states. By contrast, states and localities

Table 8–2 Effect of Education Reform on Political Consciousness

Variable	Model 1	Model 2	Model 3
Black Contribution	−.226***		
Public Contribution		.153***	
Salary Ratio			.142**
Constant	.070***	−.064**	−.050
Adjusted R^2	.589	.587	.373

N = 11 states; ***$p \leq .001$ **$p \leq .05$ *$p \leq .10$.
Y = Percent Change in Black Registered Voters, 1930–1940.

that contributed higher amounts to black education, and thus social citizenship, were also states that were less resistant to political citizenship. The final measure of education reform, shown in model 3, was the impact of the black-to-white teacher salary ratio. Like the public contribution to Rosenwald schools, this had a statistically significant and positive effect on the change in voter registration rates between 1930 and 1940.

In short, states that were more open to state-supported equalization (whether that support came from litigation or lobbying pressure from reform groups, or strategic concessions varied by state) were also states where African Americans began to take the first steps in translating their claims of social citizenship into claims of political citizenship during the 1930s.

The 1940s: The Rise of the Negro Voter

While white Jim Crow reformers approached the democratization of the white South belatedly but openly, they approached the democratization of the black South through their traditional lens of gradualism. Economic development, they argued, was good for whites and for blacks; only when sufficient progress had been made on that front could the "delicate" issue of black voting be reopened. If pressed on this issue, white reformers displayed their own class bias and paternalism, stating that they would agree to black voting only if it was restricted to highly qualified blacks, the "best people." Virginius Dabney was even more explicit, stating, "An educated and responsible Negro is a greater asset to the community and more deserving of the franchise than an unlettered [white?] swineherd from the pine barrens."[28] Again, however, this limited support for upper-class black enfranchisement was premised on the actual event happening some time in the unspecified future.

Whether poor, middle class, or wealthy, African Americans—the have-nots of the South—increasingly turned to the Democratic Party, even though the party's local representatives were more likely than not completely opposed to their aspirations.[29] African American voting in Arkansas and Florida was aided by the activities of Jim Crow reformers and their political allies (e.g., Brooks Hays in Arkansas and Claude Pepper in Florida), who led the state campaigns to change electoral laws, specifically the abolition or reform of the poll tax. In Louisiana, however, poll tax abolition did not seem to help. In that state the abolition of the poll tax in 1934 had no effect on the black voter registration rate across the state, which between 1930 and 1940 remained virtually unchanged, at less than half a percent of the black voting-age population.

JIM CROW REFORM AND THE REBIRTH OF BLACK POLITICAL CITIZENSHIP   207

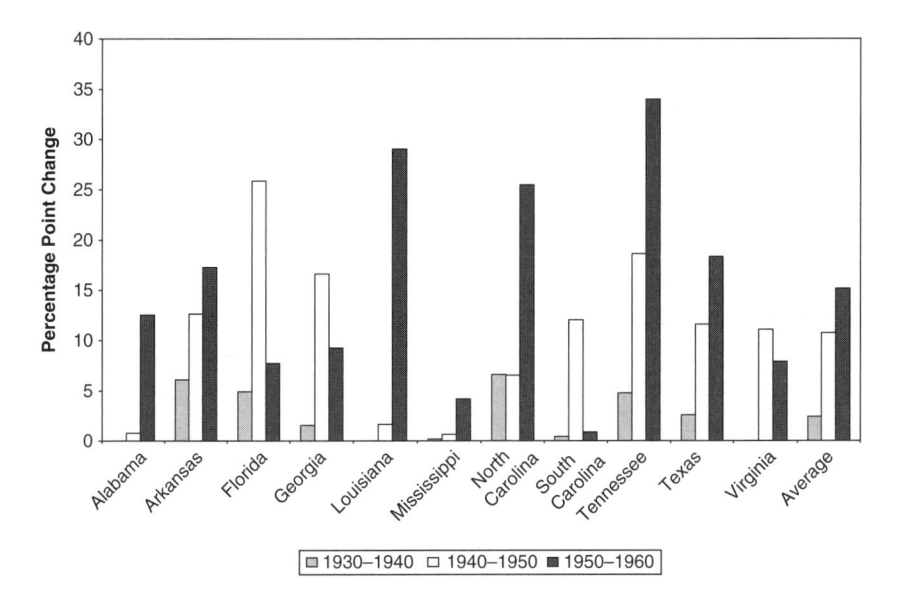

Figure 8–3 Black Voter Registration by Decade
Sources: Lawson, *Black Ballots*, 134; Lewinson, *Race, Class and Party*, App. II, Various Registration Statistics, 214–20; Price, *The Negro Voter in the South*, 5; Bureau of the Census, *Statistical Abstract of the United States, 1973*, Table 701: White and Negro Voter Registration in 11 Southern States: 1960 to 1971, 436. Numbers calculated by author.

Political change, at least measured by voter registration, had begun to occur across the South by 1940. Some of it no doubt was due to the impact of the New Deal during the 1930s.[30] The shaping of the New Deal was aided in part by the participation of white and black Jim Crow reformers like Will Alexander and Clark Foreman and research undertaken by Howard Odum, Arthur Raper, and Charles Johnson. The impact of New Deal programs had trickled down somewhat to poor African Americans, freeing them a bit from the economic control of whites but, more important, strengthening their claims to social citizenship. Middle-class blacks increasingly fulfilled what seemed to be a preordained role assigned to them by Jim Crow reformers: as the managers of other blacks in a separate and slightly more equal world.[31] These middle-class blacks were largely educated in the black colleges and universities, whose status had been strongly shaped by white foundations.

Across the South between 1930 and 1940 black voter registration increased overall by 2.9 percent, from a low of 60,000 registered voters to 168,000; this was a fraction (3.5 percent) of the South's black voting-age population (see Figure 8–3). Alabama, Mississippi, and Virginia had little growth or even a decline in black voter registration; in Arkansas, Florida, North Carolina, and

Tennessee black voter registration increased by approximately 5 percent. The decade 1940–50 saw another increase in black voter registration, to about 12 percent of the black voting-age population. Again there were variations across states; not only did Arkansas, Tennessee, and Florida again make large gains, but Georgia (16 percent), South Carolina (12), and Virginia (11) had impressive increases as well.

The impact of World War II in terms of democratic rhetoric, economic growth, and military participation contributed to strengthening black claims to political citizenship. The black press nurtured and popularized the famous "Double V" campaign for victory against fascism abroad and for democracy at home.[32] This campaign for a renewed commitment to the ideals of American democracy was given a singular focus when the Supreme Court invalidated the white primary in *Smith v. Allwright* (1944).

The White Primary

The white primary, unlike other disenfranchising devices, was based on explicit racial exclusion. As a result it had a far more immediate impact on black political participation than registration laws. Throughout most of the South almost all blacks, regardless of education, occupation, or wealth, were barred from participating in the Democratic primary. Thus blacks were effectively excluded from meaningful political participation. At the same time because the white primary was explicitly based on racial exclusion it offered an opportunity for legal challenge that the poll tax and voter registration laws did not offer.

Since 1903, with the enactment of the Terrell Election Law, blacks in Texas were barred from voting in the Democratic primary by the rules of the party; in 1923 they were barred by state statute.[33] The state statute and the legal challenge against the white primary grew out of the few political openings left for blacks: urban politics and the institutional patchiness and disjunctions of the Jim Crow order.

The path to the Texas white primary began at the turn of the twentieth century. As it had elsewhere, the Populist movement roiled Texas politics and shook the state's elites. To control democracy elites led the charge in enacting a poll tax for the state in 1902, which would disenfranchise not only poor blacks but, more important, poor whites. Despite the imposition of the poll tax, in some parts of eastern Texas blacks and Mexican Americans confounded the attempts to control political participation by either continuing to pay their poll tax or by participating in the practice of candidates or local party organizations paying individual poll taxes. The latter practice led to allegations that their votes were "easily manipulated" or "purchasable," thus tainting attempts to purify the state's democratic process. Whether from their own initiative or via poll tax payment schemes, African Americans and Mexican Americans still had the ability to "swing a Democratic primary." With minority votes available, white politicians were continually tempted by the "forbidden fruit of black votes."[34] Black voting undermined white solidarity because it magnified rather than dampened "divisions among white men"; in turn, this allowed blacks some political leverage. Black political citizenship and white supremacy could not coexist; thus the problem of black voting had to be dealt with decisively. Texas, like other southern states, turned to the white primary as a nearly perfect solution. In 1903 the state enacted the Terrell Election Law, which would clarify and further regulate the primary system.

Despite these attempts by state legislators to finish off black political participation, local party organizations and politicians were resistant to fully implementing or abiding by these rules. The lure of black votes, especially in areas of intense political competition, was hard to resist. Bexar County, home of the city of San Antonio, was one of the few places left in Texas where the door of political participation for blacks had not completely swung closed. In a close primary race for district attorney in 1918, two white candidates tried to marshal black electoral support. One candidate, John Tobin, was successful and narrowly won. After the election D. A. McAskill, who lost, approached the state legislature for new legislation to avert the possibility of "the direful domination of local government…by the colored people."[35] The state legislature did not act on his pleas. In 1922 McAskill won the next primary election, this time narrowly defeating an opponent who tried to enlist the black vote. McAskill again approached the state legislature, and this time the state acted.

The state legislature in 1923 codified black exclusion from the white primary into Texas state law. The new law stated: "In no event shall a negro be eligible to participate in a Democratic primary election held in the State of Texas and should a negro vote in a Democratic primary such ballot shall be void and election officials are herein directed to throw out such ballot and not count the same." Initially this formal exclusion seemed to be constitutional, as the Texas Supreme Court had earlier ruled that "political parties were private organizations," thus "outside the boundaries of the Fourteenth and Fifteenth Amendments." The rulings were supported by a U.S. Supreme Court ruling, *Newberry v. United States*. Texas, like its other southern brethren, had at last seemed to find the final answer to the problem of black voting.

In the long run this codification of black exclusion "as a matter of state law" turned out to be a mistake for Texas and the rest of the states that relied on the white primary. White primary laws violated the rule that North Carolina governor Charles Aycock had devised in the early days of the Jim Crow order: "silent management" through bureaucratic discretion rather than state laws and regulations that directly challenged the civil rights amendments were the key to maintaining the Jim Crow order and protecting it from challengers. By violating these rules and putting racial exclusion explicitly into state law, white Texans had broken the rules of "silent management" and thus provided blacks an opening from which to challenge their political exclusion.

The campaign to overturn the white primary was begun by African Americans in Texas, who at times cooperated with NAACP and at times acted on their own. The funding for the litigation largely came from the Texas Colored Teachers Association as well as a wide variety of African American civic and fraternal groups. Jim Crow reform had helped to strengthen the teachers of the state as they tackled multiple challenges. They learned valuable skills and built important links across class, gender, urban, and rural divisions as they lobbied for educational resources such as increased state funding for primary schools, the establishment of out-of-state tuition grants for black undergraduates, and even the establishment of a full-fledged university for black Texans. This local control over direction and funding challenged a widespread, though waning belief that the Jim Crow order was largely destabilized by challengers from outside the order.

This black-led campaign against the white primary also challenged the contours of Jim Crow reform during the New Deal, especially the economistic orientations of some white Jim Crow reformers. In particular the interests of Texas blacks clashed with the interests of San Antonio's mayor Maury Maverick. Maverick, a leading New Deal and Jim Crow reformer, was a prominent southern voice in the ongoing campaign against the poll tax campaign. Yet like many other white southern liberals, he learned that attacking a practice such as the white primary that harmed only blacks was far more difficult to do than to support poll tax reform, which was seen as hurting more whites than blacks. Attacking the white primary was not in the best interests of southern reform, according to those who believed that the problems of the South were due to economics, not race.[36] Beyond their philosophical problems was the fact that southern New Deal politicians like Maverick and Claude Pepper, as well as white Jim Crow reformers, were still reluctant to be associated with any action that threatened to erase rather than soften the color line.

The belief that the best path to reclaiming political citizenship for southern blacks lay through the courts was primarily advocated by the NAACP. This strategy, however, had produced few successes up through the 1930s, as the U.S. Supreme Court was reluctant to focus on the reality that the poll tax and the white primary constituted targeted disenfranchisement that violated both the Fourteenth and Fifteenth Amendments. Despite the Court's reluctance, the blatant nature of the Texas law opened the door to a cautious intervention by the Court. In *Nixon v. Herndon* (1927) the Court overturned narrow aspects of the Texas primary system, focusing on the extent that the Texas law violated the Fourteenth Amendment's prohibition of state action.[37] Having broken the rule of silent management Texas had "invited" this judicial "slap."[38]

The state of Texas evaded the decision by changing the primary rules once again, giving the state's Democratic Party the power to determine membership. The party duly did so, and barred blacks, this time as a private organization. Texas blacks returned to court. In *Nixon v. Condon* (1932), they again seemed to have won a partial victory when the Court ruled that the Texas Democratic Party was "*not* a simple voluntary association." Once again the state changed its rules, and once again Texas blacks went back to court, this time without the support of the NAACP, who wanted to rethink the case. This time, black Texans were handed a defeat. In *Grovey v. Townsend* (1932) the Supreme Court upheld the state's and party's actions.[39] This defeat would reveal significant rifts between blacks in Texas, who felt that the NAACP was too far away and too disengaged to address their concerns, and the NAACP, who had urged the Texans not to take the case back to court for fear of setting an unfavorable precedent.

Despite this setback, the initial ruling had inspired blacks in Arkansas, Florida, and Virginia to take action. In Florida Sylvanus Hart, a World War I veteran from Jacksonville, brought a suit against Duval County, This action was not surprising as the city was one in which blacks still had some involvement in city politics. Hart, however, lost his suit, as the Duval County Circuit Court ruled that the Florida Democratic Party was a private organization.[40] In Arkansas, where black leadership of the Arkansas Negro Democratic Association had previously been resistant to the NAACP, they now invited the organization to join forces to bring a suit against the state. The NAACP was cool to this invitation, given the lack of past support from the state's black leaders. Although the Arkansas Negro Democratic Association got an injunction blocking the removal of blacks from the state's democratic primaries, this injunction was overturned by the state supreme court.[41]

In Virginia the outcome was slightly more successful. A group of African Americans decided to challenge Virginia's white primary law, which the General Assembly had adopted in 1912. To the surprise of everyone, the Federal District Court ruled in *West v. Bliley* (1929) that Virginia's primary rules did indeed violate the Fourteenth and Fifteenth Amendments.[42] The Byrd "Organization," Virginia's dominant political faction, determined to maintain its control over local and state party organizations and unwilling to give up this centralized control that evading the constitution required, reluctantly acceded to this decision. Part of this acceptance rested on the belief that the poll tax as well as the hostility of local registrars constituted a significant and formidable barrier to increased African American political participation.[43]

Despite the success in Virginia, the struggle to end the white primary seemed to have come to an end with the *Grove* decision. But in 1941 there seemed to be a slight opening. The Roosevelt judicial selections created a Supreme Court with a different perspective, including a willingness to develop a new racial order.[44] In addition, another case had emerged, *United States v. Classic*; this case, though not directly concerning the white primary issue, was very closely tied to the issue of primary elections and the question of state action. The Court ruled that primaries for *federal* offices could be governed by the federal government. Another challenge to the white primary was mounted, this time with cooperation between the NAACP and black Texans, and this time the challengers were successful. In an "unprecedented reversal" the Court ruled in *Smith v. Allwright* that the white primary could not stand; it was a violation of the Fifteenth Amendment's prohibition against voting discrimination based on race.[45]

The reaction of the white South to the decision was initially calm. At first editorials in the white newspapers reassured white southerners that nothing would change. However, as southern blacks moved more or less immediately to probe this opening emotions began to run high across the region. Overall white acceptance of or resistance to the decision varied across states, and was in many ways linked to broader issues in the Jim Crow order. In Georgia, as discussed in the previous chapter, Governor Ellis Arnall, locked in fierce competition with Eugene Talmadge, chose to not fight the decisions. When Arnall and his faction lost control of the state government, Talmadge's machine wasted no time enacting a range of new laws to purge Georgia's *Smith* voters. Florida and South Carolina went back to court to try to block the ruling; they also tried, with little success, to once again evade the courts by trying to purge the party from the state. In both of these states as well as Georgia good government groups quickly objected, arguing that the "cure" of a private electoral system would lead to even more chaos and corruption in state and local politics. Alabama and to some extent Virginia enacted or at least tried to enact new laws that would give local registrars greater discretionary power. Alabama's Boswell Amendment would eventually be declared unconstitutional by the Supreme Court in *Davis v. Schnell* (1949).[46] Mississippi largely eschewed legal maneuverings in favor of threats of violent reprisals against any blacks who tried to vote. The *Jackson Daily News* gave a typically blunt warning: "DON'T TRY IT!...Staying away from the poll...will be the best way to prevent unhealthy and unhappy results."[47]

The defeat of the white primary was the necessary, though not the only ingredient that sparked the movement among African Americans to reclaim their lost political citizenship. The political mobilization of southern African

Americans was linked to preexisting social and political networks that had been created, sustained, or even strengthened during the development of the Jim Crow order.

Citizenship Politics and the Rise in Voter Registration During the 1940s

Jim Crow reform politics, the poll tax reform campaign, and the end of the white primary were three factors that stimulated the rise in southern black voter registration in the South during the 1940s. What brought these factors together into a coherent whole and contributed to a decisive shift in the ending the dominance of the Jim Crow reform model was the emergence of citizenship politics.

Citizenship politics grew out of the dense network of African American occupational, professional, religious, civic, and fraternal groups and identities that emerged behind the veil of the Jim Crow South. Throughout the 1930s and more rapidly in the 1940s civic leagues and voters groups were created by African Americans throughout the South. In almost every state in the South by the mid-1940s African American civic leagues and voter groups, both partisan and nonpartisan, existed in every major city. They ranged from groups such as the Durham Committee on Negro Affairs, which was heavily influenced by the city's black elite, to the Orleans Parish Progressive Voters League, which was involved in New Orleans politics.[48] In almost every state there existed a statewide "association of associations," umbrella organizations that would aid activists in "prepar[ing] communities for collective action."[49] In Arkansas this role was taken by the Committee on Negro Associations, established in 1940; Virginia had the Virginia Voters League; and Texas had the Texas Council of Negro Organizations, which was organized in 1941.[50] The Texas Council had an affiliated membership of forty-five statewide organizations, a leadership of two hundred, and an aggregate membership of 600,000. One of the leaders of the Council argued, "Since the Council acted as a clearing house it managed to avoid the effects of those 'divide and conquer' techniques."[51]

The emergence of these new organizational forms and new leadership marked a decisive shift away from the interracialism and elitism of the earlier period of black political life. The growth in a new kind of political citizenship took place within and increasingly apart from the South's managed race relations model. The goal of all of these groups was to create a new sense of engagement in American democracy. For southern African Americans Jim Crow reform politics created the strategic and institutional bases for the modern civil rights movement. Within the framework of

American political development citizenship politics was the connective tissue that linked the ideas, interests, and institutions that emerged out of Jim Crow reform into a transformative racial order.

This new political identity and sense of efficacy was developed through a rich network of local civic leagues and voter groups that both overlapped with and stood independently of the NAACP. Made up of ordinary middle-class and working-class citizens, these groups helped to reconnect ordinary blacks to the political system. Some of the most important members were teachers and the state and local teachers associations that represented them.

Many black teachers were located in schools that were financed by Rosenwald Foundation funds as well as by the funds of local blacks; they were responsible for mobilizing communities to raise the funds and were charged with interacting with the white political structure in order to gain access to further resources. In the late 1930s some of these teachers started to organize salary equalization cases and pressure the states to create graduate school programs in order to combat their second-class status in the southern educational system. Their own efforts at empowerment coincided with a greater recognition of their role in inculcating a sense of citizenship and hope in their students in American democracy.

A brief list of some of the activities of these groups gives a sense of the important role teachers organizations played. In Texas, the Texas Colored Teachers Association helped to fund and organize community pressure in support of the *Smith* white primary case and the *Sweatt* graduate school integration case. The statewide Virginia Teachers Association provided the organizational superstructure on which the Virginia Voters League was launched. Black teachers in the South played critical multiple roles. Harry T. Moore used his association with the Florida State Teachers Association to build the Progressive Voters League. In Arkansas the salary equalization case filed by the Little Rock Colored Teachers Association finally enabled the NAACP to begin to develop a more productive relationship with the state's black leadership.

These civic leagues were a critical transmission link in persuading ordinary people, the old and especially the young, that politics was not only everyone's business but was in fact critical to the material and social well-being of their community. For example, the goal of the Petersburg Civic League of Virginia was "to train Negro citizen people to be 100 per cent citizens; to teach the use and power of voting; to notify and explain to members local, state and national government issues; to conduct public forums pertaining to civic matters; to publish a list annually of Negro Citizens who have paid their voting poll tax; to bring to public hearing the merits and demerits of candidates whose beliefs are to promote the civic welfare of Negro people."[52] Although Ralph Bunche would decry the rise of citizenship politics as the "fetishization of the ballot," to advocates of citizenship politics the quest for the vote could lead to practical short-term results and long-term transformations. To believe in democracy was perhaps too abstract a notion for many African Americans. Instead advocates of citizenship politics listed more specific ways that the vote could make a difference: "increasing teachers' salaries, assuring just treatment by police and in the courts; building a new high school; paving streets in Negro sections of town; calling Negroes for jury service; and helping Negroes secure employment in state and local governmental service."

The first step of this citizenship politics was to provide political education of the most practical kind. Key to this strategy was encouraging the payment of poll taxes, helping fellow community members to register to vote, and providing the courage to exercise the vote.

The quest for the ballot also reflected a belief in American democracy and in an essentially reformist approach to politics. Thus for Luther Jackson, who spearheaded the birth of the Virginia Voters League, "the ballot [was] the recognized instrument by which minority groups, under a democratic government, may defend their civil liberties." Jackson's professed belief was that at least in Virginia, blacks were being held back not by electoral rules, but by the attitudes and beliefs of the blacks themselves. African Americans needed to develop a "keen appreciation of their obligation, under a democratic form of government, for participation in the civic and political life."[53] Whether or not the barriers were as minimal as Jackson believed, he and others proceeded on the belief that only though a process of education linked to political activity could blacks in the South begin to reclaim and exercise their citizenship.

In short by linking the need for educating voters to the practical benefits of voting, teachers organizations and civic leagues provided an important ingredient in creating the ideal of citizenship politics that was fundamental to reform politics. While local elites and middle-class blacks often dominated the leadership of these leagues, many of the leagues worked hard at representing and reflecting a cross-section of the local black community. Meetings were often used to motivate and educate potential voters. For example, Virginia Voters League meetings were part revival meetings and part strategy sessions, which allowed ordinary citizens a means to reengage with politics. The meetings were designed to give public recognition to individuals who had embraced "100% citizenship." Thus one meeting program directed registered voters to sit in the front of the meeting space, those who had paid their poll taxes immediately behind, and then all others.

The knowledge gained through civic leagues and the citizenship schools that they offered helped these ordinary people help others and provided the solidarity needed to confront recalcitrant registrars. Confronting white authority was not insignificant, especially when that confrontation transgressed one or more rules of Jim Crow. Having the support of someone with knowledge of state and local voting laws and regulations and who could also get backing from a local civic group was an important factor in overcoming the reluctance that many southern blacks had in pressing for political rights.

In 1949 the activities of these civic groups and voter leagues and their long-standing message of civic engagement dovetailed quite neatly with the NAACP's First Class Citizenship Drive. What local political activists had articulated and supported for the past decade was now embraced by the nation's most important civil rights organization. According to this campaign:

> A first class citizen can live, travel, work, have a voice in his government just as any other American citizen regardless of color or religion. The second class citizenship so many of us tolerate is a shame upon humanity. What is worse, we do nothing about it, except complain. The ballot will do the work. Instances were mentioned where the white candidate wanted the Negro vote, and word was sent down—not to keep Negroes from registering and voting. The Negro put the person in question in the seat of civic life.[54]

The growth of the NAACP reflected the resurgence of black political citizenship as well as the flowering of black social citizenship. In some places in the South, such as Florida, Georgia, and Texas, the unfolding of social and political citizenship emerged alongside of and was intertwined with the growth of local and state chapters of the NAACP. In other places the NAACP emerged after this process had already significantly begun, as was the case in Arkansas and Virginia. In Alabama and Mississippi the growth in black associational life was not reflected in the growth in NAACP membership; there white hostility toward the NAACP was unrelenting, making few blacks willing to openly associate themselves with the NAACP.

In 1940 there 11,576 southern members of the NAACP scattered across 132 branches through the South; by 1946 southern membership rose to 115,036 in 299 branches (see Figure 8–4).[55] There was considerable within-region variation. Not surprisingly, Mississippi had the fewest NAACP members and branches in 1940 and in 1950. Yet despite the hostility of white Mississippians, there was still a marked increase in the number of members and chapters, from three to eighteen, in one of the most repressive of southern states.[56] By 1950 the postwar surge in NAACP membership was waning, partly due to the end of the wartime economy and wages, partly as a result of the increase in NAACP membership dues that

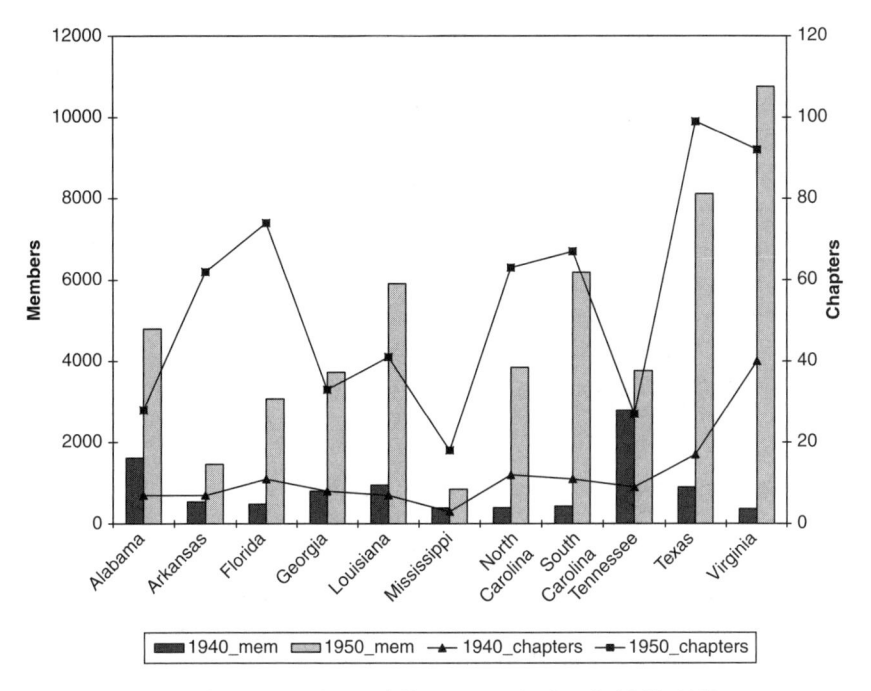

Figure 8–4 NAACP Membership and Chapters in the South, 1940–1950
Source: NAACP membership figures from Richard Valelly, Swarthmore College. NAACP chapter numbers compiled from NAACP Annual Reports, 1939 through 1960; also Anglin, "A Sociological Analysis of a Pressure Group," 128.

occurred in 1948, and partly as a result of the effort of some states to limit the activities of the NAACP operations.[57] Richard M. Valelly argues that the NAACP was a "party-in-waiting" that would translate black political demands into action, but the different patterns of membership growth suggest that the emergence of the NAACP reflected local conditions and local actions as much as the top-down preferences and successes of the organization itself.[58]

Analysis of the rise and fall of the NAACP during this pre–civil rights period should weaken one of the most enduring myths about the organization and its members: that its orientation was elitist and alienated from ordinary African Americans. Certainly leaders of the NAACP, as in other reform organizations, came from educated backgrounds, but the sheer growth in numbers of new members, as well as information gleaned from NAACP membership applications and branch charters, reveals that membership spanned the spectrum of southern black life in the Jim Crow order, from domestics and manual laborers to seamstresses and rail porters, doctors and teachers. The struggle for political citizenship, with rallies, voter registration drives, and rousing speeches, became a tangible means for many African Americans to experience some measure of the political citizenship that was denied to them. As the decade of the 1940s unfolded, the struggle for political citizenship in some southern states and cities became more and more tangible. Of all the southern states, African Americans in Virginia were the most enthusiastic supporters of the NAACP. The state went from having one of the lowest numbers of members in 1940 to one of the highest in the region in 1950. At the same time the number of politically engaged African Americans (as measured by voter registration numbers) in the state increased dramatically as the black civic groups and the NAACP began a sustained drive for "first-class citizenship" for Virginia's African Americans.

The Beginning of Southern Black Politics

From 1940 to 1950, but especially from 1946 onward there was a dramatic surge in the number of blacks registered to vote. Over one million southern African Americans, or about one-fifth of the southern black voting-age population, were registered to vote (see Figure 8–3). What makes this number remarkable is that at the beginning of the 1940s fewer than 200,000 blacks were eligible to vote in the eleven states of the former Confederacy. Looking at individual states, important subregional differences can be seen. For example, by 1950 there were only four states in which at least 20 percent of blacks were registered: Arkansas (21 percent), Florida (32 percent), Georgia (20 percent), Tennessee (25 percent), and Louisiana (25 percent by 1952).

We can examine these intraregional differences as well the growth in black voter registration as a whole by analyzing the impact of various institutional, political, and social capital factors of black voter registration. Certainly external factors such as the growing political power of northern blacks in the New Deal Democratic coalition could have played an indirect role in encouraging southern black political participation. President Truman's endorsement of civil rights in 1948 sent a powerful signal, strong enough to finally force many members of the southern congressional delegation to openly revolt and form the Dixiecrat Party. The growing imperatives of the cold war may have also helped to spur this quest for citizenship since the advancement of American foreign policy objectives was hampered by the country's "race problem." Although these factors may explain growth over time, they do not seem to offer an explanation for variation across regions.

Other factors, largely internal to the South, played a significant role in reshaping the southern political landscape. One of the most important changes was the poll tax reform campaign, which had significantly changed or abolished the poll tax in six of the southern states. Not only did poll tax reform and abolition open up the southern electorate to special interests, but it also stimulated political competition as white politicians sought the new white (and in some instances black) voters that electoral reform had brought into the political system. Coupled with these political and institutional changes was the flowering of black citizenship politics, which contributed to the reestablishment and growth of the NAACP from the 1940s on. To gauge how these changes affected black political engagement, I undertook a regression analysis.[59] The dependent variable in the analysis is the number African Americans registered (as a percentage of the black voter-age population) in the eleven southern states of the former Confederacy from 1940 to 1952, on a biannual basis, for a total sample of seventy-seven cases.[60] The sample ends in 1952, as the *Brown* decision may contaminate the rate of voter registration or resistance to it.[61]

I used four measures to control for change in political context. I measured political competition as the percentage of the vote won by the winner of a state's gubernatorial election nearest to the registration year. I hypothesized that states with greater political competition were more open to the growth in African American voting as white candidates and politicians sought office. I also used the percentage of each state's population that was black as a proxy of the prevalence of planter or black belt control. I measured electoral rules using two dummy variables: whether or not a state abolished the poll tax and whether or not a state attempted some type of poll tax reform during the 1940s. Florida, Georgia, Louisiana, and North Carolina all abolished the poll tax. Activists in the states of Arkansas, Tennessee, Texas, and Virginia attempted to achieve some form of poll tax reform during the study period. I hypothesized that both of these measures had positive effects on southern black voter registration.

I measured the impact of black citizenship politics by a state's NAACP membership. If the NAACP was indeed not only a "party in waiting" but also a reflection of the growth of citizenship politics within a state, the impact of membership on southern black voter registration should be positive. The results of the analysis are presented in Table 8–3.

The abolition of the poll tax had a positive and statistically significant effect on black voter registration in the South. The impact of poll tax reform on black voter registration was positive, though not statistically significant. The impact of these variables on black voter registration is not surprising. The states that abolished the poll tax during the 1930s included Florida and Louisiana, where African Americans had begun to reengage in urban politics during the 1930s. By contrast, although poll tax abolition in Georgia and Tennessee was a much more contested process, in both states African Americans were highly mobilized as a result.[62] Although an anti–poll tax

Table 8–3 Black Voter Registration, 1940–1952: Regression Analysis

	Model 1	Model 2	Model 3
Political Competition	−.066	−.074	−.064
	(1.790)	(1.990)	(1.750)
Poll Tax Abolish	.042		.033
	(2.740)		(2.050)
Poll Tax Reform		.028	.015
		(1.900)	(.988)
Percent Black	−.483	−.474	−.454
	(4.130)	(3.850)	4.310
NAACP Membership	.093	.098	.019
	(7.360)	(7.780)	(7.260)
Constant	−.348	−.369	−.350
	(3.340)	(3.480)	(−3.450)
Adj R^2	.590	.600	.610

*N = 11 States; Standard errors in parentheses.
***$p \leq .001$ **$p \leq .05$ *$p \leq .10$.

campaign challenged a state's political elites as well as its political culture, often that was not enough to make a significant difference in black voter registration. African Americans in Texas, and to some extent in Virginia, were able to mobilize in spite of the poll tax ban, yet this mobilization did not match efforts that occurred in the states where the poll tax no longer remained. One of the most surprising results was that black voter registration was negatively affected by a state's level of political competition. This result could reflect the impact of states like Mississippi and Alabama, which had surprising levels of political competition, coupled with nearly complete exclusion of blacks from politics.

V. O. Key argued that the greatest degree of racial oppression, or racial inequality, existed in areas where African Americans were a majority of the population. My analysis supported this claim: black voter registration decreased as the size of a state's black population increased. This political exclusion was countered by the strong and statistically significant impact of citizenship politics, as measured by NAACP state membership, on black voter registration. The NAACP was indeed critical in the rise of black voter registration during the 1940s. The growth of the organization in the South concomitantly with the growth of citizenship politics was an important factor in explaining the growth and variation in African American voting registration in the South.

This analysis provides a window into the growth of black citizenship politics in the South during the beginning of the end of the Jim Crow order. The South was not a "solid South" as the 1940s and early 1950s unfolded. Intraregional variation was significant. Areas with the greatest numbers of

African Americans, the Deep South, had the greatest degree of disenfranchisement, which stemmed from political and institutional barriers such as the poll tax, as well as the difficult social, economic, and cultural conditions that constrained the emergence of black citizenship politics in these states. In other states, however, the poll tax reform campaign movement made a difference. That difference was magnified if it was coupled with the growth in black citizenship politics. Thus Georgia and South Carolina stand out as states where reform and citizenship politics was able to significantly increase black voter registration during the 1940s. By 1952 change, bitterly contested by most whites and cautiously imagined by many blacks, had come to even these states. Registration rates in Alabama and Mississippi crept up to the 4 to 5 percent range.

The Unintended Consequences of Reform

In the late 1940s some white politicians began to pay attention to a new (yet still small) black electorate; this did not go unnoticed by blacks or whites. This new attention persuaded some blacks to try to achieve material benefits as the result of electoral politics and as a symbol of their status as citizens, not supplicants. Under the managed race relations model, material benefits for African Americans relied on the goodwill of white elites who decided in the end where and when these benefits would be dispensed. Ultimately some white Jim Crow reformers, such as Virginius Dabney, were forced by changing circumstances to carefully sound out a limited political inclusion of blacks as a necessary step if the South was to retain the most important elements of Jim Crow: social separation and inequality.

For white conservatives, however, this new African American political participation threatened the social and political order. For example, political factions such as the Talmadge wing of the Georgia Democratic Party and the Byrd organization of Virginia were threatened by the emergence of new groups of voters, including union members, the growing number of suburban voters, and African Americans. Although there is still debate about the roots of Virginia's massive resistance, the speed at which the Byrd organization embraced it may have partly been based on their fear of these new political threats. While most discussions of Virginia politics during the 1940s have focused on the battles between the Byrd organization, dominated by Senator Harry Byrd, and insurgents, more attention should be paid to how whites and blacks attempted to grapple with the newly emerging black vote. In Georgia the rapid emergence of a significant black vote in Atlanta and Savannah, where it had led to the defeat of one the state's most reactionary segregationists, led to wholesale purging and disenfranchising of blacks from 1948 onward. In Florida black voter mobilization on a statewide level was effectively shut down with the 1951 assassination of Harry T. Moore, the leader of the Progressive Voters League.

The rapid mobilization of the South's new black voters was usually followed by a concerted attempt to suppress their votes. Whereas states like Florida, Tennessee, and Virginia had at times been in the forefront of (or at least keeping pace with) average levels of black voter registration in the South, by the mid-1950s this kind of political mobilization had stalled. The democratization of the black South would have to wait until the civil rights movement pushed away the last vestiges of the Jim Crow reform order and brought pressure from below and above to bring down the order. The end of the political Jim Crow order would come not come about until the enactment of two key voting rules that had eluded reformers: the ratification in of the Twenty-fourth Amendment, which prohibited the poll tax payment, and the Voting Rights Act of 1965.

While social integration as embodied by the *Brown v. Board of Education* case may have been the last straw for the South's whites, especially its conservatives, it was preceded by a growing uneasiness about the African American vote and the political and social ramifications of that power. The separate and multiple battles over social citizenship and then political citizenship that took place throughout the South in the late 1940s up until the *Brown* decision developed into a much larger battle over first-class and full citizenship for African Americans. Jim Crow reform having helped to create the conditions for social citizenship and having given limited support to political citizenship could not stop a quest for full citizenship emerging as the new step in the evolution of the Jim Crow order.

Chapter 9

The End of Jim Crow Reform

> There is no power in the world—not even all the mechanized armies of the earth, Allied and Axis—which could now force the Southern white people to the abandonment of the principle of social segregation.
>
> Mark Ethridge, quoted in Sosna, *In Search of the Silent South*

Mark Ethridge, a white journalist and longtime white member of the Jim Crow reform movement, was flustered and angered by what he saw as a sudden assertiveness of blacks during World War II.[1] The boundaries of the Jim Crow order that had been carefully and painstakingly drawn by Ethridge and his colleagues were now being challenged. This challenge was not met with reason and cool-headed pragmatism, but with a hot flash of anger: no armies in the world could violate social segregation.

The response of Ethridge was not unusual among white Jim Crow reformers. Jim Crow reform first flourished and then died in the shadow of war. Like World War I, World War II created massive waves of change. In both instances, the mobilization of society and state called for in total war challenged existing social, economic, and political boundaries. In both eras millions of whites and blacks migrated in search of the new economic and social opportunities provided by wartime spending. Military service, especially for blacks, subverted and challenged the beliefs of many whites about the status of African American citizenship. At the end of the first war Jim

Crow reform emerged to strengthen the weakened political, civil, and social citizenship boundaries of the Jim Crow order.

The impact of World War II on the South and on the nation, however, was not simply a repeat of the impact of World War I. Nearly two decades had passed in which political, economic, and social conditions within the South had changed. Some of these changes were the result of external forces. For example, as a result of New Deal policy and then the war, the South was the beneficiary of a massive inflow of funds, people, and new ideas. New Deal agricultural policy, the economic stimulus of war jobs, as well as the continued mechanization of farming hastened the shift of white and black southerners from farm to city and from the South to points north and west.

Internal forces also played a role in transforming the South between the wars. The educational system created by white southerners as an additional means of social control of southern blacks was in turn subverted by blacks. Education policy and politics became one of the building blocks for the creation of new types of black social capital and citizenship, which in turn supported the quest for full restoration of African Americans' political and civil rights citizenship. The struggle for white democracy extended into a tentative and brief moment of democratization for southern African Americans as well.

Jim Crow reform, however, was unable to effectively respond to the new challenges of the war and the successes and failures produced under its own aegis. White reformers had largely accepted the confines of vertical segregation; indeed many saw no need to even question its existence. And black reformers accepted vertical segregation to the extent that other alternatives were foreclosed. However, as the struggles to create a biracial order unfolded and the contradictions and evasions of this process were revealed, the ability of the order to absorb these challenges—through the actions of white reformers and the acquiescence of blacks—by the quiet management of southern technocrats increasingly failed.

The broader political order in which the Jim Crow order was enmeshed was significantly different from the political order that had existed at the end of World War I. Then the South controlled significant elements of the national political structure, having the presidency and Congress in their hands. Ideologically the Jim Crow order both created and supported the flourishing of biological racism and the revisionism of the Civil War, which had written in the white South as history's victims and written blacks out of history and American culture, except in the most degrading and minimal of roles.

As World War II unfolded the Jim Crow order found itself in a different position. Blacks, at least in the North, were no longer on the far margins of American politics. Under the prodding and pressure of newly energized northern black voters and black interest groups such as the NAACP and leaders such as A. Philip Randolph and his national March on Washington Movement the Roosevelt administration began to slowly allow blacks the right to participate in meaningful military service and to economically benefit from wartime spending.

Despite their protestations of eternal stability, many whites could sense that some of the lines of the Jim Crow order were being challenged. In the face of these changes rumors flew across the white South at a furious pace: African American women were joining Eleanor Clubs, where they "whispered among themselves and plotted insurrection."[2] Meanwhile other rumors alleged that African American men in Charleston, Memphis, New Orleans, and elsewhere were arming themselves, sometimes with the aid of the Sears Roebuck catalogue. Indeed the pervasiveness of these rumors inspired Howard Odum and Charles Johnson to separately collect and analyze them to show how unsubstantiated they were. There were no Eleanor Clubs, nor were black men stockpiling weapons from the store founded by Julius Rosenwald.

These studies showed that average whites were unsettled by the strange new times that had descended upon the South, and conversely that southern blacks perceived a slight weakening of the old order. The rumors were backed up by more visible signs of African American militancy. Military bases in the South became the sites of armed conflict between African American soldiers and local white civilians. In the cities bus drivers, often the front-line enforcers of the Jim Crow order, reported "numerous recent instances of insolent, impudent conduct on the part of Negro passengers that necessitated 'calling the law.'"[3]

The creation of the Fair Employment Practice Committee (whose head was Mark Ethridge) inserted a symbolic layer of bureaucratic power and enforcement between southern whites and blacks that weakened the already loosening hold that whites had exerted over black economic advancement and rights. The influx of tens of thousands of black men in uniform throughout the region signaled the attainment of civil rights and moral citizenship that many white southerners were uncomfortable with.

For the first time since its establishment defenders of the Jim Crow order were forced to defend its ideational basis. The racial ideology of Nazism made biological racism increasingly unpalatable for public consumption. The war's focus, a battle against fascism and the protection of democracy and freedom, forced whites, especially southerners, to grapple with the lack of democratic citizenship for southern whites and for southern African Americans. The war for democracy was particularly painful for white Jim Crow reformers like Mark Ethridge, a former New Dealer, the editor of the Louisville *Courier-Journal*, and a member of the CIC. At a Fair Employment Practice Committee hearing in 1941 Ethridge refused to concede that there was a war for democracy abroad *and* at home. For him and many other white Jim Crow reformers segregation in the South was "now and forever," a "fact as sure as science" that no power in the world could dislodge.[4]

The fear of whites and the rising militancy of blacks showed that the Jim Crow order that reformers had tried to perfect was in fact crumbling under its own contradictions. While many of these contradictions and conflicts came from forces outside of the South, an equal number came from within the South. Southern reformers, especially whites, had failed to secure the South from within. Walter White, the head of the NAACP, and others quipped that one of the first casualties of the war seemed to be white southern liberals, but it was Jim Crow reform, its white and black adherents, and its ethos of interracial and elite leadership that was mortally wounded.[5]

"Sane and Sensible" Policy in a World of Inequality

Jim Crow reformers had pushed for "sane and sensible" solutions to the shortcomings of the Jim Crow order. Reformers relied on what they called "interracialism": cooperation and communication between the races through education, through appeals to religious sentiment, and by elite leadership. The sane and sensible approach relied on an explicit power differential. The lines of segregation, the lines that demarcated the boundaries of political civil rights and social citizenship, had largely been drawn by whites. These lines, however, were never as rigid as white reformers or conservatives had liked; they were subject to contestation from within the Jim Crow order.

One of the goals of Jim Crow reform was to strengthen, reshape, and control the southern government. This effort began with the antilynching campaign, which revealed the gendered approach and the Progressive roots of Jim Crow reform: women organized and men studied. The antilynching campaign chronologically and ideologically led to and intersected with the southern New Deal, which rested on the belief that the southern political economy could be transformed through objective analysis, rational planning, and a professional bureaucracy. From the New Deal onward it was an article of faith among many white reformers as well as some blacks that the economic transformation of the South would gradually weaken the color line as white workers would no longer be in economic competition with black workers. This decrease in competition would make white workers more open to politicians friendly to the New Deal and less susceptible to southern demagogues.

The antilynching campaign was a success to the extent that it was no longer politically or socially acceptable to advocate lynching. Lynching became the unacceptable exception rather than the rule. "Respectable" southern whites and newspapers removed the tacit public approval that they had earlier given to lynching. The attempt by southern reformers to extend their control over the state was not as successful. Their campaign to reform southern government was a much larger and more amorphous goal. Their reliance on word portraiture and thick description that drove home the reality of lynching did not easily translate into the policy arena; it provided no easily understood and translated platform of policy ideas for a politician to enact. When politicians did take notice of these state reformers and their plans, rather than the Progressive outcome they expected reformers found in states like Alabama and Virginia that clean politics and neo-Progressive governance was not necessarily in alignment with the ideals of Jim Crow reform.[6]

Indeed racial and economic conservatives were quick to embrace the southern state reformers' agenda in order to protect white elite interests. As a result of this incongruence, the expansion of southern government occurred on terms set by political and economic elites, not by state planners and technocrats. New Deal planning boards were shut down or transformed into economic development agencies, which, like the earlier New South boosters, attempted to woo northern manufacturers with the promise of cheap, nonunion labor. The failure of the CIO's Operation Dixie and the passage of the Taft-Hartley Act of 1947, which sharply limited unions' ability to organize workers, was another blow to the prospect of a more egalitarian southern economy. The economic transformation of the South that had been accelerated by the war created a new set of southern political elites who were not necessarily the natural allies of Jim Crow reformers.

Education policy was central to the growth of the Jim Crow reform and was the area where reformers had their most visible success. Education also played a key role in the downfall of the Jim Crow order. Jim Crow reform was responsible for the development and expansion of black primary education in the South. Northern foundations played a critical role in directing and funding the construction of schools and the establishment of state bureaucratic organizations that would provide long-term oversight of these schools and serve as a permanent advocate for these schools within the state bureaucracy.

At the beginning of the reform era "silent management" assured inequality in public education; education officials had the power to set budgets, curricula, and any other issue for black schools without any oversight or accountability. By the end of the reform era the establishment and institutionalization of state education bureaucracies and state inspectors directly accountable for black schools made black education a visible (though still fundamentally and grossly unequal) part of the state's administrative portfolio.

During the Jim Crow reform era northern foundations had facilitated the creation of black social capital that could be directed toward quasi-political activities. Foundation funding as well as personnel selection created opportunities not only for local self-help, but also for the development and strengthening of networks, as in the case of southern black teachers, that crossed local and state lines with the creation of state and national teachers associations. These networks sometimes crossed even racial boundaries as black teachers worked with white teachers on employment issues such as the establishment of retirement and pension plans or even higher education funding (albeit initially within the separate framework).

By the end of the 1940s equalization became the means by which white southerners attempted to forestall integration of schools. Governor James Byrnes of South Carolina, while leading a fight to keep the state's white primary, also called for a massive school equalization program. Under his plan a 3 percent sales tax would be collected to fund the upgrading of black public schools. In announcing his "new deal" for South Carolina's blacks, Byrnes argued:

> It is our duty to provide for the races substantial equality in school facilities. We should do it because it is right. For me that is sufficient reason.... If we demand respect for state rights, we must discharge state responsibilities. A primary responsibility of a state is the education of its children. We have made great progress in that field. We spend for education more in proportion to the income of the state than is spent on the average nationally. While we have done much, we must do more.... It must be our goal to provide for every child in this state, white or colored, at least a grade school education.[7]

Byrnes could speak for other white conservatives who rued their past lack of support for equalization. In a belated and probably futile plan of catch-up funding, southern state governments like South Carolina's were, according to Byrnes, being "forced to do what we should have been doing for the past fifty years" in order to try and avert integration.[8] Behind the pragmatism lay a warning and a threat: southern governors like Byrnes, Fielding Wright of Mississippi, and Herman Talmadge of Georgia all vowed in 1951 that they would close down the public school system before allowing integration.

Attempts to reform southern higher education were where the disjunctions within the Jim Crow order and between the Jim Crow order and the American political order became manifest. The *Gaines v. Canada* (1938) decision, which required states with segregated systems to provide equal in-state resources, provided a pivotal turning point in this reform process. Black educators and communities faced a quandary: Did they accept funding that would strengthen segregated education (institutionally as well as intellectually), or did they reject equalization, as the NAACP in the mid- to late 1940s was increasingly suggesting that they do?

For whites the *Gaines* decision and the equalization strategy offered an opportunity to justify to nonsoutherners as well as blacks that separate and equal was truly a viable alternative. At first, few states proved willing to take the equalization path, and instead remained content with a continuing pattern of shortchanging black higher education. As political and demographic pressure grew, however, southern states embraced equalization as a means of averting an even worse alternative: integration.

The policy decisions made in the wake of *Gaines*, which were partially due to the lobbying and maneuvering of white and black southern educators, led to three negative outcomes for the Jim Crow order. First, the failure of most southern governments to live up to "fair play" segregation became a symbol of the failure of Jim Crow reform to live up to the goals and methods that it advocated. Second, the failure of southern government to effectively counter the threat posed by *Gaines* and equalization arguments led to higher education becoming the opening wedge for dismantling the Jim Crow order. Third, the *Gaines* decision and its aftermath demonstrated the impossibility that the South could maintain a dual system that would be credible and legitimate under rapidly changing political and ideological circumstances.

Alongside education reform was a slower and even more contested change occurring in the southern political structure. The southern New Deal gave ideological support and limited political power to Jim Crow reformers. Initially aided by the Roosevelt administration, southern reformers began an assault on the poll tax. Though not the most fundamental problem of the South's variety of discriminatory electoral practices, it was the most widespread and strategically seemed to harm whites the most. Some reformers embraced poll tax reform as a reflection of white privilege that was wrongfully withheld; others saw poll tax reform as the means to other ends: the enfranchisement of a huge pool of have-not whites, which in turn would "naturally" support New Deal–friendly politicians. For some blacks poll tax reform signaled the beginning a new campaign to reclaim political citizenship.

As the nation entered World War II in a fight to protect democracy, the Jim Crow order as well as the nation at large faced issues of legitimacy. Poll taxes denied worthy white voters, and particularly white soldiers, the right to vote. The presence of the poll tax, at least for whites, became increasingly problematic and embarrassing. Blacks noted this contradiction and used it to strengthen their own "Double V" campaign for freedom (and equality) at home and abroad. The result of poll tax reform was the (re)enfranchisement of millions of white voters across the South.

This broader battle for political citizenship for whites influenced blacks. Some Jim Crow reformers, aided again by social science research, argued that limited democratization ought to be extended to the right sort of southern blacks. V. O. Key, whose work on the South would be considered the bible of pre–civil rights movement southern politics, argued that this political gradualism was also unsustainable: "The fact is that southern whites have a bear by the tail and don't know what to do about it."[9] The democratization of the white South opened a brief window for blacks to engage in Jim Crow politics, and to the extent they could blacks jumped through that window. Between 1946 and 1954 nearly a million black southerners registered to vote. Judicial decisions such as *Smith v. Allwright*, which outlawed the white primary in 1946, were important in unlocking the ballot box for southern blacks, as were the poll tax reforms that a number of southern states enacted during the 1930s and 1940s.

The impact of the *Smith* decision and poll tax reform varied; in Mississippi, where there was no poll tax reform but plenty of undiluted hostility toward the *Smith* decision, the number of new black registered voters barely increased. In Georgia the number of new black voters was in the tens of thousands as a result of a liberal governor who sponsored the repeal of the state's poll tax and also refused to lend political or institutional support to opposing the *Smith* ruling.

The experience of black Virginians during the 1940s was emblematic of this narrow window of political inclusion. African Americans in Virginia went from a largely voteless group in 1930 to a group in which 20 percent of all potential black voters were registered by the mid-1950s. Education politics and managed race relations had created a particularly strong southern reform movement in the state, as well as a network of institutions led by and for African Americans. The presence of these institutions and organizations did not presume unanimity; sharp disagreements remained within the African American community over tactics and goals. The engagement of blacks in Virginia politics shows the possibilities as well as limitations of Jim Crow politics.

Political mobilization in the wake of the *Smith* decision appeared quickly; in addition to Virginia, the flowering of African American political mobilization occurred in Georgia, Arkansas, Florida, and Texas. However, this nascent mobilization was ultimately constrained by "Boswellianism," as the white South quickly attempted to contain if not eliminate mobilization through changes in electoral laws such as Alabama's Boswell Amendment as well as through the usual tactics of intimidation and outright violence.[10] Thus in Virginia the curtailment of voter mobilization helped to reenergize the Byrd machine. In Georgia black political mobilization was weakened by the result of the resurgent Talmadge forces, who took over the state government after Arnall and his reform forces lost power.[11]

In Florida in 1951 Harry T. Moore, the head of the NAACP, and his wife were killed by a bomb planted in their house by racial terrorists. In contrast to the lack of response to such murders in the beginning of the Jim Crow era, there was an investigation, which produced significant national coverage and boosted the profile of the NAACP. Changed national circumstances and internal pressure forced Florida's officials to conduct a formal and semicredible investigation. However, some things did not change; not surprisingly there were no arrests. The murders of the Moores and increased state repression against the NAACP had a significant effect on the political mobilization of black Floridians, which faltered and then stalled for over a decade afterward.[12]

By contrast, attempts to limit white political participation virtually collapsed by the end of World War II. Alabama introduced poll tax reform in the early 1950s, as did South Carolina. The size of the southern white electorate swelled, and turnout in presidential elections increased. The average turnout in the core southern states of Alabama, Georgia, Louisiana, Mississippi, and South Carolina increased from 18 percent of the electorate in 1948 to 29 percent in 1952. The rest of the southern states also experienced an increase in turnout, from 28 percent in 1948 to 42 percent in 1952.

The emergence of mass white turnout was coupled with the return of white veterans, would eventually shake up southern politics. Many of the more reformist veterans had begun to make linkages between the fight for democracy abroad and the limitations of southern government at home. Some of these white veterans, such as Sid McMath of Arkansas, would ally themselves with other reformers, white and black, to chart a new postwar course for the South. On the other hand, white veterans like Strom Thurmond and Herman Talmadge (Eugene's son) would hold on to equal if not more reactionary beliefs. For them the fight to protect democracy was also a fight to protect the southern way of life. What united these disparate veterans was their willingness to challenge an entrenched southern political structure and to use the newly enfranchised white electorate as a means to challenge the southern power structure.[13] For some of the new southern politicians these new challenges would take the risky and electorally unproven road of racial moderation; for others the traditional politics of racism provided a more optimal strategy and a tried and true path toward achieving political power.

The political backlash of the white South was formally born with the emergence of the Dixiecrats in 1947 as a result of the national Democratic Party's decisive shift away from its wholesale and largely uncritical support of the Jim Crow order since the Wilson era. What some historians have described as "white backlash" and later "massive resistance" actually grew out of efforts by the white political leaders of the Jim Crow order to create a new means of defending the order by white elites, but also by the white masses. Thus, for example, at the same time that Alabama moved to block any further growth in black political activity in 1949, it also moved to increase the size of the white electorate through significant poll tax reform in 1952. The southern black vote was still too fragile to withstand the assault begun against it, and it as well as any other kind of nascent racial moderation that had emerged after World War II was decisively killed off before *Brown* had even wound its way through the courts.

New voters always provide fertile ground for ambitious politicians. The rapid expansion of the southern white electorate in the late 1940s and early 1950s proved to be irresistible to entrepreneurial politicians, who seized on white fears of change. Charging that other politicians were "soft on segregation" proved to be just as effective as charging a politician with being "soft on communism." There was no moderate middle ground available. By 1952 many of the remaining southern New Deal liberals, as well as some of the liberal-reformist veterans—Frank Porter Graham and W. Kerr Clark of North Carolina, Claude Pepper of Florida, Howard Rainey of Texas, Sid McMath of Arkansas, and James Folsom of Mississippi—had disappeared from the political scene.

The Battle between the States: Southern Blacks and Northern Blacks

For southern African Americans the process of Jim Crow reform exacerbated the long-standing division between accommodationist and expansive approaches to confronting the color line and highlighted the growing isolation of African American liberals.[14] For African American reformers such as Charles S. Johnson, a sociologist and the president of Fisk University, Jim Crow reform offered tangible (albeit more limited) material as well political benefits. At the same time Jim Crow reform also resonated deeply with their wary yet firm belief in the redemptive power of the American creed.[15]

Yet this vision of limited inclusion offered by the black Jim Crow reformers conflicted with other groups in the African American community. At the beginning of the Jim Crow era reforms threatened long-standing power relationships and concessions that individual African Americans had developed between themselves and white elites. The *Gaines* decision revealed a range of competing private, institutional, and community interests within the southern African American community. By the late 1940s another dynamic had emerged: between desegregation and integration. For blacks this was an important and still unsettled distinction. The fact that if pressed, white reformers reluctantly favored desegregation made this debate within the

African American community even more contentious. Gordon B. Hancock, one of the South's preeminent black reformers, expressed this viewpoint in the volume *What the Negro Wants*, which was published in 1944. He argued that there was no way that the postwar United States, and by extension the South, could "avoid a head-on collision with the color question," but he did raise a number of questions about the conditions racial adjustment should demand:

> In our fight for our rights, shall we make a frontal or a flank attack?... What proportion of our moral and material energies shall we use fighting segregation and what proportion shall we employ making the most of it, to gain strength with which further to fight it? Shall we exhaust our energies in efforts at integration or shall we make the very most of a separate economy that is forced upon us...? Shall we adopt the same type of education current among whites or shall we seek a type of education that meets the needs of the millions of Negroes rather than a type that meets the needs of the few Negroes in the higher brackets of life? In the first case we too often satisfy merely our pride; in the second we satisfy the demands of an inexorable situation.[16]

For desegregation advocates like Hancock integration was desirable in the abstract. In light of the immediate conditions of southern African Americans, integration could possibly undermine, if not destroy African American institutions and communities that were often the only bulwark against a hostile Jim Crow order. Indeed overlooked in the integration approach were the African American teachers and principals and the schools, including those funded by the Rosenwald Foundation, which were eliminated from the integrated but white-controlled southern school systems. The hard-earned African American social capital created by Jim Crow reform collapsed; one-way integration was its replacement.

For those who advocated the integrationist approach Jim Crow reform underlined the utter perversion of the American creed: separate simply could not be equal; either one was a full citizen of the polity, or one was not. Anything in between was simply delusion and evasion of the fundamental essence of American democracy. Beyond this belief was the argument that the "Negro problem" was not a southern problem (if it had ever really been a problem at all); it was a national problem "so long as trains, automobiles, planes, the telephone, telegraph, printing presses, and nation-wide business, church, educational, labor and other national organizations exist." According to Rayford Logan, "The only way by which the South can make its problem exclusively a southern problem is for it to secede from the Union."[17] First-class citizenship could not be effectively addressed on a sectional basis. Nonetheless southern whites, and less willingly southern blacks, continued to play out the roles assigned to them within the Jim Crow order. It was a search for a moderate middle ground that did not fundamentally alter the dividing lines of southern state and society.

Increasingly, though, this middle ground would be abandoned by southern black reformers as the strategies they adopted under the Jim Crow order became increasingly attacked as overly accommodationist at best, and possibly racial treachery at worst. The problems of race were increasingly defined by and for northern blacks.

The Durham Conference

While the tensions created by wartime mobilization and migration caused some southern white reformers to reaffirm their commitment to segregation, other reformers attempted once again to find a sensible middle ground. Their attempt to find this middle ground occurred as a result of the ground shifting beneath them. White reformers believed that white southerners had been the victims of "inexorable [forces] conditioned in cultural complexes, suffering terribly and needing sympathy and help as few peoples ever needed it in the annals of man." Yet suddenly the white South found itself in "retrogression in comparison with what was demanded and with the commitments of the American people to global democracy."[18]

For southern white reformers Jim Crow reform became less about envisioning new strategies and more about controlling southern blacks in a rearguard action: defense rather than offense became the order of the day. Southern whites, in the words of John Temple Graves, were convinced that the unrest among black southerners was fomented by "Northern agitators," whose activity in turn lent support to "Southern agitators of the white man."[19] In the view of some white reformers there was no difference between the NAACP and the Ku Klux Klan.

Despite this growing intransigence, some white reformers attempted to initiate an interracial dialogue. In 1942 Jesse Daniel Ames, now the de facto head of an increasingly moribund CIC, contacted Gordon Hancock, a staunch black reformer and the president of Virginia Union College. Hancock was invited to pull together a conference of southern blacks to draft a "new charter on race relations for the South."

Hancock acceded to Ames's request and invited a roster of safe and sensible black southerners, mostly drawn from southern educational institutions. The group met in Durham, North Carolina, in October 1942 as the Southern Conference on Race Relations. P. B. Young was the chair, Luther P. Jackson the secretary-treasurer, and Hancock the director. The conference statement was signed by Charles S. Johnson of Fisk, Frederick D. Patterson of Tuskegee, Benjamin E. Mays of Morehouse College, Rufus E. Clement of Atlanta University, and Horace Mann Bond of Fort Valley State College. Aside from Young there were a few representatives from groups outside of academe, most notably a representative from the CIO and one from the AFL. With the exception of these two, all of those in attendance had links, professional and otherwise, to the social and educational structure created by Jim Crow reform. This was by design, as Ames felt that such a conference would be able to paint a true picture of southern black opinion untainted by northern or federal interests.

At first the results of the Durham Conference were welcomed by white reformers, although the tone of the report was a little unsettling. The report was an unabashed declaration of independence from interracial paternalism. Its introduction stated, "[The] southern Negro today is speaking for himself... [and setting forth] just what the Negro wants and is expecting of the post-war South and the nation." A stunned Ames would read that the safe and sane black elites of the South were in a decorous revolt.

> We are proposing to draft a New Charter of Race Relations in the South. The old charter is paternalistic and traditional; we want a new Charter that is fraternalistic and scientific; for the old charter is not compatible with the manhood and security of the Negro, neither is it compatible with the dignity and self-respect of the South.... The Negro has paid the full price of citizenship in the South and nation, and the Negro wants to enjoy the full exercise of this citizenship, no more and no less.... We therefore need not cringe and crawl, tremble or truckle or even tip-toe, as we deliberate on a possible way to relieve a pressure that is already becoming critical.[20]

The Durham conference offered white reformers what would become a problematic bone for southern black leadership: an agreement to not challenge segregation for the duration of the war. By the following summer even this concession was not enough, as some white reformers became even more unhinged by the changes in southern society created by the war. At the follow-on conference that was held in Richmond, a long-time white CIC member, M. Ashby Jones, denounced the Durham statement as an example of southern blacks pushing too hard, and too unrealistically, for change.

The Durham conference was followed by other attempts to create a middle ground. Two years later William T. Crouch proposed to publish under the auspices of the University of North Carolina Press an edited volume by blacks. This work would enlighten the nation and the (white) South in answering the question of "what the Negro wants." To Crouch's chagrin this group of contributors (which included southern and nonsouthern blacks) declared, "Negroes eventually [want] to enjoy the same rights, opportunities and privileges that are vouchsafed to all other Americans and to fulfill all the obligations that are required of all other Americans. Americans who profess to believe in democracy will have to face the dilemma of cooperating in the implementation of these aspirations or of limiting their ideals to white Americans only."[21] In a publisher's introduction hastily added to the book, Crouch would disavow these statements of what African Americans wanted. Instead he argued that these blacks, as well as people such as Gunnar Myrdal, were operating under "gross misapprehensions of what such ideas as equality, freedom, democracy, human right, have meant, and of what they can be made to mean." What blacks needed, argued Crouch, was a return to the ideals and leadership of Booker T. Washington.[22]

The Durham Conference and its aftermath signaled the intellectual exhaustion of Jim Crow reform. Southern blacks, based on their own conviction as well as increased pressure from northern blacks, had gone on the record as refusing to countenance a permanent state of segregation. White reformers had also reached an impasse and ultimately a split in the ranks that shattered any notion of a powerful moderating force in southern politics. White southern liberals like Mark Ethridge and Virginius Dabney increasingly turned into outright conservatives. Blacks, especially southerners, were demanding too much and too soon. This betrayal was also taken personally.

In the dark days of the 1920s, which in retrospect was the beginning of the golden age of the Jim Crow order, these white reformers had taken what they believed were courageous stands. In a system governed by the dictum of separate and (un)equal, it was incumbent upon the white South for purposes of legitimacy and morality to live up to its political and ideological commitments. The work of these white liberals—in newspaper columns, committees and study groups, and behind-the-scenes lobbying—had all been focused on the perfection of the Jim Crow order. Now their work as well as the political and social order that they thought was consistent with American traditions of self-determination and majoritarian democracy was under attack. This attack was coming not just from outside the order, which was to be expected, but from inside the order as well. To soon-to-be former reformers such as Virginius Dabney, the South, the Jim Crow order, and southern reform were all standing "nearer and nearer" on a "dangerous precipice."[23] World War II had shattered the beginning of a new golden age in which the southern reformers had developed almost complete "unanimity in plans for cooperative arrangements, in which Negroes and whites were enthusiastic": "Today...there is practically none of this left."[24]

The end of this grand coalition of willing partners in the perfection of racial harmony was symbolized best by the feeble end of the CIC and the initial lackluster performance of its successor organization, the Southern

Regional Council. Moribund since the mid-1930s with the departure of Will Alexander and others to Roosevelt's New Deal administration, the CIC had come under the increasing control of Jessie Daniel Ames. An earlier attempt by Howard Odum to take over the organization and transform it into a vehicle that would advance his regionalism agenda also failed. By the beginning of the war only a skeleton staff remained. The Durham Conference and the later Richmond debacle demonstrated the exhaustion of the biracial doctrine and the growing dissent over what Charles Johnson called the "next steps."[25] This dissent occurred within and between whites and blacks.

The uncertainty over the next steps was seen in the creation of the Southern Regional Council, which was incorporated in January 1944. The issue of segregation by then was clearly on the table (though whether it was welcome was another issue), at least in the reform- and liberal-minded southern community.[26] Although many of the earlier names that had been involved in the CIC were also involved in the SRC, this involvement did not extend beyond figurehead status. For whites like Virginius Dabney, uncertainty over whether the SRC would ultimately publicly renounce segregation would lead them to distance themselves from and ultimately resign from the SRC. For blacks and increasingly more integrationist-minded whites, the SRC's refusal to take a stand on segregation also meant a distancing; they believed the SRC was not liberal enough, especially for the few northern foundations still interested in "the South" as opposed to civil rights. By the time the organization took an official stand against segregation in 1949, the moment for southern reform had passed. The SRC would spend the next decade scrambling for funds, members, and attention until it found a new role in the modern civil rights movement.

The Death of Jim Crow Reform

The death of the CIC and the birth of the SRC mirrored in one sense the literal death as well as the dispersal of Jim Crow reformers. The intellectual father of race relations, Robert Parks, died in 1944, and Charles Merriam, Parks's intellectual counterpart in the social sciences at Chicago and the mentor of the state reformers, died in 1953. Jackson Davis, a long-time southern field agent for the GEB, died in 1947. Edwin Embree, head of the Rosenwald Foundation, died in 1950, after the Foundation finally shut its doors in 1948. Will Alexander retired to North Carolina in 1948.

The social scientists who had provided the analytical structure on which the support and the eventual critique of the Jim Crow order rested also died or left the South. Luther Jackson died in 1950, Howard Odum in 1954, Charles Johnson in 1956. Meanwhile the cadre of southern researchers who had provided the analyses central to the rational planning of the Jim Crow order had moved on, in some cases out of the South. Roscoe Martin, the public administration reformer and political scientist based at the University of Alabama, left the South for Syracuse University after his organization sponsored V. O. Key's *Southern Politics*. Arthur Raper, Odum's student and the author of the *Tragedy of Lynching*, left the South deeply pessimistic about prospects for change; he would eventually make a career in the federal government, seeking to apply his New Deal experiences abroad. Ralph Bunche also moved on, first to the federal government during the war and then into a long career at the United Nations, reinventing himself as an international diplomat and subsequently being awarded a Nobel Peace Prize.

Their physical absence was echoed in the intellectual weakness and ultimately collapse of Jim Crow reform thought. This weakness was first thrown into sharp relief by Gunnar Myrdal's *An American Dilemma*, the template of the racial liberalism that would define mid-twentieth-century American politics and society and the civil rights movement that emerged in its wake.[27] Under this new intellectual regime the South and its white southerners were no longer central to the race problem. Race was *the nation's* political, economic, social, and in particular moral problem. The South was simply an extreme manifestation of this broader problem. Because race was a national problem, the South—and by extension white southerners—could no longer claim any special status or legitimacy, nor could they be expected to hold any special privileges. The South could not monopolize the issue, shape the debate, or control the agenda. Unlike Jim Crow reform, racial change could and should be directed by the government. Under this new racial liberalism, reliance on the slow change of white folkways—change instigated by reliance on vague gradualism and appeasement—gave way to a new and forceful immediacy. The immediate application of stateways could alter folkways. Myrdalism and, by extension, racial liberalism would argue that change could be created by individuals and by the state and that society would somehow have to follow.

From Reform to Protest

Southern reformers engaged in an approach that would ultimately prove to be unsuccessful given the internal and external forces converging on the South. The limitations of white southern reform and in particular its endorsement of economic growth coupled with limited social and political rights for blacks as a solution to the crisis of the Jim Crow state, rested on three unstable legs. First, central to Jim Crow reform was its belief that white southerners would give a fair hearing to a rational discourse on race that was buttressed by the findings of objective, yet sympathetic social science. Southern reformers were convinced that a way could be found to circumvent and somehow neuter the emotionally charged discussions produced by race-baiting demagogic politicians. Second, Jim Crow reform and the economic and class assumptions that constituted an element of it rested on an increasingly unrealistic belief that African Americans would accept a still separate but slightly less unequal vision of American citizenship. Southern liberals were blind, in some cases by choice and in other cases by their environment, to a growing reality of African Americans as active agents in a quest for full and inclusive American citizenship.

The third leg of Jim Crow reform, adherence to the maintenance of social inequality, was shattered by the *Brown v. Board of Education* decision in 1954. Unlike voting cases, the *Brown* decision went straight to the heart of the Jim Crow order; vertical segregation was never the point. Segregation was about the right of whites to dominate blacks. *Brown* stripped away the distractions of vertical segregation and theoretically ended the political and economic institutions that maintained social inequality and created the benefits derived from white privilege. In the face of such an egregious assault on southern culture and white privilege any concession—political, economic, or social—was unacceptable to many southern whites.

What made the time right for Rosa Parks and others? Reform had brought about some changes in the South, but those changes were too much for some and not enough for others. In the midst of this the time arrived for the civil rights movement to begin, as there simply was no other alternative left but to fight.

Race, Region, and American Political Development: An Analytical Coda

> I must confess that over the past few years I have been gravely disappointed with the white moderate. I have almost reached the regrettable conclusion that the Negro's great stumbling block in his stride toward freedom is not the White Citizen's Counciler or the Ku Klux Klanner, but the white moderate, who is more devoted to "order" than to justice; who prefers a negative peace which is the absence of tension to a positive peace which is the presence of justice; who constantly says: "I agree with you in the goal you seek, but I cannot agree with your methods of direct action"; who paternalistically believes he can set the timetable for another man's freedom; who lives by a mythical concept of time and who constantly advises the Negro to wait for a "more convenient season." Shallow understanding from people of good will is more frustrating than absolute misunderstanding from people of ill will. Lukewarm acceptance is much more bewildering than outright rejection.

As quoted above, Martin Luther King Jr.'s *Letter from a Birmingham Jail* captures the quickening pace of the civil rights movement and the inability of the few remaining self-proclaimed southern white moderates to understand what King would later call the "fierce urgency of now."[1] Nearly fifty years later, in a successful bid to become the first African American president, Barack Obama invoked some of those same words and some of King's spirit. Yet the world in which Obama made his historic run was vastly different from the world of King and the world of Jim Crow reformers. If the notion that segregation would be outlawed was fantastical to white and black southerners in 1940, then the notion that a black man—let alone one of mixed racial heritage and national origin (Kenyan and Kansan) that was sanctioned by law—would become president within their children's lifetime would have left most southerners (as well as most Americans) simply shaking their heads in disbelief and doubtful of the sanity of the prognosticator of such a prediction.

Nonetheless even with the vast changes in American politics and society that took place in the wake of the civil rights movement, there were many who doubted the timing or efficacy of Obama's candidacy. Like the southern moderates in King's era, there were many moderates who thought that Obama's campaign was "too soon"; not only would it fail (because everyone knew someone who wouldn't vote for Obama), but his failure would harm America's race relations by increasing racial tension. The campaign would threaten the Democratic Party by pitting its constituent groups against each other, from women who felt that it was their (i.e., Hillary Clinton's) turn to Latinos who allegedly "wouldn't vote for a black candidate." Obama's success would threaten whites, pushing the white working class into the further embrace of the Republican Party, and his almost certain failure would disillusion blacks and other minorities, leading to future political apathy and, more alarmingly, possible riots. Given the improbability of his winning, whites who voted for Obama in the primaries were chided that their choice wasn't a rational one, it was rather a delusional belief that voting for Obama was gaining a "cool black friend." Looking back, Obama's campaign brought out much of the anxiety, resentment, anger, fear, and hope that lay in American politics at the beginning of the twenty-first century. In the upcoming years his election, and the success or failure of his presidency, will provide political scientists and historians with much to analyze and debate. For this book, however, Obama's election calls for an analytic coda.

When this book project began, George W. Bush, the former governor of Texas, had just been elected president of the United States. His election rested on the Supreme Court's interpretation of and ruling on irregularities in Florida's voting process, from confusing ballot design to alleged massive disenfranchisement of African American voters. Bush's presidency was accompanied by the ascendancy of southern Republicans to key leadership positions in Congress. Karl Rove, Bush's advisor, spoke of a permanent Republican majority made up of stalwart white southern Republican, NASCAR, and evangelical "values" voters. The South, or at least individuals who claimed to speak for the region's people and values, seemed to be firmly in control of the national political agenda. Political maps showed the United States divided into red states and blue states, with a "liberal, latte sipping, Volvo driving" coastal elite pitted against the heartland of the "real America" of "values voters" and NASCAR dads. Others saw a replaying or recurrence of an older, enduring sectional division between the North and the South. This interpretation was not surprising, as the rise of southern Republicans from the 1960s onward is one of the fundamental developments in American politics. Understanding the causes and consequences of this political development has been the focus of politicians, political analysts, and scholars.[2]

For liberal Democrats, the continued success of the Republican Party and the dominance of its southern wing led to a variety of attempts to create alternative paths to political power, or at least the achievement of policy goals that could get past the seemingly durable hold that southern conservatives had on American politics. Despite research showing that many Americans agreed with Democratic Party positions, Democrats could not win the presidency unless the party fielded a white southerner. The Republicans seemed to hold an electoral lock on the presidency, and the key to that lock was the solid South.[3]

In this atmosphere of constrained political opportunities in which the red state/blue state, and by extension North and South, divide seemed insurmountable, I saw parallels to an earlier time, when a different, yet similar solid South played an influential role in American politics. For those on the losing side of political contests, what shape does a politics of waiting look like?

The similarities between the solid South of the early twentieth century and that of the late twentieth century were of course limited. The first solid South, the Jim Crow order, unlike the second, was characterized by legally sanctioned racial discrimination, limited democracy, and minimal economic development. Beyond these obvious and crucial differences emerged an interesting puzzle.

For a region and a period that played a pivotal role in the shaping of modern politics, political scientists had paid very little attention to its actual workings. Embedded within the American state was another political order that was the antithesis of American democracy. For many political scientists, understanding the functioning of that symbiotic order, how it was constructed, how it gained legitimacy and authority not only within the broader national arena but within the South itself, was not a primary focus of research.

This neglect was especially surprising to find in the field of American political development, given that the creation, maintenance, and ending of political orders, both as a unique set of arrangements and in concurrence with others, is now seen as central to the field's focus.[4] Indeed the presence of the Jim Crow order, the interplay between ideas, interests, and institutions, the formation and development of its political and institutional arrangements and structures, presents a challenge to the questions and concepts that form the core of analysis in American political development: the interplay between power, legitimacy, and authority; the connection, if any, between democratization and modernization; and the durability and scope of American exceptionalism and liberalism versus the alternative of multiple traditions of liberalism and illiberalism.[5]

The Jim Crow order also presents a way to understand a more basic question of politics: How exactly does the politics of who gets what and how play out in a regime based on racial inequality and limited democracy? V. O. Key writes, "The simple fact is that a government founded on a democratic doctrine becomes some other sort of regime when large proportions of its citizens refrain [or are excluded] from voting."[6] What was the nature of this "other sort of regime"? For political scientists this question remained a mystery in which they seemed to evince little interest.

The behavioral revolution of the 1950s relegated the Jim Crow order to the past and to historians. The political environment of the South as defined by Key (and largely hewed to by his heirs) was one in which black disenfranchisement was a fait accompli and ongoing challenges to disenfranchisement were seen as aberrations rather than a pattern of sustained, though intermittent challenge.[7] It was a universe in which the political activism of southern white women in leading poll tax reform and establishing and defending the nascent southern welfare state was not seen as distinctive enough to be included in first "real" analysis of political science.[8] Instead southern politics was defined by the political actors that could be easily measured and understood: white elite males.

Although Key relied heavily on the qualitative data provided by interviews, in his correspondence with Roscoe Martin he repeatedly emphasized the need for a more rigorous analysis based on empirical data. As Key's book went to press, the need for empirical data was answered in the emergence of large-scale surveys such as the American National Election Studies. The need for historical context, timing, and sequence ended and modern southern politics began with the first surveys. That the emergence of wide-scale survey research also coincided with the emergence of the civil rights movement made the need to go back in time less interesting and less compelling as the dramatic changes of the 1950s and 1960s unfolded.[9] Thus the South of 1948 was seen as very similar to the South of 1910: as a political order run by and for white men.[10] There was nothing of interest for political scientists to know that wasn't already measured by surveys.

This is not to say that the Jim Crow order or its political institutional legacy was completely ignored. Rather the Jim Crow South as an issue of race and region has been largely treated as an indivisible variable. In statistical analyses the "South" variable is an unexplored acknowledgment of regional difference. Depending on the study, it stood for extreme racial inequality, limited economic development, or a lack of state capacity. Understanding the ways race and region separately and in combination affect politics and policy outcomes has been undeveloped.

At the table of American political development inquiry, race and region are the silent and awkward guests; their presence is acknowledged, but they are very rarely drawn into substantive conversation. The regime that the union of race and region presents, the Jim Crow order, remains opaque to the others at the table, who see only the part of the order that most readily and visibly intersects with the national order. For example, to the extent that race has entered into debates over the shaping of the American welfare state, it has until recently been wholly wrapped up with region. The Jim Crow order—as the source of the southern conservative voting bloc in Congress—gave a distinctive and enduring stamp to America's welfare state by creating a two-tier welfare state. Due to the "southern imposition," one level of this welfare state was locally controlled, with inequality based on race and gender inscribed into its institutional structure; the tier of national social insurance was controlled by the national government and was more egalitarian and inclusive.[11] The "southern imposition" is only one facet of the political, economic, and social order that was the Jim Crow order.

Part of that limited engagement is due to the nature of the field of American political development itself. Its focus has been almost entirely on the development of the national state. While the fact that the United States operated under a strong decentralized and fragmented federal structure has always been acknowledged by work in the field, decentralization and fragmentation, rather than being the substance of study themselves, have been problems that the field has sought to explain away (while leaving them largely unexplored black boxes). It has been an implicit assumption of the field that overcoming this decentralization and fragmentation is central to the political modernization of the American state. Thus less attention has been paid to subnational actors, institutions, and orders in their own right, and instead the focus has been on the extent to which these actors impede or facilitate national political development. This has led bizarrely to the neglect of one long-standing political order in particular: the South.

In their recent work, *The Search for American Political Development*, Skowronek and Orren call the Jim Crow era a "notorious 80-year time-out."[12] Even recent works in American political development that focus on race also leave much of the Jim Crow order in a state of analytic limbo.[13] Although critical and needed attention is paid to the processes by which the withdrawal and later restoration of political citizenship of southern African Americans took place, the focus is on linking each episode to a distinctive moment in national political development. These works and others largely focus on white and black elites in the setting of national politics.[14] What happened in the South between these critical junctures is not part of these analyses.

One can take away from these works, at least among political scientists, a sense that during this interregnum in democracy, history and political development stopped in the South between the end of Reconstruction and the start of the civil rights movement in the 1950s. In a very cursory reading of southern history and with a narrow understanding of political development (elites and nonelites, voters and nonvoters), perhaps history and development did terminate: a small group of white elites controlled the politics and economy of this region until external pressure from national institutions and interests, the secular pressures of economic development and urbanization, and internal pressure from below in the form of African Americans' protest and mobilization challenged and ultimately defeated them. Yet as this book has shown, this story is too simplistic and misleading. The political development of the South did not remain in a state of suspended animation. Few if any orders do. If that is the case, why have political scientists, especially those in American political development, skirted a serious analysis of the Jim Crow order itself, not simply the outward manifestations of the regime?

I suggest that there could be long-term costs of this state of analytic limbo and long-term analytical payoffs from a change in focus. Methodologically the field of American political development threatens to become a caricature of that which it rejected. From its origins, the field has grappled with the concept of American exceptionalism and liberalism; on the other hand, the field has worked to free political analysis from the methodological individualism of behaviorism that gave short shrift to institutions and to broader theoretical concepts such as power, legitimacy, and authority. Yet despite these challenges to mainstream political science, the Jim Crow order has implicitly been given a pass by the field on the issue of exceptionalism; issues of power, authority, and legitimacy have been largely unaddressed. Racial and gender ordering is a thread that runs though the development of the American state, and nowhere was it more visible than in the Jim Crow South, where democracy was defined as the provenance of white male elites; white women were mythologized as "southern ladies," to be excluded from the public sphere and protected from black men demonized as sexual predators; and black women were simply servants or field hands.[15] Yet the field of American political development, like its behaviorist brethren, is dangerously attracted to a methodical approach more akin to a "drunkard's search."[16]

Despite its rejection of behaviorism, research on American political development has largely focused on elite state actors such as politicians and bureaucrats, or on groups such as white clubwomen or farmers, that have had the resources to organize and engage state institutions. The claim that the field of American political development uncovers the heretofore hidden or ignored role of state actors, or the state itself, often devolves into an analysis of a different set of elites (mostly at the national level) not easily captured by the behaviorist survey-based approach. Nonstate actors and nonelites play almost as minor a role in American political development research as they did under the behaviorist paradigm. While scholars such as Key and other behaviorists narrowed the study of the political realm to those who could formally participate (e.g., vote), American political development scholars have only slightly opened the door to exploring nonelectoral forms of political participation, albeit focusing on those who could claim some level of legitimacy as quasi-political actors. Even more disconcerting is the conspicuous absence of state-level actors. This absence is critical as the states were where the American state largely resided until the dawn of the twentieth century. The federal structure was the political, institutional, economic, and ideological terrain on which the emergence of a modern national and centralized state had to emerge.[17]

As a result of this drunkard's search, the American political development narrative presents the civil rights movement as almost entirely a product of a changing configuration of ideas, interests, and institutions of the national political order. How and why *southern* African Americans decided to sit down like Rosa Parks and begin the civil rights movement remains largely absent from the world of American political development. Why some southern white political leaders quickly turned to massive resistance while others, after initial resistance, pursued racial moderation remains unknown. The extent to which the actions of each group may have critically shaped the emergence of the southern Republican Party as well as the transformation of the Democratic Party is a story that only in the past few year has begun to be explored by political scientists.[18]

The Jim Crow order fell between the intradisciplinary cracks of political science and became the subject of research in other fields. Important questions about the development of the Jim Crow order (and thus the development of the American state) were relegated to history, economics, and sociology. The impact on the South of order-changing or least challenging events such as the New Deal and the two world wars has been comprehensively addressed by historians and economists. The varied paths toward (and away from) political mobilization of women, farmers, labor, and African Americans have been the domain of historians and sociologists. The latter two fields have also provided much of the analytical structure for understanding the emergence of the civil rights movement in the South. Historians and economists have also dominated the discussion of political economy and the modernization of the southern economy. For understanding the politics of race and class within the Jim Crow order, it is sociologists who have taken the lead with the development of theories of local racial states. Sociologists have been in the forefront of answering the basic questions of politics—who got what—in the Jim Crow order through detailed empirical analysis of AAA cotton referenda voting, the distribution of emergency relief funding, and allocation of vocational education. Sociologists, especially those interested in social movements, not political scientists, reached for and found a hidden politics of the Jim Crow order that went beyond simply the counting of votes and revealed the internal tensions that beset the Jim Crow order.[19] Historians exposed the intense activity in the Jim Crow order beneath the apparent acquiescence.[20]

Far from occurring in a vacuum of time and space, the ordering of the Jim Crow order and in particular Jim Crow reform had an effect on southern and American politics that belies its relative brevity. For example, what "separate but equal" meant changed over time from the initial *Plessy v. Ferguson* ruling in 1896, to the *Gaines v. Canada* decision in 1939, to the *Brown v. Board of Education* decision in 1954. While the Court may have set down its rulings, local people, politicians and bureaucrats, foundation officials, and teachers, whites and blacks, all brought these decisions to life and gave them institutional meaning and structure. Jim Crow reform accepted the boundaries of separate but pushed the limitations of equal beyond simple and grudging inclusion. "Equal" was pushed to have substantive meaning in terms of schools, curricula, and financing. For southern African Americans, social welfare citizenship for blacks and a quasi-political sphere for political reengagement were the results.

The debate over the acceptability of separate and equal, coupled with the white South's by and large complete inability and unwillingness to fulfill the spirit of *Plessy* or *Gaines*, intersected at a critical moment with broader challenges to American ideals of democracy and liberalism. The result of this critical intersection was both the civil rights movement and white backlash. The civil rights movement led to a host of other social movements, for women, Latinos, Native Americans, Asian Americans, gays and lesbians, and other groups marginalized or disempowered in America's incomplete democracy. For many people this new assertion of rights and identities was unwarranted and unwanted. White backlash began with antipathy to the civil rights movement, but by Nixon's election had spread from the South across the country to a so-called silent majority of "the heartland" of "real Americans."[21]

Consideration of the Jim Crow order—its formation, maintenance, and subsequent demise—allows those interested in pushing the boundaries of American political development to confront concepts such as timing and sequence. Consider two scenarios of southern politics. In the first scenario, southern blacks (or at least the elite leadership) by and large believed in the

American Creed, to the extent that they also bitterly resented white America's deviation from the Creed and its hypocrisy about doing so. With such a belief system, the decision to engage in noninstitutional politics in the 1950s was radical. Why, then, was the late 1950s the beginning of the civil rights movement, and not the late 1940s, a time of war against fascism and racism that only highlighted the stark deviation between American ideals and institutions? Why was the the late 1940s the right time for challenging the political system outside of existing political channels?

While sociologists such as Doug McAdam can point to cognitive liberation, political scientists have limited concepts to apply in such a situation.[22] What was in the political context of the South that sequenced the decision to engage in protest rather than reform? In McAdam's study, politics plays a role in explaining the shift from reform to protest. How did the emergence of a southern black electorate affect the timing and emergence of the civil rights movement? If formal electoral politics had not emerged when it did in the late 1940s as a result of *Smith v. Allwright* and local black political mobilization, would the choice to engage in protest have been made sooner or later? Was the inability to transform southern state and local politics, despite having obtained the vote, linked to a subsequent decision to engage in noninstitutional politics? If so, why? To get at these questions, a better understanding of how and why these new southern African American political actors emerged at this time must be developed.

In the second scenario, a counterfactual situation can be considered. What if, in *Brown* or in the cases leading up to it, the Court had decided in favor of the defendants, not the plaintiffs? That is, what if the Court had decided that in keeping with its earlier decision in *Gaines v. Canada*, the provision of truly equal schools would in fact be sufficient, and that students educated in segregated schools incurred no significant degree of psychological harm? The hold of *Brown* as a critical juncture has made it hard to envision such an outcome. Yet if one examines the Court's decisions prior to *Brown* as well as the current state of "race relations," as it was called in the 1940s, one could argue that as long as political rights (e.g., the right to vote, serve on juries, run for office) as guaranteed in the current interpretations of the Fourteenth and Fifteenth Amendments were enforced, the Court could have decided that no further action on the part of the state was necessary, and in fact could be detrimental.[23]

These possibilities raise an intriguing question. What would the South—and by extension the American state—have looked like without *Brown*? The process of Jim Crow reform offers a glimpse of a peculiar model of American democracy, a regional reform movement that engaged in a politics of limited political equality within a framework of social separateness. By contrast, *Brown* would unleash a national movement for full political and social equality. Returning to the puzzles of the 1940s will open up the limited way that political scientists think about race and political science, but also reshape previously accepted views on patterns of American political development.

An American political development approach can alter our understanding of political events, processes, and institutions that we have come to take for granted. For example, when trying to determine the origins of the Civil Rights movement such an approach can shift the focus away from the presidency, Congress, or the judiciary to look at the South itself. A more nuanced approach offered by American political development can also offer insights into and qualifications of the bottom-up perspective of the social movement literature of sociology and the grassroots approach of history by looking systematically across all southern states at state-level political and institutional factors, social capital formation, and political mobilization. Methodologically, by focusing on a mixture of qualitative as well as quantitative evidence, we can surmount the data limitations of past analyses of southern politics. The end result is a better model of the timing and sequence of this critical juncture in southern and American politics. An approach that seriously considers the role of state-level political actors can qualify the dominant interpretations of the timing and sequence of the partisan shift in the South.[24]

Thus the 2008 election would have presented a rich degree of complexity and irony for Jim Crow reformers. Barack Obama, whose parents' marriage was illegal in every southern state until six years after his birth, was the candidate of the Democratic Party, which sixty years previously had sustained its first serious revolt by the southern Democrats. His running mate was Joe Biden, a white Catholic who had made his own case for becoming president by declaring himself the senator of a former slave state, thereby intimating in his inimitable Bidenesque way that he was the best candidate to lure white southerners back to the Democratic fold.

Running against the Democratic ticket was Senator John McCain, a decorated Vietnam veteran born in the Panama Canal Zone (an American outpost governed along explicit Jim Crow lines), whose great-grandfathers owned a vast Mississippi plantation. McCain, however, was a resident of Arizona, part of the sunbelt, a creation of the mid- to late twentieth-century political economy that unified former southern Democrats with conservative western Republicans. McCain's running mate was Sarah Palin, the governor of Alaska, which became a state five years after *Brown*. A proud working mother of five, including a special needs infant, Palin the "hockey mom" symbolized in some ways the success of the women's movement. And indeed Palin and many of her female supporters embraced a rhetoric of female empowerment that came out of the feminist movement. At the same time, Palin also took the position that she and McCain, not Obama (possibly foreign-born and possibly a non-Christian), the Ivy League elitist, represented the real America.

In the end Obama won the election, winning along the way three southern states: Florida, North Carolina, and Virginia. At least in the 2008 presidential election, the solid Republican South was not so solid. Whether this was a one-time instance or the beginning of a new partisan shift remains to be seen. The election itself, however, was historic. The four people who ran for the highest office in the nation reflected a United States probably unrecognizable to the Jim Crow reformers of the 1920s, yet the world those reformers made—intentionally or not—helped to create the political world we have today. Rosa Parks died in 2005, before she could see this historic election, yet her simple affirmation of citizenship still resonates today at the dawn of the twenty-first century.

Notes

INTRODUCTION

1. Shabazz, *Advancing Democracy*, 10.
2. J. Douglas Smith discusses "managed race relations and the role of black and white elites" in *Managing White Supremacy*.
3. For "fair play" segregationists, see Newberry, "Without Urgency or Ardor."
4. For discussion of racial orders, see King and Smith, "Racial Orders." See also Omi and Winant, *Racial Formation*.
5. On democratization in the United States, see Gonzalez and King, "The State and Democratization."
6. See Lemann, *Redemption*.
7. On modernization and white supremacy, see Cell, *The Highest Stage*; Reed, "Looking Back."
8. Skocpol's definition is given in *Protecting Soldiers and Mothers*, 57–59. See also P. Pierson, *Politics in Time*, for further discussion of policy feedback.
9. On the NAACP in the South during the 1920s, see Autrey, "'Can These Bones Live?'"; Reich, "Soldiers of Democracy." On Garveyism in the South, see Rolinson, *Grassroots Garveyism*.
10. See Hale, *Making Whiteness*.
11. On other interpretations of the post–World War II South, see Mickey, "Paths out of Dixie"; Brooks, *Defining the Peace*.
12. See, for example, J. J. Kilpatrick, *The Sovereign States*.
13. As is well known, Washington's seeming acquiescence masked an active, though secret, financial support of litigation and other actions that would weaken

the Jim Crow order. On Washington's "double life," see Harlan, *Booker T. Washington*. For a different perspective see Norrell, *Up from History*.

14. See Cash, *The Mind of the South;* Gaston, *The New South Creed*.

15. King and Smith define this as "internal tensions, by the conflicts of the orders with each other, by the defection of actors and institutions from one order to its rival, and by their interactions with other actors and institutions comprising American life" ("Racial Orders," 77).

16. Robert Lieberman argues that ideas are a "medium by which people can imagine a state of affairs other than the status quo and such imaginings might plausibly spur them to act to try and make changes." However, he argues also that "ideas alone do not create the incentives or opportunities for action, and not all holders of ideas act on them" ("Ideas, Institutions," 698).

17. On the multiple Souths, see Woodward, *The Strange Career;* Key, *Southern Politics*.

18. See Kelley, "'We Are Not What We Seem,'" and more generally his *Race Rebels*.

19. See Nye, *Soft Power*, 14–32.

20. In *Citizenship and Social Class* T. H. Marshall argues that citizenship evolves in the following order: civil, political, social. In *The Price of Citizenship* Michael Katz critiques this approach, noting that in the American case social citizenship rights can come before or despite the lack of other types of citizenship. See also Jill Quadagno's *The Color of Welfare* for this perspective.

21. This expands Pierre Van den Berghe's work on Herrenvolk democracy, in which political citizenship rests upon racial status. See his *Race and Racism*. See also Vickery, "'Herrenvolk' Democracy."

22. For lynching statistics, see Tolnay and Beck, *A Festival of Violence*.

23. Indeed an argument can be made that the lack of civil rights citizenship acted as a weight on southern economic development as it made the enforcement of property rights insecure. See Carden, "Trial by Fury."

24. For discussion of the South's haves and have-nots, see Key, *Southern Politics*.

25. See Gorman, "Confederate Pensions."

26. Gilmore, *Gender and Jim Crow*, 120.

27. For discussion of this event, see Kluger, *Simple Justice*, 4.

28. See Jacqueline Dowd Hall's "The Long Civil Rights Movement."

29. Paul Lewinson calls this politeness "the exquisite finesse which is part of every Southern Negro's protective coloration" (*Race, Class, and Party*, 143).

CHAPTER 1

1. Grantham, "The Regional Imagination."

2. See Tindall, "Business Progressivism."

3. African Americans are largely invisible in the two definitive accounts of southern liberalism: Sosna, *In Search of the Silent South*, and Kneebone, *Southern Liberal Journalists*.

4. For recent criticism, see Steinberg, *Race Relations*. For extensive discussion, see Stanfield, *Philanthropy*.

5. On the politics of knowledge, see Lagemann, *The Politics of Knowledge*. For a more recent discussion, see O'Connor, *Poverty Knowledge*.

6. Sumner, *Folkways*, 78–79.

7. Kirby, *Darkness*, 4. For further discussion of southern progressivism, see Dittmer, *Black Georgia*; Grantham, *Southern Progressivism*; W. A. Link, *The Paradox*. Also see Tindall, *The Emergence*; Woodward, *Origins of the New South*; Kousser, "Progressivism." For the link between progressivism and white supremacy see Cell, *The Highest Stages*.

8. For a key to new southern reform, see Owsley, "A Key."

9. Indeed Weatherford's first book was one of the first texts to be adopted in early sociology and race relations courses and study groups. His second major work on the topic, *Race Relations: Adjustment of Whites and Negroes in the United States*, a formal treatment cowritten with Charles Johnson, was a widespread standard text for college courses in this era.

10. Egerton, *Speak Now*, 44–46; Kirby, *Darkness*, 51–52.

11. McCulloch, *The Call of the New South*, 5–6.

12. The Southern Publicity Committee was financed by the Phelps-Stokes Fund. See Ellis, "Commission on Interracial Cooperation," 5. See Tindall, *The Emergence*, 175–83, for a brief overview of this period. Weatherford, *Interracial Cooperation* provides a listing of the organizations in this early period.

13. W. A. Link, *Paradox*, 241.

14. Locke, "The New Negro," 3. For "nadir" see Logan, *The Negro in American Life*.

15. Cash, *Mind of the South*, 316.

16. For discussion of soldier citizenship, see Valelly, *Two Reconstructions*, 34–35.

17. See Rolinson, *Grassroots Garveyism*.

18. See E. J. Scott, "Letters." For discussion of the impact of migration, see Hahn, *A Nation*.

19. For an overview of the meaning of World War I to blacks and whites, see Klinker and Smith, *The Unsteady March*, 111–16.

20. For a discussion of the race riots during the Red Summer, see Tuttle, *Race Riot*.

21. The historians Morton Sosna and John Kneebone have argued that the views of these white reformers were shaped in response to their historical interpretation of the Reconstruction era (itself shaped by the emerging Columbia University–based Dunning School as well as the Lost Cause mythology). See Sosna, *In Search*, 11–19; Kneebone, *Southern Liberal Journalists*, 3–19.

22. Karl, *Charles E. Merriam*, x.

23. See Karl, *Charles E. Merriam*, 107–8; Merriam, "The Present State."

24. See Stanfield, *Philanthropy*, 9.

25. For discussions of race relations theory, see Stanfield, *Philanthropy*, 38–56; Steinberg, *Race Relations*, 42–57. For Park's formulations of this theory, see "Racial Assimilation" and "The Bases of Race Prejudice."

26. Stanfield, *Philanthropy*, 9.

27. For more discussion of vertical segregation, see Kneebone, *Southern Liberal Journalists*, 76–96.

28. Park, "The Bases of Race Prejudice," 20.

29. For a discussion of Hayes's concert, see Kneebone, *Southern Liberal Journalists*, 74.

30. See Stanfield, *Philanthropy*, 191. Stanfield further argues that this approach "tore history from the hands and minds of men and thus conveniently ignored the fact that reality is a social construct. Societal organization is a product of a collective consciousness representative of human interests. Social structures and processes do not appear out of nowhere" (*Philanthropy*, 191).

31. According to Stanfield, "The legitimization of empiricism in social research justified labeling data presentations as science, while theorizing became speculation. Empiricism fits nicely into a society in which the handling of racial problems was increasingly assigned to bureaucratic organization[s] more interested in 'facts' than in 'interpretations'" (*Philanthropy*, 192).

32. Other indirect or temporary sources of funds were the Southern Education Board, Carnegie Foundation, Hand Fund, Cushing Fund, Memorial Conference for Education in the South, University Commission on Race Relations, Interracial Commission, Blanchard Fund, and Phelps-Stokes Fund. See Leavell, *Philanthropy*, especially 57–82, 58, n. 8. See also Fosdick, *Adventure in Giving*, 3; General Education Board, *Review and Final Report*, 18.

33. In addition to Lagemann, "The Politics of Knowledge," see also Ross, *The Origins*.

34. J. D. Anderson, "Northern Foundations," 378, and *The Education of Blacks*.

35. James Anderson argues that foundations were "equal partners in [the] southern project of education as [a] means of social control and subordination" ("Northern Foundations," 371).

36. On the concept of state leveraging, see David Strong et al., "Leveraging the State," 660.

37. GEB, *Final Report*, 59–60. This route was clearly through whites, since according to Raymond Fosdick of the GEB, "Whatever the economic consequences of the Civil War, the psychological effects of defeat [presumably for whites] were profound" (*Adventure in Giving*, 320). Fosdick would also argue, "Hindsight [was] making unjust demands upon the past.... Sixty years ago there was no alternative to this approach; there was no public opinion to support any other course" (323).

38. To be sure, these universities also housed in all likelihood an even larger number of scholars who ranged from indifferent to active supporters of the Jim Crow order. On the improvement of southern higher education, see Dennis, *Lessons in Progress*.

39. For an overview of Odum, see Sosna's chapter on Odum in *In Search*; Tindall, "The Significance."

40. With the *Gaines v. Canada* (1938) decision, this situation began to change, with some states very slowly increasing funding to black institutions.

41. On the transformation of black higher education it the 1920s, see, for example, Wolters, *The New Negro*.

42. See Gavins, "Gordon Blaine Hancock," 216.

43. See Gilpin and Gasman, *Charles S. Johnson;* Dunne, "Next Steps." 1–34.

44. For quotation see C. S. Johnson, "The Present Status," especially 323.

45. Stanfield, *Philanthropy*, 88–89. See also J. S. Holloway, *Confronting the Veil*; J. S. Holloway and Keppel, *Black Scholars*.

46. On southern women's activism, see Gordon, "Black and White"; M. E. Frederickson, "'Each One.'"

47. For a discussion of "maternalist politics," see Skocpol, *Protecting Soldiers and Mothers*, especially 29–38. On the "domestication of politics," see P. Baker, "The Domestication of Politics."

48. For discussions of this early period, see M. E. Frederickson, "'Each One,'" Hall, *Revolt*; Ellis, "The Commission on Interracial Cooperation," 23–24.

49. See Hammond, *In Black and White*, xl; Ellis, "The Commission on Interracial Cooperation," 23–24.

50. A. F. Scott, Southern Lady: From Pedestal to Politics, 1830–1930.

51. A. F. Scott, "After Suffrage."

52. Gilmore, *Gender and Jim Crow*, 149.

53. In a letter Lugenia Hope called Moton "weak, very weak…she is too compromising in her attitude on race relationship[s]." Quoted in Ellis, "The Commission on Interracial Cooperation," 30.

54. Linda Gordon notes that African American settlements were often called missions as they were more overtly religious than ones created by whites ("Black and White," 560). See also Shivery and Smythe, "The Neighborhood Union"; Rouse, *Lugenia Hope Burns*, xx.

55. Ellis, "The Commission on Interracial Cooperation," 33–34.

56. Stivers, "Settlement Women," 523–24.

57. See Gilmore, *Gender and Jim Crow*, 203–12.

58. On gender and the state, for a review see Tolleson-Rinehart and Carroll, "'Far from Ideal'" On the intersection of black women and "statemaking," see F. R. Wilson, *The Segregated Scholars*, 90–114, 173–214.

59. Ellis, "The Commission on Interracial Cooperation," 27.

60. Will Alexander, quoted in Ellis, "The Commission on Interracial Cooperation," 24.

61. For discussions of the black middle-class and the expansion of the Jim Crow state, see Hine, "Black Professionals"; Ferguson, *Black Politics*.

62. Martin Luther King, "Letter from Birmingham Jail," 1963. The sentence follows "never quite knowing what to expect next, and are plagued with inner fears and outer resentments; when you are forever fighting a degenerating sense of 'nobodiness.'"

63. For example, Oscar DePriest from Chicago's South Side was elected to the U.S. House of Representatives in 1929, the first African American elected to that body in the twentieth century, and the first since the ascendance of the Jim Crow order. For a contemporary perspective on African American urban politics in the North, see H. Gosnell, *Negro Politicians*.

64. "Lifting as We Climb" was the motto of the National Association of Colored Women. See E. L. Davis, *Lifting as We Climb*. On the black women's club movement, see Rouse, *Lugenia Burns Hope*; Shaw, *What a Woman*; A. F. Scott, "Most Invisible."

65. Weare, *Black Business*, 212–13.

66. Wesley quoted in "*Texas Observer*, prepared by Texas Commission on Inter-Racial Cooperation, 1932, p. 4," in Lanier, "The History," 103.

67. For a discussion of managed race relations, see J. D. Smith, *Managing White Supremacy*.

68. All quoted in Stanfield, *Philanthropy*, 73, 76, 107.

69. W. B. White, "Decline," 43.

70. Thompson, "Editorial Comment: Best Practices," 127.

71. Bunche, *The Political Status*, 39, 42. Also on southern liberals, see Myrdal, *An American Dilemma*, 466–74, 842–50.

72. Quoted in Bunche, *The Political Status*, 211.

73. Gavins, "Gordon Blaine Hancock," 217–18.

CHAPTER 2

1. For discussion of "savage ideal," see Cash, *Mind of the South*, 134–35.

2. Woodward, *Origins of the New South*, 107.

3. For an example of this belief, see F. L. Hoffman, "Race Traits," especially 235–38.

4. Wilson quoted in Mancini, *One Dies*, 32.

5. See Cox, "Lynching," especially 579.

6. On the festival aspect of lynching, see Clarke, "Without Fear." There is a substantial literature on lynching; for an overview, see Tolnay and Beck, *A Festival of Violence*; Brundage, *Lynching*. Brundage identified three types of lynchings: those carried out by small groups, often in secret; "quasi-legal posses"; and mass mobs (7–45).

7. See Tindall, *Emergence of the New South*, 172.

8. For recent work on Ida Wells-Barnett, see Giddings, *Ida*; Schechter, *Ida B. Wells-Barnett*. For Wells-Barnett's writings, see T. Harris, *Selected Works*.

9. The following discussion of the NAACP's work in the Dyer antilynching bill draws on the following works: Zangrando, *The NAACP Crusade*; Rable, "The South"; Ferrell, "Nightmare and Dream." See also Tindall's *Emergence of the New South*, 170–74.

10. Tindall, *Emergence of the New South*, 174.

11. "Turn It Around," *Daily Telegraph* (Macon, GA), December 21, 1921, NAACP Microfilm Collection, Reel 11.

12. Quoted in Hall, *Revolt against Chivalry*, 197.

13. Ellis, "Commission on Interracial Cooperation," 11.

14. On the formation of the CIC, see Sosna, *In Search*; Newberry, "Without Urgency"; Pilkington, "The Trials of Brotherhood"; Burrows, "The Commission on Interracial Cooperation"; Ellis, "The Commission on Interracial Cooperation"; McDonough, "Men and Women of Good Will."

15. Lanier, "History of Higher Education for Negroes," 102, quoting Jessie Daniel Ames, *Condensed Report of Conditions in Texas from November 1925 to February 1928*, Texas Commission on Inter-Racial Cooperation, 1928, foreword, p. 3.

16. McDonough, "Men and Women of Good Will," 55–59.

17. Ellis, "Commission on Interracial Cooperation," 15–16.

18. See Burrows, "Commission on Interracial Cooperation," 129.

19. Ellis, "Commission on Interracial Cooperation," 5, 22.

20. Suggs, *P. B. Young*. On Carter Wesley, see Shabazz, *Advancing Democracy*, 42–44; Lanier, "History of Higher Education for Negroes," 99–108; Pitre, "Black Houstonians."

21. Ellis, "Commission on Interracial Cooperation," 22, 21.

22. Ellis, "Commission on Interracial Cooperation," 37–40, 41. Brundage agues that because of the state's conservative political culture, the Virginia CIC was "virtually stillborn" in that state (*Lynching*, 188).

23. For a discussion of the "Louisville way" and James Bond's role in it, see G. C. Wright, *Life behind a Veil*, especially 268–74.

24. Ellis, "Commission on Interracial Cooperation," 36.

25. According to Ellis, fieldwork stopped in Oklahoma, South Carolina, Arkansas, Mississippi, Florida, and Louisiana but not in Virginia and North Carolina ("Commission on Interracial Cooperation," 48–49).

26. See Chadbourn, *Lynching and the Law*, 166–73, 201–3, 208–10. Chadbourn's work, partially funded by foundation monies, was criticized by some southern reformers as too academic and not sufficiently linked to a program of action. On this latter point, see Ellis, "Commission on Interracial Cooperation," 80–82.

27. Quoted in Hall, *Revolt against Chivalry*, 226.

28. See McDonough, "Men and Women of Good Will," 81–82; Ellis, "Commission on Interracial Cooperation," 66–69.

29. See Ames, "Report of the Executive Director," January 10, 1935, ASWPL Papers, Woodruff Library, Atlanta University. The definitive work on the ASWPL and Ames is Hall's *Revolt against Chivalry*, but see also Barber, "The Association"; J. S. Reed, "An Evaluation."

30. See Barber, "The Association," 379.

31. "Resolutions," Conference of Southern White Women, Georgia, November 1, 1930, ASWPL papers, Woodruff Library, Atlanta University.

32. See Hall, *Revolt against Chivalry*; Barber, "The Association," 380–81.

33. Quoted in Hall, *Revolt against Chivalry*, 181–82.

34. On the importance of black women's political activity in antilynching activities, see Gilmore, *Gender and Jim Crow*, 147–95; M. J. Brown, *Eradicating This Evil*; Powell, "United in Gender."

35. See Hall, *Revolt against Chivalry*, 165–67; M. J. Brown, *Eradicating This Evil*, 57–94.

36. Quoted in Barber, "The Association," 385.

37. See Burrows, "Commission on Interracial Commission," 156–62.

38. See L. Reed, *Simple Decency*, 91–92; Rable, "The South," 211–20; Zangrando, *The NAACP Crusade*.

39. See Raper, *Tragedy of Lynching*, introduction, n.p.

40. See Minutes, Commission on the Study of Lynching, September 5, 1930, CIC Papers; Dykeman and Stokely, *Seeds of Southern Change*, 134–37.

41. Walter Chivers received his training—though like many African American scholars of the day, he was unable to receive his doctorate—from New York University. At Morehouse he was the undergraduate advisor of Martin Luther King Jr. See Stanfield, "A Neglected Chapter"; Willie, "Walter R. Chivers."

42. In addition to the Raper report, the CIC published or sponsored Chadbourn's study as well as two studies of its own: "Lynchings and What They Mean" and "The Mob Murder of S. S. Mincey"; see Hall, *Revolt against Chivalry*, 161.

43. See, for example, Wells-Barnett's writings and speeches, as well as W. B. White, *Rope and Faggot*.

44. Raper, *Tragedy of Lynching*, 38.

45. Raper, *Tragedy of Lynching*, 37–38, 53.

46. See Cooper, "The State Police Movement." For further discussion of the early development of state police forces, see Conover, "State Police Developments"; G. W. Ray, "From Cossack to Trooper"; B. Smith, "Factors"; Dulaney, *Black Police*.

47. Cooper, "The State Police Movement," 420.

48. Ray, "From Cossack to Trooper," 565–66; B. Smith, "Factors," 716. Ray argues that the use of the National Guard on an ongoing basis was expensive and logistically difficult for state governments.

49. Ray, "From Cossack to Trooper," 571.

50. Quoted in Conover, "The State Police Movement," 780–81.

51. Myrdal, *An American Dilemma*, 540. See Clarke, "Without Fear," who argues that capital punishment effectively replaces the social control role played by lynching.

52. For discussions of the early CIC's role in addressing policing in black communities, see Dulaney, *Black Police*, 39–41; CIC papers, Reel 51, Robert B. Eleazar survey of police chiefs, October 5, 1933. On the post–World War II push for better "minority-police relations," see McEntire and Weckler, "The Role of the Police"; Rudwick, "The Southern Negro Policeman."

53. Quoted in Hall, *Revolt against Chivalry*, 196–97. Hall cites a common ASWPL meeting topic during this period, "Which is Better—A Lynching or the prostitution of the Courts and a prevented Lynching?"

54. Quoted in Hall, *Revolt against Chivalry*, 197.

55. Cox, "Lynching and the Status Quo," 380, 382. For Ames quotation, see Hall, *Revolt against Chivalry*, 224–26.

CHAPTER 3

1. Key, *Southern Politics*, 4.

2. On the "central theme" of southern history, see Phillips, "The Central Theme." For a discussion of the struggle over the control of government as the central motif of southern history, see Woodard, *Origins of the New South*, especially 51–74.

3. Wiebe, *Search for Order*. See also Brownell, "The Commercial-Civic Elite."

4. On these connections, see Grantham, *Southern Progressivism*; W. A. Link, *The Paradox*; Fosdick, *Adventure in Giving*.

5. See O'Toole, "Harry F. Byrd." See also Key, *Southern Politics*, who speculates on the intersection of party organization and state reform and reorganization (306, n. 7).

6. See Kousser, "Progressivism"; Woodward, *Origins of the New South*, 369–95.

7. See Clapp, "Public Administration," 169.

8. See Sitkoff, *A New Deal*, 77.

9. See Lieberman, *Shifting*.

10. See Sitkoff, *A New Deal*, 44; King, *Separate and Unequal*, 39–70.

11. Sosna, *In Search*, 63–64.

12. Sitkoff, *A New Deal*, 78–79. For discussion of the informal women's cabinet in the FDR administration, see Gordon, "Black and White," 564.

13. For Foreman's experience in the Roosevelt administration, see Clark Foreman, interview, *Documenting the American South*, November 1974, http://docsouth.unc.edu/sohp/A-027/menu.html (accessed October 20, 2008). Alexander's appointment is discussed in Sosna, *In Search*, 64, and is covered extensively in Dykeman and Stokely, *Seeds*.

14. Quoted in Sitkoff, *A New Deal*, 77. Karen Ferguson's book *Black Politics in New Deal Atlanta* also provides a detailed local analysis of this new black middle class. On gender, see Chirhart, "Gender."

15. On the hostility of Roosevelt toward black activists during his first term, see Sitkoff, *A New Deal*, 42–55.

16. See Stanfield, *Philanthropy*, 28–29. Raper's other CIC/UNC sponsored works included *Sharecroppers All* (1941), coauthored with the African American sociologist, Ira DeA. Reid, and *Tenants of the Almighty* (1943). Raper would later become an important part of Myrdal's research team for *American Dilemma*.

17. See Dykeman and Stokely, *Seeds*; Eagles, *Jonathan Daniels*.

18. Odum believed in "balance as an important concept in societal well-being...the organic nature of society...the inevitability of progress, of gradualism as the best strategy for obtaining social change, or pragmatism as the wisest approach to social action." (G. B. Johnson and Johnson, *Research in Service to Society*, 162–64). Odum would clarify that "technicways in contemporary society...arise from the pressure of technological forces and procedures to impel conformity of individual and group to quick-changing patterns, regardless of empirical considerations or of mass sanction." Howard Odum, "Notes on the Technicways in Contemporary Society," *American Sociological Review* 2, no. 3 (1937), 339. See also Thomas, "Conservative Currents."

19. Vance, "Howard Odum's Technicways," 457.

20. Quoted in Sosna, *In Search*, 56–57. See also Southern Regional Council, *Into the Mainstream*.

21. See Nixon, "Politics," 123. In some ways these administrationists paralleled Odum's regional approach in their use of social science to address the South's problems.

22. Clapp, "Public Administration," 169.

23. Martin received his B.A. and M.A. degrees from the University of Texas, where he was part of the "Texas Mafia," a group of political scientists that included V. O. Key Jr., who was Martin's student while both were at Texas. Heard, "Introduction"; Spragens, "R. Taylor Cole."

24. Karl, *Charles E. Merriam*, x, 107–8. See Merriam, "The Present State," 185.

25. Texas's Bureau was considered one of the strongest in the South in the 1920s. See R. J. Harris and Cooper, "Roscoe Coleman Martin."

26. Their identification as fellow southerners was strong. In descriptions and reminiscences these southern administrationists repeatedly emphasized the southern characteristics and qualities of their former colleagues. For discussions of the formation of southern political science, see Clapp, "Public Administration"; R. J. Harris and Cooper, "Roscoe Coleman Martin"; Vaughan, "Political Science"; Havard and Dauer, "The Southern Political Science Association." Gender also mattered. When considering the appointment of a woman to join the bureau of a southern university, Martin argued that she would have difficulty inspiring credibility. Despite this hesitation, the woman was hired. See Davis to file, November 12, 1946, Rockefeller Foundation Archives, GEB Files, Box 493, File 5252.

27. Brookings Institution, Institute for Government Research., *Report on a Survey of the Organization and Administration of the State and County Governments of Alabama; Submitted to Governor G. M. Miller by Institute for Government Research of the Brookings Institution, Washington, D.C., 1932.* 5 vols. (Montgomery, AL: Wilson Printing Company, 1932). See also R. C. Martin, "Alabama's Administrative Reorganization."

28. On Alabama politics, see Key, *Southern Politics*, 36–57; Nixon, "Politics"; Webb and Armbrester, *Alabama Governors*.

29. Patterson, *The New Deal*; E. C. Green, *The New Deal*.

30. See Bosworth, *Tennessee Valley County*, 113.

31. See Martin to Rockefeller Foundation, October 21, 1937, Rockefeller Foundation Archives, GEB Files, box 493, Folder 5251.

32. See Burdine, "Trends"; H. White, "The Southern Regional Training Program"; Egger and Cooper, *Research*.

33. Dixon was educated at Columbia University and received a law degree from University of Virginia. After serving in France, he returned to Birmingham to private law practice. (K. A. Frederickson, *The Dixiecrat Revolt*, 89). Martin alleges that Dixon lost the 1934 Democratic nomination largely due to his "sweeping demands for reform" (R. C. Martin, "Alabama's Administrative Reorganization," 436). See Webb and Armbrester, *Alabama's Governors*.

34. See Tindall, "Business Progressivism." On Graves, according to the Alabama state website, "Although Graves was Grand Dragon of the Alabama Ku Klux Klan when he took office, he advocated a progressive program that included increased aid to educational and social services. During his first term as governor, funding for schools increased, the price of textbooks decreased, and several new schools were built. The Highway Department was organized and a $25 million road bond and a two-cent gasoline tax were passed that resulted in more paved and graveled roads. Fifteen toll bridges were constructed. The State Docks were completed and several new boards and commissions were created including the Alabama Industrial Development Board, the Realty Board and the Muscle Shoals Commission. In addition, the Veteran's Bureau was created to assist Alabama's servicemen. The convict lease system was abolished and convicts were used to work on state roads instead of being leased to private businesses." See also Webb and Armbrester, *Alabama's Governors*.

35. New departments were created (Finance, Industrial Relations, Conservation, Personnel, Commerce, Revenue, and State Docks and Terminals), while other ones

were consolidated or eliminated. A Pardon and Parole Board was also established in response to critical reports. For further information, see R. C. Martin (1940), "Alabama's Administrative Reorganization."

36. Patronage had come to dominate almost every Alabama governor's administration. Indeed at Dixon's inauguration, he was pressed to fill twenty thousand applications for appointments to state positions. The creation of a merit system, in Martin's view, would "save [the governor] 40 percent of all the time previously devoted to the affairs of office, and it will save him no end of grief through poor administration and through the misunderstandings of his friends and the attacks of his enemies." See Roscoe Martin to Fred McCuistion, "An Approach to State Administrative Reorganization," December 8, 1942, Rockefeller Foundation Archives, GEB Files, Box 493, Folder 5251.

37. See J. M. Ray, "American Government."

38. On the role of GEB support for Odum's new regionalism, see Fosdick, *Adventure in Giving*, 269–70; A. Roberts, "Demonstrating Neutrality."

39. Richard Foster to Rockefeller Foundation, October 1937, Rockefeller Foundation Archives, GEB Files, Box 93, Folder 5251.

40. See Fosdick, *Adventure in Giving*, 266–73.

41. Mann to File, December 7, 1945, Rockefeller Foundation Archives, GEB Files, Box 493, File 5252.

42. Burdine, "Trends"; H. White, "The Southern Regional Training Program"; Egger and Cooper, *Research*.

43. The University of Georgia was one of the original partners, but organizational politics at the university forced it to withdraw from the program after a year's participation; it was replaced by Kentucky. Material from the GEB papers in the Rockefeller Archives suggests that Martin's relationship with the defeated liberal governor of Georgia, Ellis Arnall, may have played a role in the sudden lack of cooperation.

44. Egger and Cooper, *Research*, 151.

45. See H. White, "The Southern Regional Training Program," 75.

46. The internship was then followed by nine months of coursework in public administration. The pedagogy of the program was interesting; it stressed the importance of fieldwork prior to any formal introduction to the theory and methods of public administration.

47. Egger and Cooper, *Research*, 43.

48. Egger and Cooper, *Research*, 180–82.

49. File Memo, September 13, 1943, GEB.

50. See, for example, Chirhart, "Gender."

51. Memo to GEB from Dr. L. Vaughn Howard, University of Georgia, November 14, 1944.

52. Mann to File Memo, December 3, 1943, GEB.

53. See Memo, "Regional Program in Public Administration," April 17, 1944, and letter from Harmon Caldwell, to Albert Mann, August 9, 1944, GEB.

54. See Cobb, *The Selling of the South*; Schulman, *From Cottonbelt to Sunbelt*; Gavin Wright, *Old South*.

55. For discussions of the Southern Policy Committee, see Leuchtenberg, *The White House*, 102–13; Sullivan, *Days of Hope*, 63–67; Foreman, "The Decade of Hope."

56. Durr was a lawyer for the Reconstruction Finance Corporation. His wife, Virginia Durr, also a prominent activist, was Supreme Court Justice Hugo Black's sister-in-law. See Durr, *Outside the Magic Circle*.

57. For following quotations from Hugo Black, see Bunche, *The Political Status*, 386. Bunche called this economic liberalism a "kind of infantile economic determinism" (39).

58. See Leuchtenberg, *The White House*, 117.

59. For a discussion of the ideological evolution of Dabney and Graves, see J. M. Matthews, "Virginius Dabney."

60. For a brief discussion of Odum, see Sosna, *In Search*; Thomas, "Conservative Currents"; Grantham, "The Regional Imagination."

61. See Albert Lepawsky's assessment in *State Planning*. Lepawsky was a faculty member at Alabama. On the decline of New Deal planning more generally, see Reagan, *Designing a New America*.

62. See File Memo, December 14, 1948, Rockefeller Foundation Archives, GEB Files, Box 493, File 52530.

CHAPTER 4

1. W. M. Brewer, "The Poll Tax," 299.

2. Bunche, *The Political Status*, 210.

3. For excellent discussions of the SCHW, see Klibaner, *Conscience*; L. Reed, *Simple Decency*; Krueger, *And Promises*.

4. See, for example, Stoney, "Suffrage, Part I"; Virginius Dabney, "Shall the South's Poll Tax Go?," *New York Times Magazine*, February 12, 1939.

5. This antidemocratic view is reported in a number of sources, including Woodward, *Origins*, especially 339–43; Kousser *The Shaping*. For specific reference, see Donald Strong, "American Government," 697–98; Stoney, "Suffrage, Part I."

6. On poll tax politics and African Americans in Arkansas, see Cothran and Phillips, "Expansion"; Kirk, *Redefining*, 11–33.

7. Quoted in Lawson, *Black Ballots*, 55.

8. See Wilkerson-Freeman, "The Second Battle"; Podolefsky, "The Illusion."

9. See Durr, *Outside*, 131. Durr believed that women's organizations such as the American Association of University Women, the League of Women Voters, and the Woman's Party provided little support to the SCHW on the poll tax issue (135, 153).

10. See Gilmore, "But She Can't Find."

11. On the role of poll taxes in the South, see Woodward, *Origins*; Lawson, *Black Ballots*; Lewinson, *Race, Class*; Kousser, *The Shaping*; Key, *Southern Politics*, 578–618; Ogden, *The Poll Tax*.

12. See Feldman, *The Disenfranchisement Myth*.

13. Feldman, *The Disenfranchisement Myth*, 115–42.

14. Brinkley, *The End*; Katznelson, Geiger, and Kryder, "Limiting Liberalism."

15. Rowan, "America's Rotten Districts."

16. National Committee to Abolish the Poll Tax, *Fact Sheet*, April 1943.

17. See L. Reed, *Simple Decency*, 73.

18. See Rable, "The South."

19. Ogden, *Poll Tax*, 241–80.

20. Sosna, "World War II," 2.

21. For example, in Senate hearings in 1943 the United Christian Council for Democracy argued, "We shall be in a much stronger moral position to be the champions of freedom and democracy among the nations if this injustice in our own country is corrected at once." Senate hearings on S. 1280, part I, p. 330, March 14, 1942.

22. See, for example, Odum, *Race*, 14–17; Jonathan Daniels, "Dictators and Poll Taxes," *Nation*, February 22, 1941; Maury Maverick, "Let's Join the United States," *Nation*, May 11, 1940; Langston Hughes, "What Shall We Do about the South?," *Common Ground* 3 (Winter 1943); Louis B. Wright, "Myth Makers and the South's Dilemma," *Sewanee Review* 53 (October–December 1945).

23. See Odum, *Race*, 17–21; Cash, *Mind of the South*.

24. See Cothran and Phillips, "Expansion"; Dennis, *Luther P. Jackson*; Kirk, *Redefining*.

25. In fact the legislation was perhaps more symbolic than practical. There was a daunting logistical problem of distributing ballots to millions of service members located all over the world and covered under hundreds of different electoral jurisdictions. See B. C. Martin, "The Service Vote"; Lawson, *Black Ballots*, 66–85.

26. Quoted in K. A. Frederickson, *The Dixiecrat Revolt*, 37.

27. Lawson, *Black Ballots*, 67.

28. For discussions of Arnall's political career, see Arnall, *The Shore*; Henderson, *The Politics of Change*; Henderson and Roberts, *Georgia Governors*.

29. In fact Arnall told an audience, "If a Negro ever tried to get into a white school in the section [of the state] where I live, the sun would not set on his head. And we wouldn't call on the governor or the State Guard, either." Quoted in Henderson, *The Politics of Change*, 49, quoting Atlanta *Journal* 1, no. 10 (1942). In his autobiography Arnall acknowledges these statements but probably rightfully asserts that in that era and under those circumstances his response to Talmadge's charges was the only politically viable one for a politician who wanted to get elected.

30. See Henderson, *The Politics of Change*, 33–50.

31. See Citizens' Fact Finding Commission, "Political System: Democracy's First Line of Defense," Atlanta, May 1940.

32. Henderson, *The Politics of Change*, 80. The proceedings of the committee are covered in Albert B. Sayre, ed., *Records of the Commission of 1943–1944 to Revise the Constitution of Georgia*, 2 vols. (Atlanta, GA: n.p., 1946).

33. Atlanta *Journal*, May 29, 1944.

34. Quoted in Henderson, *The Politics of Change*, 85.

35. See Sayre, *Records of the Commission*, 95–101. The dissenting votes were cast by Beatrice H. Haas, the sole female member of the commission and a member of the Georgia League of Women Voters, and James V. Carmichael.

36. For positions of the senators, see Atlanta *Constitution*, January 4, 1945; "The Discredited Poll Tax," Atlanta *Journal*, January 8, 1945.

37. Quoted in Memphis *Commercial Appeal*, December 19, 1944; *New York Times*, October 25, 1944. Frederic Ogden's stated purpose for his book, *The Poll Tax in the South*, was to provide an "objective, factual analysis as a voting prerequisite" (vii).

38. Arnall, *The Shore*, 101.

39. See Ogden, *The Poll Tax*, 181–87; Henderson, *The Politics of Change*, 92.

40. Henderson, *The Politics of Change*, 94.

41. Quoted in Memphis *Commercial Appeal*, December 19, 1944.

42. Arnall's comments on equality were made during a news conference in Louisville, Kentucky. See *Louisville Times*, June 26, 1945. See also Arnall, *The Shore*, 87, 96–100; Henderson, *The Politics of Change*, 138.

43. Quoted in *Atlanta Journal*, January 23, 1945.

44. Henderson, *The Politics of Change*, 90. Despite Talmadge's efforts, Georgia's voters, including the voters in Talmadge's home district, overwhelmingly ratified the new constitution.

45. *Atlanta Journal*, January 8, 1945.

46. Henderson, *The Politics of Change*, 91.

47. See Clark Foreman, "Georgia Kills the Poll Tax," *New Republic* 112 (February 26, 1945): 291; *Atlanta Constitution*, February 11, 1945; *Atlanta Journal*, March 28, 1945.

48. See Bernd and Holland, "Recent Restrictions."

49. Key, *Southern Politics*, 15–18.

50. Quoted in Ogden, *The Poll Tax*, 187.

51. Bunche, *The Political Status*, 75–76.

52. On role of World War II veterans, see Brooks, *Defining the Peace*; Lester, *A Man*; Spinney, "Municipal Government."

53. See J. Perry, *Democracy*.

54. On Texas liberals, see J. K. Doyle, "Maury Maverick"; Hine, *Black Victory*. On Mexican American veterans, see Allsup, *The American G.I. Forum*. See also Stoney, "Suffrage, Part I"; Ogden, *Poll Tax*, 215–24.

55. On the Byrd machine's poll tax strategy, see Buni, *The Negro*, 133–41; Atkinson, *Dynamic Dominion*, 18–44; Dennis, *Luther P. Jackson*, 177–91; Ogden, *Poll Tax*, 201–15.

56. Wilkerson-Freeman, "The Second Battle"; Podolefsky, "The Illusion"; Stetson, "Found Women."

57. Ogden, *The Poll Tax*, 252.

58. Key, *Southern Politics*, 617; Ogden, *The Poll Tax*, 138.

59. On the impact of poll tax reform and democratization and the Dixiecrats, see Sullivan, *Days of Hope*, 185–89.

60. On this point, see Thornton, *Dividing Lines*.

61. Massive white resistance was not mobilized by a unified southern elite. While some elites were strategic politicians using racial antagonism as an electoral resource, other elites saw massive resistance as potentially undermining the

political and economic gains that were beginning to accrue from the South's repositioning as part of the Sunbelt. See, for example, Black and Black, *Politics and Society*; and Jacoway and Colburn, *Southern Businessmen*.

62. For an overview, see, "The South Fights Back: Boswellianism and Bilboism," in Lawson, *Black Ballots*; Bernd and Holland, "Recent Restrictions"; Bernd, "White Supremacy."

63. See W. M. Brewer, "The Poll Tax," 299.

CHAPTER 5

1. See Fisher, "Multiplying Dollars," 153. For broad historical treatments of black education in the late nineteenth century and early twentieth, see E. Anderson and Moss, *Dangerous Donations*; J. D. Anderson, *The Education of Blacks* and "Northern Foundations"; Bond, *The Education of the Negro* and *Negro Education*; Dennis, "Schooling"; Harlan, *Separate and Unequal*; Kluger, *Simple Justice*; Margo, *Race and Schooling*.

2. For example, see C. V. Harris, "Stability."

3. Kirby, *Darkness*, 100.

4. Fosdick, *Adventure in Giving*, 3, quoting Baker's *Color Line*.

5. For discussion of the attitudes of the planter class toward black education, see Woodruff, "Mississippi Delta Planters."

6. Quoted in Dennis, *Luther P. Jackson*, 112.

7. Bond, "Negro Education," especially 49.

8. Gilmore, *Gender and Jim Crow*, [page TK].

9. Fisher, "Multiplying Dollars."

10. According to J. Morgan Kousser, education politics is "central to any discussion of the distribution of government in the South in this period [Progressive era], for state and local government there provided no other services, except possibly the courts, which directly affected large numbers of people or which could possibly have redistributed societal resources from race to race or class to class" ("Progressivism," 173). David Strong et al. echo this, arguing that "not only was education an early social right, it remained among the most *important* social benefits provided by the state—albeit at the local and state levels—until the social assistance and social insurance programs of the early twentieth century were instituted" ("Leveraging the State," 659, n. 1).

11. For discussions of the southern educational "constitutional moment," see Tyack and Lowe, "The Constitutional Moment," and more broadly, Ackerman, *We the People*, 6–7.

12. On the North Carolina case, see Kousser, "Progressivism," 185–86. For the Alabama case, see Bond, "Negro Education." For more discussion of North Carolina, see Thuesen, "Classes." At the Alabama state convention a motion to include this provision was defeated, 90 to 31. Of the thirty-one delegates in favor of exclusion, twenty-four were from white counties, and seven were from black belt counties. Of the seven favorable votes, three delegates represented a district with only a slight black majority. Instead of exclusion, the convention agreed on separation (Bond, "Negro Education").

13. Bond, "Negro Education," 157. Kousser also comes to the same conclusion in "Progressivism," See also Kousser, "Separate."

14. Kousser, "Progressivism," 185.

15. For discussion of Aycock and "quiet management," see Kousser, "Progressivism," 186–87, n. 31 for full citation. See also Kirby, *Darkness*, 102–5.

16. On educational funding, see generally, Bond, *The Education of the Negro*; Margo's *Race*. See also Washington, "Availability."

17. GEB, *Final Report*, 25.

18. GEB, *Final Report*, 1–2.

19. C. V. Harris, "Stability," 377. For comparisons of Atlanta and Memphis, see Plank and Turner. "Changing Patterns," and "Contrasting Patterns."

20. Link, *Paradox*, 75.

21. Leavell, "The Program," 157.

22. Leavell, "The Program," 157.

23. See, for example, Johnson, *Governing*; Wiebe, *The Search*.

24. GEB, *Final Report*, 5; in the case of Georgia, it would be to repeal laws that banned publicly supported high schools.

25. Fosdick, *Adventure in Giving*, 122–24.

26. Calculated from GEB, *Final Report*, appendix II, 82–83.

27. Thus the black community of Birmingham, Alabama, "realized that [to achieve black school progress] the necessary numbers of schoolteachers, unlike the smaller leadership staffs of black churches and fraternal organizations, could not be sustained with the voluntary resources that the black community could generate from within itself. Schools depended upon tax revenue collected and allocated by the white dominated state and local governments" (C. V. Harris, "Stability," 376).

28. David Strong et al. "Leveraging the State," 662.

29. On the asymmetrical relationship between blacks and white administrators, Harris argues, "Strategies recognized as explicitly political at the time would not have met with outright resistance, if not repression.... Black leaders typically phrased their requests to white leaders cautiously, asking for specific programs or buildings or for specific improvements needed to maintain basic standards of decency but not explicitly requesting relative advancement toward the white level" (C.V. Harris, "Stability," 414).

30. Fosdick, *Adventure in Giving*, 93.

31. See GEB, *Annual Report, 1936–1937*, 35–36.

32. Fosdick, *Adventure in Giving*, 94.

33. Thuesen, "Classes," 65, 66–67, 68.

34. The Jeanes Fund was created from the bequest of Anna T. Jeanes, a Philadelphia Quaker who left her money for the "purpose of assisting, in the southern United States, community, country or rural schools for that great class of Negroes to whom the small...schools alone are available" (GEB, *Final Report*, 18).

35. See Pincham, "A League"; Walker, *Their Highest Potential*. See also Fairclough, *A Class of Their Own*, 251–61.

36. Fosdick, *Adventures in Giving*, 89–93; see also Brewton, "Educational Research."

37. GEB, *Review*, 19.

38. For discussions of this, see Mohr, "Schooling"; Walker, *Their Highest Potential*, xx.

39. See Brewton, "Educational Research," 168.

40. In a sense it restores political activity and agency to lower-class African Americans that are more purposive than Robin Kelley's rude acts (*Race Rebels*, xx).

41. David Strong et al. define leveraging as a strategy that involved "using private funds in combination with partial public funding to directly establish new public schools and then negotiate a state commitment to ongoing support of the new public schools" ("Leveraging the State," 660).

42. Fosdick, *Adventure in Giving*, 99–115.

43. A report by Fred McCuistion found that "more than 18,130 of the Negro teaching force in 15 Southern states had less than a high school education. Mississippi alone had 1,312 Negro elementary teachers who only had an elementary school background." McCuistion, "The South's Negro Teaching Force," 17; See also Redcay, Pioneering"; McCuistion, "The South's Negro Teaching Force."

44. Redcay suggests that the names came form the fact that schools were intended to be centrally located, to train teachers for elementary schools, and to offer industrial training ("Pioneering," 44, n. 9).

45. The minimum salary appropriation would rise to $1,000 in 1923 and $1,500 in 1932 (Redcay, "Pioneering," 42).

46. Fosdick reports that at the time of his publication, 1961, that there were "1,939 public high schools for colored children...of which 541 [were] accredited...furnish[ing] convincing evidence of the trend of the last forty-five years" (*Adventure in Giving*, 113). See also Redcay, "Pioneering"; GEB, *Annual Report, 1936–1937*, 25.

47. Embree and Waxman, *Investment in People*, 17.

48. David Strong et al., "Leveraging the State," 674.

49. Indeed Rosenwald argued, "Should any of our projects become permanently dependent upon our help, we should feel that we had failed." Quoted in McCormick, "The Julius Rosenwald Fund," 605.

50. In 1920, with the establishment of a larger building program, the administration of the program (including site selection, design, and teacher training) was shifted from Tuskegee (which retained teacher training) to a new headquarters in Nashville (see McCormick, "The Julius Rosenwald Fund," 613).

51. Figures from Newbold, "Common Schools," 222. See McCormick, "The Julius Rosenwald Fund" 615, for slightly different (though close) figures. See Fisher, "Multiplying Dollars," 149, for statistics through 1920.

52. See Leavell, *Philanthropy*, 144.

53. See McCormick, "The Julius Rosenwald Fund," 614.

54. For a discussion and history of African American teachers associations in the 1930s, see Daniel, "Current Trends," For discussions of specific states, see Dennis, *Luther P. Jackson*, for Virginia; Fairclough, "'Being in the Field'"; Fultz,

"African American Teachers"; Lanier, "The History"; Middleton, "The Louisiana Education Association."

55. The Association of Colleges and Secondary Schools for Negroes was reorganized in 1934. It was previously the Association of Colleges for Negro Youth, founded in 1913. See Daniel, "Current Trends," 286.

56. Quotations in this paragraph from Dennis, *Luther P. Jackson*, 110–11.

57. See the discussion of Mississippi equalization legislation in Bolton, "Mississippi's School Equalization Program," 104.

58. The equalization legislation was supported by Dr. T. R. M. Hamilton, an African American physician from Dallas County, who was also the leader the Regional Council of Negro Leadership. See Dittmer, *Local People*, 32–36; and especially Beito and Beito, "T. R. M. Howard."

59. Dennis, *Luther P. Jackson*, 110–11.

60. See McCuistion, "The South's Negro Teaching Force."

61. Fosdick, *Adventure in Giving*, 124–26.

62. Dennis, *Luther P. Jackson*, 114.

63. These teachers organizations also began "emphasizing...teacher's salaries, federal involvement in education, the improvement of school budgets, and lobbying for favorable school legislation" (Dennis, *Luther P. Jackson*, 114).

64. By 1950 "salary differentials had become the exception rather than the rule in the South" (Dennis, *Luther P. Jackson*, 131). This did not mean that officials did not find other criteria on which to discriminate. See Fultz, "Teacher Training."

65. Thuesen, *Classes*, 122.

66. Thompson, "Court Action" 421.

67. Williams, "Court Action," 439.

68. For an example of the Jim Crow reform stance, see G. Graham, "Negro Education."

69. Michael Dennis discusses the Aline Black case in some detail. He argues that "as a middle-class movement rooted as much in professional self-interest as in racial justice, the salary equalization cause afforded individual teachers ample opportunities to satisfy their own interests with little consideration for larger issues." Teachers eventually settled for a compromise: equalization phased in over three years; however, the city failed to honor this agreement. Compromise was not the end point; the case "opened the floodgates of litigation for equal salaries throughout Virginia, demonstrating that legal action could achieve results while highlighting the uncomfortable contradictions of the entire system of segregated education.... It exemplified the development of the teachers association as an instrument of racial advocacy." Indeed,"salary equalization meant more than additional equal earnings; it implied recognition of professional status and social equality. It would confer a sense of dignity that African Americans had granted their teachers but that most whites jealously withheld" (Dennis, *Luther P. Jackson*, 114–27). In *The NAACP's Legal Strategy*, 77–81, Mark Tushnet argues that the Black case polarized advocates of immediate action and conservatives. Nonetheless "before the advent of mass demonstrations and sit-ins, the protest activities of organizations such as the [Virginia Teachers Association] were

chronically fragile, susceptible to white opposition and internal dissention" (Dennis, *Luther P. Jackson*, 131).
70. Thuesen, *Classes*, 111.
71. See Embree and Waxman, *Investment in People*. The GEB closed in 1952.
72. Quoted in Beilke, "The Changing Emphasis," 7.
73. GEB, *Final Report*, 27.

CHAPTER 6

1. Gates quoted in Fosdick, *Adventure in Giving*, 129.
2. The Flexner Report: "If...college training is provided for carefully selected Negroes, it is inevitable that some of those thus trained will enter the professions; and there appears, indeed, to be a distinct opening for the well-trained Negro physician" (quoted in Fosdick, *Adventure in Giving*, 174–76).
3. See Klarman, *From Jim Crow*; McMahon, *Reconsidering Roosevelt*.
4. See Lanier, "The History," 204. For further discussion of Texas, see Shabazz, *Advancing Democracy*; Bullock, "Negro Higher"; Hornsby, "The 'Colored Branch University.'"
5. On the black bourgeoisie, see Frazier, *The Black Black Bourgeoisie*; Hine, "Black Professionals"; Fairclough, "Being in the Field."
6. See J. W. Davis, "The Negro Land-Grant College," 324. For a discussion of Gandy, see Dennis, *Luther P. Jackson*.
7. Fosdick, *Adventure in Giving*, 190.
8. Fosdick, *Adventure in Giving*, 189.
9. Although the offer was made in 1935, the legislature did not act until 1940, and then it only appropriated $10,000 to transform it into a two-year training college for rural elementary teachers (Fosdick, *Adventure in Giving*, 209–10). In 1942 the GEB and the Rosenwald Foundation granted $30,000. Later that year the state legislature gave it the status of a four-year institution. By 1955 the state had raised its funding to the "regal sum" of $325,000. By contrast, the GEB contributed approximately $500,000 to the college during the same period, paying for new buildings. See Fosdick, *Adventure in Giving*, 210.
10. For this quotation and following, see Fosdick, *Adventure in Giving*, 197.
11. This atypical budgetary performance on the part of Mississippi might be due to its having relatively fewer state supported institutions for African Americans.
12. See Lanier, "The History"; Shabazz, *Advancing Democracy*.
13. See Bond, *Negro Education*; Kluger, *Simple Justice*; Tushnet, *The NAACP's Legal Strategy*; McCuistion, "Graduate Instruction."
14. See Kluger, *Simple Justice*; Ransom, "Education."
15. See especially Bluford, "The Lloyd Gaines Story"; Kelleher, "The Case."
16. See Burke and Hine, "The School," 52.
17. Quoted in Fosdick, *Adventure in Giving*, 183.
18. Charles Thompson, the editor of the *Journal of Negro Education*, had a series of editorials on this issue; the quotation is from "Editorial Comment: Negro Higher Education in Maryland," 128.

19. Weaver and Page, "The Black Press," 17.

20. Shepard quoted in Burns, "Graduate Education," 197.

21. Burns, "Graduate Education," 206.

22. On this point, see Weaver and Page, "The Black Press," 21. Other black colleges and universities also indirectly benefited from the *Gaines* effect. Fort Valley Junior College in Georgia was raised to a four-year institution in 1939, and Albany State College, also in Georgia, also became a four-year institution.

23. This is discussed in R. E. Jackson, "Financial Aid." See *Wrighten v. Board of Trustees University of South Carolina*, 1947. For discussions of the contentiousness of the issue, see E. D. Hoffman, "The Genesis"; Lau, "Freedom Road"; Roefs, "The Impact."

24. On Mississippi's equalization strategy, see F. O. Alexander and Whiteside, "Negro Higher"; J. D. Anderson, "Philanthropy"; Bolton, "Mississippi's School Equalization Program"; Woodruff, "Mississippi Delta Planters."

25. The following works discuss these grants: R. E. Jackson, "Financial Aid"; Capps, "The Virginia Out-of-State Graduate Aid Program"; Clement, "Legal Provisions."

26. See Daniel, "Negro Higher Education."

27. In CPI-adjusted 2005 dollars, the amounts would be approximately $56,000 (DE), $100,000 (WV), $334,000 (MO), $389,000 (MD), $445,000 (VA).

28. Clement, "Legal Provisions," 146.

29. Thompson, "Editorial Comment: Extension," 440.

30. Capps, "The Virginia Out-of-State Graduate Aid Program," 33. See also Clement, "Legal Provisions," for state-by-state description of these programs' administration.

31. Toppin, *Loyal*; Atwood, "The Origin"; Wennersten, "The Travail."

32. Daniel, "Negro Higher Education," 383.

33. See Capps, "The Virginia Out-of-State Graduate Aid Program"; Smith, *Managing White Supremacy*, 244–49.

34. Jenkins, "Negro Higher Education."

35. Quoted in J. D. Smith, *Managing White* Supremacy, 248.

36. F. O. Alexander and Whiteside, "Negro Higher"; Daniel, "Negro Higher Education"; Thompson, "Editorial Comment: Extension"; Thompson, "Editorial Comment: Administrators"; Thompson, "Editorial Comment: Why"; Weaver, "The Black Press."

37. See Ivey, "Regional Education"; Thompson, "Editorial Comment: Why."

38. See Virginia State College, 1946, John M. Gandy Papers, Virginia State Univeristy Archives; Thompson, "Editorial Comment: Some," 520.

39. See Picott, "The Negro"; J. L. Johnson, "The Supply," 351.

40. "Court Backs Negro on Full Education," *New York Times*, December 13, 1938.

41. Bunche, "The Programs," 546.

42. Thompson, "Editorial Comment: Some," 516.

43. Gray, "Recommendation," 604.

44. Thompson, "Editorial Comment: Administrators," 442.

45. Redd, "Present Status," 403.

46. Bond, "The Evolution," especially 230–31.

47. Quoted in Burke and Hine, "The School," 53.

48. "No Gaines Fiasco for Texas Negroes," *Houston Informer*, June 10, 1950.

49. See Capps, "Virginia Out-of-State Aid Program."

50. On of Gaines, see Bluford, "The Lloyd Gaines Story." On Bailey, see Burke and Hine, "The School of Law," 36. On Hocutt, see G. Ware, "Hocutt," 233.

CHAPTER 7

1. Quoted in Clement, "Legal Provisions," 143.

2. For historical overviews of southern universities and their challenges, see Dennis, *Lessons*; Wells, "From Ideas."

3. Gee, *Research Barriers*.

4. Although many black colleges and universities received some type of GEB funding, from the 1920s on the GEB decided to concentrate on four academic centers for southern blacks. See Fosdick, *Adventure in Giving*.

5. Odum, *Southern Regions*, 520.

6. On early discussion on regional approaches, see Coffman, "Regional Planning"; Kendrick, "A Southern Confederation; Pipkin, "Southern Philosophy."

7. See G. Graham, "Negro Education"; R. S. Baker, "The Paradoxes."

8. Bluford, "Lloyd Gaines," 244. This is equivalent to about $2.5 million in 2005 dollars.

9. C. Wilson, "Racial Dialectic," 2089.

10. Despite these limitations, Lincoln University Law School did have an impact. For example, the second dean of the law school, Scovell Richardson, would win an important civil rights case, defeating attempts to enforce a restrictive covenant when he attempted to move into an all-white St. Louis neighborhood. In 1957 Richardson would become the second African American named to the U.S. Customs Court. Despite these attempts at institutionalization, like Missouri and Oklahoma, SCSCN's law school was closed in 1966 after awarding fifty-one law degrees.

11. In response to a second equalization case, this time brought against the University of Missouri's School of Journalism (*Bluford v. Canada*, D.C., 32 F. Supp. 707), the state directed Lincoln University to create a school of journalism. Like its law school counterpart, the inequality of the journalism program was readily apparent in its lack of faculty and resources. Again the dilemma of *Gaines* was apparent: the new dean was hired from Howard University.

12. Burns, "Graduate Education," 209.

13. See Hine, "South Carolina State," 156–57.

14. Burke and Hine, "The School of Law," 30–37.

15. Hine, "South Carolina State," 162.

16. Quoted in Burke and Hine, "The School of Law," 44.

17. R. S. Baker, *Paradoxes of Desegregation*, 82; *Wrighten v. Board of Trustees of the University of South Carolina*, 72 F. Supp. 948 (E.D.S.C. 1947).

18. Burke and Hine, "The School of Law," 46.

19. Indeed Wrighten would pay a price for what he called "sticking his neck out." Presaging what would happen to other overt challengers to the Jim Crow order and what had happened to Lloyd Gaines, Wrighten was unable to secure

employment in South Carolina. When he approached Judge Waring's wife for financial support in order to attend law school, Marshall reportedly denounced Wrighten's "extremely bad taste." See Klarman, *From Jim Crow*, 255.

20. Kluger, *Simple Justice*, 288.

21. Sipuel's parents had originally settled in Tulsa, but they lost their home (and her minister father was briefly imprisoned) in the Tulsa Race Riots of 1921, when whites burned down substantial parts of the city's thriving African American community. The family of John Hope Franklin, the African American historian, was also harmed by the Tulsa Riot (see his autobiography, *Mirror to America*).

22. *Sipuel v. Oklahoma State Board of Regents* 332 U.S. 631 (1948).

23. See Hubbell, "The Desegregation."

24. Quoted in *Texas Observer*, prepared by Texas Commission on Inter-Racial Cooperation, 1932.

25. On Texas, see Lanier, "The History," especially 100–101, 104; Shabazz, *Advancing Democracy*, 34–65. See also Bullock, "Negro Higher"; Hornsby, "The 'Colored Branch University'"; Pitre, "Black Houstonians" and *In Struggle*.

26. Lanier, "History," 106–10.

27. See Memo (1/22/41) from President Charles T. McCormick to George Wilford Stumberg, McCormick Papers, Tarlton Law Library, University of Texas at Austin.

28. See Lanier, "History," 113.

29. Lanier, "History," 111–13.

30. See, for example, Gee, *Research Barriers*; Pipkin, "Southern Philosophy 182–95; Kendrick, "A Southern Confederation"; M. B. Pierson, *Graduate Work*; Wells, "Contested Ground."

31. Sugg and Jones, *The Southern Regional Education Board*, 6; Haskew, "Impact"; Benjamin Fine, "Education in Review: Regional System is Seen as a Great Advance in Higher Education in the South," *New York Times*, July 24, 1949.

32. On early discussion on regional approaches, see Coffman, "Regional Planning"; Pipkin, "Southern Philosophy," and Kendrick, "A Southern Confederation"; Tindall, Significance of Howard T. Odum."

33. Odum, *Southern Regions*, 520.

34. On Odum's influence, see Tindall, *The Emergence*, 560–649.

35. Funkhouser, "Conferences," 125.

36. Sugg and Jones, Southern Regional Education Board, 13.

37. In 1941 southern law school deans began to quietly discuss the possible impact of *Gaines* and whether a "regional law school for the colored present[s] a fair and...economic solution of the problem." Letter, October 20, 1941, to McCormick from Henry Witham, University of Tennessee, McCormick Papers, Tarlton Law Library, University of Texas at Austin.

38. John N. Popham, "Medical College Offered to the South," *New York Times*, January 19, 1948; "Regional Colleges Charted for South," *New York Times*, February 9, 1948.

39. Sugg and Jones, *The Southern Regional Education Board*, 14.

40. Sugg and Jones, *The Southern Regional Education Board*, 18–19.

41. See Fosdick, *Adventure in Giving*, 178–79.

42. Fosdick, *Adventure in Giving*, 179. Fosdick states that Fisk had "long been the object of deep distrust and dislike on the part of white citizens of Nashville" (190).

43. See Fosdick, *Adventure in Giving*, 174–87; Summerville, *Educating*.

44. GEB, *Final Report*, 37.

45. Dillard University was created as a result of GEB intervention. In 1930 two struggling New Orleans colleges for blacks (Straight College and New Orleans University) were merged as a result of the growing inability of their largely northern-based churches to continue supporting these institutions. Will Alexander, one of the South's preeminent Jim Crow reformers and the director of the CIC, became its first president. The chair of Dillard University's board of trustees, who would eventually become one of the most important southern philanthropists that supported Jim Crow reformers, was Edgar Stern, who was also Julius Rosenwald's son-in-law. See Richardson, "Edgar B. Stern."

46. Fosdick, *Adventure in Giving*, 181.

47. Fosdick, *Adventure in Giving*, 180–83.

48. Fosdick, *Adventure in Giving*, 182.

49. Norfolk, Virginia, *Journal and Guide*, April 29, 1944, quoted in Fosdick, *Adventure in Giving*, 182.

50. Ivey, "Regional Education," 388.

51. Ivey reports slightly different numbers for 1949–50: 208 whites and 181 blacks, with a budget of $1.5 million ("Regional Education," 385–86).

52. Thompson, "Editorial Comment: Why," 7–8. Rufus Clement, president of Atlanta University, denied allegations that he had endorsed the regional plan. See Memo from Atlanta All Citizens Committee on the Southern Regional Education Plan, n.d., Stetson Kennedy Papers.

53. "Top Ten Reasons Why the Regional School Plan Is Opposed," Southern Conference Educational Fund, n.d., folder 57, Stetson Kennedy papers.

54. Stetson Kennedy, "Southern Educators Reject Regional Jim Crow Colleges," n.d., folder 57, Stetson Kennedy papers.

55. Adam Fairclough has a sympathetic treatment of the position of black college presidents in "'Being in the Field" and "Tuskegee's Robert R. Moton."

56. Fairclough, *Race and Democracy*, 134.

57. Burke and Hine report that with the closing of the last law school open to African Americans in 1905, only ten black lawyers were admitted to the South Carolina Bar between 1901 and 1924. The next African American to be admitted to the bar was Harold Boulware in 1940. Boulware, a graduate of the revamped Howard University Law School, would eventually serve as co-counsel with Marshall on *Briggs v. Elliot* ("The School of Law," 38–39). Unlike the case of Missouri, Oklahoma, and South Carolina, the three other law schools created in the wake of the *Gaines* decision (Texas Southern, North Carolina Central, and Southern University) are still in operation. See A. L. Davis, "The Role."

CHAPTER 8

1. On the role of labor, see Sullivan, *Days of Hope*; Korstad and Lichtenstein, "Opportunities"; Norrell, "Labor"; Honey, *Southern Labor*.

2. See L. P. Jackson, "The Voting Status"; Lewinson, *Race, Class*.

3. On voter registration numbers, see Farris, "The Re-Enfranchisement"; L. P. Jackson, "Race and Suffrage"; Lawson, *Black Ballots*; H. D. Price, "The Negro and Florida Politics" *The Negro and Southern Politics*; M. Price, *The Negro Voter* and *The Negro and the Ballot*; Donald S. Strong, "The Rise"; Southern Regional Council, "The Negro Voter in the South," special report, Atlanta, July 18, 1957.

4. The intersection of discriminatory tactics and the social culture of the South is discussed in L. P. Jackson, "Race and Suffrage"; M. Price, *The Negro Voter*, 11–22.

5. For a definition and discussion of "cognitive liberation," see McAdam, *Political Process*, 48–49.

6. J. D. Smith, *Managing White Supremacy*, 26; and R. E. Baker, "Negro Voter."

7. On the Republican Party's periodic attempts to purge blacks form its attenuated southern ranks, see Gilmore, "False Friends."

8. For discussions of the "southern imposition," the effect of southern ideology and power on public policy, see Farhang and Katznelson, "The Southern Imposition"; Katznelson, Geiger, and Kryder, "Limiting Liberalism."

9. The numbers of African Americans registered in the South comes from Lewinson, *Race, Class*.

10. This is not to say that no blacks participated in the white primary. In his research notes for Myrdal's *The American Dilemma* Ralph Bunche reports that in a very few locations and on very rare occasions, a small (meaning about a hundred or so) blacks were allowed to participate. These notes were published in his *Political Status of the Negro*. See also Broady, "Will Two."

11. Glen Feldman challenges Kousser's argument on this point. In *The Disenfranchisement Myth* Feldman argues that in fact whites supported disenfranchisement that would ultimately harm them as well. See also Kousser, *The Shaping*.

12. "What the People Think about Voting in Petersburg" Folder 524, Box 18, Luther P. Jackson papers.

13. On the post–World War I collapse of the NAACP, see Autrey, "Can These"; Reich, "Soldiers"; Berg, *"Ticket to Freedom."*

14. For a discussion of Garveyism, see Rolinson, *Grassroots Garveyism*.

15. Lewinson, *Race, Class*, 150; Bunche, *The Political Status*, 460–85.

16. On the "protective anonymity" of the urban South, see Lewinson, *Race, Class*, 133–38.

17. Lewinson, *Race, Class*, 135.

18. Bunche, *The Political Status*, 570.

19. For a discussion of Atlanta politics during this period, see Ferguson, *Black Politics* and Bayor, *Race and the Shaping*.

20. On blacks in Tennessee politics, see Valien, "Expansion"; Plank and Turner, "Contrasting Patterns."

21. Plank and Turner, "Contrasting Patterns," 208. See also Lewison, *Race, Class*, 140–41 for the role of black Republican leaders in this election.

22. Plank and Turner, "Contrasting Patterns," 213.

23. For Bunche's discussion of black urban political activity, see *The Political Status*, 477–502.

24. Lewinson discusses this kind of attack in a 1923 Savannah election (*Race, Class*, 148–49). In *Dividing Lines* Thornton discusses this situation in the context of Alabama urban elections during the 1940s and 1950s.

25. See Smith, *Managing White Supremacy*, 251–55.

26. Bunche, *The Political Status*, 78.

27. On the Little Rock suit, see Kirk, *Redefining*, 30; Tushnet, *The NAACP's Legal Strategy*.

28. Quoted in Kneebone, *Southern Liberal*, 54, 48, 125–43. On elite sentiments, see the interview with Dabney in Bunche, *The Political Status*, 210–13; Sosna, *In Search*, 27, 96–98.

29. For broad discussions of political changes in the 1930s and 1940s, see Kellogg, "Civil Rights"; McCoy and Ruetten, "The Civil Rights Movement" and *Quest and Response*; Sitkoff, "Harry Truman" and *A New Deal*; Sternsher, *The Negro*.

30. Some of the shift in party affiliation among African Americans began in 1928 as the result of the presidential campaign of Al Smith, which polarized the southern white political establishment. See Weiss, *Farewell*. Moon describes how blacks were pushed-pulled out of the Republican Party by Smith's political attractiveness and Hoover's "lily-white" campaign (*Balance of Power*, 105–9). Bunche and Lewinson each describe the impact of the Smith campaign (Lewinson, *Race, Class*, 171–76; Bunche, *Political Status*, 193–98).

31. On the role of New Deal programs in making Atlanta's black middle class, see Ferguson, *Black Politics*, 186–218.

32. On the role of the black press, see Finkle, "The Conservative Aims."

33. Another Texas law, passed in 1905, made it illegal to pay someone else's poll tax, allegedly a common occurrence in Texas. For discussions of the white primary, see Alilunas, "The Rise"; Hine, *Black Victory*; Lawson, *Black Ballots*; Zelden, *The Battle*. Also see Klarman, *From Jim Crow*, 196–204.

34. Zelden, *The Battle*, 38. According to Zelden, the Terrell Law was actually a set of measures that included "rules outlining the use of primaries," rules requiring "mandatory declaration by voters of their party membership in order to vote," rules governing "the use of official ballots," as well as further stiffening of the poll tax requirements (37, 38, 40). A subsequent law enacted in 1905 made it illegal to pay someone else's poll tax.

35. Quoted in Zelden, *The Battle*, 43.

36. J. K. Doyle, "Maury Maverick."

37. *Nixon v. Herndon*, 273 U.S. 536 (1927). This case was followed by *Nixon v. Condon*, 286 U.S. 73 (1932).

38. Berg, *"The Ticket to Freedom,"* 79.

39. *Grovey v. Townsend*, 295 U.S. 45, 55 S. Ct. 622 (1932).

40. The Florida case was *State* ex. Rel. *Hart v. Price*, Case No. 12842L, Circuit Court, Duval County, Florida (1934). The case is briefly mentioned in Berg, *"The Ticket to Freedom,"* 80; and is discussed in Farris, "The Re-Enfranchisement," 266–67.

41. On the lack of support for the NAACP in Arkansas, see Berg, *"The Ticket to Freedom,"* 75, 80; and more generally Kirk, *Redefining*, 20–21.

42. *West v. Bliley*, 33 F.2d. 177 (E.D. Va. 1929).

43. J. D. Smith, *Managing White Supremacy*, 199–204.

44. On impact of Roosevelt court selections, see McMahon, *Reconsidering Roosevelt*, 7, 12–13.

45. Klarman, *From Jim Crow*, 236–53.

46. *Davis v. Schnell*, 336 U.S. 933 (1949). See also Foster, "'Boswellianism.'"

47. Quoted in Dittmer, *Local People*, 1–2.

48. On local political activity, especially voter groups see Bunche, *The Political Status*, 253–327; Weare, *Black Business*, 24–257. On Louisiana, see Fairclough, *Race and Democracy*, 179–86.

49. See Morris, *Origins*.

50. For discussions of these state leagues, see Kirk, *Redefining*, 26–33; B. Green, *Before*, 54; H. D. Price, *The Negro and Southern Politics*, 67–77; Dennis, *Luther P. Jackson*, 72–96.

51. Quoted in Lanier, "History of Higher Education," 113.

52. Following quotations are from "Why Negroes Should Vote in Petersburg and How They May Qualify," 1935, Folder 525, Luther P. Jackson papers.

53. Draft of Virginia Voters League constitution, n.d., Box 18, Luther P. Jackson papers.

54. Record of Regional Meeting of Virginia Voters League, March 30, 1949, Folder 524, Luther P. Jackson papers.

55. NAACP membership numbers were collected and shared with the author by Richard Valelly, Swarthmore College. The membership numbers come from figures that Valelly and his assistants compiled from NAACP papers in the Library of Congress. NAACP chapter and branch information compiled by author from NAACP annual reports, 1920–1960, and cross-checked with Anglin, "Sociological Analysis."

56. See Berg, *"The Ticket to Freedom,"* 110.

57. For a discussion of the rise and decline of the NAACP during the 1940s, see Berg, *"The Ticket to Freedom,"* chapters 3 and 4.

58. Valelly, *The Two Reconstructions*, 167–70. For a picture on nonelite participation in the NAACP, see Presnell, "The Impact."

59. Following Stimpson's recommendations for time series models dominated by cross-sections, a random-effects panel model was estimated.

60. Voting registration data are drawn from a variety of sources, including data gathered by Luther Jackson that was later incorporated into his study, "Race and Suffrage." See also M. Price, *The Negro Voter* and *The Negro and the Ballot*.

61. On the attempt to shut down the NAACP in the South in the wake of *Brown*, see Valelly, who notes the emergence of laws aimed at restricting the activities of the NAACP (*The Two Reconstructions*, 178–18); Berg, *"Ticket to Freedom,"* 156–57; Klarman, *From Jim Crow*, 335–40. See also Murphy, "The South."

62. Tennessee's state legislature repealed the tax in 1943; however, the repeal was ruled unconstitutional by the state supreme court. In 1949 state law changed to exempt women and veterans and abolished requiring payment for voting in primaries. See Valien, "Expansion," 362–68.

CHAPTER 9

1. According to Sosna, Ethridge made the comment in the epigraph to mollify conservative white critics (*In Search*, 109).

2. On "Eleanor Clubs," see Odum, *Race*, 67–89. African American researchers at Fisk University also examined the tensions created by the war; see C. S. Johnson et al., *To Stem*.

3. Graves, "The Southern Negro," 502. For the political significance of African American "insolence," see Kelley, *Race Rebels*, 55–75. For other discussions of African Americans and World War II, see Kryder, *Divided Arsenal*; Wynn, *The Afro-American*.

4. Quoted in Graves, "The Southern Negro." On the history of South and the impact of World War II, see Bartley, *The New South*; Sosna, "More Important"; McMillen, *Remaking Dixie*; Tyler, "The Impact." For discussions of the economic changes in the South due to the war, see Schulman, *From Cotton Belt*; Cobb, *The Selling*.

5. For White's comment, see Kneebone, *Southern Liberal Journalists*, 198.

6. See, for example, O'Toole, "Harry F. Byrd, Sr."

7. Quoted in G. Graham, "Negro Education, 429."

8. Quoted in Black and Black, *Politics*, 91. The gap between the value of school for whites and for blacks was huge in South Carolina. Public schools for whites were valued at a total of $89 million, while public schools for blacks were worth a total of $17 million. W. E. Solomon, "Desegregation in Public Education in South Carolina," *Journal of Negro Education* 24, no. 3 (1955): 327–32.

9. Key, *Southern Politics*, 650.

10. See Foster, "'Boswellianism'"; Franklin, "'Legal' Disenfranchisement"; Gomillion, "The Negro Voter."

11. On Georgia, see Bernd, "White Supremacy"; Bernd and Holland, "Recent Restrictions."

12. On the murder of Harry T. Moore and its impact on black political mobilization in Florida and the crisis in the United States, see B. Greene, *Before His Time*; H. D. Price, *The Negro*, 55–58.

13. For discussions of the role of veterans in post-WWII southern politics, see Brooks, *Defining the Peace*; Wynn, *The Afro-American*; Dittmer, *Local People*.

14. This expansive approach would later be strongly identified as liberal integrationism. I suggest that liberal integrationism had not yet become the reigning approach.

15. See Gilpin and Gasman, *Charles S. Johnson*.

16. Hancock, "Race Relations," 242.

17. Logan, "The Negro Wants First-Class Citizenship," in *What the Negro Wants*, 18.

18. Odum, *Race*, 13–15.

19. Graves, "The Southern Negro," 500. See also Sosna on the equivalence some white reformers made between the NAACP and the Klan (*In Search*, 108–9).

20. Hancock, "Race Relations," 239.

21. Quoted in Logan, *What the Negro Wants*, vii–viii.

22. Quoted in Logan, *What the Negro Wants*, xv, xxi–xxiii.
23. Dabney, "Nearer."
24. Sosna, *In Search*, 111–12.
25. On Johnson's "next steps," see Dunne, "Next Steps."
26. On the birth of the Southern Regional Council, see McDonough, "Men and Women"; Dunbar, "The Southern Regional Council"; Allred, "The Southern Regional Council." For recent work on the SRC, see Norrell, "Triangles"; L. D. Smith, "'The Ordeal"; Sosna, "World War II."
27. In addition to Myrdal's work, see Southern, "*An American Dilemma Revisited*" and *Gunnar Myrdal*. See also discussions of this new regime in Steinberg, *Race Relations*, 84–94; Stanfield, *Philanthropy*, 85–197.

CODA

1. For *Letter from a Birmingham Jail*, see Clayborne Carson and Kris Shephard, eds., *A Call to Conscience: The Landmark Speeches of Dr. Martin Luther King, Jr.* (New York: Intellectual Properties Management, Warner Books, 2001).

2. For an early analysis of the rise of the sunbelt and its significance as a core component of the modern Republican Party, see Kevin Phillips, *The Emerging Republican Majority* (Garden City, NY: Anchor Books, 1970); Earl Black and Merle Black, *The Rise of Southern Republicans* (Cambridge, MA: Harvard University Press, 2002); David Lublin, *Republican South: Democratization and Partisan Change* (Princeton, NJ: Princeton University Press, 2004), and Shafer and Johnston, *The End of Southern Exceptionalism*.

3. For an analysis of the durability of Democratic support, see John B. Judis and Ruy Teixeira, *The Emerging Democratic Majority* (New York: Scribner, 2002). For example of Democratic party strategy, see Thomas F. Schaller, *Whistling Past Dixie: How Democrats Can Win Without the South* (New York: Simon & Schuster, 2008).

4. For overview of the state of American political development, see Orren and Skowronek, *The Search*.

5. On theory of multiple traditions, see R. Smith, "Beyond Toqueville" and Stevens, "Beyond Toqueville, Please!"

6. Key, *Southern Politics*, 508.

7. For challenges to Key's thesis, see Woodward, *Origins*; Kousser, *The Shaping*.

8. On Key's decision to excise a chapter on southern women's politics from *Southern Politics*, see Wilkerson-Freeman, "The Second Battle"; Gilmore, "But She Can't."

9. Although this is not to say that the civil rights movement became a center of scholarly focus in political science, as it did in sociology, history, and even economics. See E. Wilson, "Why." The study of the civil rights movement did not influence the development of new theoretical approaches such as social movements research. See Rogers Smith's critique, "The Puzzling Place of Race in American Political Science," *PS: Political Science and Politics* 37 (2004): 41–45.

10. Key makes this argument explicitly throughout *Southern Politics*, Shafer and Johnston in their *End of Southern Exceptionalism* make the argument implicitly through their methodological approach.

11. On race and the shaping of the American welfare state, see Lieberman, *Shifting*; Quadagno, *The Color of Welfare*. On gender and the welfare state, see Suzanne Mettler, *Dividing Citizens: Gender and Federalism in New Deal Public Policy* (Ithaca, NY: Cornell University Press, 1998). On the southern imposition, see Farhang and Katznelson, "The Southern Imposition."

12. Orren and Skowronek, *The Search*, 179.

13. For an exception, see Julie Novkov, *Racial Union: Law, Intimacy, and the White State in Alabama, 1865–1954* (Ann Arbor: University of Michigan Press, 2008).

14. See Valelly, *The Two Reconstructions*; King and Smith, "Racial Orders"; Frymer, *Uneasy Alliances*. On black-white elite interaction, see Kryder, *Divided Arsenal*; King, *Separate and Unequal*.

15. Black women inhabited a slightly different, though no less subordinated, position compared to black men. See Paula Giddings, *When and Where I Enter: The Impact of Black Women on Race and Sex in America* (New York: Morrow, 1984).

16. For new work that addresses the issue of the drunkard's search, race, and American political development, see Joseph Lowndes, Julie Novkov, and Dorian Warren's introduction to *Race and American Political Development* (2008).

17. See Kimberley S. Johnson, *Governing the American State*, and Elisabeth S. Clemens, "Lineages of the Rube Goldberg State: Building and Blurring Public Programs, 1900–1940." In *Rethinking Political Institutions: The Art of the State*, eds. Ian Shapiro, Stephen Skowronek, and Daniel Galvin (New York: New York University Press, 2006): 380–443.

18. See Joseph Lowndes, *From the New Deal to the New Right: The Southern Origins of Modern Conservatism* (New Haven, CT: Yale University Press, 2008).

19. On racial states, see Omi and Winant, *Racial Formation*. On local racial states, see James, "The Transformation." For further work on southern politics by sociologists, see, for example, Caleb Southworth, "Aid to Sharecroppers: How Agrarian Class Structure and Tenant-Farmer Politics Influenced Federal Relief in the South, 1933–1935," *Social Science History* 26 (2002): 37–74; Werum, "Elite Control"; Regina Werum, "Sectionalism and Racial Politics: Federal Vocational Policies and Programs in the Pre-Desegregation South," *Social Science History* 21 (1997): 399–453.

20. For subversive acts, see Kelley, *Race Rebels*; Glenda Gilmore, *Defying Dixie: The Radical Roots of Civil Rights, 1919–1950's* (New York: Norton, 2008).

21. On the transformation of southern white backlash into modern conservatism, see, for example, Kruse, *White Flight*; Matthew D. Lassiter, *The Silent Majority: Suburban Politics in the Sunbelt South* (Princeton, NJ: Princeton University Press, 2006). For conservatism and the silent majority, see Thomas Sugrue, *The Origins of the Urban Crisis: Race and Inequality in Postwar Detroit* (Princeton, NJ: Princeton University Press, 1996); Lisa McGirr, *Suburban Warriors: The Origins of the New American Right* (Princeton, NJ: Princeton University Press, 2002).

22. McAdam, *Political Process*.

23. See footnote 1 in *Brown v. Board of Education* 347 U.S. 483 (1954).

24. For such an approach, see Robert Mickey, *Paths Out of Dixie*.

Bibliography

NEWSPAPERS AND PERIODICALS

Atlanta Constitution
Atlanta Daily World
Chicago Defender
Crisis
Nation
New Republic
New York Times
Pittsburgh Courier

ORAL HISTORY COLLECTIONS

Alexander, Will W. Interview by Dean Albertson, 1952, Columbia Oral History Collection, Butler Memorial Library, Columbia University, New York.
Arnall, Ellis. Interview by James F. Cook, March 17, 1986, Ellis Arnall, Georgia Governors Series, Box A-1, Georgia Government Documentation Project, Special Collections and Archives, Georgia State University, Atlanta.
Daniels, Jonathan. Interview by Daniel Singal, 1972, Southern Intellectual Leaders Project, Columbia Oral History Collection, Butler Memorial Library, Columbia University, New York.
Johnson, Guy Benton. Interview by Daniel Singal, 1972, Southern Intellectual Leaders Project, Columbia Oral History Collection, Butler Memorial Library, Columbia University, New York.

Raper, Arthur F. Interview by Daniel Singal, 1971, Southern Intellectual Leaders Project, Columbia Oral History Collection, Butler Memorial Library, Columbia University, New York.

Vance, Rupert. Interview by Daniel Singal, 1971, Southern Intellectual Leaders Project, Columbia Oral History Collection, Butler Memorial Library, Columbia University, New York.

MANUSCRIPT COLLECTIONS

AFL-CIO Region 5 and Region 8 records, 1940–1974, Southern Labor Archives, Special Collections and Archives, Georgia State University, Atlanta.

Clarence A. Bacote papers, Robert W. Woodruff Library, Atlanta History Center.

Citizens' Fact Finding Movement Records, L1984–30, Southern Labor Archives, Special Collections and Archives, Georgia State University, Atlanta.

Luther Foster papers, Special Collections, Virginia State University, Petersburg.

John M. Gandy papers, Special Collections, Virginia State University, Petersburg.

General Education Board Archives, Rockefeller Archive Center, North Tarrytown, New York.

Grace Towns Hamilton papers, Robert W. Woodruff Library, Atlanta History Center.

Luther P. Jackson papers, Special Collections, Virginia State University, Petersburg.

Stetson Kennedy papers, Special Collections and Archives, Georgia State University, Atlanta.

Don McKee papers, Special Collections and Archives, Georgia State University, Atlanta.

Rockefeller Foundation Archives, Rockefeller Archive Center, North Tarrytown, New York.

Southern Conference for Human Welfare Collection 1938–1972, Robert W. Woodruff Library, Atlanta History Center.

Virginia Teachers Association, Special Collections, Virginia State University, Petersburg.

MICROFILM

Association of Southern Women for the Prevention of Lynching, Robert W. Woodruff Library, Atlanta History Center.

Commission on Interracial Cooperation, Robert W. Woodruff Library, Atlanta History Center.

National Association for the Advancement of Colored People (NAACP) papers, Columbia University, New York.

Southern Regional Council Papers 1944–1968, Robert W. Woodruff Library, Atlanta History Center.

BOOKS AND ESSAYS

Abbott, Frank C. *A History of the Western Interstate Commission for Higher Education: The First 40 Years.* Publication No. 2A348B, WICHE Publications. Boulder, CO: Western Interstate Commission for Higher Education, 2004.

Ackerman, Bruce. *We the People:* Vol. 1, *Foundations.* Cambridge, MA: Belknap Press of Harvard University Press, 1983.

Alexander, Florence O., and Mary G. Whiteside. "Negro Higher and Professional Education in Mississippi." *Journal of Negro Education* 17, no. 3 (1948): 312–30.

Alexander, Will W. "Southern White Schools Study Race Questions." *Journal of Negro Education* 2, no. 2 (1933): 139–46.

Alilunas, Leo. "Political Participation of the Negro in the North and South." *Journal of Negro History* 25, no. 2 (1940): 180–202.

———. "The Rise of The 'White Primary' Movement as a Means of Barring the Negro from the Polls." *Journal of Negro History* 25, no. 2 (1940): 161–72.

———. "A Study of Judicial Cases Which Have Developed as the Result of 'White Primary' Laws." *Journal of Negro History* 25, no. 2 (1940): 172–80.

Alimard, Amin. "Origins, History and Directions of the University Bureau Movement in the United States." In *The Research Function of University Bureaus and Institutes for Government Related Research*, edited by Dwight Waldo. Berkeley: University of California Press, 1960.

Allred, William Clifton. "The Southern Regional Council, 1943–1961." Master's thesis, Emory University, 1966.

Allsup, Carl. *The American G.I. Forum: Origins and Evolution.* Austin: Center for Mexican American Studies, University of Texas at Austin, 1982.

Ames, Jesse Daniel. *The Changing Character of Lynching.* Atlanta, GA: Commission of Interracial Cooperation, 1942.

Anderson, Eric, Jr., and Alfred A. Moss. *Dangerous Donations: Northern Philanthropy and Southern Black Education, 1902–1930.* Columbia: University of Missouri Press, 1999.

Anderson, James D. *The Education of Blacks in the South, 1860–1935.* Chapel Hill: University of North Carolina Press, 1988.

———. "Northern Foundations and the Shaping of Southern Black Rural Education, 1902–1935." *History of Education Quarterly* 18, no. 4 (1978): 371–96.

———. "Philanthropy, the State and the Development of Historically Black Public Colleges: The Case of Mississippi." *Minerva* 35 (1997): 295–309.

Anderson, W. E. "Negro Higher and Professional Education in Alabama." *Journal of Negro Education* 17, no. 3 (1948): 249–54.

Anderson, William. *The Wild Man from Sugar Creek: The Political Career of Eugene Talmadge.* Baton Rouge: Louisiana State University Press, 1975.

Anglin, Roland A. "A Sociological Analysis of a Pressure Group." PhD diss., Indiana University, 1949.

Aptheker, Herbert. "South Carolina Poll Tax, 1737–1895." *Journal of Negro History* 31, no. 2 (1946): 131–39.

Arnall, Ellis. *Messages and Addresses, 1943–1946*. Atlanta: Executive Department, State of Georgia, 1946.
———. *The Shore Dimly Seen*. New York: J. B. Lippincott, 1946.
———. *What the People Want*. Philadelphia: J. B. Lippincott, 1947.
Atkins, James A. "Negro Educational Institutions and the Veteran's Educational Facilities Program." *Journal of Negro Education* 17, no. 2 (1948): 141–53.
Atkinson, Frank B. *The Dynamic Dominion: Realignment and the Rise of Two-Party Competition in Virginia, 1945–1980*. 2d rev. ed. Lanham, MD: Rowman and Littlefield, 2006.
Atwood, Rufus B. "The Origin and Development of the Negro Public College, with Especial Reference to the Land-Grant College." *Journal of Negro Education* 31, no. 3 (1962): 240–50.
Autrey, Dorothy. "'Can These Bones Live?' The National Association for the Advancement of Colored People in Alabama, 1918–1930." *Journal of Negro History* 82, no. 1 (1997): 1–12.
Bacote, Clarence A. "The Negro in Atlanta Politics." *Phylon* 15 (December 1955): 333–50.
———. "The Negro Voter in Georgia Politics Today." *Journal of Negro Education* 22, no. 3 (1957): 307–18.
Baker, Paula. "The Domestication of Politics: Women and American Political Society, 1780–1920." *American Historical Review* 89, no. 3 (1984): 620–47.
Baker, R. Scott. "A New Racial Order in Education: South Carolina's Response to the African American Struggle for Equality and Access, 1945–1975." Paper presented at the Civil Rights Movement in South Carolina Conference, March 2003.
———. "The Paradoxes of Desegregation: Race, Class, and Education, 1935–1975." *American Journal of Education* 109, no. 3 (2001): 320–43.
Baker, Riley E. "Negro Voter Registration in Louisiana, 1879–1964." *Louisiana Studies* 4, no. 3 (1965): 332–50.
Balogh, Brian. "Reorganizing the Organizational Synthesis: Federal Professional Relations in Modern America." *Studies in American Political Development* 5 (1991): 119–72.
Barber, Henry E. "The Association of Southern Women for the Prevention of Lynching, 1930–1942." *Phylon* 34, no. 4 (1973): 378–89.
Barnard, William D. *Dixiecrats and Democrats: Alabama Politics, 1942–1950*. Tuscaloosa: University of Alabama Press, 1974.
Barrows, Edward Flud. "The Commission on Interracial Cooperation: A Case Study in the History of the Interracial Movement in the South." PhD diss., University of Wisconsin, 1955.
Bartley, Numan V. *The Creation of Modern Georgia*. Athens: University of Georgia Press, 1983.
———. *The Rise of Massive Resistance: Race and Politics in the South during the 1950s*. Baton Rouge: Louisiana State University Press, 1969.
———. *The New South, 1945–1980*. Baton Rouge: Louisiana State University Press, 1995.

Bartley, Numan V., and Hugh D. Graham. *Southern Politics and the Second Reconstruction*. Baltimore: Johns Hopkins University Press, 1975.
Bates, Beth Tomkins. "A New Crowd Challenges the Old Agenda of the Old Guard in the NAACP, 1933–1941." *American Historical Review* 102, no. 2 (1997): 340–77.
Bayor, Ronald H. *Race and the Shaping of Twentieth Century Atlanta*. Chapel Hill: University of North Carolina Press, 2000.
Beezer, Bruce. "North Carolina's Rationale for Mandating Separate Schools: A Legal History." *Journal of Negro Education* 52, no. (1983): 213–26.
Beilke, Jayne R. "The Changing Emphasis of the Rosenwald Fellowship Foundation Program, 1928–1948." *Journal of Negro Education* 66, no. 1 (1997): 3–13.
Beito, David T., and Linda Royster Beito. "T. R. M. Howard: Pragmatism over Strict Integrationist Ideology in the Mississippi Delta, 1942–1954." In *Before Brown: Civil Rights and White Backlash in the Modern South*, edited by Glenn Feldman. Tuscaloosa: University of Alabama Press, 2004.
Bensel, Richard M. *Sectionalism and American Political Development, 1880–1980*. Madison: University of Wisconsin Press, 1984.
Berg, Manfred. *"The Ticket to Freedom": The NAACP and the Struggle for Black Political Integration*. Gainesville: University Press of Florida, 2005.
Berman, William C. *The Politics of Civil Rights in the Truman Administration*. Columbus: Ohio University Press, 1970.
Bernd, Joseph L. "White Supremacy and the Disenfranchisement of Blacks in Georgia, 1946." *Georgia Historical Quarterly* 66, no. 4 (1982): 492–513.
Bernd, Joseph L., and Lynwood M. Holland. "Recent Restrictions upon Negro Suffrage: The Case of Georgia." *Journal of Politics* 21, no. 3 (1959): 487–513.
Biles, Roger. *The South and the New Deal*. Lexington: University Press of Kentucky, 1994.
Black, Earl. "Southern Governors and Political Change: Campaign Stances on Racial Segregation and Economic Development, 1950–69." *Journal of Politics* 33, no. 3 (1971): 703–34.
Black, Earl, and Merle Black. *Politics and Society in the South*. Cambridge, MA: Harvard University Press, 1987.
Blackmar, F. W. "Review: *Studies in the American Race Problem* by Alfred Holt Stone." *American Journal of Sociology* 14, no. 6 (1909): 837–39.
Bluford, Lucile H. "The Lloyd Gaines Story." *Journal of Educational Sociology* 32, no. 6 (1959): 242–46.
Bolton, Charles C. "Mississippi's School Equalization Program: A Last Gasp to Try to Maintain a Segregated Educational System." *Journal of Southern History* 66, no. 4 (2000): 781–814.
Bond, Horace Mann. *The Education of the Negro in the American Social Order*. New York: Octagon, 1934.
———. "The Evolution and Present Status of Negro Higher and Professional Education in the United States." *Journal of Negro Education* 17, no. 3 (1948): 224–35.
———. *Negro Education in Alabama: A Study in Cotton and Steel*. Washington, DC: Associated Publishers, 1939.

———. "Negro Education: A Debate in the Alabama Constitutional Convention of 1901." *Journal of Negro Education* 1, no. 1 (1932): 49–59.
Bontecou, Eleanor. *The Poll Tax*. Washington, DC: AAUW, 1942.
Borstelmann, Thomas. *The Cold War and the Color Line: American Race Relations in the Global Arena*. Cambridge, MA: Harvard University Press, 2003.
Bosworth, Karl A. *Black Belt County: Rural Government in the Cotton Country of Alabama*. Tuscaloosa: Bureau of Public Administration, University of Alabama, 1941.
———. *Tennessee Valley County: Rural Government in the Hill Country of Alabama*. Tuscaloosa: University of Alabama Press, 1941.
Boykin, Leander. "The Status and Trend Differentials between White and Negro Teachers' Salaries in the Southern States, 1900–1046." *Journal of Negro Education* 18, no. 1 (1949): 40–47.
Bracey, Helen Harris. "Negro Higher and Professional Education in Florida." *Journal of Negro Education* 17, no. 3 (1948): 272–79.
Bradley, Gladyce Helene. "Negro Higher and Professional Education in Maryland." *Journal of Negro Education* 17, no. 3 (1948): 303–11.
Branch, Taylor. *Parting the Waters: America in the King Years, 1954–63*. New York: Simon & Schuster, 1988.
Brattain, Michelle. *The Politics of Whiteness: Race, Workers, and Culture in the Modern South*. Princeton, NJ: Princeton University Press, 2001.
Brewer, James H. "Editorials from the Damned." *Journal of Southern History* 28, no. 2 (1962): 225–33.
Brewer, William M. "The Poll Tax and Poll Taxers." *Journal of Negro History* 29, no. 3 (1944): 260–99.
Brewton, John E. "Educational Research in the South Related to Action Programs." *Peabody Journal of Education* 25, no. 5 (1948): 195–203.
———. "The Status of Supervision of Schools for Negroes in the Southeastern States." *Journal of Negro Education* 8, no. 2 (1939): 164–69.
Brigham, R. I. "Negro Public Colleges in St. Louis and Kansas City, Missouri." *Journal of Negro Education* 17, no. 1 (1948): 50–57.
Brinkley, Alan. *The End of Reform: New Deal Liberalism in Recession and War*. New York: Knopf, 1995.
Brittain, Joseph Matt. "Negro Suffrage and Politics in Alabama since 1870." PhD diss., Indiana University, 1958.
———. "Some Reflections on Negro Suffrage and Politics in Alabama: Past and Present." *Journal of Negro History* 47, no. 2 (1962): 127–38.
Broady, Tally R. "Will Two Good White Men Vouch for You?" *Crisis*, January 1947.
Brookings Institution. Instututute for Government Research. "Report on a Survey of the Organization and Administration of the State and County Governments of Alabama; Submitted to Governor G. M. Miller." Washington, DC: Brookings Institution, 1932.
Brooks, Jennifer. *Defining the Peace: World War II Veterans, Race and the Remaking of Southern Political Tradition*. Chapel Hill: University of North Carolina Press, 2004.
Brown, Aaron. "Negro Higher and Professional Education in Georgia." *Journal of Negro Education* 17, no. 3 (1948): 280–88.

Brown, Mary Jane. *Eradicating This Evil: Women in the Anti-Lynching Movement.* New York: Routledge, 2000.
Brown, Michael. "State Capacity and Political Choice: Interpreting the Failure of the Third New Deal." *Studies in American Political Development* 9 (1995): 187–212.
Brownell, Blaine A. "The Commercial-Civic Elite and City Planning in Atlanta, Memphis, and New Orleans in the 1920s." *Journal of Southern History* 41 (1975): 339–68.
———. *The Urban Ethos in the South, 1920–1930.* Baton Rouge: Louisiana State University Press, 1975.
Brundage, W. Fitzhugh. *Lynching in the New South: Georgia and Virginia 1880–1930.* Chicago: University of Illinois Press, 1993.
Bryant, Lawrence C. "Graduate Training in Negro Colleges." *Journal of Negro Education* 30, no. 1 (1961): 69–71.
Bullock, Henry Allen. "Expansion of Negro Suffrage in Texas." *Journal of Negro Education* 26, no. 3 (Summer 1957): 369–77.
———. "Negro Higher and Professional Education in Texas." *Journal of Negro Education* 17, no. 3 (1948): 373–81.
Bulmer, Martin, and Joan Bulmer. "Philanthropy and Social Science in the 1920s: Beardsly Ruml and the Laura Spellman Rockefeller Memorial 1922–1929." *Minerva* 19, no. 3 (1981): 347–408.
Bunche, Ralph J. *A Brief and Tentative Analysis of Negro Leadership.* Edited by Jonathan Scott Holloway. New York: New York University Press, 2005.
———. "The Negro in the Political Life of the United States." *Journal of Negro Education* 10, no. 3 (1941): 567–84.
———. *The Political Status of the Negro in the Age of FDR.* Edited by Dewey W. Grantham. Chicago: University of Chicago Press, 1973.
———. "The Programs of Organizations Devoted to the Improvement of the Status of the American Negro." *Journal of Negro Education* 8, no. 3 (1939): 539–50.
Buni, Andrew. *The Negro in Virginia Politics, 1902–1965.* Charlottesville: University of Virginia Press, 1967.
Burdine, J. Alton. "Trends in Public Administration in the South." *Journal of Politics* 10, no. 3 (1948): 419–40.
Burke, W. Lewis, and William C. Hine. "The School of Law at South Carolina State College: Its Creation and Legacy "In *Matthew J. Perry: The Man, His Times and His Legacy*, edited by W. Lewis Burke and Belinda F. Gergel. Columbia: University of South Carolina Press, 2004.
Burns III, Augustus M. "Graduate Education for Blacks in North Carolina, 1930–1951." *Journal of Southern History* 46, no. 2 (1980): 195–218.
Burrows, Edward Flud. "The Commission on Interracial Cooperation, 1919–1944: A Case Study of the History of an Interracial Movement in the South." PhD diss., University of Wisconsin, 1954.
Cade, J. B., and Elsie L. Hebert. "Negro Higher and Professional Education in Louisiana." *Journal of Negro Education* 17, no. 3 (1948): 296–302.
Caliver, Ambrose, ed. *Fundamentals in the Education of Negroes.* National Conference on Fundamental Problems in the Education of Negroes. Washington, DC: GPO, 1935.

Campbell, Alan K. "Roscoe C. Martin." *PS* 5, no. 4 (1972): 509–10.

Capps, Marian P. "The Virginia Out-of-State Graduate Aid Program, 1936–1950." *Journal of Negro Education* 25, no. 1 (1956): 25–35.

Carden, Art. "Trial by Fury: Institutions and Southern Productivity." Working Paper No. 2005–070, Contracting and Organizations Research Institute, University of Missouri, Columbia, 2006.

Carpenter, Daniel. *The Forging of Bureaucratic Autonomy: Reputations, Networks, and Policy Innovation in Executive Agencies, 1862–1928*. Princeton, NJ: Princeton University Press, 2001.

Cash, W. J. *The Mind of the South*. New York: Random House, 1991.

Cell, John W. *The Highest Stages of White Supremacy: The Origins of Segregation in South Africa and the American South*. New York: Cambridge University Press, 1982.

Chadbourn, James. *Lynching and the Law*. Chapel Hill: University of North Carolina Press, 1933.

Chafe, William H. *Civilities and Civil Rights: Greensboro North Carolina and the Black Struggle for Freedom*. New York: Oxford University Press, 1980.

Chappell, David. *Inside Agitators: White Southerners in the Civil Rights Movement*. Baltimore: Johns Hopkins University Press, 1996.

———. "Southern Liberalism and Constitutional Equality." Paper presented at Conference on the Southern Regional Council and the Civil Rights Movement. University of Florida, Gainesville, October 2003.

Chirhart, Ann. "Gender, Jim Crow, and Eugene Talmadge: The Politics of Social Change in Georgia." In *The New Deal and Beyond: Social Welfare in the South since 1930*, edited by Elna C. Green. Athens: University of Georgia Press, 2003.

Citizen's Fact Finding Commission. "Political System: Democracy's First Line of Defense." Atlanta, GA, May 1940.

Clapp, Gordon R. "Public Administration in an Advancing South." *Public Administration Review* 8 (1948): 169–75.

———. *The TVA: An Approach to the Development of a Region*. Chicago: University of Chicago Press, 1955.

Clark, Elizabeth Hughes. "The Genesis of the *Journal of Politics*." *PS* 21, no. 3 (1988): 674–78.

Clarke, James W. "Without Fear or Shame: Lynching, Capital Punishment and the Subculture of Violence in the American South." *British Journal of Political Science* 28, no. (1998): 269–89.

Clement, Rufus E. "Educational Programs for the Improvement of Race Relations: Interracial Committees." *Journal of Negro Education* 13, no. 3 (1944): 316–28.

———. "Legal Provisions for Graduate and Professional Instruction for Negroes in States Operating Separate School Systems." *Journal of Negro Education* 8, no. 2 (1939): 142–49.

Clubok, Alfred B., John M. DeGrave, and Charles D. Farris. "The Manipulated Negro Vote: Some Pre-Conditions and Consequences." *Journal of Politics* 26, no. 1 (1964): 112–29.

Cobb, James C. *The Selling of the South: The Southern Crusade for Industrial Development 1936–1990*. Urbana: University of Illinois Press, 1993.
Coffman, L. D. "Regional Planning of Higher Education." *Journal of Educational Sociology* 8, no. 4 (1934): 215–22.
Cole, Taylor, and John H. Hallowell, eds. *The Southern Political Scene, 1938–1948*. Gainesville, FL: Southern Political Science Association, 1948.
Colson, Edna M. "The Negro Teachers' College and Normal School." *Journal of Negro Education* 2, no. 3 (1933): 284–98.
Committee for Georgia. "Your Participation in Georgia's Politics." Atlanta, GA, August 1945.
Conover, Milton. "State Police Developments: 1921–1924." *American Political Science Review* 18, no. 4 (1924): 773–81.
Cooper, Weldon. *Municipal Government and Administration in Alabama*. Tuscaloosa: University of Alabama Press, 1940.
———. "The State Police Movement in the South." *Journal of Politics* 1, no. 4 (1939): 414–33.
Cothran, Tilman, and William M. Phillips Jr. "Expansion of Negro Suffrage in Arkansas." *Journal of Negro Education* 26, no. 3 (1957): 287–96.
Cox, Oliver C. "Lynching and the Status Quo." *Journal of Negro Education* 14, no. 4 (1945): 576–88.
Crick, Bernard R. *The American Science of Politics: Its Origins and Conditions*. Berkeley: University of California Press, 1959.
Curtis, L. Simington. "The Negro Publicly-Supported College in Missouri." *Journal of Negro Education* 31, no. 3 (1962): 251–59.
Dabney, Virginius. *Liberalism in the South*. Chapel Hill: University of North Carolina Press, 1932.
———. "Nearer and Nearer the Precipice." *Atlantic Monthly*, January 1943, 94–100.
Dahmer, Claude, Jr., and Elliott McGinnies. "Shifting Sentiments towards Civil Rights in a Southern University." *Public Opinion Quarterly* 13, no. 2 (1949): 241–51.
Dalfiume, Richard M. "The 'Forgotten Years' of the Negro Revolution." *Journal of American History* 55 (1968): 90–106.
Danhof, Clarence H. "Four Decades of Thought on the South's Economic Problems." In *Essays in Southern Economic Development*, edited by Melvin L. Greenhut and W. Tate Whitman. Chapel Hill: University of North Carolina Press, 1964.
Daniel, Walter G. "Current Trends and State Activities." *Journal of Negro Education* 6, no. 4 (1937): 661–72.
———. "Negro Higher Education and Professional Education in Virginia." *Journal of Negro Education* 17, no. 3 (1948): 382–92.
Dauer, Manning J. "Recent Southern Political Thought." In *The Southern Political Scene, 1938–1948*, edited by Taylor Cole and John H. Hallowell. Gainesville, FL: Kallman Publishing Corp., 1948.
Davis, Abraham L. "The Role of Black Colleges and Black Law Schools in the Training of Black Lawyers and Judges: 1960–1980." *Journal of Negro History* 70, nos. 1–2 (1985): 24–34.

Davis, Elizabeth Lindsay. *Lifting as We Climb: National Association of Colored Women.* Washington, DC: National Association of Colored Women, 1933.

Davis, John W. "The Negro Land-Grant College." *Journal of Negro Education* 2, no. 3 (1933): 312–28.

Dawson, Michael C., and Ernest Wilson III. "Paradigms and Paradoxes: Political Science and African-American Politics." In *Political Science: Looking to the Future*, edited by William Crotty. Evanston, IL: Northwestern University Press, 1991.

DeCosta, Frank A. "Negro Higher and Professional Education in South Carolina." *Journal of Negro Education* 17, no. 3 (1948): 350–60.

Dennis, Michael. "The Idea of Citizenship in the Early Civil Rights Movement." *Citizenship Studies* 9, no. 2 (2005): 181–203.

———. *Lessons in Progress: State Universities and Progressivism in the New South, 1880–1920.* Urbana: University of Illinois Press, 2001.

———. *Luther P. Jackson and a Life for Civil Rights.* Gainesville: University Press of Florida, 2004.

———. "Schooling along the Color Line: Progressives and the Education of Blacks in the New South." *Journal of Negro Education* 67, no. 2 (1998): 142–56.

Dittmer, John. *Black Georgia in the Progressive Era.* Urbana: University of Illinois Press, 1977.

———. *Local People: The Struggle for Civil Rights in Mississippi.* Urbana: University of Illinois Press, 1994.

Dove, Rita. *On the Bus with Rosa Parks: Poems.* New York: Norton, 1999.

Doyle, Don H. *Nashville since the 1920s.* Knoxville: University of Tennessee Press, 1985.

Doyle, Judith Kaaz. "Maury Maverick and Racial Politics in San Antonio, Texas, 1938–1941." *Journal of Southern History* 53, no. 2 (1987): 194–224.

DuBois, W. E. B. *Black Reconstruction in America, 1860–1880.* 1935. New York: Atheneum Press, 1992.

Dudley, Julius Wayne. "A History of Southern Women for the Prevention of Lynching, 1930–1942." PhD diss., University of Cincinnati, 1979.

Dudziak, Mary L. *Cold War Civil Rights: Race and the Image of American Democracy.* Princeton, NJ: Princeton University Press, 2000.

Dulaney, W. Marvin. *Black Police in America.* Bloomington: Indiana University Press, 1996.

Dunbar, Leslie. "The Southern Regional Council." *Annals of the American Academy of Political and Social Science* 357 (1965): 108–12.

Dunne, Matthew W. "Next Steps: Charles S. Johnson and Southern Liberalism." *Journal of Negro History* 83, no. 1 (1998): 1–34.

Durisch, Lawrence L. "Southern Regional Planning and Development." *Journal of Politics* 26 (1964): 41–59.

———. "TVA and State and Local Development." In *TVA: The First Twenty Years: A Staff Report*, edited by Roscoe C. Martin. Tuscaloosa: University of Alabama Press, 1956.

Durr, Virginia Foster. *Outside the Magic Circle: The Autobiography of Virginia Foster Durr.* Tuscaloosa: University of Alabama Press, 1985.

Dykeman, Wilma, and James Stokely. *Seeds of Southern Change: The Life of Will Alexander*. Chicago: University of Chicago Press, 1962.
Eagles, Charles W. *Jonathan Daniels and Race Relations: The Evolution of a Southern Liberal*. Knoxville: University of Tennessee Press, 1982.
———. "Toward New Histories of the Civil Rights Era." *Journal of Southern History* 66, no. 4 (2000): 815–48.
Edwards, Carolyn Hinshaw. *Hallie Farmer: Crusader for Legislative Reform in Alabama*. Huntsville, AL: Strode, 1979.
Egerton, John. *The Americanization of Dixie: The Southernization of America*. New York: Harper's Magazine Press, 1974.
———. *Speak Now against the Day: The Generation before the Civil Rights Movement in the South*. New York: Knopf, 1994.
Egger, Rowland, and Weldon Cooper. *Research, Education and Regionalism: The Bureau of Public Administration of the University of Alabama, 1938–1948*. Tuscaloosa: University of Alabama, Bureau of Public Administration, 1949.
Ellis, Ann Wells. "The Commission on Interracial Cooperation, 1919–1944: Its Activities and Results." PhD diss., Georgia State University, 1976.
Ely, James W., Jr. *The Crisis of Conservative Virginia: The Byrd Organization and the Politics of Mass Resistance*. Knoxville: University of Tennessee Press, 1976.
Embree, Edwin R., and Julia Waxman. *Investment in People: The Story of the Julius Rosenwald Foundation*. New York: Harper and Brothers, 1949.
Enck, Henry S. "Black Self-Help in the Progressive Era: The 'Northern Campaigns' of Smaller Southern Black Industrial Schools, 1900–1915." *Journal of Negro History* 61, no. 1 (1976): 73–87.
Evans, Ivan T. *Bureaucracy and Race: Native Administration in South Africa*. Berkeley: University of California Press, 1997.
Fairclough, Adam. *A Class of Their Own: Black Teachers in the Segregated South*. Cambridge, MA: Belknap Press of Harvard University Press, 2007.
———. "'Being in the Field of Education and Also Being a Negro...Seems...Tragic': Black Teachers in the Jim Crow South." *Journal of American History* 87, no. 1 (2000): 65–91.
———. "The Costs of *Brown*: Black School Teachers and School Integration." *Journal of American History* 91, no. 1 (2004): 43–55.
———. *Race and Democracy: The Civil Rights Struggle in Louisiana, 1915–1972*. Athens: University of Georgia Press, 1995.
———. *Teaching Equality: Black Schools in the Age of Jim Crow*. Mercer University Lamar Memorial Lectures, 43. Athens: University of Georgia Press. 2001.
———. "Tuskegee's Robert R. Moton and the Travails of the Early Black College President." *Journal of Blacks in Higher Education* 31 (2001): 94–105.
Farhang, Sean, and Ira Katznelson. "The Southern Imposition: Congress and Labor in the New Deal and Fair Deal." *Studies in American Political Development* 19 (2005): 1–30.
Farmer, Hallie. "Legislative Planning and Research in Alabama." *Journal of Politics* 9, no. 3 (1947): 429–38.
———. *The Legislative Process in Alabama*. Tuscaloosa: University of Alabama Press, 1949.

Farris, Charles D. "Effects of Negro Voting upon the Politics of a Southern City: An Intensive Study, 1946–48." PhD diss., University of Chicago, 1953.

———. "The Re-Enfranchisement of Negroes in Florida." *Journal of Negro History* 39, no. 4 (1954): 259–83.

Feldman, Glenn, ed. *Before Brown: Civil Rights and White Backlash in the Modern South*. Tuscaloosa: University of Alabama Press, 2004.

———. *The Disenfranchisement Myth: Poor Whites and Suffrage Restriction in Alabama*. Athens: University of Georgia Press, 2004.

———. *Politics, Society, and the Klan in Alabama*. Tuscaloosa: University of Alabama Press, 1999.

Fenton, John H. "The Negro Voter in Louisiana." *Journal of Negro Education* 26, no. (1957): 319–28.

Fenton, John H., and Kenneth N. Vines. "Negro Registration in Louisiana." *American Political Science Review* 51, no. 3 (1957): 704–13.

Ferguson, Karen. *Black Politics in New Deal Atlanta*. Chapel Hill: University of North Carolina Press, 2002.

Ferrell, Claudine L. "Nightmare and Dream: Anti-Lynching in Congress, 1917–1922." PhD diss., Rice University, 1983.

Fields, Barbara J. "*Origins of the New South* and the Negro Question." *Journal of Southern History* 67, no. 4 (2001): 811–26.

Finkle, Lee. "The Conservative Aims of Militant Rhetoric: Black Protest During World War II." *Journal of American History* 60, no. 3 (1973): 692–713.

Fisher, Isaac. "Multiplying Dollars for Negro Education." *Journal of Social Forces* 1, no. 2 (1923): 149–53.

Fletcher, Allen A. "Poll Tax Politics." *New Republic*, May 20, 1940.

Flynt, Wayne. "The Flowering of Alabama Liberalism: Politics and Society During the 1940s and 1950s." In *Alabama: The History of a Deep South State*, edited by William Warren Rogers, Roger Ward, David, Atkins, Leah Rawls, and Wayne Flynt. Tuscaloosa: University of Alabama Press, 1994.

Foreman, Clark. "The Decade of Hope." *Phylon* 12, no. 2 (1951): 137–50.

Fosdick, Raymond Blaine. *Adventure in Giving: The Story of the General Education Board, a Foundation Established by John D. Rockefeller*. New York: Harper & Row, 1962.

Foster, Vera Chandler. "'Boswellianism': A Technique in the Restriction of Negro Voting." *Phylon* 10 (1949): 26–37.

Franklin, John Hope. "'Legal' Disenfranchisement of the Negro." *Journal of Negro Education* 26 no. (1957): 241–48.

———. *Mirror to America: The Autobiography of John Hope Franklin*. New York: Farrar, Straus and Giroux, 2006.

Frazier, E. Franklin. *The Black Bourgeoisie: The Rise of a New Middle Class in the United States*. New York: Collier Books, 1962.

Frederickson, Kari A. *The Dixiecrat Revolt and the End of the Solid South, 1932–1968*. Chapel Hill: University of North Carolina Press, 2001.

Frederickson, Mary E. "'Each One Is Dependent on the Other': Southern Churchwomen, Racial Reform, and the Process of Transformation, 1880–1940." In *Visible Women: New Essays on American Activism*, edited by Nancy A. Hewitt and Suzanne Lebsock. Urbana: University of Illinois Press, 1993.

Freidel, Frank. *F.D.R. and the South*. Baton Rouge: Louisiana State University Press, 1965.
Frymer, Paul. *Uneasy Alliances: Race and Party Competition*. Princeton, NJ: Princeton University Press, 1999.
Fultz, Michael. "African American Teachers in the South: Powerlessness and the Ironies of Expectations and Protest." *History of Education Quarterly* 35, no. 4 (1995): 401–22.
———. "Teacher Training and African American Education in the South, 1900–1940." *Journal of Negro Education* 64, no. 2 (1995): 196–210.
Funkhouser, W. D. "Conferences on Graduate Work in Negro Institutions in the South." *Journal of Negro Education* 15, no. 1 (1946): 122–27.
"Gallup and Fortune Poll." *Public Opinion Quarterly* 5 (Autumn 1941): 470–97.
Gaston, Paul M. *The New South Creed: A Study in Southern Mythmaking*. 1970; Montgomery, AL: New South Books, 2002.
Gavins, Raymond. "Gordon Blaine Hancock: A Black Profile from the New South." *Journal of Negro History* 59 (1974): 207–27.
———. *The Perils and Prospects of Southern Black Leadership: Gordon Blaine Hancock, 1884–1970*. Durham, NC: Duke University Press, 1977.
Gee, Wilson. *Research Barriers in the South*. New York: Century, 1932.
General Education Board. *The General Education Board: An Account of Its Activities, 1902–1914*. New York: General Education Board, 1915.
———. Annual Report, 1936–1937. New York: General Education Board, 1937.
———. *Review and Final Report, 1902–1964*. New York: General Education Board, 1964.
Giddings, Paula. *Ida: A Sword among Lions: Ida B. Wells and the Campaign against Lynching*. New York: Harper Collins/Amistad, 2008.
Gilmore, Glenda. "But She Can't Find Her [V. O.] Key." *Feminist Studies* 25, no. 1 (1999): 133–53.
———. "False Friends and Avowed Enemies: Southern African Americans and Party Allegiances in the 1920s." In *Jumpin' Jim Crow: Southern Politics from Civil War to Civil Rights*, edited by Jane Elizabeth Dailey, Glenda Elizabeth Gilmore, and Bryant Simon. Princeton, NJ: Princeton University Press, 2000.
———. *Gender and Jim Crow: Women and the Politics of White Supremacy in North Carolina, 1896–1920*. Chapel Hill: University of North Carolina Press, 1996.
Gilpin, Patrick J., and Marybeth Gasman. *Charles S. Johnson: Leadership beyond the Veil in the Age of Jim Crow*. Albany: State University of New York Press, 2003.
Goldfield, David R. *Promised Land: The South since 1945*. Arlington Heights, IL: H. Davidson, Inc., 1987.
———. "The Urban South: A Regional Framework." *American Historical Review* 86, no. 4 (1981): 1009–34.
Gomillion, Charles G. "The Negro Voter in Alabama." *Journal of Negro Education* 26, no. 3 (1957): 281–86.
Gonzalez, Francisco E., and Desmond King. "The State and Democratization: The United States in Comparative Perspective." *British Journal of Political Science* 34 (2004): 193–211.

Goodenow, Ronald K. "Paradox in Progressive Educational Reform: The South and the Education of Blacks in the Depression Years." *Phylon* 39, no. 1 (1978): 49–65.

Gordon, Linda. "Black and White Visions of Welfare: Women's Welfare Activism, 1890–1945." *Journal of American History* 78 (September 1991): 559–90.

Gorman, Kathleen. "Confederate Pensions as Southern Social Welfare." In *Before the New Deal: Social Welfare in the South, 1830–1930*, edited by Elna Green. Athens: University of Georgia Press, 1999.

Gosnell, Cullen B. "Historical Note on the Southern Political Science Association." *Journal of Politics* 16 (1954): 406–7.

Gosnell, Harold. *Negro Politicians: The Rise of Negro Politics in Chicago*. 1935. 2nd ed. Chicago: University of Chicago, 1968.

Graham, Grace. "Negro Education Progresses in South Carolina." *Social Forces* 30 (1952): 429–38.

Graham, Hugh Davis. *The Civil Rights Era: Origins and Development of National Policy*. New York: Oxford University Press, 1990.

Grantham, Dewey. "The Contours of Southern Progressivism." *American Historical Review* 86, no. 5 (1981): 1035–59.

———. *The Democratic South*. Athens: University of Georgia Press, 1963.

———. "Georgia Politics and the Disenfranchisement of the Negro." *Georgia Historical Quarterly* 32 (1948): 1–21.

———. "Hoke Smith: Progressive Governor of Georgia, 1907–1909." *Journal of Southern History* 15, no. 4 (1949): 423–40.

———. "The Regional Imagination: Social Scientists and the American South." *Journal of Southern History* 34, no. 1 (1968): 3–32.

———. *Southern Progressivism: The Reconciliation of Progress and Tradition*. Knoxville: University of Tennessee Press, 1983.

Graves, John Temple. "The Southern Negro and the War Crisis." *Virginia Quarterly Review* 18, no. 4 (1942): 500–517.

Gray, William H. "Recommendation of an Out-of-State Scholarship Fund for Negroes in Florida." *Journal of Negro Education* 16, no. 4 (1947): 604–9.

Green, Ben. *Before His Time: The Untold Story of Harry T. Moore: America's First Civil Rights Martyr*. 1999; Gainesville: University of Florida Press, 2005.

Green, Elna C., ed. *The New Deal and Beyond: Social Welfare in the South since 1930*. Athens: University of Georgia Press, 2003.

Greene, Harry W. "Negro Higher and Professional Education in West Virginia." *Journal of Negro Education* 17, no. 3 (1948): 393–99.

Greene, Lee S. "Regional Research and Training in Public Administration." *Public Administration Review* 7 (1947): 245–53.

Guinier, Lani. "From Racial Liberalism to Racial Literacy: *Brown v. Board of Education* and the Interest-Divergence Dilemma." *Journal of American History* 91, no. 1 (2004): 92–118.

Guy, Mary E. "The Ties That Bind: The Link between Public Administration and Political Science." *Journal of Politics* 65, no. 3 (2003): 641–55.

Hackney, Sheldon. *Populism to Progressivism in Alabama*. Princeton, NJ: Princeton University Press, 1969.

Hahn, Steve. *A Nation under Our Feet: Black Political Struggles in the Rural South from Slavery to the Great Migration*. Cambridge, MA: Belknap Press of Harvard University Press, 2003.

Hale, Grace Elizabeth. *Making Whiteness: The Culture of Segregation in the South, 1890–1940*. New York: Pantheon, 1998.

Hall, Jacqueline Dowd. "The Long Civil Rights Movement and the Political Uses of the Past." *Journal of American History* 91, no. 4 (2005): 1233–63.

———. *Revolt against Chivalry: Jessie Daniel Ames and the Women's Campaign against Lynching*. New York: Columbia University Press, 1993.

Hammond, Lily. *In Black and White: An Interpretation if the South*. Edited by Elna C. Green. Athens: University of Georgia Press, 2008.

Hancock, Gordon B. "Race Relations in the United States: A Summary." In *What the Negro Wants*, edited by Rayford Logan. Chapel Hill: University of North Carolina Press, 1944.

Harlan, Louis R. *Booker T. Washington: The Wizard of Tuskegee, 1901–1915*. New York: Oxford University Press, 1983.

———. *Separate and Unequal: Public School Campaigns and Racism in the Southern Seaboard States 1901–1915*. Chapel Hill: University of North Carolina Press, 1958.

———. "The Southern Education Board and the Race Issue in Public Education." *Journal of Southern History* 23, no. 2 (1957): 189–202.

Harris, Carl V. "Stability and Change in Discrimination against Black Public Schools, Birmingham, Alabama, 1871–1931." *Journal of Southern History* 51, no. 3 (1985): 375–416.

Harris, Nelson H. "Negro Higher and Professional Education in North Carolina." *Journal of Negro Education* 17, no. 3 (1948): 335–40.

Harris, Robert J., and Weldon Cooper. "Roscoe Coleman Martin, 1903–1972." *Journal of Politics* 34, no. 4 (1972): 1341–44.

Harris, Trudier, ed. *Selected Works of Ida B. Wells-Barnett*. New York: Oxford University Press, 1991.

Haskew, Lawrence D. "Impact of the Southern Regional Education Board in Its First Twenty Years." In *The Future South and Higher Education*. Atlanta: Southern Regional Education Board, 1968.

Havard, William C., and Manning J. Dauer. "The Southern Political Science Association: A Fifty Year Legacy." *Journal of Politics* 42, no. 3 (1980): 664–86.

Heard, Alexander. "Introduction to the New Edition." In *Southern Politics in State and Nation*. 1949; Knoxville: University of Tennessee Press, 1984.

———. *A Two Party South?* Chapel Hill: University of North Carolina Press, 1952.

Henderson, Harold Paulk. *The Politics of Change: A Political Biography of Ellis Arnall*. Athens: University of Georgia Press, 1991.

Henderson, Harold Paulk, and Gary L. Roberts. *Georgia Governors in an Age of Change: From Ellis Arnall to George Busbee*. Athens: University of Georgia Press, 1988.

Hesseltine, William B. "Odum to Southern History: A Preliminary Estimate." *Journal of Southern History* 24 (1958): 285–307.

———. "Sectionalism and Regionalism in American History." *Journal of Southern History* 26 (1960): 25–34.

Hine, Darlene Clark. "Black Professionals and Race Consciousness: Origins of the Civil Rights Movement, 1890–1950." *Journal of American History* 89, no. 4 (2003): 1279–94.

———. *Black Victory: The Rise and Fall of the White Primary in Texas*. Columbia: University of Missouri Press, 2003.

Hine, William C. "South Carolina State College: A Legacy of Education and Public Service." *Agricultural History* 65 (1991): 149–67.

Hobson, Wayne K. "Professionals, Progressives, and Bureaucratization: A Reassessment." *Historica* 39 (1977): 639–58.

Hodge, Clarence Lewis. *The Tennessee Valley Authority: A National Experiment in Regionalism*. Washington, DC: American University Press, 1938.

Hoffman, Edwin D. "The Genesis of the Modern Movement for Equal Rights in South Carolina, 1930–1939." *Journal of Negro History* 44, no. 4 (1959): 346–69.

Hoffman, Frederic L. "The Race Traits and Tendencies of the American Negro." *Publications of the American Economic Association* 11, no. 1/3 (1896): 1–329.

Holloway, Harry. "The Negro and the Vote: The Case of Texas." *Journal of Politics* 23 (1961): 526–56.

Holloway, Jonathan Scott. *Confronting the Veil: Abram Harris Jr., E. Franklin Frazier, and Ralph Bunche, 1919–1941*. Chapel Hill: University of North Carolina Press, 2002.

Holloway, Jonathan Scott, and Ben Keppel, eds. *Black Scholars on the Line: Race, Social Science, and American Thought in the 20th Century*. Notre Dame, IN: University of Notre Dame Press, 2007.

Holmes, Michael S. *The New Deal in Georgia: An Administrative History*. Westport, CT: Greenwood Press, 1974.

Honey, Michael. *Southern Labor and Black Civil Rights*. Urbana: University of Illinois Press, 1993.

Hornsby, Alton, Jr. "The 'Colored Branch University' Issue in Texas: Prelude to Sweatt vs. Painter." *Journal of Negro History* 61, no. 1 (1976): 51–60.

Hubbard, Maceo, and Raymond Alexander. "Types of Potentially Favorable Court Cases Relative to the Separate School." *Journal of Negro Education* 4 (1935): 375–405.

Hubbell, John T. "The Desegregation of the University of Oklahoma, 1946–1950." *Journal of Negro Education* 57, no. 4 (1972): 370–84.

Hudson, J. Blaine. "The Establishment of Louisville Municipal College: A Case Study in Racial Conflict and Compromise." *Journal of Negro Education* 64, no. 2 (1995): 111–23.

Irving, Florence B. "The Future of the Negro Voter in the South." *Journal of Negro Education* 26, no. (1957): 390–99.

Ivey, John E., Jr. "Regional Education: An Experiment in Democracy." *Phylon* 10, no. 4 (1949): 381–88.

Jackson, Luther P. "Citizenship Training: A Neglected Area in Adult Education." *Journal of Negro Education* 14, no. 3 (1945): 477–87.

———. "Race and Suffrage in the South since 1940." *New South*, June–July 1948.
———. "The Voting Status of Negroes in Virginia, 1947–1948." In *Eighth Annual Report*. Petersburg: Virginia Voters League, 1948.
Jackson, Reid E. "Financial Aid Given by Southern States to Negroes for Out-of-State Study." *Journal of Negro Education* 13, no. 1 (1944): 30–39.
Jackson, Walter A. *Gunnar Myrdal and America's Conscience: Social Engineering and Racial Liberalism, 1938–1987*. Chapel Hill: University of North Carolina Press, 1990.
Jacoway, Elizabeth R., and David R. Colburn. *Southern Businessmen and Desegregation*. Baton Rouge: Louisiana State University Press, 1982.
James, David R. "The Transformation of the Southern Racial State: Class and Race Determinants of Local-State Structures." *American Sociological Review* 53 (1988): 191–208.
Jenkins, Martin D. "The Availability of Higher Education for Negroes in the Southern States." *Journal of Negro Education* 16, no. 3 (1947): 459–73.
———. "The Future of the Desegregated Negro College: A Critical Summary." *Journal of Negro Education* 27, no. 3 (1958): 419–29.
———. "Negro Higher Education." *Journal of Negro Education* 5, no. 4 (1936): 666–70.
Johnson, Charles S. "Next Steps in Education in the South." *Phylon* 15, no. 1 (1954): 7–20.
———. "The Present Status of Race Relations, with Particular Reference to the Negro." *Journal of Negro Education* 8, no. 3 (1939): 323–35.
———. "Southern Race Relations Conference." *Journal of Negro Education* 12, no. 1 (1943): 133–39.
Johnson, Charles S., Elizabeth Allen, Horace Mann Bond, Margaret McCulloch, and Alma Forrest Polk. *Into the Main Street: A Survey of Best Practice in Race Relations in the South*. Chapel Hill: University of North Carolina Press, 1947.
Johnson, Charles S., et al. *To Stem This Tide: A Survey of Racial Tension in the United States*. Boston: Pilgrim Press, 1943.
Johnson, Guy B., and Guion Johnson. *Research in Service to Society: The First Fifty Years of the Institute for Research in the Social Sciences at the University of North Carolina*. Chapel Hill: University of North Carolina Press, 1980.
Johnson, Joseph L. "The Supply of Negro Health Personnel-Physicians." *Journal of Negro Education* 18, no. 3 (1949): 346–56.
Johnson, Kate Burr, and Nell Battle Lewis. "A Decade of Social Progress in North Carolina." *Journal of Social Forces* 1, no. 4 (1923): 400–403.
Johnson, Kimberley S. *Governing the American State: Congress and the New Federalism, 1877–1929*. Princeton, NJ: Princeton University Press, 2006.
Johnson, Phillip J. "The Limits of Interracial Compromise: Louisiana, 1941." *Journal of Southern History* 69, no. 2 (2003): 319–48.
Jones, Allan Quinn, Jr. "Negro Suffrage in Florida." Master's thesis, Atlanta University, 1948.
Jones, B. A. "New Legal Requirements of Race Relations in the South." *Phylon* 13, no. 2 (1952): 97–106.

Jordan, Elizabeth Cobb. "The Impact of the Negro Organization Society on Public Support for Education in Virginia, 1912–1950." PhD diss., University of Virginia, 1978.

Kallenbach, Joseph E. "Constitutional Aspects of Federal Anti-Poll Tax Legislation." *Michigan Law Review* 45, no. 6 (1947): 717–32.

Kammerer, Gladys. *Thirteen Years of Achievement: The Southern Regional Training Program.* Tuscaloosa: Bureau of Public Administration, University of Alabama, 1958.

Karl, Barry. *Charles E. Merriam and the Study of Politics.* Chicago: University of Chicago Press, 1974.

Katz, Michael. *The Price of Citizenship: Redefining the American Welfare State.* New York: Metropolitan Books, 2001.

Katznelson, Ira, Kim Geiger, and Daniel Kryder. "Limiting Liberalism: The Southern Veto in Congress, 1933–1950." *Political Science Quarterly* 108 (1993): 283–306.

Katznelson, Ira, and Bruce Pietrykowski. "Rebuilding the American State: Evidence from the 1940s." *Studies in American Political Development* 5 (1991): 301–39.

Kean, Melissa F. "Guiding Desegregation: The Role of 'Intelligent White Men of the South,' 1945–1954." *History of Higher Education Annual* 19 (1999): 57–83.

Keech, William R. *The Impact of Negro Voting.* Chicago: Rand McNally, 1968.

Keefe, William J. "Southern Politics Revisited." *Public Opinion Quarterly* 20, no. 2 (1956): 405–12.

Kelleher, Daniel T. "The Case of Lloyd Lionel Gaines: The Demise of the Separate but Equal Doctrine." *Journal of Negro History* 56, no. 4 (1971): 262–71.

Kelley, Robin D. G. *Race Rebels: Culture, Politics, and the Black Working Class.* New York: Free Press, 1994.

———. "'We Are Not What We Seem': Rethinking Black Working-Class Opposition in the Jim Crow South." *Journal of American History* 80, no. 1 (1993): 75–112.

Kellogg, Peter J. "Civil Rights Consciousness in the 1940s." *Historian* 42 (1979): 18–41.

Kendrick, Benjamin. "A Southern Confederation of Learning: Higher Education and the New Regionalism." *Southwest Review* 19 (1934): 182–95.

Key, V. O. *Southern Politics in State and Nation.* 1949; Knoxville: University of Tennessee Press, 1984.

Kilpatrick, James Jackson. *The Sovereign States: Notes of a Citizen of Virginia.* Chicago: Henry Regnery, 1957.

Kilpatrick, William H. "Resort to Courts by Negroes to Improve Their Schools a Conditional Alternative." *Journal of Negro Education* 4, no. 3 (1935): 412–18.

King, Desmond. *In the Name of Liberalism: Illiberal Social Policy in the United States and Britain.* Oxford: Oxford University Press, 1999.

———. *Separate and Unequal: African Americans and the U.S. Federal Government.* 2nd ed. Oxford: Oxford University Press, 2007.

King, Desmond, and Rogers Smith. "Racial Orders in American Political Development." *American Political Science Review* 99, no. 1 (2005): 75–92.

Kirby, Jack Temple. *Darkness at the Dawning: Race and Reform in the Progressive South.* New York: J. B. Lippincott, 1972.

Kirk, John A. *Redefining the Color Line: Black Activism in Little Rock, Arkansas, 1940–1970*. Gainesville: University of Florida Press, 2002.

Klarman, Michael J. *From Jim Crow to Civil Rights: The Supreme Court and the Struggle for Racial Equality*. New York: Oxford University Press, 2004.

———. "How *Brown* Changed Race Relations: The Backlash Thesis." *Journal of American History* 81, no. 1 (1994): 81–118.

Klibaner, Irwin. *Conscience of a Troubled South: The Southern Conference Education Fund, 1946–1966*. Brooklyn, NY: Carlson, 1989.

———. "The Travail of Southern Radicals: The Southern Conference Educational Fund, 1946–1976." *Journal of Southern History* 49, no. 2 (1983): 179–202.

Klinker, Philip A., and Rogers M. Smith. *The Unsteady March: The Rise and Decline of Racial Equality in America*. Chicago: University of Chicago Press, 1999.

Kluger, Richard. *Simple Justice: The History of Brown v. Board of Education and Black America's Struggle for Equality*. New York: Knopf, 1976.

Kneebone, John T. *Southern Liberal Journalists and the Issue of Race, 1920–1944*. Chapel Hill: University of North Carolina Press, 1985.

Koeniger, A. Cash. "The New Deal and the States: Roosevelt versus the Byrd Organization in Virginia." *Journal of American History* 68, no. 4 (1982): 876–96.

Korstad, Robert, and Nelson Lichtenstein. "Opportunities Found and Lost: Labor, Radicals, and the Early Civil Rights Movement." *Journal of American History* 75 (1988): 786–811.

Kousser, J. Morgan. "Progressivism—for Middle-Class Whites Only: North Carolina Education, 1880–1910." *Journal of Southern History* 46, no. 2 (1980): 169–94.

———. "Separate but *Not* Equal: The Supreme Court's Decision on Racial Discrimination in Schools." *Journal of Southern History* 46, no. 1 (1980): 17–44.

———. *The Shaping of Southern Politics: Suffrage Restriction and the Establishment of the One-Party South, 1880–1910*. New Haven, CT: Yale University Press, 1974.

Krueger, Thomas A. *And Promises to Keep: The Southern Conference for Human Welfare, 1938–1948*. Nashville, TN: Vanderbilt University Press, 1967.

Kruse, Kevin M. "Personal Rights, Public Wrongs: The *Gaines* Case and the Beginnings of the End of Segregation." *Journal of Supreme Court History* 2 (1997): 113–30.

———. *White Flight: Atlanta and the Making of Modern Conservatism*. Princeton, NJ: Princeton University Press, 2005.

Kryder, Daniel. *Divided Arsenal: Race and the American State During World War II*. Cambridge: Cambridge University Press, 2000.

Lacy, Michael J., and Mary Furner. *The State and Social Investigation in Britain and the United States*. New York: Cambridge University Press, 1993.

Lagemann, Ellen Condliffe. "The Politics of Knowledge: The Carnegie Corporation and the Formulation of Public Policy." *History of Education Quarterly* 27, no. 2 (1987): 205–20.

———. *The Politics of Knowledge: The Carnegie Corporation, Philanthropy, and Public Policy*. Chicago: University of Chicago Press, 1992.

Lamis, Alexander P., and Nathan C. Goldman. "V. O. Key's Southern Politics: The Writing of a Classic." *Georgia Historical Quarterly* 71 (1987): 261–85.

Lane, Russell A. "The Legal Trend towards Increased Provisions for Negro Education in the United States between 1920 and 1930." *Journal of Negro Education* 1, no. 3/4 (1932): 396–99.

Lanier, Raphael O'Hara. "The History of Higher Education for Negroes in Texas 1930–1955 with Particular Reference to Texas Southern University." PhD diss., New York University, 1957.

Larkin, Vernell Danae. "Dreams Denied: The Anderson Mayer State Aid Act, 1936–1950." PhD diss., University of Kentucky, 2001.

Lassiter, Matthew, and Andrew B. Lewis, eds. *The Moderates' Dilemma: Massive Resistance to School Desegregation in Virginia*. Charlottesville: University of Virginia Press, 1998.

Lau, Peter F. "Freedom Road Territory: The Politics of Civil Rights Struggle in South Carolina During the Jim Crow Era." PhD diss., Rutgers, The State University of New Jersey, 2002.

———. *Democracy Rising: South Carolina and the Fight for Black Equality since 1865*. Lexington: University of Kentucky Press, 2006.

Lawson, Steven. *Black Ballots: Voting Rights in the South, 1944–1969*. New York: Columbia University Press, 1976.

———. "Freedom Then, Freedom Now: The History of the Civil Rights Movement." *American Historical Review* 96, no. (1991): 456–71.

Leavell, Ullin W. *Philanthropy in Negro Education*. Nashville, TN: George Peabody College for Teachers, 1930.

———. "The Program of Dual Education and Racial Adjustment of George Peabody College for Teachers." *Journal of Negro Education* 2, no. 2 (1933): 157–64.

Lee, Eliza Wing-Yee. "Political Science, Public Administration and the Rise of the American Administrative State." *Public Administration Review* 55, no. 6 (1995): 538–46.

Leloudis, James L. *Schooling in the New South: Pedagogy, Self and Society in North Carolina*. Chapel Hill: University of North Carolina Press, 1996.

Lemann, Nicholas. *Redemption: The Last Battle of the Civil War*. New York: Farrar, Straus and Giroux, 2006.

Lepawsky, Albert. *State Planning and Economic Development in the South*. NPA Committee of the South, Report No. 4. Kingsport, TN: National Planning Association, 1949.

Lester, Jim. *A Man for Arkansas: Sid McMath and the Southern Reform Tradition*. Little Rock, AR: Rose Publishing, 1976.

Leuchtenberg, William. *The White House Looks South*. Baton Rouge: Louisiana State University Press, 2005.

Lewinson, Paul. *Race, Class, and Party: A History of Negro Suffrage and White Politics in the South*. 1932; New York: Russell & Russell, 1963.

Lewis, Earl. *In Their Own Interests: Race, Class and Power in Twentieth Century Norfolk, Virginia*. Berkeley: University of California Press, 1991.

Lewis, Earl M. "The Negro Voter in Mississippi." *Journal of Negro Education* 26, no. 3 (1957): 329–50.

Lichtenstein, Alex. "Good Roads and Chain Gangs in the Progressive South: The Negro Convict Is a Slave." *Journal of Southern History* 59, no. 1 (1993): 5–110.

Lieberman, Robert. "Ideas, Institutions, and Political Order: Explaining Political Change." *American Political Science Review* 96, no. 4 (2002): 697–712.

———. *Shifting the Color Line: Race and the American Welfare State.* Cambridge, MA: Harvard University Press, 1998.

Link, Arthur S. "Correspondence Relating to the Progressive Party's 'Lily White' Policy in 1912." *Journal of Southern History* 10, no. 4 (1944): 480–90.

Link, William A. *A Hard Country and a Lonely Place: Schooling, Society and Reform in Rural Virginia.* Chapel Hill: University of North Carolina Press, 1986.

———. *The Paradox of Southern Progressivism, 1880–1930.* Chapel Hill: University of North Carolina Press, 1992.

———. "Privies, Progressivism, and Public Schools: Health Reform and Education in the Rural South, 1909–1920." *Journal of Southern History* 54 (1988): 623–24.

Locke, Alain. "The New Negro." In *The New Negro*, edited by Alain Locke. New York: Atheneum, 1970.

Logan, Rayford, ed. *The Attitude of the Southern White Press toward Negro Suffrage, 1932–1940.* Washington, DC: Foundation Publishers, 1940.

———. *The Negro and American Life: The Nadir, 1877–1901.* New York: Dial Press, 1954.

———, ed. *What the Negro Wants.* Chapel Hill: University of North Carolina Press, 1944.

Lowndes, Joseph, Julie Novkov, and Dorian T. Warren. *Race and American Political Development.* New York: Routledge, 2008.

Lucker, Andrew M. *V.O. Key, Jr.: The Quintessential Political Scientist.* Major Concepts in Politics and Political Theory, 19. New York: Peter Lang, 2001.

Mancini, Matthew J. *One Dies, Get Another: Convict Leasing in the American South, 1866–1928.* Columbia: University of South Carolina Press, 1996.

Margo, Robert. "Race Differences in Public School Expenditures: Disenfranchisement and School Finance in Louisiana, 1890–1910." *Social Science History* 6 (1982): 9–33.

———. *Race and Schooling in the South, 1880–1950: An Economic History.* Chicago: University of Chicago Press, 1990.

Marshall, T. H., and Tom Bottomore. *Citizenship and Social Class.* Concord, MA: Pluto Press, 1992.

Marshall, Thurgood. "The Rise and Collapse of the 'White Democratic Primary.'" *Journal of Negro Education* 26, no. 3 (1957): 249–54.

Martin, Boyd C. "The Service Vote in the Elections of 1944." *American Political Science Review* 39, no. 4 (1945): 720–32.

Martin, Roscoe C. "Alabama's Administrative Reorganization of 1939." *Journal of Politics* 2, no. 4 (1940): 436–47.

———. *The Growth of State Administration in Alabama.* Tuscaloosa: University of Alabama Press, 1942.

———. "Political Science and Public Administration: A Note on the State of the Union." *American Political Science Review* 46, no. 3 (1952): 660–76.

———, ed. *The University Bureaus of Administration*. Tuscaloosa: Bureau of Public Administration, University of Alabama, 1946.

Martin, William H. "Negro Higher and Professional Education in Arkansas." *Journal of Negro Education* 17, no. 3 (1948): 255–64.

Marx, Anthony. *Making Race and Nation*. New York: Cambridge University Press, 1998.

Matthews, Donald R., and James W. Prothro. *Negroes and the New Southern Politics*. New York: Harcourt Brace World, 1966.

Matthews, John Michael. "Virginius Dabney, John Temple Graves, and What Happened to Southern Liberalism." *Mississippi Quarterly* 45, no. 4 (1992): 405–20.

McAdam, Doug. *Political Process and the Development of Black Insurgency 1930–1970*. Chicago: University of Chicago Press, 1982.

McCormick, J. Scott. "The Julius Rosenwald Fund." *Journal of Negro Education* 3, no. 4 (1934): 605–26.

McCoy, Donald R., and Richard T. Ruetten. "The Civil Rights Movement: 1940–1954." *Midwest Quarterly* 11 (1969): 11–34.

McCoy, Donald R., and Richard T. Ruetten. *Quest and Response: Minority Rights and the Truman Administration*. Lawrence: University Press of Kansas, 1973.

McCrary, Peyton, and Steven F. Lawson, "Race and Reapportionment, 1962: The Case of Georgia Senate Redistricting." *Journal of Policy History* 12, no. 3 (2000): 293–320.

McCuistion, Fred B. "Graduate Instruction for Negroes in the United States." Nashville, TN: George Peabody College for Teachers, 1939.

———. "Higher Education of Negroes (a Summary)." Nashville, TN: Association of Colleges and Secondary Schools of the Southern States, 1933.

———. "The Present Status of Higher Education of Negroes." *Journal of Negro Education* 2, no. 3 (1933): 379–96.

———. "The South's Negro Teaching Force." *Journal of Negro Education* 1, no. 1 (1932): 16–24.

———. "The South's Negro Teaching Force (a Brief Study)." Nashville, TN: Julius Rosenwald Fund, Southern Office, 1931.

———. "The Support of Public Education in the United States: With Special Reference to Negro Schools." *Journal of Educational Sociology* 12, no. 5 (1939): 257–63.

McCulloch, James E., ed. *The Call of the New South: Addresses Delivered at the Southern Sociological Congress, Nashville, Tennessee, May 7 to 10, 1912*. Nashville, TN: Southern Sociological Congress, 1912.

McDonough, Julia Anne. "Men and Women of Good Will: A History of the Commission on Interracial Cooperation and the Southern Regional Council, 1919–1954." PhD diss., University of Virginia, 1993.

McEntire, Davis, and Joseph Weckler. "The Role of the Police." *Annals of the American Academy of Political and Social Science* 244 (1946): 82–89.

McGill, Ralph. "Civil Rights for the Negro." *Atlantic Monthly*, November 1949.

McKissack, Rosetta Sangster. "Attitudes towards Negro Political Participation in Georgia." Master's thesis, Atlanta University, 1954.

McMahon, Kevin J. *Reconsidering Roosevelt on Race*. Chicago: University of Chicago Press, 2004.

McMillan, Lewis K. "Negro Higher Education as I Have Known It." *Journal of Negro Education* 8, no. 1 (1939): 9–18.

McMillen, Neil R. *Dark Journey: Black Mississippians in the Age of Jim Crow*. Urbana: University of Illinois Press, 1989.

———. "Perry W. Howard, Boss of Black-and-Tan Republicanism in Mississippi, 1924–1960." *Journal of Southern History* 48, no. 2 (1982): 205–24.

———, ed. *Remaking Dixie: The Impact of World War II on the American South*. Jackson: University Press of Mississippi, 1997.

Meier, August, and John H. Bracey Jr. "The NAACP as a Reform Movement, 1909–1965: 'To Reach the Conscience of America.'" *Journal of Southern History* 59, no. 1 (1993): 3–30.

Merriam, Charles. "The Present State of the Study of Politics." *American Political Science Review* 15 (1921): 173–85.

Messick, J. D. "Negro Education in the South." *Journal of Educational Sociology* 21, no. 2 (1947): 88–96.

Meyer, John W., David Tyack, Joanne Nagel, and Audri Gordon. "Public Education as Nation-Building in America: Enrollments and Bureaucratization in the American States, 1870–1930." *American Journal of Sociology* 85 (1979): 591–613.

Mickey, Robert W. *Paths Out of Dixie: The Democratization of Authoritarian Enclaves in America's Deep South, 1944–1972*. Princeton, NJ: Princeton University Press, forthcoming.

Middleton, Ernest J. "The Louisiana Education Association, 1901–1970." *Journal of Negro Education* 47, no. 4 (1978): 363–78.

Miller, J. Erroll. "The Negro in Present Day Politics with Special Reference to Philadelphia." *Journal of Negro History* 33 (1948): 303–43.

Mitchell, Broadus. "Southern Quackery." *Southern Economic Journal* 3, no. 2 (1936): 143–47.

Mohr, Clarence L. "Schooling, Modernization, and Race: The Continuing Dilemma of the American South." *American Journal of Education* 106, no. 3 (1998): 439–50.

Moon, Henry Lee. *Balance of Power: The Negro Vote*. Garden City, NY: Doubleday, 1948.

———. "Counted Out and In." *Survey Graphic*, January 1947, 8–10.

———. "The Negro Voter in the Presidential Election of 1956." *Journal of Negro Education* 26 (1957): 219–30.

———. "The Southern Scene." *Phylon* 16, no. 4 (1955): 351–58.

Moos, Malcolm C. *State Penal Administration in Alabama*. Tuscaloosa: University of Alabama Press, 1942.

Morphet, Edgar L., and Roe L. Johns. "State School Organization and Administration (in Administration and Organization Other Than in Local Schools)." *Review of Educational Research* 16, no. 4 (1946): 364–69.

Morris, Aldon D. *The Origins of the Civil Rights Movement: Black Communities Organizing for Change*. New York: Free Press, 1984.

Murphy, Walter F. "The South Counter-attacks: The Anti-NAACP Laws." *Western Political Quarterly* 12, no. 1 (1959): 371–90.

Murray, Florence, ed. *The Negro Handbook*. New York: Current Books, 1942, 1944, 1946–47, 1949.

Myrdal, Gunnar. *An American Dilemma: The Negro Problem and Modern Democracy*. New York: Harper & Brothers, 1944.

Nabrit, James, Jr. "The Future of the Negro Voter in the South." *Journal of Negro Education* 26 (1957): 418–23.

National Committee to Abolish the Poll Tax. "Labor's Stake in Abolishing the Poll Tax." Washington, DC, 1947.

Newberry, Anthony Lake. "Without Urgency or Ardor: The South's Middle-of-the-Road Liberals and Civil Rights, 1945–1960." PhD diss., Ohio University, 1982.

Newbold, N. C. "Common Schools for Negroes in the South." *The American Negro*, special issue of *Annals of the American Academy of Political and Social Science*, 140 (1928): 209–23.

———. "Money: An Indisputable Argument." *Journal of Social Forces* 2, no. 1 (1923): 88–89.

Newby, I. A. *Challenge to the Court: Social Scientists and the Defense of Segregation 1954–1966*. Baton Rouge: Louisiana State University Press, 1967.

Newton, J. G. "Expansion of Negro Suffrage in North Carolina." *Journal of Negro Education* 26, no. (1957): 351–58.

Nixon, H. C. "Politics of the Hills." *Journal of Politics* 8, no. 2 (1946): 123–33.

Norrell, Robert J. "Labor at the Ballot Box: Alabama Politics from the New Deal to the Dixiecrat Movement." *Journal of Southern History* 57, no. 2 (1991): 201–34.

———. *Reaping the Whirlwind: The Civil Rights Movement in Tuskegee*. 1985; Chapel Hill: University of North Carolina Press, 1998.

———. "Triangles of Change: The Southern Regional Council in the Civil Rights Movement." Paper presented at Conference on the Southern Regional Council and the Civil Rights Movement, University of Florida, Gainesville, October 2003.

———. *Up from Slavery: The Life of Booker T. Washington*. Cambridge: Belknap Press of Harvard University Press, 2009.

Nye, Joseph S. *Soft Power: The Means to Success in World Politics*. New York: Public Affairs, 2004.

O'Brien, Thomas V. "The Dog That Didn't Bark: Aaron V. Cook and the NAACP Strategy in Georgia before Brown." *Journal of Negro History* 84, no. 1 (1999): 79–88.

O'Connor, Alice. *Poverty Knowledge: Social Science, Social Policy and the Poor in 20th Century U.S. History*. Princeton, NJ: Princeton University Press, 2001.

O'Donnell, Guillermo. "On the State, Democratization, and Some Conceptual Problems: A Latin American View with Glances at Some Postcommunist Countries." *World Politics* 21 (August 1993): 1355–69.

Odum, Howard. *Race and Rumors of Race: Challenge to American Crisis*. 1943; Baltimore: Johns Hopkins University Press, 1997.

———. *Southern Regions of the United States*. Chapel Hill: University of North Carolina Press, 1936.

Ogden, Frederic. *The Poll Tax in the South*. Tuscaloosa: University of Alabama Press, 1958.

O'Kelly, Charlotte G. "Black Newspapers and the Black Protest Movement, 1946–1972." *Phylon* 41, no. 4 (1980): 313–24.

Omi, Michael, and Howard Winant. *Racial Formation in the United States: From the 1960s to the 1990s*. 2nd ed. New York: Routledge, 1994.

Orren, Karen, and Stephen Skowronek. "Regimes and Regime Building in American Government: A Review of the Literature on the 1940s." *Political Science Quarterly* 113, no. 4 (1998–99): 689–702.

———. *The Search for American Political Development*. New York: Cambridge University Press, 2004.

O'Toole, Laurence J. "Harry F. Byrd, Sr. and the New York Bureau of Municipal Research: Lessons from an Ironic Alliance." *Public Administration Review* 46, no. 2 (1986): 113–23.

Owsley, Frank. "A Key to Southern Liberalism." *Southern Review* 3 (1937): 28–38.

Park, Robert E. "The Bases of Race Prejudice." *Annals of the American Academy of Political and Social Science* 140 (1928): 11–20.

———. "Racial Assimilation in Secondary Groups with Particular Reference to the Negro." *American Journal of Sociology* 19, no. 5 (1914): 606–23.

Parrish, C. H. "Negro Higher and Professional Education in Kentucky." *Journal of Negro Education* 17, no. 3 (1948): 289–95.

Patterson, James. *The New Deal and the States: Federalism in Transition*. Princeton, NJ: Princeton University Press, 1969.

Peeps, Stephen J. "Northern Philanthropy and the Emergence of Black Higher Education: Do-Gooders, Compromisers, or Co-Conspirators?" *Journal of Negro Education* 50, no. 3 (1981): 251–69.

Perloff, Richard M. "The Press and Lynchings of African Americans." *Journal of Black Studies* 30, no. 3 (2000): 315–33.

Permaloff, Anne, and Carl Grafton. *Political Power in Alabama: The More Things Change*. Athens: University of Georgia Press, 1995.

Perry, Jennings. *Democracy Begins at Home: The Tennessee Fight on the Poll Tax*. Philadelphia: Lippincott, 1944.

———. *Should the Anti-Poll Tax Bill Be Passed Now?* New York: American Education Press, 1944.

Perry, Thelma D. *History of the American Teachers Association*. Washington, DC: National Education Association, 1975.

Peterson, Gladys Tignor. "The Present Status of the Negro Separate School as Defined by Court Decisions." *Journal of Negro Education* 4, no. 3 (1935): 351–74.

Phillips, Ulrich B. "The Central Theme of Southern History." *American Historical Review* 24 (1928): 30–43.

Picott, J. Rupert. "The Negro Public College in Virginia." *Journal of Negro Education* 31, no. 3 (1962): 275–83.

Pierson, Mary Bynum. *Graduate Work in the South*. Chapel Hill: University of North Carolina Press, 1947.

Pierson, Paul. *Politics in Time: History, Institutions and Social Analysis*. Princeton, NJ: Princeton University Press, 2004.

Pilkington, Charles Kirk. "The Trials of Brotherhood: The Founding of the Commission on Interracial Cooperation." *Georgia Historical Quarterly* 69, no. 1 (1985): 55–80.

Pincham, Linda B. "A League of Willing Workers: The Impact of Northern Philanthropy, Virginia Estelle Randolph and the Jeanes Teachers in Early Twentieth-Century Virginia." *Journal of Negro Education* 74, no. 2 (2005): 112–23.

Pipkin, Charles W. "The Southern Philosophy of State's Rights: The Old Sectionalism and the New Regionalism." *Southwest Review* 19 (1934): 182–95.

———. "Graduate Work in the South: Some Phases of Graduate Work in the Southern Regions since 1935." *South Atlantic Bulletin* 7, no. 1 (1941).

Pitre, Merline. "Black Houstonians and the 'Separate and Equal' Doctrine: Carter W. Wesley versus Lulu B. White." In *The African American Experience in Texas*, edited by Bruce A. Glasrud and James M. Smallwood. Lubbock: Texas Tech University Press, 2007.

———. *In Struggle against Jim Crow: Lulu B. White and the NAACP, 1900–1957*. College Station: Texas A&M University Press, 1999.

Plank, David N., and Rick Ginsberg, eds. *Southern Schools, Southern Cities: Public Education in the Urban South*. Westport, CT: Greenwood Press, 1990.

Plank, David N., and Marcia Turner. "Changing Patterns in Black School Politics: Atlanta, 1872–1973." *American Journal of Education* 95, no. 4 (1987): 584–608.

Plank, David N., and Marcia Turner. "Contrasting Patterns in Black School Politics: Atlanta and Memphis, 1865–1985." *Journal of Negro Education* 60 (1991): 203–18.

Plotke, David. *Building a Democratic Political Order: Reshaping American Liberalism in the 1930s and 1940s*. New York: Cambridge University Press, 1996.

Podolefsky, Ronnie L. "The Illusion of Suffrage: Female Voting Rights and the Women's Poll Tax Repeal Movement after the Nineteenth Amendment." *Columbia Journal of Gender and Law* 7 (1997–98): 185–237.

"Poll Tax Support, 1941." *Public Opinion Quarterly* 5 (1941).

"Poll Tax Support, 1948." *Public Opinion Quarterly* 7 (1948).

"Poll Tax Support, 1949." *Public Opinion Quarterly* 13 (1949).

Powell, Kimberly A. "United in Gender, Divided by Race: Reconstruction of Issue and Identity by the Association of Southern Women for the Prevention of Lynching." *Communication Studies* 46, nos. 1–2 (1995): 34–44.

President's Committee on Civil Rights. *To Secure These Rights*. Washington, DC: GPO, 1948.

Presnell, Boyte Austin. "The Impact of World War II on Race Relations in Mobile, Alabama, 1940–1948." Master's thesis, Atlanta University, 1972.

Prewitt, Kenneth J., and Louis L. Knowles. *Institutional Racism in America*. Englewood Cliffs, NJ: Prentice-Hall, 1970.

Price, Hugh Douglas. "The Negro and Florida Politics, 1944–1954." *Journal of Politics* 17, no. 2 (1955): 198–220.

———. *The Negro and Southern Politics: A Chapter in Florida History*. New York: New York University Press, 1957.

Price, Margaret. *The Negro and the Ballot in the South*. Atlanta, GA: Southern Regional Council, 1959.

———. *The Negro Voter in the South*. Atlanta, GA: Southern Regional Council, 1957.

"Public Opinion Polls." *Public Opinion Quarterly* 7 (Autumn 1943): 478–505.

"The Quarter's Polls." *Public Opinion Quarterly* 12 (Autumn 1948): 530–77.

"The Quarter's Polls." *Public Opinion Quarterly* 13 (Autumn 1949): 537–61.

Quadagno, Jill S. *The Color of Welfare: How Racism Undermined the War on Poverty*. New York: Oxford University Press, 1994.

Rabinovitz, Howard N. "Half a Loaf: The Shift from White to Black Teachers in the Negro Schools of the Urban South, 1865–1890." *Journal of Southern History* 410 (1974): 565–94.

———. *Race Relations in the Urban South*. Urbana: University of Illinois Press, 1978.

Rable, George C. "The South and the Politics of Anti-Lynching Legislation, 1920–1940." *Journal of Southern History* 51 (1985): 201–20.

Rankin, Robert S. *Political Science in the South*. Tuscaloosa: Bureau of Public Administration, University of Alabama, 1946.

Ransom, Leon A. "Education and the Law: *Gaines v. The University of Maryland*." *Journal of Negro Education* 8, no. 1 (1939): 111–17.

Raper, Arthur. *The Tragedy of Lynching*. 1933; Mineola, NY: Dover, 2003.

Ray, Gerda W. "From Cossack to Trooper: Manliness, Police Reform and the State." *Journal of Social History* 28, no. 3 (1995): 565–86.

Ray, Joseph M. "American Government and Politics: The Influence of the Tennessee Valley Authority on Government in the South." *American Political Science Review* 43, no. 5 (1949): 922–32.

Reagan, Patrick D. *Designing a New America: The Origins of New Deal Planning, 1890–1943*. Amherst: University of Massachusetts Press, 1999.

Redcay, Edward E. "Pioneering in Negro Education." *Journal of Negro Education* 6, no. 1 (1937): 38–53.

Redd, George N. "Present Status of Negro Higher and Professional Education: A Critical Summary." *Journal of Negro Education* 17, no. 3 (1948): 400–409.

———. "Resources for Graduate Work for Negroes in the States of Alabama, Kentucky, and Tennessee." *Journal of Negro Education* 15, no. 2 (1948): 161–71.

Reed, Adolph, Jr. "Looking Back at 'Brown.'" *The Progressive* 58, no. 6 (June 1994): 20–22.

Reed, John Shelton. "An Evaluation of an Anti-Lynching Organization." *Social Problems* 16, no. 2 (1968): 172–82.

Reed, Linda. *Simple Decency and Common Sense: The Southern Conference Movement, 1938–1963*. Bloomington: Indiana University Press, 1991.

Reedy, Sidney J. "Negro Higher and Professional Education in Missouri." *Journal of Negro Education* 17, no. 3 (1948): 321–34.

Reich, Steven A. "Soldiers of Democracy: Black Texans and the Fight for Citizenship, 1917–1921." *Journal of American History* 82, no. 4 (1996): 1478–504.

Reid, Herbert O., and James M. Nabrit. "Remedies under Statutes Granting Federal Aid to Land Grant Colleges." *Journal of Negro Education* 17, no. 3 (1948): 410–25.

Richardson, Joe M. "Edgar B. Stern: A White New Orleans Philanthropist Helps Build a Black University." *Journal of Negro History* 82, no. 3 (1997): 328–42.

Roady, Elston E. "The Expansion of Negro Suffrage in Florida." *Journal of Negro Education* 26, no. 3 (1957): 297–306.

Roberts, Alisdair. "Demonstrating Neutrality: The Rockefeller Philanthropies and the Evolution of Public Administration, 1927–1936." *Public Administration Review* 54, no. 3 (1994): 221–28.

Roberts, S. O. "Negro Higher and Professional Education in Tennessee." *Journal of Negro Education* 17, no. 3 (1948): 361–72.

Robinson, Armstead L., and Patricia Sullivan, eds. *New Directions in Civil Rights Studies*. Charlottesville: University Press of Virginia, 1991.

Roefs, Wim. "The Impact of 1940s Civil Rights Activism on the State's 1960s Civil Rights Scene: A Hypothesis and Historiographical Discussion." In *Toward the Meeting of the Waters*, edited by Winfred B Moore and Orville Vernon Burton. Columbia: University of South Carolina Press, 2008.

Rolinson, Mary G. *Grassroots Garveyism: The Universal Negro Improvement Association in the Rural South, 1920–1927*. Chapel Hill: University of North Carolina Press, 2007.

Ross, Dorothy. *The Origins of American Social Science*. New York: Cambridge University Press, 1991.

Rouse, Jacqueline Anne. *Lugenia Hope Burns: Black Southern Reformer*. Athens: University of Georgia Press, 1989.

Rowan, Stanley. "America's Rotten Districts." *Common Sense*, October 1940.

Rubinson, Richard. "Class Formation, Politics, and Institutions: Schooling in the United States." *American Journal of Sociology* 92 (1986): 519–48.

Rudwick, Elliot M. "The Southern Negro Policeman and the White Offender." *Journal of Negro Education* 30, no. 4 (1961): 426–31.

Salmond, John A. *A Southern Rebel: The Life and Times of Aubrey Willis Williams, 1890–1965*. Chapel Hill: University of North Carolina Press, 1983.

Saye, Albert B., ed. *Records of the Commission of 1943–1944 to Revise the Constitution of Georgia*. 2 vols. Atlanta: State of Georgia, 1946.

Sayre, Albert B. "American Government and Politics: Georgia's Proposed New Constitution." *American Political Science Review* 39, no. 3 (1945): 459–63.

Schechter, Patricia. *Ida B. Wells-Barnett and American Reform, 1880–1930*. Chapel Hill: University of North Carolina Press, 2001.

Schiesl, Martin J. *The Politics of Efficiency: Municipal Administration and Reform in America, 1800–1920*. Berkeley: University of California Press, 1977.

Schulman, Bruce J. *From Cotton Belt to Sun Belt: Federal Policy, Economic Development, and the Transformation of the South, 1938–1980*. New York: Oxford University Press, 1991.

Scott, Anne Firor. "After Suffrage: Southern Women in the Twenties." *Journal of Southern History* 30, no. 3 (1964): 298–318.

———. "Most Invisible of All: Black Women's Voluntary Associations." *Journal of Southern History* 56, no. 1 (1990): 3–22.

Scott, Emmett J. "Letters of Negro Migrants of 1916–1918." *Journal of Negro History* 4, no. 3 (1919): 290–340.

Scribner, Christopher MacGregor. *Renewing Birmingham: Federal Funding and the Promise of Change, 1929–1979*. Athens: University of Georgia Press, 2002.

Seidelman, Raymond, and Edward Harpham. *Disenchanted Realists: Political Science and the American Crisis, 1884–1984*. Albany: State University of New York Press, 1985.

Seidemann, Henry P. "Report on a Survey of the Organization and Administration of the State and County Governments of Alabama; Submitted to Governor G. M. Miller." Washington, DC: Brookings Institution, 1932.

Shabazz, Amilcar. *Advancing Democracy and the Struggle for Access and Equity in Higher Education in Texas*. Chapel Hill: University of North Carolina Press, 2004.

Shade, William G. "'Revolutions Can Go Backwards': The American Civil War and the Problem of Political Development." *Social Science Quarterly* 55, no. 3 (1974): 753–67.

Shafer, Byron, and Richard Johnston. *The End of Southern Exceptionalism*. Cambridge, MA: Harvard University Press, 2006.

Shaw, Stephanie. *What a Woman Ought to Be and to Do: Black Professional Women Workers During the Jim Crow Era*. Chicago: University of Chicago Press, 1996.

Shivery, Louie Davis, and Hugh H. Smythe. "The Neighborhood Union: A Survey of the Beginnings of Social Welfare Movements among Negroes in Atlanta." *Phylon* 3, no. 2 (1942): 149–62.

Simpson, George L., Jr. "Howard W. Odum and American Regionalism." *Social Forces* 34 (1955): 101–6.

Sindler, Allan P. *Huey Long's Louisiana, State Politics, 1920–1952*. Baltimore: Johns Hopkins University Press, 1956.

Singal, Daniel. *The War Within: From Victorian to Modernist Thought in the South, 1919–1945*. Chapel Hill: University of North Carolina Press, 1982.

Singh, Nikhil Pal. *Black Is a Country: Race and the Unfinished Struggle for Democracy*. Cambridge, MA: Harvard University Press, 2005.

Sitkoff, Harvard. "Harry Truman and the Election of 1948: The Coming of Age of Civil Rights in American Politics." *Journal of Southern History* 37 (1971): 597–616.

———. *A New Deal for Blacks: The Emergence of Civil Rights as a National Issue: The Depression Decade*. New York: Oxford University Press, 1978.

———. "Racial Militancy and Interracial Violence in the Second World War." *Journal of American History* 58, no. 3 (1971): 661–81.

Skocpol, Theda. *Protecting Soldiers and Mothers: The Political Origins of Social Policy in the United States* Cambridge, MA: Belknap Press of Harvard University Press, 2002.

Skowronek, Stephen. *Building a New American State: The Expansion of National Administrative Capacities, 1877–1920*. New York: Cambridge University Press, 1982.

———. *The Politics Presidents Make: Leadership from John Adams to Bill Clinton*. Cambridge, MA: Harvard University Press, 1997.

———. "The Reassociation of Ideas and Purposes: Racism, Liberalism, and the American Political Tradition." *American Political Science Review* 100, no. 3 (2006): 385–401.

Smith, Bruce. "Factors Influencing the Future Development of State Police." *Journal of Criminal Law and Criminology* 23, no. 4 (1932): 713–18.

Smith, C. Calvin. "The Politics of Evasion: Arkansas' Reaction to *Smith v. Allwright*, 1944." *Journal of Negro History* 67, no. 1 (1982): 40–51.

Smith, Gerald L. *A Black Educator in the Segregated South: Kentucky's Rufus B. Atwood*. Lexington: University of Kentucky Press, 1994.

Smith, J. Douglas. *Managing White Supremacy: Race, Politics, and Citizenship in Jim Crow Virginia*. Chapel Hill: University of North Carolina Press, 2002.

———. *The New Deal in the Urban South*. Baton Rouge: Louisiana State University Press, 1988.

———. "'The Ordeal of Virginius Dabney': A Southern Liberal, the Southern Regional Council and the Limits of Managed Race Relations." Paper presented at Conference on the Southern Regional Council and the Civil Rights Movement, University of Florida, Gainesville, October 2003.

Smith, Larissa M. "Where the South Begins: Black Politics and Civil Rights Activism in Virginia, 1930–1951." PhD diss., Emory University, 2001.

Smith, Marjorie. "Racial Confrontation in Columbia, Tennessee: 1946." Master's thesis, Atlanta University, 1971.

Smith, Rogers M. "Beyond Tocqueville, Myrdal and Hartz: The Multiple Traditions in America." *American Political Science Review* 87, no. 3 (1993): 549–66.

———. "The Puzzling Place of Race in American Political Science." *PS: Political Science and Politics* 37, no. 1 (2004): 41–45.

Smith, S. L. "The Passing of the Hampton Library School." *Journal of Negro Education* 9, no. 1 (1940): 51–58.

Smith, Samuel L. *Builders of Goodwill: The Story of the State Agents of Negro Education in the South, 1910 to 1950*. Nashville: Tennessee Book Co., 1950.

Sosna, Morton. *In Search of the Silent South*. New York: Columbia University Press, 1977.

———. "More Important Than the Civil War? The Impact of World War II on the South." In *Perspectives on the American South: An Annual Review of Society, Politics and Culture*, edited by James C. Cobb and Charles Reagan Wilson. New York: Gordon and Breach, 1987.

———. "World War II, Democracy and the South: The Birth of the Southern Regional Council." Paper presented at Conference on the Southern Regional Council and the Civil Rights Movement, University of Florida, Gainesville, October 2003.

Southern, David W. "*An American Dilemma* Revisited: Myrdalism and White Southern Liberals." *South Atlantic Quarterly* 75, no. 2 (Spring 1976): 182–97.

———. *Gunnar Myrdal and Black-White Relations: The Use and Abuse of an American Dilemma, 1944–1969*. Baton Rouge: Louisiana State University Press, 1987.
Southern Electoral League. "Plain Facts about the Poll Tax." Atlanta, n.d.
Southern Policy Conference. "Report of the Southern Policy Conference." Atlanta, GA, April 25–28, 1935.
Southern Regional Council. "The White Primary 1944; With Special Reference to Georgia." Atlanta, 1944.
"Southern Regional Training Program for the Development of Trained Talent for Public Service in the South." Pamphlet. Tuscaloosa: Bureau of Public Administration, University of Alabama, 1945.
Spinney, Robert G. "Municipal Government in Nashville, Tennessee, 1938–1951: World War II and the Growth of the Public Sector." *Journal of Southern History* 61, no. 1 (1995): 77–112.
Spragens, Thomas A., Jr. "R. Taylor Cole." *PS: Political Science and Politics* 24, no. 3 (1991): 550–52.
Stanfield, John H. "A Neglected Chapter in the History of the Scholarship of Teaching Sociology." *Teaching Sociology* 31, no. 4 (2003): 361–65.
———. *Philanthropy and Jim Crow in American Social Science*. Westport, CT: Greenwood Press, 1985.
Steinberg, Stephen. *Race Relations: A Critique*. Stanford: Stanford University Press, 2007.
Sternsher, Bernard, ed. *The Negro in Depression and War: Prelude to Revolution, 1930–1945*. Chicago: Quadrangle, 1969.
Stetson, Dorothy McBride. "Found Women: Pioneers in Southern Political Science, Hallie Farmer." *PS* 21 (1988): 667–69.
Stevens, Jacqueline. "Beyond Tocqueville, Please!" *American Political Science Review* 89, no. 4 (1995): 987–95.
Stimson, James A. "Regression Models in Space and Time: A Statistical Essay." *American Journal of Political Science* 29, no. 4 (1985): 914–47.
Stivers, Camilla. *Bureau Men, Settlement Women: Constructing Public Administration in the Progressive Era*. Lawrence: University Press of Kansas, 2000.
———. "Settlement Women and Bureau Men: Constructing a Usable Past for Public Administration." *Public Administration Review* 55 (1995): 522–29.
Stone, Alfred Holt. "Is Race Friction between Blacks and Whites in the United States Growing and Inevitable?" *American Journal of Sociology* 13, no. 5 (1908): 676–97.
Stoney, George C. "Suffrage in the South, Part I, the Poll Tax." *Survey Graphic*, January–February 1940, 5–9.
———. "Suffrage in the South, Part II." *Survey Graphic*, March–April 1940, 163–67.
———. "Tool of the State Machines." In *The Poll Tax*. Washington, DC: American Council on Public Affairs, 1940.
Strong, David, Pamela Barnhouse Walters, Brian Driscoll, and Scott Rosenberg. "Leveraging the State: Private Money and the Development of Public Education for Blacks." *American Sociological Review* 65, no. 5 (2000): 658–81.
Strong, Donald S. "American Government and Politics: The Poll Tax: The Case of Texas." *American Political Science Review* 38, no. 4 (1944): 693–709.

———. "The Future of the Negro Voter in the South." *Journal of Negro Education* 26 (1957): 400–407.

———. *Registration of Voters in Alabama*. Tuscaloosa: University of Alabama Press, 1956.

———. "The Rise of Negro Voting in Texas." *American Political Science Review* 42 (1948): 510–22.

———. *Urban Republicanism in the South*. Tuscaloosa: Bureau of Public Administration, University of Alabama, 1960.

Sugg, Redding S., Jr., and George Hilton Jones. *The Southern Regional Education Board: Ten Years of Regional Cooperation in Education*. Baton Rouge: Louisiana State University Press, 1960.

Suggs, Henry Lewis. *P. B. Young, Newspaperman: Race, Politics, and Journalism in the New South, 1910–1962*. Charlottesville: University Press of Virginia, 1988.

Sullivan, Patricia. *Days of Hope: Race and Democracy in the New Deal Era*. Chapel Hill: University of North Carolina Press, 1996.

Summerville, James. *Educating Black Doctors: A History of Meharry Medical College*. Tuscaloosa: University of Alabama Press, 1983.

Sumner, William Graham. *Folkways: A Study of the Sociological Importance of Usages, Manners, Customs, Mores, and Morals*. 1906; New York: Dover, 1959.

Swanson, Ernest W., and John A. Griffin. *Public Education in the South Today and Tomorrow: A Statistical Survey*. Chapel Hill: University of North Carolina Press, 1955.

Teasley, C. E., III "Public Administration in a Changing South." *Southern Review of Public Administration* 1, no. 1 (1977): 25–30.

Thomas, William B. "Conservative Currents in Howard Washington Odum's Agenda for Social Reform in Southern Race Relations, 1930–1936." *Phylon* 45, no. 2 (1984): 121–34.

Thompson, Charles H. "Court Action the Only Reasonable Alternative to Remedy Immediate Abuses of the Negro Separate School." *Journal of Negro Education* 4, no. 3 (1935): 419–34.

———. "Editorial Comment: Administrators of Negro Colleges and the Color Line in Higher Education in the South." *Journal of Negro Education* 17, no. 4 (1948): 437–45.

———. "Editorial Comment: Best Practices in Race Relations in the South." *Journal of Negro Education* 16, no. 2 (1947): 123–29.

———. "Editorial Comment: Extension of Segregation through Regional Schools." *Journal of Negro Education* 17, no. 2 (1948): 101–5.

———. "Editorial Note: Negro Higher and Professional Education in the United States." *Journal of Negro Education* 17, no. 3 (1948): 221–23.

———. "Editorial Comment: Negro Higher Education in Maryland." *Journal of Negro Education* 16, no. 4 (1947): 481–90.

———. "Editorial Comment: Some Critical Aspects of the Problem of the Higher and Professional Education for Negroes." *Journal of Negro Education* 14, no. 4 (1945): 509–26.

———. "Editorial Comment: Why Negroes Are Opposed to Segregated Regional Schools." *Journal of Negro Education* 18, no. 1 (1949): 1–8.

Thornton, J. Mills, III. *Dividing Lines: Municipal Politics and the Struggle for Civil Rights in Montgomery, Birmingham and Selma*. Tuscaloosa: University of Alabama Press, 2002.

———. "Municipal Politics and the Course of the Movement." In *New Directions in Civil Rights Studies*, edited by Armstead L. Robinson and Patricia Sullivan. Charlottesville: University Press of Virginia, 1991.

Thuesen, Sarah Caroline. "Classes of Citizenship: The Culture and Politics of Black Public Education in North Carolina, 1919–1960." PhD diss., University of North Carolina, Chapel Hill, 2003.

Tindall, George B. "Business Progressivism: Southern Politics in the Twenties." *South Atlantic Quarterly* 62 (1963): 92–106.

———. "The 'Colonial Economy' and the Growth Psychology: The South in the 1930s." *South Atlantic Quarterly* 64 (1965): 465–77.

———. *The Emergence of the New South, 1913–1945*. Baton Rouge: Louisiana State University Press, 1967.

———. "The Significance of Howard W. Odum to Southern History: A Preliminary Estimate." *Journal of Southern History* 24 (1958): 285–307.

Tolleson-Rinehart, Sue, and Susan J. Carroll. "'Far from Ideal': The Gender Politics of Political Science." *American Political Science Review* 100, no. 4 (2006): 507–13.

Tolnay, Stewart E., and E. M. Beck. *A Festival of Violence: An Analysis of Southern Lynchings, 1882–1930*. Urbana: University of Illinois Press, 1992.

Toppin, Edgar. *Loyal Sons and Daughters: Virginia State University, 1892–1992*. Norfolk, VA: Pictorial Heritage Publishing, 1992.

Tushnet, Mark V. *The NAACP's Legal Strategy against Segregated Education*. Chapel Hill: University of North Carolina Press, 1987.

Tuttle, William M., Jr. *Race Riot: Chicago in the Red Summer of 1919*. New York: Atheneum, 1970.

Tyack, David, and Robert Lowe. "The Constitutional Moment: Reconstruction and Black Education in the South." *American Journal of Education* 94, no. 2 (1986): 236–56.

Tyler, Pamela. "The Impact of the New Deal and World War II on the South." In *A Companion to the American South*, edited by John B. Boles. Malden, MA: Blackwell, 2002.

Valelly, Richard M. *The Two Reconstructions: The Struggle for Black Enfranchisement*. Chicago: University of Chicago Press, 2004.

Valien, Preston. "Expansion of Negro Suffrage in Tennessee." *Journal of Negro Education* 26, no. 3 (1957): 362–68.

Vance, Rupert. "Howard Odum's Technicways: A Neglected Lead in American Sociology." *Social Forces* 50, no. 4 (1972): 456–61.

———. "The Sociological Implications of Southern Regionalism." *Journal of Southern History* 26 (1960): 44–56.

Vance, Rupert B., and Katherine Jocher. "From Community Studies to Regionalism." *Social Forces* 23 (1945): 245–58.

———. "Howard W. Odum." *Social Forces* 33 (1955): 203–17.

Van Den Berghe, Pierre. *Race and Racism: A Comparative Perspective*. New York: Wiley, 1967.

Vander Zanden, James W. "Accommodation to Undesired Change: The Case of the South." *Journal of Negro Education* 31 (1962): 30–35.

———. "Resistance and Social Movements." *Social Forces* 31 (1959): 312–15.

———. "The Southern White Resistance Movement to Integration." PhD diss., University of North Carolina, 1958.

Vaughan, Donald S. "Political Science in the South—Then and Now." *Journal of Politics* 51, no. 3 (1989): 497–522.

Vickerey, Kenneth P. "'Herrenvolk' Democracy and Egalitarianism in South Africa and the U.S. South." *Comparative Studies in Society and History* 16, no. 3 (1974): 309–28.

Vogel, Jeffrey E. "Redefining Reconciliation: Confederate Veterans and the Southern Responses to Federal Civil War Pensions." *Civil War History* 51, no. 1 (2005): 67–93.

Walker, Vanessa Siddle. *Their Highest Potential: An African American School Community in the Segregated South*. Chapel Hill: University of North Carolina Press, 1996.

Wallenstein, Peter. "Black Southerners and Non-Black Universities: Desegregating Higher Education, 1935–1967." *History of Higher Education Annual* 19 (1999): 121–48.

Walters, Pamela Barnhouse, David R. James, and Holly J. McCammon. "Citizenship and Public Schools: Accounting for Racial Inequality in Education in the Pre- and Post-Disenfranchisement South." *American Sociological Review* 62, no. 1 (1997): 34–52.

Ward, Deborah E. *The White Welfare State: The Racialization of U.S. Welfare Policy*. Ann Arbor: University of Michigan Press, 2005.

Ware, Arthur W. "Defining Public Welfare as a Function of Government in Virginia." *Social Forces* 6, no. 4 (1928): 622–26.

Ware, Gilbert. "Hocutt: Genesis of Brown." *Journal of Negro Education* 52, no. 3 (1983): 227–33.

Washington, Althea. "Availability of Education for Negroes in the Elementary School." *Journal of Negro Education* 16, no. 3 (1947): 439–49.

Weare, Walter B. *Black Business in the New South*. Chicago: University of Illinois Press, 1973.

Weatherford, Willis D. *Interracial Cooperation: A Study of the Various Agencies Working in the Field of Racial Welfare*. New York: Interracial Committee of the War Work Council of YMCA, 1920.

Weatherford, Willis D., and Charles S. Johnson. *Race Relations: Adjustment of Whites and Negroes in the United States*. 1934; New York: Negro Universities Press, 1969.

Weaver, Bill, and Oscar C. Page. "The Black Press and the Drive for Integrated Graduate and Professional Schools." *Phylon* 43, no. 1 (1982): 15–28.

Webb, Samuel L., and Margaret E. Armbrester, eds. *Alabama Governors: A Political History of the State*. Tuscaloosa: University of Alabama Press, 2001.

Weeks, O. Douglas. "The White Primary." *Mississippi Law Journal* 8, no. 2 (1935): 135–38.
———. "The White Primary: 1944–1948." *American Political Science Review*, 42, no. 3 (1948): 500–510.
Weiss, Nancy J. *Farewell to the Party of Lincoln*. Princeton, NJ: Princeton University Press, 1983.
Wells, Amy E. "Contested Ground: Howard Odum, the Southern Agrarians, and the Emerging University in the South during the 1930s." *History of Higher Education Annual* (2001): 79–101.
———. "From Ideas to Institutions: Southern Scholars and Emerging Universities in the South, circa 1920–1950." PhD diss., University of Kentucky, 2001.
———. "Mischief Making on the Eve of *Brown v. Board of Education*: The Origins and Early Controversies of the Southern Regional Education Board." Paper presented at American Educational Research Association meeting, San Diego, 2004.
Wennersten, John R. "The Travail of Black Land-Grant Schools in the South, 1890–1917." *Agricultural History* 65, no. 2 (1991): 54–62.
Werum, Regina. "Elite Control in State and Nation: Racial Inequalities in Vocational Funding in North Carolina, Georgia, and Mississippi, 1918–1936." *Social Forces* 78, no. 1 (1999): 145–86.
———. "Tug-of-War: Political Mobilization and Access to Schooling in the Southern Racial State." *Sociology of Education* 72, no. 2 (1999): 89–110.
Westin, Richard B. "The State and Segregated Schools: Negro Public Education in North Carolina, 1852–1956." PhD diss., Duke University, 1966.
White, Howard. "The Southern Regional Training Program in Public Administration." *Journal of Politics* 8, no. 1 (1946): 74–85.
White, Walter B. "Decline of Southern Liberals." *Negro Digest*, January 1943, 43.
———. *Rope and Faggot: A Biography of Judge Lynch*. 1929; Notre Dame, IN: University of Notre Dame Press, 2002.
Wiebe, Robert H. *The Search for Order, 1877–1920*. New York: Hill and Wang, 1966.
Wilkerson, Doxey A. "Conscious and Impersonal Forces in Recent Trends toward Negro-White Equality in Virginia." *Journal of Educational Sociology* 32, no. 8 (1959): 402–8.
———. "The Negro School Movement in Virginia: From 'Equalization' to 'Integration.'" *Journal of Negro Education* 29, no. 1 (1960): 17–29.
———. "Some Correlates of Recent Progress toward Equalizing White and Negro Schools in Virginia." PhD diss., New York University, 1958.
Wilkerson-Freeman, Sarah. "The Second Battle for Woman Suffrage: Alabama White Women, the Poll Tax, and V. O. Key's Master Narrative of Southern Politics." *Journal of Southern History* 68, no. 2 (2002): 333–74.
Wilkins, Roy. "Future of the Negro Voter in the United States." *Journal of Negro Education* 26 (1957): 424–31.
Williams, W. T. B. "Court Action by Negroes to Improve Their Schools a Doubtful Remedy." *Journal of Negro Education* 4, no. 3 (1935): 435–41.

Willie, Charles V. "Walter R. Chivers: An Advocate of Situation Sociology." *Phylon* 43, no. 3 (1982): 242–48.

Wilson, Carey. "Racial Dialectic: Missouri Style." *The Nation*, February 24, 1945, 208–9.

Wilson, Ernest. "Why Political Scientists Don't Study Black Politics, but Historians and Sociologists Do." *PS: Political Science and Politics* 18, no. 3 (1985): 600–607.

Wilson, Francille Rusan. *The Segregated Scholars: Black Social Scientists and the Creation of Labor Studies, 1890–1950*. Charlottesville: University of Virginia Press, 2006.

Wilson, Louis R. *The University of North Carolina, 1900–1930: The Making of a Modern University*. Chapel Hill: University of North Carolina Press, 1957.

Wolters, Raymond. *The New Negro on Campus: Black College Rebellions of the 1920s*. Princeton, NJ: Princeton University Press, 1975.

Woodruff, Nan Elizabeth. "Mississippi Delta Planters and Debates over Mechanization, Labor and Civil Rights in the 1940s." *Journal of Southern History* 60, no. 2 (1994): 263–84.

Woodward, C. Vann. *Origins of the New South 1877–1913*. 1951; Baton Rouge: Louisiana State University Press, 1971.

———. *The Strange Career of Jim Crow*. 3rd rev. ed. New York: Oxford University Press, 1974.

———. *Thinking Back: The Perils of Writing History*. Baton Rouge: Louisiana State University Press, 1986.

Wright, Gavin. *Old South, New South: Revolutions in the Southern Economy since the Civil War*. Baton Rouge: Louisiana State University Press, 1996.

Wright, George C. *Life behind a Veil: Blacks in Louisville, Kentucky, 1865–1930*. Baton Rouge: Louisiana State University Press, 1985.

Wright, Marion Thompson. "Negro Higher and Professional Education in Delaware." *Journal of Negro Education* 17, no. 3 (1948): 265–71.

Wright, William E. *Memphis Politics: A Study in Racial Bloc Voting*. New Brunswick, NJ: Eagleton Institute of Politics, Studies in Practical Politics, 1962.

Wright-Austin, Sharon D. *The Transformation of Plantation Politics: Black Politics, Concentrated Poverty and Social Capital in the Mississippi Delta*. Albany: State University of New York Press, 2006.

Wynes, Charles E. "The Evolution of Jim Crow Laws in Twentieth Century Virginia." *Phylon* 28, no. 4 (1967): 416–25.

Wynn, Neil A. *The Afro-American and the Second World War*. 1975; New York: Holmes and Meier, 1993.

Zangrando, Robert. *The NAACP Crusade against Lynching, 1909–1950*. Philadelphia: Temple University Press, 1980.

Zelden, Charles L. *The Battle for the Black Ballot: Smith v. Allwright and the Defeat of the Texas All-White Primary*. Lawrence: University Press of Kansas, 2004.

Index

abolition, 219
academics, 33
accommodationism, 10
achievement, 15, 174
activism, 18
adaptation, 168
administration, 85, 261n36
advocacy, 137, 215, 227
African American. *See* black(s)
agency, 141
agenda, 19, 108, 169
agitators, 88, 234
Alabama, 83, 260n34
Alexander, Will, 142, 207, 273n45
alignment, 198
AMA (American Medical Association), 184
An American Dilemma (Myrdal), 238
American Medical Association. *See* AMA
Ames, Jessie Daniel, 55, 237
analysis, 202, 219, 220t, 243
Anderson, Charles, 136
animosity, 76
antagonism, 264n61
apartheid, 5
Arkansas, 207f
Arnall, Ellis, 101–02
arrest, 13
assimilation, 29

Association of Southern Women for the Prevention of Lynching. *See* ASWPL
ASWPL (Association of Southern Women for the Prevention of Lynching), 59
Atlanta, 201
attitude, 192
authority, 169, 216
Aycock, Charles B., 121

baccalaureate degrees, 176
ballot, 263n25
Banks, W.R., 178
bargaining, 190
Beale Street, 200
bias, 206
Big Mule alliance, 78
Bilbo, Theodore, 46
Bill, Taylor, 175
biracialism, 29, 56
black(s)
  agency, 141
  assertiveness of, 25
  assimilation, 29
  belief reinforced by, 70
  benefits for, 143
  children, 122
  community, 34, 125, 152
  critique, 138

317

black(s) (*continued*)
  education, 118
  elections participated in by, 199
  elite, 39, 213
  high school, 128
  inclusion of, 73
  juries excluding, 44
  labor, 26
  leadership, 201
  litigation, 140
  lobby, 129
  majority, 265n12
  men, 127
  middle-class, 38, 200, 207
  militancy, 226
  obligations to, 2
  opportunity for, 174
  option, 235
  ordinary, 214
  police, 63, 193
  population, 149
  pragmatism, 117
  protest, 245
  reformers, 92
  Republican Party remnant, 198
  self-help, 132
  settlements, 255n54
  sexuality, 48
  teachers, 134–35
  universities, 145
  urban, 203
  vote, 106, 194*f*, 207*f*
  whites reaching out to, 40
  whites threatened by, 127
  World War II effect on, 223
Black, Aline, 268n69
Black, Hugo, 87
black-belt counties, 120
black women, 57–58
  subordination of, 279n15
  teachers, 126–28
Blease, Cole, 46
Bond, Horace Mann, 120, 165
bond referendum, 199
Boswellianism, 230
boundaries, 177
boycotts, 201
Breedlove v. Suttles, 197
bribes, 139
Briggs v. Elliott, 18
Brown v. Board of Education, 5
budget, 269n11
Bunche, Ralph, 41, 164
bureaucrats, 117
business, 20, 89, 200

Caldwell, Millard, 183
campaign, 16, 229
capital, 119
the Carnegie Corporation, 172
carpetbaggers, 100
caste, 35, 117
chapters, 217*f*
charity, 15
chauvinism, 45
children, 72, 122, 205
Christians, 4, 24
church, 233, 266n27
CIC (Commission on Interracial Cooperation), 3, 21
  base of, 52
  control of, 237
  evolution, 64
  Jim Crow reform led by, 67
  promise, 90
CIO. *See* Congress of Industrial Organizations
citizenship
  advocacy, 215
  civil rights, 13
  evolving, 252n20
  exercising, 205
  politics, 142
  reclaiming, 39
  reemerging, 191
  social, 15
civil rights
  beginning of, 1
  citizenship, 13
  Democrat support of, 114
  litigation, 203
  modern, 165, 237
  pre, 192
the Civil War, 7, 249, 254n37
class, 128, 145
  bias, 206
  working, 191
coalition, 14, 19
cold war, 87
college, 151*t*, 253n9
colonialism, 105
color
  line, 33, 47, 181
  people of, 37
Colored Teachers Association. *See* CTA
Commission on Interracial Cooperation. *See* CIC
Committee on Negro Associations, 213
community
  black, 34, 125, 152

building, 39
business, 200
divided, 180
expense born by, 141
involvement, 128
leadership, 117
organizing, 191
well-being, 214
white, 51
conference, 178, 181
conformity, 259n18
Congress of Industrial Organizations (CIO), 9
conscience, 48
consciousness, 254n30
political, 205t
conservatives, 244
constituency, 172
constitution, 64, 157
reform, 102
state, 147
conviction, 236
cooperation, 181, 236
corruption, 68, 93
cost of, 108
state, 212
credit, 197
creed, 98
crime, 61
Crump, E.H., 201
CTA (Colored Teachers Association), 178
culture, 274n3
customs, 74

Dabney, Virginius, 221
Darden, Colgate, 202
data, 249
death, 197, 237–38
debate, 110, 172
race entering into, 244
resistance, 222
decency, 266n26
Delaine, Joseph, 17
democracy
essence of, 233
interregnum, 245
limited, 105
paths to, 115
redefining, 108
repudiation of, 5
rhetoric of, 100
struggle for, 94
white, 99
democratization, 230, 243
Democrat Party, 114, 242

desegregation, 102, 143, 232
limited, 189
meaningful, 167
staving off, 159
discourse, 144
discrimination, 274n3
disenfranchisement, 6, 221
Dixiecrat, 88, 196, 218
revolt, 112
vote, 113f
doctors, 167
doctrine, 106
Double V campaign, 16, 208
Douglass, Frederick, 196
DuBois, W.E.B., 10
dues, 134–35
Durham Committee on Negro Affairs, 213
Durham conference, 234–37
Durr, Clifford, 86

economics, 278n9
economy, 122, 171, 254n37
elites of, 68
wartime, 216
education, 15
associations, 134–35t
black, 118
board of, 159
dual system of, 143
funding of, 121
politics, 265n10
primary, 130, 144
professional, 164
reform, 140, 204
regional, 180
rural, 127
segregated, 116–20
vocational, 247
Educational Equality Act, 161
egalitarianism, 120
elections, 199, 219, 250
presidential, 111
reform, 14
stolen, 203
un-competitive, 194
electorate, 104, 108, 113
elites, 51, 68, 250
black, 39, 213
Delta, 118
non southern, 46
white, 133
emotions, 23
empiricism, 254n31
employment, 161, 197
endowment, 185

enfranchisement, 229
enrollment, 163, 181
entitlement, 147
entrepreneurs, 114
environment, 239
equality, 4, 136, 170
equalization, 268n69
  integration forestalled with, 228
  staving off, 182
ethos, 34, 49, 136
etiquette, 35, 38, 192–93
eugenics, 23
exclusionists, 120

farming, 148, 224
fear, 61, 226
feminists, 94, 249
Fifteenth Amendment, 94
Fisk University, 34
Florida, 112
folkways, 44, 74, 141
  stateways tension with, 55
  strength of, 22
  white, 152
Foreman, Clark, 207
Fortas, Abe, 86
foundations, 185, 257n26
  Jim Crow reform, 73
  northern-based, 30
Fourteenth Amendment, 96
fraud, 103, 110
freedom, 13, 229, 263n21
fundamentalism, 242
funding, 121, 171, 228
  GEB, 184
  graduate, 162
  indirect, 254n32
  litigation, 210
  partial, 267n41
  public, 204*f*
  relief, 247
  the South, 224
  special, 175
fundraising, 127–28

Gaines, Lloyd, 153
Gaines v. Canada, 136, 153–58, 166
Gandy, John, 162
gangs, 71
Garvey, Marcus, 8
GEB (General Education Board), 16, 31
  fiscal limits of, 137
  funding, 184
  goals, 145
  intervention, 273n45

papers, 261n43
sponsorship, 182
strategies, 123
support for, 82–83
gender, 55, 71, 245
General Education Board. *See* GEB
geographical divide, 77
Georgia, 84–86, 104
G.I. Bill, 174
government, 70, 76, 157
  aegis of, 170
  business-friendly, 89
  control over, 120
  distribution of, 265n10
  intervention, 62
  New South, 22
  oversight, 103
  reform, 227
  reorienting, 14
  white, 147
gradualism, 188, 259n18
Grand Dragon, 260n34
grandfather clause, 155
Grantham, Dewey, 20
grants, 151*t*, 158*t*, 160*t*
grassroots approach, 249
the Great Depression, 66, 137, 156
Great Migration, 12
Grovey v. Townsend, 211

habits, 74
Hancock, Gordon B., 233
Harlem Renaissance, 26
have-nots, 75, 111
heritage, 241
hierarchy, 3, 71, 173
the Highlander School, 2
high school, 124, 128
historians, 246
Hocutt, Thomas, 167
hope, 155
Hope, Lugenia Burns, 36
House of Representatives, 98*t*
hypocrisy, 248

ideas, 7
identity, 9, 193
  fact rooted, 75
  national, 6
ideology, 58, 169, 225
illiteracy, 93
imprisonment, 13
incarceration, 12
independence, 147, 235
injunction, 211

institutionalization, 140*t*
instructor, 179
integration, 9, 175, 187
  desegregation separated from, 232
  equalization forestalling, 228
  unimaginable, 154
intermarriage, 38
interracialism, 21, 52, 169
  new, 187
  organizations centered on, 2
  paternalist, 235
  shift away from, 213
intimidation, 139, 230
intransigence, 234
Ivey, John E., 185

Jackson, Alice C., 161
Jackson College, 149
Jeanes Teachers Program, 126
Jim Crow
  doctrine, 106
  elaboration of, 155
  etiquette, 192–93
  evolution of, 9
  variety of, 11
Jim Crow order, 25, 84, 255n63
  defenders of, 88, 180
  development, 213
  early decades of, 143
  elaborating, 169
  ending, 115
  establishment of, 40
  hierarchy, 173
  limits of, 65, 122, 146
  myths, 67
  perfection, 236
  personal enforcing, 45
  reform, 188
  securing, 94
  stateways shaped by, 66
  transformation, 99
  violence, 43
Jim Crow reform, 33, 41, 91
  axis, 71
  biracialism, 56
  CIC led, 67
  death of, 237–38
  essence of, 105
  foundations, 73
  limitations, 166
  movement, 50
  rationale, 115
jobs, 224
John F. Slater Fund, 31
Johnson, Lyndon, 86

journalists, 50
Journal of Negro Education (Thompson), 164
Journal of Social Forces (Odum), 119
judiciary, 249
Julius Rosenwald Fund, 31
juries, 44
jurisdiction, 263n25

Kellogg Foundation, 172
Kentucky, 83
Key, V.O., 22
King, Martin Luther, Jr., 240, 257n41
King v. Chapman, 107
Kluger, Richard, 177
Ku Klux Klan, 4, 51, 81
  Alabama, 260n34
  resurgence of, 27

labor, 44, 116
  black, 26
  unionized, 89, 138
Lagemann, Ellen Condliffe, 23
Latino, 241
Laura Spelman Rockefeller Memorial, 172
law, 13, 53
  school, 273n57
  violation of, 210
leadership, 32, 162
  black, 201
  community, 117
  NAACP, 192
legacy, 17
legislation, 97
Letter from a Birmingham, Jail (King), 240
liberal arts, 172
liberals, 41
  New Deal, 101–02, 232
  southerner, 21
library, 175
the Library of Congress, 276n55
life, 41
Lincoln University Law School, 271n10
literacy, 117
litigation, 140, 251n13
  civil rights, 203
  funding, 210
living expenses, 159
lobby, 129, 206
lower-class, 27, 44, 95
lynching, 43, 47*f*, 255n6
  justification, 61
  legislative sanctions against, 54*t*
  newspapers announcing, 56
  organizations preventing, 57*f*
  pledges to stop, 60*f*

lynching (*continued*)
  studies, 197
  tacit support of, 12

mainstream thinking, 124
management, 143, 209
manufacturing, 8
marches, 201
markets, 161
Marshall, Thurgood, 155
Martin, Roscoe, 76, 84
McAdam, Doug, 248
McLaurin v. Oklahoma State Regents for Higher Education, 177
Meharry Medical College, 184–88
membership, 133, 216, 222
merit system, 78
middle-class, 58, 191
  blacks, 38, 200, 207
  movement, 268n69
  size of, 8
migrants, 98
migration, 11, 25
militancy, 226
military, 100, 103, 223
minorities, 241
missions, 255n54
Mississippi, 52
mob, 43, 53
mobilization, 16
  eliminating, 230
  era of, 107
  lower-class, 44
modernity, 142
modernization, 18, 70, 243
Moore, Harry T., 231
morality, 4
movements, 19, 59
  Garvey, 198
  Jim Crow reform, 50
  middle-class, 268n69
  Populist, 208
  white led, 72
Murray v. Maryland, 153
Myrdal, Gunnar, 236, 238
myth, 67, 75

NAACP (National Association for the Advancement of Colored People), 2, 133, 146
  chapters, 217f
  involvement of, 174
  leadership, 192
  membership, 216
  resistance, 211
  strategy, 153

nation, 6
National Association for the Advancement of Colored People. *See* NAACP
the National Guard, 258n48
nationalism, 8
Nazism, 225
negotiations, 22
Negro, 26, 28, 32
Negro Life in the South (Weatherford), 24
neighborhood, 271n10
neutrality, 81
Newberry v. United States, 209
the New Deal, 2, 86, 91
  height of, 77
  liberals, 101–02, 232
  material benefits of, 96
  shaping, 207
New South, 22
newspapers, 56
New York City, 167
Nineteenth Amendment, 36
Nixon v. Herdon, 211
Nobel Peace Prize, 238
norms, 11
North Carolina, 207f

Obama, Barack, 240
obligation, 2, 24
Odum, Howard, 33, 119, 259n18
Ogden, Frederic, 104
Oklahoma, 177
opportunity, 161
organizations
  fraternal, 148
  interracial, 2
  local, 211
  lynching prevention by, 57f
  reform, 150
  umbrella, 92
  women's, 35
Owlsey, Frank, 24

pamphlets, 52, 187
Park, Robert, 21
Parks, Rosa, 1, 250
passion, 43
paternalism, 4, 49
  end of, 137–39
  interracialist, 235
patronage, 261n36
Peabody Education Board, 31
peace, 240
Pepper, Claude, 97
Perry, Matthew, 188
philanthropy, 30, 118, 273n45

plaintiff, 177
plantations, 77, 249
Plessy v. Ferguson, 5
police
  black, 63, 193
  establishment of, 63t
  state, 62
policy
  changing, 22
  makers, 171
  outcomes of, 244
  Reconstruction, 123
politeness, 252n29
politics
  bifurcation of, 196
  citizenship, 142
  consciousness in, 205t
  education, 265n10
  indirect, 190
  Ku Klux Klan, 51
  local, 202
  modern, 242
  participation in, 196
  urban, 208
poll tax, 6
  abolition, 219
  enacting, 95t
  fraud, 110
  legislation, 97
  paying, 215, 275n33
  reform, 92–94, 111f
  repeal, 105–07
  study, 104
population, 112, 149, 218
power, 63
pragmatism, 223
precedent, 157
Present Forces in Negro Progress (Weatherford), 24
press, 62
pride, 233
privilege, 15
progress, 20
Progressivism, 4
  business, 20
  ethos, 49
  ethos of, 34
protest, 201, 245
Public Administration Bureau, 79–83
punishment, 197

race
  baiting, 102, 239
  debate entered by, 244
  ideology based on, 225
  mixed, 241
  privilege of, 15
  relations, 144, 169
  riots, 27–28, 272n21
  role of, 101
  salary based on, 138
  settlement, 23
  status by, 7
  understanding between, 76
racism
  biological, 21, 225
  legitimated, 3
  rants of, 48
  war against, 248
Randolph, A. Philip, 225
rape, 47
Raper, Authur, 238
ratification, 105
rationalization, 47
reconciliation, 20
the Reconstruction, 6, 15, 123
records, 161
reform
  bounded, 88
  consequences of, 221–22
  constitution, 102
  demands of, 260n33
  education, 140, 204
  electoral, 14
  government, 227
  gradualism of, 18
  Jim Crow order, 188
  limitations of, 158
  opponents of, 108
  organizations, 150
  piecemeal, 9
  poll tax, 92–94, 111f
  southerner, 21
  state, 109
reformers
  black, 92
  conclusions of, 49
  contradiction among, 14
  government, 76
  male, 45
  white, 60
regionalism, 72
registration
  by decade, 207f
  rates, 221
  restrictive, 93
  vote, 17, 193, 195t
regression analysis, 220f
rejection, 162
relief, 247

Republican Party
  black remnant of, 198
  lily-whitism of, 194
  modern, 278n2
  reemergence of, 9
  success, 242
research, 30, 82, 242
resistance, 107, 205
  debate on, 222
  NAACP, 211
  white, 264n61
resources, 124, 266n27
revival meetings, 215
revolt, 112, 218, 235
revolution, 1, 113
rhetoric, 37
Richardson, Scovell, 271n10
rights, 10
riots, 27–28, 272n21
Rockefeller Foundation, 31, 82
roles, 207
Roosevelt, Eleanor, 92
Roosevelt, Franklin, 71, 85
roots, 7
the Rosenwald Foundation, 16, 129–30, 204
Rotary Club, 102

sacrifice, 96
salary
  equalization, 268n69
  race-based, 138
  teacher's, 139*t*
sanitation, 127
scholarships, 160
schools. *See also* high school
  building, 203
  country, 266n34
  county training, 129
  elementary, 267n43
  foundation supported, 185
  free, 121
  law, 273n57
  makeshift, 165
  overcrowded, 126
  rural, 130
  temporary, 179
  value of, 277n8
SCHW (Southern Conference for Human Welfare), 3, 92
Scottsboro Boys, 63
Scruggs, Sherman, 156
SCSCN (South Carolina State College for Negroes), 176

Second Morrill Act, 146
segregation
  de jure, 146
  education, 116–20
  extreme, 85
  horizontal v. vertical, 29–30
  mandated, 125–26
  ordinances, 92
  seating, 148
  social, 32
  strategy, 177
  systems of, 228
  undergraduate, 189
  vertical, 150, 239
segregationists, 4
self-defense, 64
sentiment, 226
service
  domestic, 34, 148
  members, 263n25
  military, 103, 223
  sector, 8
servility, 10
settlement, 23
sexuality, 38, 48
Shepard, James, 156
Simkins, Mojdeska, 165
slaves, 123
Smith, Al, 275n30
Smith Hughes Vocational Training Act, 129
Smith v. Allwright, 17, 103
social science, 101
Social Security, 72
society
  citizenship in, 15
  hierarchy within, 3
  organic nature of, 259n18
  segregated, 32
Sociological Congress, 25
sociologists, 246
Soldier's Vote Act, 100
sop, 162
the South
  autonomy, 48
  characteristics of, 260n26
  funding, 224
  good faith efforts of, 170
  problems of, 42, 210
  redefinition of, 65
  scrutiny of, 99
  stabilizing, 144
  symbols of, 173
  traditions of, 68
  United States rejoined by, 1

INDEX   325

South Carolina State College for Negroes.
    See SCSCN
Southern Conference for Human Welfare.
    See SCHW
Southern Education Board, 31
southerners
    credo, 99
    liberal, 21
    native, 19
    reforming, 21
    white, 53
Southern Methodist Church, 49
Southern Policy Committee, 86
Southern Publicity Committee, 25
Southern Regional Council. *See* SRC
Southern Regional Education Board.
    See SREB
The Southern Regional Education
    Plan, 186
Southern Universities, 32–35
Sparks, Chauncey, 182
speech, 218
SRC (Southern Regional Council), 75,
    237–38
SREB (Southern Regional Education
    Board), 183
state(s)
    academics, 33
    actors, 245
    border, 132
    commitment, 267n41
    constitution, 147
    contributions, 131*t*
    corruption, 212
    employees, 157
    functionaries, 14
    modern, 42
    networks, 59
    officials, 175
    planning board, 79–80
    police, 62
    positions, 261n36
    power, 116
    provisions, 121*t*
    reform, 109
    representation, 96
    resistance, 205
    resources, 124
    revenue, 69*t*
    rights, 10
    statute, 208
    supreme court, 166
    tuition, 154, 163*f*
    violence sponsored by, 12
statesmanship, 186

statesmen, 178
stateways, 55, 66
statistics, 69*t*, 206, 221
status, 7, 14, 117
status quo, 101, 188, 252n16
statute, 208
strategy, 177, 187
students
    distribution of, 186
    exiled, 165
    new, 171
    Virginia, 161*f*
studies, 104, 197, 252n9
subordination, 279n15
suffrage, 27, 100
sunbelt, 278n2
supremacy, 2, 43
Supreme Court, 87, 166
survey, 243
Sweatt v. Painter, 158
sympathy, 170, 234

Taft-Hartley Act, 227
Talmadge, Eugene, 106, 263 n29
tax, 151. *See also* poll tax
TCDE (Texas Commission on Democracy
    in Education), 179
teachers
    black, 134–35
    black women, 126–28
    qualification of, 137, 174
    salaries, 139*t*
    training, 267n44
technicways, 74
technocrats, 66
Tennessee, 83, 220, 276n62
Tennessee Valley Authority. *See* TVA
tension, 172
Terrell Election Law, 208
terrorists, 231
Texas Commission on Democracy in
    Education. *See* TCDE
theory, 261n46
Thompson, Charles, 155, 164
Thurmond, Strom, 183
tradition, 20, 68, 236
Tragedy of Lynching (Raper), 238
training, 83, 148
    teacher, 267n44
    voter, 214
transportation, 160*t*
treaty, 182
tuition, 136
    grants, 158*t*, 160*t*
    state, 154, 163*f*

326 INDEX

Tuskegee model, 148–50
TVA (Tennessee Valley Authority), 78, 81

unions, 138, 222
United Nations, 238
United States
  creed of, 98
  exceptionalism, 245
  the South rejoining, 1
  traditions, 236
United States v. Classic, 212
university, 13, 145, 182
University Commission on Southern Race Questions, 25
urbanization, 114, 199
the Urban League, 187, 199

veterans
  enrollment of, 181
  liberal, 232
  white, 231
  World War I, 211
  World War II, 109
violence, 11–12, 43
Virginia, 161*f*
Virginia Electoral Reform League, 110
virtue, 37
voting
  AAA cotton referenda, 247
  black, 106, 194*f*, 207*f*
  Dixiecrat, 113*f*
  fraud, 103
  House of Representatives, 98*t*
  manipulation, 93
  NASCAR, 241
  popular, 112*f*
  population, 218
  registration, 17, 193, 195*t*
  suburban, 109, 222
  training, 214
  turnout, 231

wage, 196
waivers, 160
war
  cold, 87
  economy in times of, 216
  ideas leading to, 7
  jobs, 224
  racism goes to, 248
  violence post, 11
Washington, Booker T., 10, 26, 39
Washington, Margaret Murray, 36
Weatherford, Willis D., 24
welfare, 243
Wells, Ida B., 58
West v. Bliley, 212
white(s)
  allies, 141
  authority, 216
  average, 61, 225
  backlash, 139, 156
  black men threatening, 127
  blacks reached out to by, 40
  community, 51
  control, 107
  counterparts, 132
  democracy, 99
  dominance of, 70
  electorate, 108, 113
  elite, 133
  expectations, 151
  fear of, 226
  folkways, 152
  government, 147
  hostility, 125
  individual, 145
  liberals, 41
  lower-class, 27, 95
  moderate, 240
  movements, 72
  needs of, 118
  neighborhood, 271n10
  poor, 63
  primary, 192, 208–12, 274n10
  reformers, 60
  resistance, 264n61
  southern, 53
  veterans, 231
  women, 55
White, Walter, 226
Wilson, Woodrow, 46
Woman's Missionary Society, 35
women, 27, 35, 260n26. *See also* black women
Works Progress Administration, 73
worldview, 19
World War I, 28, 211
World War II, 91
  beginnings of, 98
  black's assertiveness during, 223
  post, 277n13
  veterans, 109
Wright, Fielding, 183
Wrighten, John, 188

YWCA, 36